THE ORIGINS AND
DEVELOPMENT OF
EUROPEAN
INTEGRATION

THE ORIGINS AND
DEVELOPMENT OF

EUROPEAN
INTEGRATION

A READER AND COMMENTARY

EDITED BY

PETER M. R. STIRK AND DAVID WEIGALL

PINTER

London and New York

PINTER

A Cassell imprint

Wellington House, 125 Strand, London WC2R 0BB
370 Lexington Avenue, New York, NY 10017-6550

First published 1999
Introductions and selection © Peter M. R. Stirk and David
Weigall 1999

British Library Cataloguing-in-Publication Data
A catalogue record for this book is available from the British
Library.

ISBN 1–85567–516–1 (hardback)
      1–85567–517–1 (paperback)

Library of Congress Cataloging-in-Publication Data
The origins and development of European integration: a reader
and commentary / edited by Peter M. R. Stirk and David
Weigall.
      p.   cm.
Includes bibliographical references and index.
ISBN 1–85567–516–1 (hardcover). – ISBN   1–85567–517–X
(pbk.)
1. Europe – Economic integration – History.   I. Stirk,
   Peter M. R., 1954–   . II. Weigall, David.
   HC241.0765 1998
   337.1'4–dc21   98–20773
                                                            CIP

Typeset by York House Typographic Ltd
Printed and bound in Great Britain by Biddles Ltd, Guildford
and King's Lynn

CONTENTS

ACKNOWLEDGEMENTS

The editors are grateful to George Wilkes for assistance in the selection of documents, Joan Haddock for assistance in the preparation of the typescript and Sue Stirk for the formatting of the final text. The editors are also grateful to Petra Recter at Cassell, who has been encouraging and patient in equal measure throughout the project.

Every effort has been made to identify copyright holders of sources. Should any material from works still in copyright have been included inadvertently without acknowledgement, the publishers should be notified so that any omissions may be included in future editions.

For all HMSO material, Crown Copyright is reproduced with the permission of the Controller of Her Majesty's Staionery Office. For extracts from the *Current Digest of the Soviet Press* the editors are grateful for the translation copyright of the *Current Digest of the Soviet Press*, published weekly at Columbus, Ohio, reprinted by permission of the *Digest*. The extract in Document 5.9 is reproduced with the permission of *Keesing's Worldwide*, Washington. The editors acknowledge the US rights to the extract in Document 6.6 held by Librairie Arthème Fayard, Paris. All other rights are acknowledged after the title of each individual document.

INTRODUCTION

Since the fall of the Berlin Wall, the symbol of the cold war division of Europe, it has become customary to write of the 'new European architecture' whose structural components range from the European Union to the Organization for Security and Co-operation in Europe and the North Atlantic Treaty Organization. The fact that the latter two include non-European states does not disqualify them from this architecture. The centrality of the European Union, poised as it is to embrace most of what the early prophets of European integration had in mind, is self-evident. Yet the Union started as a set of communities which did not even embrace the majority of west European states – and even now there are west European states which are not members of the Union. The construction and development of these organizations has also been affected by elements of Europe's pre-1989 architecture which have crumbled into dust, notably the Council for Mutual Economic Assistance (CMEA) and the Warsaw Pact, and by structures which never advanced beyond their architects' drawing board. This volume seeks to take account of all these structures, though pride of place is given to the European Union.

The fact that the elements of Europe's architecture overlap and are usually regarded either as incomplete or as already teetering under their own weight is at the very least an indication that they are not the product of some semi-divine plan encoded in long-term economic trends. They are, rather, the product of specific constellations of events, often unexpected and unwanted events, in which competing visions and interests have led to compromises, which in turn have had unanticipated, and sometimes unwanted, consequences.

In selecting documents to illustrate this process, we have given preference to those which illuminate the underlying debate. Formal treaties, even important ones, are either omitted altogether or represented by only a few articles. They are readily available elsewhere. Preference has been given to the debate in the larger states, notably Britain, France, Germany and the United States, although smaller states are also represented, both because their influence has sometimes been greater than their size would suggest and because of the intrinsic interest of the debate within them.

Any selection of documents is bound to leave gaps and others would undoubtedly have chosen differently, leaving other gaps. The introductions to each chapter are intended to fill in as many of these as space has permitted, and may be read independently of the documents or in conjunction with them. The overriding aim of both the introductions and the selection of documents has been to convey a sense of the vitality of the debate surrounding European integration, with all its indeterminacy and passion.

ABBREVIATIONS

ACP	African, Caribbean, Pacific states
ADAP	*Akten zur Deutschen Auswärtigen Politik*
Bull. EC	*Bulletin of the European Communities*
CAP	Common Agricultural Policy
CEEC	Committee for European Economic Cooperation
CIS	Commonwealth of Independent States
CFSP	Common Foreign and Security Policy
CMEA	Council for Mutual Economic Assistance (see also Comecon)
COCOM	Coordinating Committee on Multilateral Export Controls
Com	Commission Document
Comecon	Council for Mutual Economic Assistance (see also CMEA)
COREPER	Committee for Permanent Representatives
CSCE	Conference on Security and Cooperation in Europe
DBPO	*Documents on British Policy Overseas*
DDF	*Documents Diplomatique Français*
EAPC	Euro-Atlantic Partnership Council
EC	European Community
ECSC	European Coal and Steel Community
EDC	European Defence Community
EEC	European Economic Community
EFTA	European Free Trade Association
EMS	European Monetary System
EMU	Economic and Monetary Union

EPC	European Political Community
	or
	European Political Cooperation
ERM	Exchange Rate Mechanism
EU	European Union
Euratom	European Atomic Energy Community
FTA	Free Trade Area
FRUS	*Foreign Relations of the United States*
GATT	General Agreement on Tariffs and Trade
IGC	Intergovernmental Conference
HCNM	High Commissioner on National Minorities
MFN	Most Favoured Nation principle
NACC	North Atlantic Cooperation Council
NATO	North Atlantic Treaty Organization
The Nine	The Six plus the United Kingdom, Denmark and Ireland
ODIHR	Office of Democratic Institutions and Human Rights
OECD	Organization for Economic Cooperation and Development
OEEC	Organization for European Economic Cooperation
OSCE	Organization for Security and Cooperation in Europe
PfP	Partnership for Peace
QMV	Qualified Majority Voting
SEA	Single European Act
The Seven	Austria, Denmark, Norway, Portugal, Sweden, Switzerland, United Kingdom
The Six	France, Federal Republic of Germany, Italy, Netherlands, Belgium, Luxembourg
WTO	Warsaw Treaty Organization
WEU	Western European Union

CHRONOLOGY

1929	September	Aristide Briand issues the proposal for a United States of Europe to the Assembly of the League of Nations at Geneva
1940	June	Winston Churchill proposes Anglo-French Union
1941	July	Altiero Spinelli and associates write the Ventotene Manifesto on European union
	August	Declaration of the Atlantic Charter
1944	July	Geneva Declaration by the Resistance Movement on European Union
		Bretton Woods Agreement on fixed exchange rates
1945	February	Yalta Conference
	May	End of Second World War in Europe
	June	Establishment of Allied Control Authority in Germany
	July	Potsdam Conference
1946	April	United Nations takes over the function of the League of Nations
	September	Winston Churchill calls for Franco-German reconciliation and a 'United States of Europe' in Zürich
1947	March	United Nations establishes Economic Commission for Europe (ECE)
		Benelux agrees to form Customs union
		Announcement of the Truman Doctrine
		France and Britain sign the Treaty of Dunkirk
	June	George Marshall announces European Recovery Programme
	July	Formation of the Committee for European Economic Cooperation
	October	Establishment of General Agreement on Tariffs and Trade (GATT)
		Formation of Benelux Economic Union
1948	March	Signing of Brussels Treaty between Britain, France and Benelux
	April	Signing of OEEC Convention in Paris by sixteen states
	May	Meeting of the Hague Conference

1948	June	Yugoslavia expelled from COMINFORM
(cont'd)		Soviet Union walks out of Allied Kommandatura
		Berlin Blockade begins
1949	January	Soviet Union forms the Council of Mutual Economic Assistance (CMEA)
	April	Signing of North Atlantic Treaty in Washington by twelve states
		Establishment of the International Ruhr Authority
	May	Signing of the Statute of the Council of Europe in Strasbourg by ten states
		Ending of Berlin Blockade
1950	May	Announcement of Schuman Plan for European Coal and Steel Community
	June	Outbreak of the Korean War
	October	Pleven proposal for a European Army
1951	April	Signing of the Treaty of Paris instituting the European Coal and Steel Community (ECSC) by the Six (France, Germany, Italy and Benelux countries)
1952	May	Signing of the Treaty of Paris instituting the European Defence Community (EDC) by the Six
	August	Entry into force of the ECSC Treaty with Jean Monnet as President of the High Authority
1953	March	Death of Stalin
		The Ad Hoc Assembly adopts the plan for a European Political Community (EPC)
1954	August	The French National Assembly rejects the EDC Treaty
	October	The signing in Paris of the Treaty establishing the Western European Union by the Six plus the UK
1955	May	Germany joins NATO
		Soviet Union and allies form the Warsaw Pact
		Signing of the Austrian State Treaty
	June	The Messina Conference of the Six and Institution of the Spaak Committee to advance European integration
	October	Jean Monnet creates the Action Committee for the United States of Europe
1956	May	The Six approve Spaak Report
	June	Opening of intergovernmental conference in Brussels entrusted with formulating the treaties
	October	Soviet suppression of Hungarian uprising
1957	March	The Rome Treaties instituting the European Economic Community and Euratom (the European Atomic Energy Commission)
1958	January	Rome Treaties enter into force with Walter Hallstein as President of the Commission
	February	Benelux Treaty of Economic Union signed in the Hague

1958 (cont'd)	December	Rejection in the OEEC of British proposal for a free trade area
1959	January	First tariff reductions in the EEC
1960	January	Signing of the Stockholm Convention instituting the European Free Trade Association (EFTA): Austria, Denmark, Norway, Portugal, Sweden, Switzerland and UK
	May	EFTA comes into force
	December	OEEC becomes OECD, including Canada and the US
1961	July	The Bonn Declaration
	August	Fouchet Plan – draft treaty for political union Construction of Berlin Wall
	November	Negotiations on British entry to the EEC begin
1962	January	EEC decides on basic principles for a Common Agricultural Policy (CAP) Second Fouchet Plan and 'Draft Treaty for a European Union'
	April	Breakdown of negotiations on the Fouchet Plan
	July	US President Kennedy proposes 'Atlantic Partnership' between the US and Europe Conclusion of 1960–62 negotiations for worldwide tariff cuts in GATT; Community substantially reduces common external tariff First regulations under the CAP take effect
	December	US and Britain sign Nassau Agreement for Polaris missile system
1963	January	President de Gaulle rejects British application to join the Community and the American offer of Polaris Signing of the Elysée Treaty for Franco-German friendship and cooperation in Paris
	July	Signing of Yaoundé Convention between the Community and eighteen African states
1964	May	Opening of the GATT negotiations (Kennedy Round) in Geneva
1965	March	EEC Commission proposes a common budget and increased powers for the European Parliament
	April	Signing of the treaty merging the three 'executives' of the Community
	June	Meeting of the EEC Council of Ministers on agricultural questions ends in constitutional 'empty chair' crisis: France boycotts EEC meetings
1966	January	Crisis resolved by the 'Luxembourg Compromise', the 'agreement to disagree'. France resumes participation
	March	France withdraws from NATO's integrated military command

1966 (cont'd)	May	EEC Council agrees to complete the Customs Union by 1 July 1968, eighteen months before schedule
	July	Agreement on Common Agricultural Policy allowing free trade in agricultural products by 1 July 1968
1967	May	Britain, Denmark and Ireland reapply for Community membership
		Kennedy Round negotiations end in agreement to make major cuts in industrial tariffs
	July	The 'Merger Treaty' of April 1965 becomes effective, creating a single Council and single Commission
	November	President de Gaulle vetoes British entry for the second time
1968	July	Customs Union of the Six becomes effective: creation of a common external tariff
	August	Warsaw Pact forces invade Czechoslovakia
	December	Launching of 'Agriculture 1980': a ten-year reform plan
1969	April	President de Gaulle resigns
	July	Commission proposes that Community activities be financed from its own resources by 1974, and that the Six increase the European Parliament's budgetary powers
		President Pompidou of France announces he does not oppose UK membership of the EC in principle
	December	Summit meeting of the Heads of State and Government at the Hague
		Council agrees on the principle of providing the Community with its own resources
		Completion of the transitional twelve-year period by the EC: beginning of 'final stage'
1970	February	EEC Council agrees on final regulation for the financing of the CAP, on giving the Community its own resources and on the budgetary powers of the European Parliament
	April	Six sign treaty in Luxembourg to strengthen the powers of the European Parliament and ensure the financial autonomy of the Community
	October	Werner Report on economic and monetary union
		Adoption of Davignon Report on foreign policy cooperation
	November	West Germany recognizes Oder-Neisse in treaties with Poland and Soviet Union
1971	January	Second Yaoundé Convention comes into force
	June	EC Council agrees to the admission of Britain, Denmark, Ireland and Norway to the Community
	July	British government publishes White Paper and accepts the terms of entry as 'just and reasonable'

1972	January	The Six and the applicant countries sign the Treaty of Accession to the European Community
	February	British Parliament approves legislation enabling the UK to join the EC
	March	The Council of Ministers approves the narrowing of fluctuation margins between member currencies and closer coordination of economic policies: the 'snake'
	September	Norwegians reject EC membership in referendum
1973	January	First enlargement of the EC becomes effective
		Community adopts a common commercial policy towards Eastern Europe
	July	Conference on Security and Cooperation begins in Helsinki
	October	Mutual and Balanced Force Reduction (MBFR) talks begin in Vienna
	December	Creation of a regional development fund in Community
1974	April	British Labour government demands renegotiation of the Treaty of Accession
	December	On the initiative of the French President Valéry Giscard d'Estaing, the Paris Summit institutes the European Council to bring together on a regular basis the Heads of State and Government
1975	February	The Lomé Convention signed by the Community and forty-six African, Caribbean and Pacific (ACP) countries. Replaces and extends Yaoundé
	June	British referendum endorses membership of the Community
	August	Helsinki Final Act instituting the Conference for Security and Cooperation in Europe (CSCE)
	December	Publication of the Tindemans Report on European union
1976	September	Agreement on direct elections for the European Parliament
1978	July	President Valéry Giscard d'Estaing and the German Chancellor Helmut Schmidt initiate, and the European Council at Bremen approves, the institution of the European Monetary System (EMS)
1979	February	European Court ruling on the free movement of goods within the Community: the Cassis de Dijon case
	March	EMS comes into force
	June	First direct elections to the European Parliament
	October	Second Lomé Convention between Community and 58 ACP states
	December	The European Parliament rejects Community budget for the first time
1981	January	Greece becomes the tenth member of the Community

1981 (cont'd)	October	London Report extending EPC
1983	January	A Common Fisheries Policy agreed
	June	The European Council at Stuttgart adopts the Solemn Declaration on European Union
1984	February	The European Parliament adopts the Spinelli plan for European Union, the Draft Treaty
	June	Second direct elections to the European Parliament Meeting of European Council at Fontainebleau: British budget rebate agreed
	December	Third Lomé Convention
1985	January	Jacques Delors becomes President of the Commission
	June	Commission White Paper on the internal market published Schengen Convention on free circulation of persons within Community European Council at Milan agrees to convene an intergovernmental conference for the revision of the Treaties Signing of accession treaties between Community and Spain and Portugal
	September	Intergovernmental Conference opens
1986	January	Spain and Portugal become members of the Community
	February	Signing of the Single European Act (SEA)
1987	July	Single European Act comes into force
1988	February	The European Council adopt the 'Delors I' package with a doubling of structural funds to finance the SEA
1989	June	Third direct elections to the European Parliament The European Council in Madrid approves the Delors Report on economic and monetary union (EMU)
	November	The fall of the Berlin Wall
	December	Meeting of the European Council at Strasbourg agrees to establish economic and monetary union
1990	October	German reunification UK joins ERM
	December	Start of two intergovernmental conferences on EMU and political union
1991	February	Warsaw Pact dissolved
	December	European Council at Maastricht adopts the Treaty on European Union
1992	February	Signing of the Maastricht Treaty
	May	Creation of the European Economic Area, including the EFTA countries
	June	Danish referendum rejects Maastricht Treaty (50.7 per cent no)

1992 (cont'd)	September	French referendum ratifies Maastricht (51 per cent yes)
	December	European Council meeting at Edinburgh. Opt-outs granted to Denmark. Delors II budgetary package adopted
1993	May	Second Danish referendum supports Maastricht (56.8 per cent yes)
	June	British parliament approves Maastricht Treaty Copenhagen Summit: Heads of State and Government agree to admit east European countries to the EU, subject to a range of conditions, especially a satisfactory performance with regard to economic questions, human rights and democracy
	August– September	EU currency crisis, leading to widening of parity margins in EMS to 15 per cent for members
	October	German Constitutional Court rules Maastricht Treaty compatible with the German constitution
	November	Maastricht Treaty enters into force
	December	Final agreement in the GATT Uruguay Round negotiations (signed in April 1994)
1994	January	The European Economic Area comes into force Establishment of European monetary institution in Frankfurt-am-Main
	March	Agreement on the accession of Austria, Finland, Sweden and Norway to the European Union Disagreement about weighted voting arrangements to apply after enlargement. UK vetoes proposals to increase blocking minority in the Council of Ministers from two large states plus one small state to two large plus two small
	May	EU agrees Pact for Stability in Europe, regarding protection of borders and respecting minority rights among prospective member states of east Europe
	June	Fourth direct elections to the European Parliament Russia signs the 'Partnership for Peace' agreement with NATO
1995	January	Sweden, Finland and Austria accede to EU
	March	Schengen Convention comes into effect
1997	June	Amsterdam Treaty revising Maastricht agreed
	October	Amsterdam Treaty signed
	December	Luxembourg Summit. Invitations issued to Czech Republic, Estonia, Hungary, Poland, Slovenia and Cyprus to open negotiations in March 1998 with a view to EU entry early in the new century

CHAPTER 1

THE ORIGINS: FROM THE TREATY OF VERSAILLES TO THE END OF THE SECOND WORLD WAR

1918–1945

INTRODUCTION

Although the idea of European union had been periodically espoused before 1914, it was the First World War and the inadequacies of the peace settlement which induced the first sustained efforts to find an alternative to the fragmentation of Europe.[1] That same peace settlement had in fact compounded Europe's fragmentation, sanctioning the dismemberment of the Habsburg Empire, the cession of former German and Russian territory and the creation of new states in central and east Europe. These states, lying between a temporarily weakened Germany and the new Soviet state in Russia, were anxious about their identity, divided by mutual claims against each other and haunted by the memory of their past subordination to the empires of Germany, Russia and the Habsburgs. Supposedly representing the triumph of the principle of self-determination, most were in reality themselves mini-empires, containing substantial minorities. In the west, territorial changes had been less dramatic, though Germany had lost the rich iron ore lands of Alsace-Lorraine. More dramatic French proposals for annexation in the west had foundered on Anglo-Saxon opposition.

France, one of the victors of the war, was left with a security dilemma little less imposing than before the war. Demographic trends and underlying economic strength put France at a long-term disadvantage *vis-à-vis* Germany, while Britain and the United States reneged on the security guarantee which they had promised France during the peace negotiations. The extent of French dissatisfaction with the settlement was reflected in its characterization as '*la paix boche*'.[2] The result was that France embarked upon a policy of revisionism, intended to remedy the deficiencies of the treaty. It was more self-evident that Germany would be a revisionist power. Unreconciled to defeat, Germany looked to the recovery of lost territory, especially in the east, and was resentful of the assertion of German guilt for the war and at the imposition of reparations. Reparations, which bedevilled Franco-German relations for the next decade, were in turn the product of a refusal to confront the budgetary problems bequeathed by the war and, more precisely, a refusal to increase direct taxes. The financial embarrassment in which European victors and vanquished alike found themselves was aggravated by the insistence of the United States on the payment of inter-allied war debts. Despite the apparent retreat into isolation, the United States, the only superpower of the 1920s, was the linchpin of European economic, and arguably political, stability.[3]

The United States played an ambiguous role in inter-war Europe. On the one hand, the United States was an economic competitor, whose challenge was embodied in the polemical title of a 1930 publication, *America Conquers Britain. A Record of Economic War*.[4] On the other hand, Europe was dependent upon American finance to maintain the circle of reparations and debt payments, and much else besides. On the one hand, America exercised a magnetic attraction. On the other hand, critics excoriated its supposedly malign influence upon European culture. In general, America was both a model and a threat. America as a model was strongly evident in the work of two Italian critics of the peace settlement, the industrialist Giovanni Agnelli and an economist, Attilio Cabiati. For them, the United States of America embodied the solution to Europe's political and economic problems: federation (Document 1.1). The idea exerted little influence. The dominant vision, at least for those who sought an alternative to Europe's internecine conflicts, was that of President Wilson and the League of Nations.

It was disillusion with Wilson's creation, the League, which induced Richard Coudenhove-Kalergi to embark upon a career as publicist and prophet of European integration. He too was influenced by America, and especially by the Pan-American Union, whose name he adapted in calling for a Pan-European Union.[5] The ambivalence about America was explicit: 'For Europe, Pan-America signifies either a great danger or a great hope: a danger in the event Europe remains divided into petty states while a continent is organizing itself across the Atlantic; a hope in the event that Europe takes a lesson from her more modern daughter and supplements the

Pan-American by a Pan-European movement.'[6] Yet, as he argued in his first public declaration in favour of Pan-Europe, in November 1922, the biggest obstacle to his dream was closer to home. It was the mutual antipathy of France and Germany, 'which hangs like the sword of Damocles over Europe'.[7] There were many omens from which he took comfort, including the fact that both France and Germany now had republican forms of government. Yet by the time he published his *Pan-Europa* in 1923, Franco-German relations had reached new depths.

French policy towards Germany was not entirely consistent. Alongside hopes of promoting a separate Rhineland state or the use of coercion to enforce strict fulfilment of the Versailles Treaty and reparations policy, there were strategies for some kind of economic integration. Underlying the latter was fear of German economic strength. The French commercial expert Jacques Seydoux, and the Minster for Reconstruction, Louis Loucheur, sought to solve the problem of reparations, reconstruction and German economic strength with a package involving German deliveries in kind to be set against reparations. Even more ambitious plans lay behind the scheme. Franco-German cooperation in the reconstruction of devastated northern France was to be followed by Franco-German collaboration in the reconstruction of Russia. The more immediate steps were embodied in the Wiesbaden Agreement of August 1921, but these soon fell victim to intransigence on both sides.[8] The idea of linking reconstruction and international rapprochement was widely debated. The British Prime Minister, Lloyd George, envisaged an international consortium, again intended to promote Russian reconstruction, on an even grander scale, but that foundered amidst the recriminations following on from the Rapallo Treaty of 1922 between Germany and Russia.

As Franco-German relations worsened, French policy turned towards the idea of the occupation of the Ruhr as a means of enforcing German compliance. Underlying the gamble of occupation, which began in January 1923, was the hope of permanently altering the balance of power by detaching the Rhineland from Germany. A year later the strategy was in ruins and the French franc was in little better shape. As France, under the new government of Edouard Herriot, stepped back from its attempt to revise the Treaty of Versailles, advocates of integration took heart. The formation of an International Committee for a European Customs Union in August 1924 reflected the more optimistic mood. Herriot even spoke of his hope 'one day to see the United States of Europe realised' in a speech of 25 January 1925.[9] Yet such affirmations have to be set alongside Herriot's desperate search for security, by trying once again to elicit British guarantees through a strengthened League of Nations. When security once again eluded France, the new Foreign Minister Aristide Briand turned to the only remaining strategy, reconciliation with Germany, but without entirely abandoning the old ones.

The initiative came from the German Foreign Minister Gustav Stresemann who, with Briand, presided over the only period of optimism in Franco-German relations. Stresemann offered, in January 1925, a Rhineland pact, guaranteeing the borders. The ensuing Locarno Pact of October 1925 brought together France, Belgium and Germany, along with Britain and Italy who guaranteed the agreement. Public displays of reconciliation did much to promote the new spirit of Locarno among optimists, but little to dispel the suspicions of pessimists like the French Deputy who observed that 'It would be folly not to vote for the Treaty but ... greater folly to believe in it.'[10] There were also signs of economic reconciliation in the following two years. September 1926 witnessed the conclusion of an International Steel Cartel, bringing together the major steel producers of Germany, France and Belgium. Strictly, this was a private agreement between industrialists though government officials had played an important role in the background. The enthusiasm with which this was greeted was as effusive as it was unwarranted. A German economic journalist speculated that the steel pact would have 'an effect on the political structure of Europe similar to that which the Zollverein had on the political structure of Germany'.[11] Even in retrospect, the ex-French Prime Minister Herriot rhetorically asked 'whether public men will have as much initiative and intelligence as private individuals, or whether in politics we are going to be content to walk in the old ways, ignoring the great transformation, which is silently creating a new world'.[12] Part of the attraction of the Steel Cartel was that it seemed to offer an alternative strategy for integration to the more traditional one of a customs union (Document 1.2). It was a strategy which would reappear in subsequent years.

Locarno, despite the misgivings of some French parliamentarians, did constitute an important step towards Franco-German reconciliation. But Locarno only entailed recognition of the western borders. There were arbitration treaties between Germany and Poland and Czechoslovakia, but there was no acceptance of Germany's eastern borders. It was well known that Stresemann's long-term goal was revision of the border with Poland. Even Poland's neighbour, Czechoslovakia, did not regard the current German–Polish border as viable, and constantly evaded an alliance with Poland for fear of being dragged into a German–Polish conflict.[13] Yet for all the limitations and justified criticism of Locarno, the idea of the Locarno spirit was not entirely spurious. In the words of the historian of Locarno diplomacy, Jon Jacobson,

> To be a good European during the Locarno era did not mean that one was willing to diminish the sovereignty of one's state; it meant that one did not take unilateral action. One went to Geneva four times a year and there consulted with the other members of the Council of Europe and attempted to act in concert with them.[14]

It was at Geneva, in September 1929, that Aristide Briand put forward the proposal for 'une sorte de lien fédéral' between the European states. There had been speculation for some time that Briand would take such an initiative. Briand's own motives were complex. He had failed once again to win American protection, when the Americans evaded his request for a security guarantee and offered instead the Kellogg–Briand Pact of 1928, with its blanket renunciation of war as a means of foreign policy. There was a catalogue of economic complications, all inducing resentment of America. This spilled out in his conversation with Stresemann in June 1929 (Document 1.3). Thrown back on France's own resources, Briand made one last bid for reconciliation, the offer of European Union in a speech in September 1929, while remaining stubborn on more immediate issues.

The hesitant response of the other states was to request the French to draw up a more precise proposal. It took several months and much redrafting before the French memorandum was ready. Once again Europeans looked across the Atlantic for inspiration. Briand's *chef de cabinet*, Alexis Léger, studied the Pan-American Union in preparation for drafting the memorandum.[15] When the final text was presented to the European governments in May 1930, it was an ambiguous document (Document 1.4), though no more so than later proposals which eventually did lead to the creation of European institutions. One of the statements to cause concern was the 'necessary subordination of the economic to the political'. This was a reversal of the priority indicated in Briand's September speech, where he had declared that 'Evidently, the Association will act chiefly in the economic domain: its is the most pressing question.'[16] The changed emphasis helped to fuel suspicion that Briand was seeking to establish an eastern Locarno. This was considered by the British Foreign Office, only to be rejected as implausible (Document 1.5). Britain found still other reasons to reject the plan, notably its supposed incompatibility with the League of Nations. The British business community had already swung behind the idea of a retreat into Empire. That sentiment was embodied in the choice offered to its readers by the *Daily Express* in July 1929: 'Europe and deterioration', 'America and subservience' or the prosperity of Empire.[17]

The German response was even less charitable than the British. The idea that Briand was seeking some kind of eastern Locarno was so entrenched that the Foreign Office simply observed that Briand's goals were so well known they did not require discussion.[18] The harshness and alacrity of judgement was a reflection of a new spirit in the German Foreign Office. Stresemann had died in October 1929 and the new Foreign Minister Julius Curtius was more concerned with strengthening German influence in central and east Europe. The official responses from Britain and Germany were naturally more guarded, but the basic attitude was clear enough to a disappointed Briand. The new mood was captured by a German neo-conservative publicist, Ferdinand Fried, who enthused over 'Europe's sudden turn towards domestic politics and therefore one's own nation, towards the new and sober objectivity in politics. Before then one believed so casually in a Pan-Europe, in a borderless community of all nations.'[19] He exaggerated both the extent of interest in European union and the turn to domestic politics, but he did capture the greater scepticism about what was attainable by acting in concert.

Nevertheless, the economic pressure to do so did not disappear. Briand's warning in September 1929 about the 'pressing question' of economic problems was made before the Wall Street crash of October 1929 and the subsequent financial destabilization in Europe. Even then, in September the economic plight of east Europe was depressing. The worldwide collapse of trade aggravated the situation, but east Europe was suffering from inherent structural economic problems. What most of the east European states desperately needed was access to western markets, preferential access. Preferential treatment violated the most favoured nation (MFN) principle which was the prevalent orthodoxy, but it found favour in France. France made two efforts to gain international cooperation to aid the east Europeans and consolidate its own influence in east Europe. Both packages, the 1931 *plan constructif* and the 1932 Tardieu plan, combined preferences, agricultural credits and provisions for the management of trade by cartels. The British response (Document 1.6) was to stand behind the conventional orthodoxy of the MFN principle and argue that cartels were best left to industrialists. France was no more successful with Germany, potentially the largest market for the struggling east Europeans.

Franco-German relations had been soured by the revelation of a planned Austro-German customs union in March 1931. Officially, this union was open to other states, though that offer had only been included to fend off criticism. The whole affair had been prepared in secret and, contrary to the spirit of Locarno, sprung upon the international stage. In reality it was a preparation for union, *Anschluss*, which, it was intended, would enhance German leverage in central and east Europe. French hostility was predictable and effective. Financially weakened, the Austrians backed away from the union. Neither Germany nor France had been successful in their initiatives. The underlying economic position, however, favoured Germany. France, with its large agricultural sector, could not really offer the east Europeans the markets they needed. Germany could, but was initially held back by international objections to preferential treaties. Under the new regime of Adolf Hitler, however, consideration of foreign sensitivities was no more than tactical. More indicative of the regime's intent were the unilateral actions by which Hitler reintroduced conscription and remilitarized the Rhineland. On the economic front, the regime concluded bilateral preference agreements with several east European states, both in order to meet its raw material demands, which grew with its rearmament programme, and to turn the economic dependence of its partners into a political lever. There was another, more sinister, motive behind this strategy. If German trade could be reoriented towards central and east European sources of foodstuffs and raw materials, Germany would be safe from western blockade in the event of war. By the end of the 1930s, not only had economic dependence failed to bring Germany political concessions, but German trade remained stubbornly focused on west and north-west Europe. In April 1939, economic experts were warning that without a massive increase in war potential all the 'sacrifice of blood in the next war' would not protect Germany from a 'self incurred bitter end'.[20]

With the invasion of Poland in September 1939, Hitler embarked upon a series of gambles in which he constantly raised the stakes. The result was the devastation of large tracts of Europe, population movements on a scale not seen in this millennium, a genocidal policy towards the Jews and a fundamental change in the balance of power, For most of Europe this meant defeat and the degradation of occupation, sufficient in many quarters to shake faith in the viability of the nation state. Britain's escape from defeat and occupation allowed at least the illusion of greatness to persist throughout and beyond the war, but even there defeat came close enough to induce at least a temporary and desperate search for alternatives. The catalyst was the rapid defeat of France. Having for so long evaded the French search for security guarantees, Britain, in a last minute attempt to prevent France capitulating to the advancing Germans, offered France a political union. The union, one of whose architects was Jean Monnet, was to include common citizenship and a common war cabinet. Its rejection paved the way for a form of collaboration in France which so divided the nation that it added an element of civil war to the experience of occupation. There was sufficient uncertainty in Britain to induce speculation on some form of union with the United States, in which, as one Labour politician noted, 'Britain would become merely the European outpost of an Anglo-Saxon group concentrated in the west.'[21] There was little prospect of this, if only because there would have been no interest in the scheme from the United States.

There was also fevered speculation in Germany about what to do with the conquered territories. Czechoslovakia's fate had been decided before the war. The Czech lands were designated the Protectorate of Bohemia and Moravia, while Slovakia became a puppet state. The importance of Czech industry for the German war effort induced the Germans to postpone their more radical plans for the Germanization of part of the Czech population and the expulsion of the remainder. Poland's prospects were even worse. It was divided between Germany and the Soviet Union and much of the German half was incorporated into the Reich. What was left was given the name of the General Government of Poland; it became the centre of the Holocaust. In the west the mosaic of different forms of occupation was even more complex. Norway and the Netherlands fell under Nazi Party control, both being subordinated to Gauleiters with the title of Reichskommisar. Belgium and part of northern France remained under a military command, while the rest of France was divided into a zone of military occupation and an area under the control of a French government based in the spa town of Vichy.

In various government and party agencies there was extensive debate about the economic future of the New Order in Europe. There were suggestions of customs unions and currency unions, but all this was dismissed as hasty at a key meeting in the Economics Ministry in July 1940 (Document 1.7). The public pronouncements of the Nazis were more guarded. On 25 July 1940, Economic Minister Walther Funk promised the occupied countries that Germany would provide a 'safe export outlet for years to come', 'stable exchange rates', 'a rational economic division of labour' and a 'sense of economic community'.[22] In Britain, the government was concerned that, in the light of the depression of the 1930s, these promises could prove attractive and even sap the will to resist in occupied Europe. Among those commissioned to draw up a response was the economist John Maynard Keynes. He was not slow to point to one of the main problems which would plague allied planning for a post-war world: 'I cannot see how the rest of Europe can expect effective economic reconstruction if Germany is excluded from it and remains a festering mass in their midst; and an economically reconstructed Germany will necessarily resume leadership. This conclusion is inescapable, unless it is our intention to hand the job over to Russia.'[23] Keynes's claim that it was good propaganda to admit the prospect of post-war German leadership found little support, but his emphasis upon the importance of the German economy to Europe as a whole was more difficult to dismiss.

In occupied Europe, the Nazi's initial policy of simple plunder gradually gave way to an attempt to utilize the industrial and agricultural capacity of occupied Europe in the interests of the German war effort. Although the new strategy was inaugurated by others, Albert Speer brought it to fruition with his agreement with the French Minister, Jean Bichelonne, in September 1943. The two men agreed on a programme of collaboration, including the creation of a committee for European armaments production.[24] Even more ambitious schemes, like the development of Norway as the centre of Europe's aluminium industry, had to be postponed in favour of the exploitation of existing resources. There were severe limits to the introduction of a more rational economic order in occupied Europe. The exaction of occupation costs, the competing ambitions of different German agencies, inflation, the dislocation of traditional patterns of trade and the more direct impact of war all contributed to an economic situation which made a mockery of Funk's promises of 1940.

Economic collaboration was accompanied by political collaboration. In occupied west Europe, the Germans found men only too willing to cooperate with the occupier. The French Vichy government, convinced that Britain was finished, looked to an indefinite future characterized by German hegemony and sought to find a place for France in the New Order. That policy was launched, at the initiative of the Vichy leader Marshall Pétain, in a meeting with Hitler at Montoire in November 1940. Both parties later complained that the other had not lived up to the spirit of Montoire. Part of the problem was that the French did not know what Hitler's long-term intentions were (Document 1.8). Collaborators elsewhere suffered from the same uncertainty. While Marshall Pétain enjoyed genuine and widespread popularity, collaborators in Belgium, the Netherlands and Norway were despised by their fellow countrymen. They hoped to use their willingness to work with the Germans to secure power for themselves, and to find a place for their own nations in the New Order, often at the expense of others. Vidkun Quisling, whose name became synonymous with collaboration, thought that the way forward was through a 'greater Nordic federation' in which Norway would have its own army, albeit one subject to German command.[25] The Belgian fascist Léon Degrelle offered the services of an enlarged Belgium, enlarged at the expense of northern France and the Netherlands, as a 'chosen land for exchanges between Germany and Latin civilisation'.[26] The Dutch national socialist Anton Mussert argued in August 1942, for a 'Germanic federation' and pointed to the participation of Dutch volunteers in the war on the eastern front as the basis for 'the new Netherlands army, whose existence can only be justified as part of the future Germanic army'.[27]

The attack on the Soviet Union in the summer of 1941 had given great encouragement to the collaborators. Here at last was a common endeavour in which they could all participate: an anti-Bolshevik crusade. Their enthusiasm for this 'European' war met with little sympathy from Adolf Hitler (Document 1.9). Hitler's real attitude to their pleas for treaties and federations was evident in his comment on yet another proposal from Quisling: Norway's fate would be determined only after the end of the war, and then by a 'one-sided declaration by the Reich government'.[28] Despite Hitler's own contempt for the idea of European union, the slogans of the collaborators and of many German agencies induced distrust of the idea. As late as April 1943 one member of the French resistance warned against such 'false ideas'.[29]

Nevertheless, the idea of European union was quite widespread among the diverse resistance groups in occupied Europe. The precise form it took, the geographic extent, the institutions and the remit, varied according to the ideological persuasion of its authors as well as national traditions and interests. The various drafts produced by the German Count Helmuth von Moltke emphasized the need for moral renewal and the strengthening of local political communities, as well as Europe-wide federal institutions enjoying popular legitimacy (Document 9.2). In Italy, the source of the most detailed proposals, including several draft constitutions, Altiero Spinelli and Ernesto Rossi worried about the situation at the end of the war (Document 9.3). They were convinced that the nation state had once fulfilled a useful function but had now become a restrictive cage. Yet they acknowledged that the nation state would have its advocates in the liberated countries and that the window of opportunity for the federalists would be a small one. What they did not know was that there would be even more important opponents of European federation: the victorious allied governments.

The federalists in the resistance were not the only ones whose calculations were upset by the shifting policies of allied governments. The first victim of Hitler's war, Poland, sought to find a more secure post-war future soon after defeat. General Sikorski, head of the government in exile, pressed hard for a Polish–Czechoslovak federation with strong central powers and decision-making.[30] The Czech leader, Eduard Beneš, was more cautious. Less certain of his own position, because his government was still not recognized by Britain, and suspicious of Poland's authoritarian tradition as well as its greater size, Beneš delayed. Gradually, the Czechs moved closer to agreement, though only on a looser confederation. Finally, on 23 January 1942 both sides published their commitment to create a confederation (Document 1.12). A week earlier the Greek and Yugoslav exile governments had announced similar measures as the basis for a Balkan union, albeit under strong British pressure. There was widespread support in the British foreign policy establishment for federations in east Europe. However, Britain was not the most important consideration, especially for Beneš. Haunted by the memory of western betrayal at Munich in 1938, Beneš was convinced that post-war Czechoslovak security would be dependent upon the Soviet Union. When, in February 1942, the Soviet Union made its displeasure clear, the confederation was effectively finished.

The smaller powers in the west, especially Norway, the Netherlands and Belgium, were also considering their long-term future. The speed of their collapse in 1940 was clear proof of their vulnerability and their inability to provide for their security without outside support. The first initiatives were taken by the Norwegian Foreign Minister, Trygve Lie, as early as December 1940. By October 1941 he was speaking of 'a strong organised collaboration between the two great Atlantic powers as a basis for the reconstruction of post-war Europe'.[31] For the Netherlands this meant a break with the traditional policy of neutrality. It was a step which Foreign Minister Eelco Van Kleffens was prepared to take. Indeed, in the spring of 1942 he offered to allow Britain to establish bases on Dutch territory as part of an Atlantic security system. There was considerable interest in these suggestions in the

British government, but also caution lest precipitate action alienate the Americans.[32] By the middle of 1944 the British Chiefs-of-Staff had added another dimension to the arguments. According to a Foreign Office summary:

> The military say, quite rightly, that the only power in Europe which can, in the foreseeable future, be a danger to us is the Union of Soviet Socialist Republics. They go on to argue that the only way to meet that potential danger is to organise against it now, and ... they have recently advanced as an argument in favour of the dismemberment of Germany the theory that we might then be able to use the man-power and resources of north-west Germany in an eventual war against the Russians.[33]

The predominant view, however, was that Britain should keep to the policy of trying to maintain the alliance between the big three in the post-war world. That strategy fitted in with American policy. From the outset Churchill had been determined to avoid any formulation of war aims which might alienate the Americans. When his own preference for some kind of regional organization ran up against Roosevelt's preference for a global organization, it was the American option which prevailed. Both men were inclined to indulge in rather general speculation about the post-war order, without the detailed advice of their officials or even ministers. Thus, Churchill wrote to Roosevelt in February 1943 suggesting that, as part of the planned United Nations, there might be 'an instrument of European government' and a 'similar instrument in the Far East'.[34] According to Cordell Hull, the President was tempted by Churchill's suggestion but Hull claimed the credit for bringing back his President to the agreed line of support for a global organization and the exclusion of any regional arrangements (Document 1.14).

There was more ambivalence about the other key question of post-war planning: the fate of Germany. Churchill, Roosevelt and Stalin all expressed support for solving the German problem by the simple expedient of dividing the country. There were echoes of France's Rhineland policy at the end of the First World War in Foreign Minister Eden's hopes that the Allies would be helped out of their difficulty by German separatism, which would lead to an automatic dissolution of the country. There was, as his officials pointed out, little prospect of this. Moreover, they argued, even if dismemberment was imposed it would be necessary to allow for the economic unity of Germany which, as in the nineteenth century, would in turn lead to political unification. Despite these considerations, Anthony Eden was reluctant to abandon his hopes of dismemberment. While visiting Washington in March 1943, both he and Roosevelt speculated about separatism. According to Roosevelt's adviser, when 'asked what they would do if that spontaneous desire did not spring up ... both the President and Eden agreed that, under any circumstances, Germany must be divided into several states, one of which must, over all circum-stances, be Prussia. The Prussians cannot be permitted to dominate all Germany.'[35] Later in the same year, at Teheran, Roosevelt, Churchill and Stalin agreed on the desirability of dismembering Germany and instructed the European Advisory Commission to examine the issue. The fact that it failed to do so reflected in part its preoccupation with other issues, but also the practical problems involved and the continuing divisions within the Allied camp. At the Yalta conference in February 1945 Stalin raised the question again, and when he received an evasive response from Roosevelt, 'replied that what he wished to find out here was whether or not it was the joint intention to dismember Germany or not'.[36] Despite Stalin's call for a clear decision, the others fell back on agreement to the principle of dismemberment and further study of the details.

The equivocation at Yalta, with the defeat of Germany clearly in sight, was testimony to the difficulty of the problem and the persistence of divisions about how to treat Germany. Not long before Yalta, at the September 1944 Quebec Conference, Roosevelt and Churchill had consented to the plan of the American Secretary of the Treasury, Henry Morgenthau. According to this, not only was Germany to be dismembered: it was also to be subject to a programme of deindustrialization. When pressed to consider the consequences for the population of the Ruhr, Morgenthau was uncompromising: 'Just strip it. I don't care what happens to the population ... I would take every mine, every mill and factory, and wreck it.'[37] Confronted with opposition from their ministers and officials, Roosevelt and Churchill withdrew their support of the Morganthau plan. Even the more moderate policy of Yalta met with criticism from the British Chancellor, John Anderson, who warned that a dismembered Germany would not be able to pay reparations and would impose a heavy financial burden upon the occupying powers.[38] As after the First World War reparations would divide the victors, though this time Britain and the United States increasingly resisted Soviet pressure for reparations in the interest of reducing the cost of occupation. Another, wider consideration was also at work. This was well put by the American Secretary of War, Henry Stimson, in July 1945. He acknowledged the need to guard against the re-emergence of a war economy, but added: 'from the point of view of general European recovery it seems even more important that the area be made useful and productive ... The problem which presents itself therefore is how to render Germany harmless as a potential aggressor, and at the same time enable her to play her part in the necessary rehabilitation of Europe.'[39]

The Yalta Conference was later associated with the division of Europe between the two superpowers. Critics denounced the west for betraying the east and central Europeans, consigning them to a Soviet sphere of influence. Yet despite the concession to Stalin about Poland's eastern frontier – an issue which took up far more time at the conference than Germany – there was no decision to divide Europe at Yalta. British, and even more so American policy was oriented to continuing cooperation with the Soviet Union in the post-war world.[40] The possibility of some form of European integration, though frequently raised, had been suppressed in favour of the global condominium of the great powers. Maintaining unity was necessarily the prime goal until the final victory over Hitler's Germany. Unity was maintained only by papering over the disagreements or postponing decisions, notably over Germany, which would soon undermine that same unity.

NOTES

1. For a survey of the earlier ideas see Derek Heater, *The Idea of European Unity* (Leicester, 1992).
2. Thus the French Ambassador to Rome, quoted in Walter A. McDougal, *France's Rhineland Diplomacy 1914–1924* (Princeton, 1978), p. 70. See McDougal for the following description of French policy.
3. On reparations see Bruce Kent, *The Spoils of War* (Oxford, 1989). On the position of the United States see Gilbert Ziebura, *Weltwirtschaft und Weltpolitik 1922/24–1931* (Frankfurt am Main, 1984).
4. Ludwell Denny, *America Conquers Britain. A Record of Economic War* (New York, 1930).
5. The title had been employed by the pacifist Alfred Fried, whose book *Pan Amerika* influenced Coudenhove-Kalergi. See L. Jilek, 'Paneurope dans les années vingt', *Relations Internationales*, no. 72 (1992), p. 415.
6. *Pan-Europe* (New York, 1926), p. 81.
7. Quoted in M. Posselt, 'Ricard Coudenhove-Kalergi und die europäische Parlamentarier Union', PhD, Graz, 1987, p. 494.
8. On the Wiesbaden agreements see Carole Fink, *The Genoa Conference* (Chapel Hill, 1984), pp. 18–19.
9. Quoted in C.H. Pegg, 'Die wachsende Bedeutung der europäischen Einigungsbewegung in den zwanzigen Jahren', *Europa Archiv*, Vol. 14, no. 24 (1962), p. 866.
10. Quoted in Anthony Adamthwaite, *Grandeur & Misery. France's Bid for Power in Europe 1914–1940* (London, 1985), p. 122.
11. Quoted in C.H. Pegg, *Evolution of the European Idea 1914–1932* (Chapel Hill, 1983), p. 69.
12. Edouard Herriot, *The United States of Europe* (London, 1930).
13. Anna M. Cienciala, *Poland and the Western Powers 1938–1939* (London, 1968), pp. 13–15.
14. Jon Jacobson, *Locarno Diplomacy* (Princeton, NJ, 1972), p. 385.
15. Cornelia Navari, 'The origins of the Briand Plan', in A. Bosco (ed.), *The Federal Idea*, Vol. 1 (London, 1991), p. 225.
16. Odile Keller and Lubor Jilek (eds), *Le Plan Briand d'union fédérale européene* (Geneva, 1991), p. 2.
17. Quoted in Robert Boyce, 'British capitalism and the idea of European unity between the wars', in P.M.R. Stirk (ed.), *European Unity in Context: The Interwar Period* (London, 1989), p. 79.
18. *Akten der Reichskanzlei. Weimarer Republik. Die Kabinette Brüning I und II*, Vol. 1, doc. 40.
19. 'Hintergründe der Haager Konferenzen', *Die Tat*, Vol. 21 (1930), p. 899.
20. Thus Karl Krauch on 28 April 1939. Reinhard Opitz (ed.), *Europastratagien des deutschen Kapitals 1900–1945* (Köln, 1971), p. 651.
21. Quoted in Henry Butterfield Ryan, *The Vision of Anglo-America* (Cambridge, 1987), p. 18.
22. W. Lipgens (ed.), *Documents on the History of European Integration*, Vol. 1 (Berlin, 1985), pp. 70–1.
23. *Dokumente zur Deutschlandpolitik*, Series 1, Vol. 1, p. 242.
24. *ADAP*, Series E, Vol. 6, doc. 338. These developments are discussed in detail in A.S. Milward, *The French Economy in the New Order* (Oxford, 1970).

25. Lipgens, *Documents on the History of European Intergration*, pp. 78–80.
26. *Ibid.*, pp. 75–6.
27. *Ibid.*, p. 101.
28. *ADAP*, Series E, Vol. 3, doc. 182.
29. Lipgens, *Documents on the History of European Intergration*, pp. 301–2.
30. See P.S. Wandycz, 'Recent traditions of the quest for unity', in J. Lukaszewski (ed.), *The Peoples' Democracies after Prague* (Bruges, 1970), pp. 37–66.
31. Quoted in J. Eisen, *Anglo-Dutch Relations and European Unity 1940–1948* (Hull, 1980), p. 9.
32. *Dokumente zur Deutschlandpolitik*, Series 1, Vol. 3, pp. 883–90. Paul-Henri Spaak, *The Continuing Battle* (London, 1971), pp. 82–4.
33. Graham Ross (ed.), *The Foreign Office and the Kremlin* (Cambridge, 1984), doc. 27.
34. *Roosevelt and Churchill. Their Secret Wartime Correspondence* (New York, 1975), p. 311.
35. *Dokumente zur Deutschlandpolitik*, Series 1, Vol. 4, p. 223.
36. *FRUS: The Conferences at Malta and Yalta 1945*, p. 612.
37. Quoted in Gregory A. Fossedal, *Our Finest Hour* (Stanford, 1993), p. 164.
38. On the importance of Anderson's intervention, see Keith Sainsbury, 'British policy and German unity at the end of the Second World War', *English Historical Review*, Vol. 94 (1979), p. 800.
39. *FRUS: The Conference of Berlin*, Vol. 2, pp. 755–6.
40. So much so that the American historian Daniel Yergin later described this policy as that of the Yalta axioms. *Shattered Peace* (Harmondsworth, 1980).

FURTHER READING

J. Baylis, 'British wartime thinking about a postwar European security group', *Review of International Studies*, Vol. 9 (1983), pp. 265–81.

W.D. Boyce, 'Britain's First "no" to Europe: Britian and the Briand Plan, 1929–30', *European Studies Review*, Vol. 10 (1980), pp. 17–45.

J. Gillingham, *Ideology and Politics in the Third Reich* (London, 1985).

P. King and A. Bosco (eds), *A Constitution for Europe* (London, 1991).

W. Lipgens (ed.), *Documents on the History of European Integration* (Berlin, 1985ff).

W. Lipgens, *A History of European Integration*, Vol. 1 (Oxford, 1982).

S. Marks, *The Illusion of Peace* (London, 1976).

A.S. Milward, *The New Order and the French Economy* (Oxford, 1970).

A.S. Milward, *The Fascist Economy in Norway* (Oxford, 1972).

C.H. Pegg, *Evolution of the European Idea* (Chapel Hill, 1983).

G. Ross (ed.), *The Foreign Office and the Kremlin* (Cambridge, 1984).

M.L. Smith and P.M.R. Stirk (eds), *Making the New Europe: European Unity and the Second World War* (London, 1990).

P.M.R. Stirk (ed.), *European Unity in Context: The Interwar Period* (London, 1989).

P.M.R. Stirk, *A History of European Integration since 1914* (London, 1996).

R. Vaughan, *Twentieth Century Europe* (London, 1979).

1.1

GIOVANNI AGNELLI AND ATTILIO CABIATI: *EUROPEAN FEDERATION OR LEAGUE OF NATIONS?*, 1918

Federazioni europea o lega delle nazioni? (Turin, Fratelli Bocca, 1918), trans. in *The Federalist*, Vol. 31 (1989), pp. 71–9

Towards the end of the First World War, Giovanni Agnelli, founder of FIAT, and Attilio Cabiati, an economist, firmly rejected the projected League of Nations in favour of a European union with a strong central government. In posing the question, 'European federation or League of Nations?', they set out a strategic choice which was to bedevil attempts to forge a European union (see also Documents 1.4, 2.6, 2.8).

Without hesitation we believe that, if we really want to make war in Europe a phenomenon which cannot be repeated, there is only one way to do so and we must be outspoken enough to consider it: a federation of European states under a central power which governs them. Any other milder version is but a delusion . . . the typical example which shows how one community, for its very survival, has had to change from a league of sovereign and independent states to a more complex form of a union of states ruled by a central power, is given with unsurpassable clarity by the history of the United States of America. As is well known, they went through two constitutions: the first, drawn up by a Congress of 13 states in 1776 and approved by these same states in February 1781; the second, approved by the national Convention of September 17th 1787 and which came into force in 1788.

A comparison between the two documents explains why the first failed, threatening the independence and freedom itself of the young Union, while the second has created a Republic, which we now all admire.

The 1781 constitution started by affirming the sovereign independence of the individual states. Article 2 states: 'each State retains its Sovereignty, Freedom and Independence, and every Power, Jurisdiction and Right . . . ' It is true that Article 13 decreed that the states must 'abide by the Determinations of the United States in Congress assembled': but . . . Article 13 was in constant conflict with Article 2. The essence of sovereignty is legal omnipotence and it cannot acknowledge a higher sovereignty without destroying itself . . .

The preface of the 1788 Constitution – which is basically the one currently in force – states solemnly: 'We, the Peoples of the United States, in Order to found a more perfect Union, establish Justice, ensure domestic Tranquility, provide for the common Defence, promote the general Welfare and secure the Blessings of Liberty to ourselves and our Posterity, do ordain and establish this Constitution for the United States of America.'

And in fact it sets up a central government, with legislative and executive power ...

We also wish to dwell for a moment on another of the great benefits that only the creation of a federal Europe can bring with it: the setting up of the whole European Continent into one production market ...

In Europe we had reached this level of absurdity, that every factory that arose in one state was a thorn in the side for every other state: that while the superb inventions of steam applied to land and sea transport, of electricity as motive power, of the telegraph and telephone had by then cancelled distance and made the world one single large centre and international market, little men strove with all their might to cancel the immense benefits of the big discoveries, artificially creating isolated markets and small production and consumption centres ...

Only a federal Europe will be able to give us a more economic realization of the division of labour, with the elimination of all customs barriers ...

_____ 1.2 _____

ELÉMER HANTOS: 'THE EUROPEAN CUSTOMS UNION', 1926

'Der europäische Zollverein', _Weltwirtschaftliches Archiv_,
Vol. 23 (1926), pp. 229–30, 235–8.

Elémer Hantos, a Hungarian economist, wrote extensively on aspects of European integration. He was a member of the International Committee for a European Customs Union, founded in 1924. In the extract printed here, however, he asks whether a customs union is the most promising road towards integration.

_____

The victory of the Pan-European idea in the intellectual world of contemporary Europe has given new life, in economically oriented minds, to the idea of a European customs union ...

Why is the Pan-European idea carried over into the economic realm, appearing above all in the form of a European customs union? Is it perhaps that customs barriers most strongly thwart the free circulation of economic forces? In the times before the war one could answer this question affirmatively. To conduct trade policy meant, at that time, to utilise customs. Custom rates were the most important mechanism in trade policy. The arsenal of postwar trade policy worked with more comprehensive armaments; new weapons appear alongside the old. Exchange rate fluctuations, transfer difficulties, obstacles to transport, import and export bans, sales taxes and railway tariffs are barriers which exceed the highest customs dues in their effectiveness. Yet a European currency union or a European transport union is scarcely discussed: a trading union, on the other hand, is presented as the be all and end all of economic cooperation. The cause of this phenomenon is perhaps to be sought in this, that despite the inflation of currency advisers and theorists of money, there are yet more people who have an insight into, and trust their own opinion on, customs matters than is the case with financial policy or the technical problems of transportation. Moreover, the logic of things leads more easily from the well-known starting point of unpopular tariffs to general conclusions which are intelligible to broad circles. The syllogism, persuasive to every layman, runs: the maintenance of customs dues mean higher prices; higher prices bring a reduction in purchasing power; a reduction in purchasing power produces a shrinking market; a shrinking market leads to a reduction of production; a reduction of production creates poverty and misery. The European customs union, on the other hand, brings, through the abolition of customs dues, cheaper prices; lower prices create higher purchasing power; higher purchasing power produces an expansion of the market; expansion of the market leads to higher production; higher production creates prosperity and wealth ...

However well one may agree about borders, however convinced one may be of the correctness of the goal of a European customs union, the difficulties of managing the transition from today's divisions to a unified economic region are not thereby overcome. Even the most enthusiastic defender of the idea shrinks back from a leap out of the current situation into the desired one and wants to allow far reaching transitional measures. The sudden abolition of customs borders would condemn part of Europe's stock of factories and produce great unemployment. The considerable number of enterprises that are kept viable only by the customs tariffs of their homeland would be the first victims. Also, those factories which today can dump exports because of the high prices within their protected domestic markets, would be condemned to go under. Hardship could scarcely be avoided in the economic transformation; it could, however, be mitigated through a planned reduction which would set the date, for each branch of industry and for each customs area, at which customs must be completely set aside ...

International industrial interests could pave the way for the economic unification of Europe more effectively than the multilateral, staged reduction of customs tariffs. Syndicates and distribution agencies of individual branches of the economy, cartellization or the horizontal development in large-scale industries, could be a surrogate for customs tariffs. They could also be more effective than customs tariffs as equalization mechanisms, in the sense of protecting weaker groups against stronger ones, and may even promote the general equalization of production costs more quickly than the dismantling of customs barriers. One can see that a harmonization of the conflicts in the creation of an inter-state economic union may occur not only from state to state. The planned cooperation of private economic interests in international production, distribution, transport and consumer organizations would vigorously promote the European division of labour without deep-going damage to individual economies, without shaking productive life ...

For the near future, therefore, a regime of free trade in Europe is not to be expected. One needs only to recall how slowly and under what difficult circumstances the German customs union came about ... In that case the presuppositions were incomparably more favourable. It was a question of an understanding between peoples of the same origin and the same political aspirations. It would already signify great progress if areas that were previously economically united would return to mutual free trade. For the present it is not a question of final goals but of tendencies and movements. The realization of a European customs union will have to wait for a long time, but the idea itself must underlie all political and economic measures.

1.3

CONVERSATION BETWEEN ARISTIDE BRIAND AND GUSTAV STRESEMANN, 11 JUNE 1929

Akten zur Deutschen Auswärtigen Politik,
Series B, Vol. 12, doc. 19.

This conversation took place in Madrid, where both men were attending the Council of the League of Nations. It illustrates some of the considerations, including uncertainty about Britain and fear of American competition, which were to have lasting influence.

Mr Briand pointed out that ... the German press was being impatient and in large headlines spoke of negotiations between himself and the Reich Minister [Stresemann] ... There could be no talk of official negotiations taking place here in Madrid. It was a question only of clarifying mutual conceptions in personal talks ...

For Germany and France one could assume willing cooperation. Spain would certainly go along. In Italy the attitude was not as clear. But Italy would undoubtedly participate in a kind of 'European federation' if most of the other European states were for it. In relation to England the position was also unclear, since England would have to take account of its Dominions ...

In any event there was a pressing need to keep European cooperation in sight, in order to protect oneself from American supremacy ... The lack of cooperation had shown up, for example, with film. The current position, where there is almost no national film industry in the individual countries, but everything is crushed by American competition, could have certainly been avoided if the European states had come together in time.

The Reich Minister observed that the situation in the automobile industry was similar.

1.4

ARISTIDE BRIAND:'MEMORANDUM ON THE ORGANIZATION OF A REGIME OF EUROPEAN FEDERAL UNION', 17 MAY 1930

International Conciliation, Special Bulletin, June 1930, pp. 327, 329, 333, 335, 337, 339, 341, 343, 345.

Aristide Briand held ministerial office in several French cabinets, including the post of Premier. Together with the long-standing German Foreign Minister Gustav Stresemann, he was regarded as the most pro-European of statesmen. His proposal for a European Federal Union, first made in 1929, was the first formal proposal for European union made by a government in this century. The proposal was consigned to further study and effectively buried later in 1930.

The proposal taken under consideration by twenty-seven European Governments found its justification in the very definite sentiment of a collective responsibility in face of the danger which threatens European peace, from the political as well as the economic and social point of view, because of the lack of coordination which still prevails in the general economy of Europe. The necessity of establishing a permanent regime of conventional solidarity for the rational organization of Europe arises, in fact, from the very conditions of the security and well-being of the peoples which their geographical situation compels, in this part of the world to participate in a *de facto* solidarity . . .

This means that the search for a formula of European cooperation in connection with the League of Nations, far from weakening the authority of this latter must and can only tend to strengthen it, for it is closely connected with its aims . . .

The European organization contemplated could not oppose any ethnic group, on other continents or in Europe itself, outside of the League of Nations, any more than it could oppose the League of Nations . . .

The policy of European union to which the search for a first bond of solidarity between European Governments ought to tend, implies in fact, a conception absolutely contrary to that which may have determined formerly, in Europe, the formation of customs unions tending to abolish internal customs houses in order to erect on the boundaries of the community a more rigorous barrier against States situated outside of those unions . . .

It is important, finally, to place the proposed inquiry under the general conception that in no case and in no degree can the institution of the federal bond sought for between European Governments affect in any manner the sovereign rights of the States, members of such a *de facto* association . . .

Necessity of a mechanism adapted to assuring to the European union the organs indispensable to the accomplishment of its task:

A. Necessity of a representative and responsible organ in the form of regularly establishing the 'European Conference', composed of all the European Governments which are members of the League of Nations and which would be the essential directing organ of the European Union, in liaison with the League of Nations.

The powers of the Conference, the organization of its presidency and of its regular or extraordinary sessions, should be determined at the next meeting of the European States ...

B. Necessity of an executive organ, in the form of a Permanent Political Committee, composed only of a certain number of Members of the European Conference and assuring, in practice, to the European Union its organization for study at the same time as its instrument of action. The composition and powers of the European Committee, the manner of designation of its members, the organization of its presidency and of its regular or extraordinary sessions should be determined at the next meeting of the European States ...

C. Necessity of a secretariat service, however, restricted at the beginning to assure the administrative execution of the instructions of the President of the Conference or of the European Committee, communications between Governments signatory to the European Pact, convocations of the Conference or of the Committee, preparation of their discussions, recording and notification of their resolutions, etc. ...

A. General subordination of the Economic Problem to the Political.

All possibility of progress towards economic union being strictly determined by the question of security, and this question being intimately bound up with that of realizable progress toward political union, it is on the political plane that constructive effort looking at giving Europe its organic structure should first of all be made. It is also on this plane that the economic policy of Europe should afterwards be drawn up, in its broad outlines, as well as the special customs policy of each European State.

The contrary order would not only be useless, it would appear to the weaker nations to be likely to expose them, without guarantees or compensation, to the risks of political domination which might result from an industrial domination of the more strongly organized States.

It is therefore logical and normal that the justification of the economic sacrifices to be made to the whole should be found only in the development of a political situation warranting confidence between peoples and true pacification of minds ...

B. Conception of European political cooperation as one which ought to tend toward this essential end: a federation built not upon the idea of unity but of union; that is to say, sufficiently flexible to respect the independence and national sovereignty of each of the States, while assuring them all the benefit of collective solidarity for the settlement of political questions involving the fate of the European community or that of one of its Members.

1.5

MEMORANDUM ON M. BRIAND'S PROPOSAL FOR A EUROPEAN FEDERAL UNION, 30 MAY 1930

Documents on British Foreign Policy, Series 2, Vol. 1, doc. 189.

This memorandum was one of the more favourable in the internal British debate, which culminated in effective British rejection of the Briand plan.

The Memorandum, for which M. Briand has kept Europe waiting all these months, is, at least at first sight, a surprising and disappointing work. It is permeated by a vague and puzzling idealism expressed in such phrases as 'collective responsibility in face of the danger which threatens the peace of Europe', 'need for a permanent regime of solidarity', and much else which may mean a great deal or may mean nothing at all ...

M. Briand's proposed organisation could hardly fail to interfere with many of the practical activities already carried on by various organs of the League, and might well prove an embarrassing rival to it, while it is hard to see how it could, within a measurable period of time, become more efficient ...

It is conceivable (though very improbable) that M. Briand was not serious when he spoke of the urgency of economic reorganisation at Geneva last September; or (it may be from apprehension of British and American criticisms) he may indeed have been serious then, but has since changed his mind. In this case we are forced to take it that M. Briand is making his present proposals as a political move. He may think that the establishment of his 'European Association' would set a further seal on the sanctity of the present territorial and political organisation of Europe established by the Peace Treaties and post-War arrangements. It would be strange if he seriously believes that all or even the majority of European Powers would be likely to accept such a plan, which would offer most of them no advantages and would in their eyes appear merely to reinforce France's political hegemony in Europe. Perhaps, then, M. Briand calculates that the refusal, as is to be expected, of Germany, Italy and other Powers to entertain his proposals, ostensibly directed as they are towards a high moral ideal of stabilisation and co-operation, may both discredit the general policy of these countries in the eyes of the world, and provide him with convincing proofs on which future French Governments can dilate, that France, alone or chief among European Powers, thinks and works for the salvation of Europe. All this is possible, perhaps even probable; it is typical of a certain kind of French policy, but it does not fit in with what we know of M. Briand. Almost alone among French politicians he has in recent years consistently shown himself a good European, a friend of peace and of the improvement of international relations. It would be disappointing to have to fall back on the conclusion that M. Briand had been persuaded or coerced into the view that all there is for him to work for now, and in the future, is the maintenance of French political supremacy. Moreover the attempt is really too barefaced to be likely to succeed. Germany, Italy and other Powers are not likely to fall into the trap, if trap there be . . .

Though he emphasises the necessity of political association as a preliminary European reorganisation, it may well be that what he has in mind is not only, perhaps not even primarily, further military and political security for France (though no doubt he does desire this) but also such regrouping and consolidation of European finance and industry as to assure France and the rest of Europe against the ever-growing strength of Non-European and especially American competition. This is primarily what has always been meant by 'United States of Europe' or 'Pan-Europa' and without this it is hard to see that the word 'Pan-Europa' can mean anything at all. It is difficult to believe that M. Briand, who has repeatedly expressed his sympathy for the European idea, should not have something like this at the back of his mind; indeed, it is only the economic aspect of European reorganisation that could offer any attraction to Germany, Italy and many other European States, and if Europe is ever to be brought into a closer political formation it can surely be only as a result of closer economic ties . . .

This may be the key to M. Briand's meaning when he speaks of 'the subordination in principle of the economic problem' to 'the principle of political cooperation'. He may mean that economic experts left to themselves will always haggle about conflicting vested interests and will never reach practical results; that until the political leaders of the governments concentrate attention on the overriding common interests which European countries share, there will be little hope for 'the effective realisation in Europe of the programme laid down by the last Economic Conference of the League'.

_____ 1.6 _____

BRITISH COMMENTS ON A FRENCH PLAN FOR DEALING WITH THE CRISIS IN EAST CENTRAL EUROPE, MAY 1931

Documents on British Foreign Policy, Series 2, Vol. 2, doc. 37.

These objections by the British Foreign Office to the French plan for a solution to the economic crisis in east Europe contributed to the failure of the French scheme. Another French proposal in 1932 met with similar objections.

As these comments will be in the nature of criticism, it is desired at the outset to make it clear that we do not wish to be obstructive or hostile, but, on the contrary, sincerely hope that these tentative observations may help in the formulation of the French scheme to be put forward at Geneva.

1. *Inability of the Countries of Central and east Europe to Dispose of Their Cereals*

So far as the United Kingdom is concerned, we are, of course, little interested in the duties levied on cereals by European consuming countries, though this is by no means the case as regards other parts of the Empire. It should, however, be mentioned that the United Kingdom are substantial exporters of flour to Europe, and that if any preference were extended to that commodity our interest would at once be aroused ...

Also when M. Arnal originally outlined the scheme at the Foreign Office, he specified France, Germany, Czechoslovakia, Austria, Italy and Switzerland as being the six countries who were to grant this agrarian preference. Is this still the intention? Is not considerable difficulty foreseen in inducing Germany to agree to this unless a big counter-concession is offered to her? ...

It was gathered from M. Arnal that the French Government did not anticipate that the non-European grain-exporting countries would raise any difficulties over the preference scheme now proposed. It must be admitted, however, that this is by no means the impression derived by the British representative at recent meetings when this question has been discussed. At the Rome Wheat Conference the representative of the Argentine was the first to state that this country would not relax the most-favoured-nation clause in its treaties with European countries in order to allow them to give preference to wheat grown in Central Europe; the representatives of Canada and Australia then took the same line. They also pointed out that the chief sufferers in the present crisis were the overseas countries, such as Australia, Canada and the Argentine, which exported about 60 per cent. of their combined harvest, while the Danubian countries only had to export about 6 per cent. of theirs.

2. *The Crisis in Industrial Countries*

While we are in no way opposed to the development of the cartel system in appropriate cases, we feel that the effect of this policy on the general situation must be very limited, and that, taken by itself, this policy would be quite inadequate to remedy the existing crisis. Experience shows that cartels often take several years to build up; it is only in a few industries that the system is applicable, and it is difficult or impossible to apply in industries where there are a large number of small concerns or a strong tradition in favour of individualism. The formation of cartels is a matter for the industrialists concerned, and not for Governments, and where their formation has not been found possible or desirable up to the present there is a strong presumption that grave difficulties exist in organising industry in this way. We are, therefore, firmly convinced that cartels, whatever their eventual advantages, cannot in any way be regarded as an adequate alternative to tariff reductions.

3. *Financial Proposals*

We cordially endorse the view that the resumption of foreign lending on the part of those countries which have capital available for lending abroad must be an essential feature in any scheme for economic co-operation. But we must recognise that it is not enough to express an abstract sympathy with this view, and that it is necessary to devise concrete methods for ensuring a regular and adequate flow of credit to the countries which require it ...

_____ 1.7 _____

MEETING AT THE REICH ECONOMIC MINISTRY, 22 JULY 1940

W. Lipgens (ed.), *Documents on the History of European Integration*, Vol. 1 (Berlin: de Gruyter, 1985), pp. 62–5.

Military success in the west induced extensive speculation on the 'New Order' in Europe. At this meeting, Nazi Economic Minister Walther Funk rejected the more ambitious plans and revealed the exploitative nature of the 'New Order'.

The preparatory work to be undertaken under the Minister's overall direction was to include the following:

1. Coordination of the incorporated and occupied territories within the Great German economy.
2. Economic settlement with the enemy states.
3. Reorganization of the continental economy directed by Germany, and its relations with the world economy ...

1. Currency questions . . .
    It was fantasy to talk at this stage of a unified economy on a European scale, and in the same way it was harmful to use slogans like 'Currency and customs union' and to expect them to solve all difficulties. A currency or customs union could only be envisaged with a country having a similar standard of life to our own. This was not the case in south-east Europe, for instance, and it was not at all in our interest to confer on that area a similar standard of life to ours. This could only impair the efficiency of the local economy. In discussing post-war organization we must always be clear what immediate measures were necessary and what might be called for in the long run.

2. . . . Germany now had the political power to reorganize the European economy in accordance with her own needs. There was also the political intention to use that power, so that other countries would have to adapt themselves and their economies to our plans and needs. But all our needs could not be met in Europe. The needs of Europe (apart from Russia and Italy) for raw materials were such that, even counting parts of Africa and Asia as colonies, there would still be a considerable import requirement. This requirement must be decreased by intensifying European production: only thus could we regain our economic freedom. But we wanted more than this, as it was the Führer's special aim to improve the living standards of German workers. In order to satisfy needs that went beyond the bare minimum, we would have to trade with overseas countries.
    . . .

4. Foreign trade
    German foreign trade was based on bilateral arrangements. This had worked well so far, but it had the disadvantage that one was tied to a particular partner and could not start importing at will from some other country that might for a time have more of the commodity in question. Hence the bilateral system must be enlarged into a multilateral one.
    . . .

6. Questions of organization
    To enable the other countries in our sphere of interest to take similar measures, which must be agreed with us as a matter of principle, their respective economies must be reorganized. The Reich organization for agriculture could set up corresponding bodies in other countries, so supervise the whole economic process including production, processing and distribution to consumers. Similar cooperation is envisaged in industry and trade.

7. Two groups of countries
    The European countries within the German sphere of interest fall into two groups. The first comprises countries with a similar price, wage and salary, tax and income level to ours: e.g. Denmark, Holland and Switzerland. The south-eastern countries form the second group. While the first are to be organized similarly to ourselves and treated more generously in the matter of payments, the others are too different from us for a payments and currency union to be considered.

—————————————————————— 1.8 ——————————————————————

CONVERSATION BETWEEN ADOLF HITLER AND ADMIRAL DARLAN, 11 MAY 1941

Documents on German Foreign Policy,
Series D, Vol. 12, doc. 491.

At this meeting, Admiral Darlan, Deputy Prime Minister of the Vichy regime, sought to revive Hitler's interest in collaboration and to gain concessions for France. He was not successful.

... [Darlan] welcomed this opportunity to stress once more the extent to which Marshal Pétain and he himself were convinced of the need for cooperation between France and Germany ...

The Führer had conquered Europe. The formation of a European confederation of states therefore depended on him ... To be sure, the permanence and continuity of such a European confederation required the voluntary and sincere cooperation of all its members. From this also followed the unavoidable necessity of Franco-German collaboration ...

In the further course of his remarks Darlan then quoted a statement by Marshall Pétain, in which the latter expressed the wish for promoting the rapprochement between France and Germany but at the same time pointed out that at the moment France was unfortunately marching 'in the dark'; he hoped that the Führer would light up the dark road along which France was moving, so that the French nation could get a clearer picture of its future ...

The Führer replied that ... even now he did not understand why France and England had declared war on Germany. There were no practical or sensible reasons for it, unless the two countries wished to keep a great nation from existing ...

All measures which could be taken at the moment were merely emergency measures. France had to realize that real recovery could not begin until after England had finally been beaten ...

Admiral Darlan thanked the Führer for his statements and agreed with his view that nothing definitive could be done until England was defeated.

_____ 1.9 _____

MARTIN BORMANN: RECORD OF MEETING ON NAZI AIMS IN EAST EUROPE, 16 JULY 1941

W. Lipgens (ed.), *Documents on the History of European Integration*, Vol. 1 (Berlin: de Gruyter, 1985), pp. 85–6.

While collaborators greeted the attack on the Soviet Union as the beginning of a collective war against Bolshevism, Hitler privately asserted German hegemony.

By way of introduction the Führer emphasized that he wished first of all to make some basic statements. Various measures were now necessary; this was confirmed, among other events, by the assertion in an impudent Vichy newspaper that the war against the Soviet Union was Europe's war and that, therefore, it had to be conducted for Europe as a whole. Apparently the Vichy paper meant by these hints that it ought not to be the Germans alone who benefited from this war, but that all European states ought to benefit from it.

It was essential that we should not proclaim our aims before the whole world; this was in any case not necessary, but the chief thing was that we ourselves should know what we wanted. In no event should our own course be made more difficult by superfluous declarations. Such declarations were superfluous because we could do everything wherever we had the power, and what was beyond our power we would not be able to do anyway ...

We shall therefore emphasize again that we were forced to occupy, administer, and secure a certain area; it was in the interests of the inhabitants that we provide order, food, traffic, etc., hence our measures. It should not be recognizable thereby that a final settlement is being initiated. We can nevertheless take all necessary measures – shooting, resettling, etc. – and we shall take them.

But we do not want to make any people into enemies prematurely and unnecessarily. Therefore we shall act as though we wanted to exercise a mandate only. It must be clear to us, however, that we shall never withdraw from these areas.

Accordingly we should:

(1) do nothing which might obstruct the final settlement, but prepare for it only in secret;

(2) emphasize that we are liberators.

1.10

HELMUTH VON MOLTKE: 'INITIAL SITUATION, AIMS AND TASKS', 24 APRIL 1941

W. Lipgens (ed.), *Documents on the History of European Integration*, Vol. 1 (Berlin: de Gruyter, 1985), pp. 385–6.

Helmuth von Moltke was a member of the German resistance to Hitler. He was killed by the Nazis on 23 January 1945.

III. Expected political and military situation at the end of the war.

A) External Relations
1. Germany has been defeated ... For our purposes, the possibility of a German victory is of little interest since it would defer the conditions on which the fulfillment of our objectives depends to a much later period ...

B) Domestic Politics
1. The European demobilization has led to the creation of a large economic organization, directed by an inter-European economic bureaucracy and by economic self-governing bodies. Economic policy has been unequivocally subordinated to the rest of domestic policy.

2. Europe is divided into self-governing administrative units, formed in accordance with historical traditions. They are somewhat similar in size and have special relations with each other within groups. In this way the absolute domination of the former Great Powers, Germany and France, has been broken without creating resentment.

3. The administration of cultural affairs is de-centralized, but the possibility for regular exchanges between the regions remains. The confessional communities are disestablished, but they still have strong claims to be supplied with resources.

4. The constitutions of the individual states are entirely different. They all agree, however, in fostering the growth of all small communities. These latter enjoy certain rights in public law and they have an acknowledged claim to a share of public resources.

5. The highest legislative body in the European state is responsible to the individual citizens and not to the self-governing bodies. As a matter of principle, eligibility for both active and passive electoral rights will not be attained on the basis of age, but rather on the basis of specific constructive activities for the community. Whether universal suffrage ought to follow from this or whether the highest legislative body ought to be formed otherwise are questions of technique rather than principle.

6. Life and limb are to be protected by a legal process that allows no opportunity

for the employment of police methods. Economic activity is to be assured by conferring on certain occupations a status similar to that enjoyed by property. A private sector in housing and consumer goods is to be safeguarded.

7. Non-functional rights over the means of production are to be further restricted, without removing the pleasure that can be derived from responsibility and initiative.

8. The highest executive power is exercised by a cabinet consisting of five persons: the Prime Minister, Foreign Minister, Defense Minister, Minister of the Interior and Minster of Economics. In addition there will be a number of junior ministerial posts which will be represented at Cabinet level by one of the five senior ministers.

_____1.11_____

ALTIERO SPINELLI AND ERNESTO ROSSI: *THE VENTOTENE MANIFESTO*, July 1941

The Ventotene Manifesto (London: Altiero Spinelli Institute, n.d.), pp. 26, 31.

This manifesto is named after an island on which opponents of the Italian fascist regime were imprisoned. Spinelli played a long and important role in post-war European integration.

Germany's defeat would not automatically lead to the reorientation of Europe in accordance with our ideal of civilization.

In the brief, intense period of general crisis (when the States will lie broken, when the masses will be anxiously waiting for a new message, like molten matter, burning, and easily shaped into new moulds capable of accommodating the guidance of serious internationalist-minded men), the most privileged classes in the old national systems will attempt, by underhand or violent methods, to dampen the wave of internationalist feelings and passions and will ostentatiously begin to reconstruct the old State institutions. Most probably, the British leaders, perhaps in agreement with the Americans, will try to restore the balance-of-power politics, in the apparent immediate interests of their empires ...

The question which must be resolved first, failing which progress is no more than mere appearance, is the definitive abolition of the division of Europe into national, sovereign States. The collapse of the majority of the States on the Continent under the German steam-roller has given the people of Europe a common destiny: either they will all submit to Hitler's dominion, or, after his fall, they will all enter a revolutionary crisis and thus will not find themselves separated by, and entrenched in, solid State structures. Feelings today are already far more disposed than they were in the past to accept a federal reorganization of Europe. The harsh experience of recent decades has opened the eyes even of those who refused to see, and has matured many circumstances favourable to our ideal.

_____1.12_____

AGREEMENT ON A POLISH-CZECHOSLOVAK CONFEDERATION, 23 JANUARY 1941

Journal of Central European Affairs, Vol. 2 (April 1942), pp. 91–2.

This agreement was not implemented, largely because of Stalin's opposition.

1. The two Governments desire that the Polish-Czechoslovak Confederation should embrace other States of the European area with which the vital interests of Poland and Czechoslovakia are linked up.
2. The purpose of the Confederation is to assure common policy with regard to foreign affairs, defense, economic and financial matters, social questions, transport, posts and telegraphs.
3. The Confederation will have a common general staff, whose task it will be to prepare the means of defense, while in the event of war a unified supreme command will be appointed.
4. The Confederation will coordinate the policy of foreign trade and customs tariffs of the States forming the Confederation with a view to the conclusion of a customs union.
5. The Confederation will have an agreed monetary policy. Autonomous banks of issue of the States forming the Confederation will be maintained. It will be their task to assure that the parity established between the various national currencies shall be permanently maintained ... Questions of nationality will remain within the competence of the individual States forming the Confederation.

_____1.13_____

THE MEMOIRS OF CORDELL HULL, 1948

The Memoirs of Cordell Hull, Vol. 2 (London, Hodder & Stoughton, 1948), pp. 642–6.

The Secretary of State of the United States, Cordell Hull, was an ardent supporter of worldwide international organization, and saw European integration as a threat to this broader ambition.

President Roosevelt agreed in general with the Prime Minister's regional ideas. During the spring of 1943 I found there was a basic cleavage between him and me on the very nature of the postwar organization ...

At that time he did not want an over-all world organization. He did favour the creation of regional organizations, but it was the four big powers that would handle all security questions ...

The more advanced regional ideas of President Roosevelt and Prime Minister Churchill, however, might lead to questions of balance of power, and regional organizations of the type they envisaged might deal arbitrarily with one another and in the internal affairs of their members, whether by military force or economic pressure or their equivalent. This would open the door to abuses and the exercise of undue privileges by greedy, grasping nations possessing great military and economic strength.

In various meetings at the White House, my associates and I presented these arguments to the President with all the force we could. As summer arrived he began to turn toward our point of view.

EUROPE BETWEEN THE SUPERPOWERS

1945–1949

INTRODUCTION

At the end of the Second World War many of the problems which the victors of the First World War had signally failed to solve were still there, including French insecurity in the face of the underlying economic strength of Germany. French policy resembled that after 1918. Indeed, it was if anything even more demanding. De Gaulle wanted French troops 'from one end of the Rhine to the other and the detachment of the left-bank of the Rhine and the Ruhr zone'.[1] He was so committed to this that he even made British assent to these principles a condition of an

Anglo-French treaty, a condition which Britain rejected. France had gained a zone of occupation in Germany, by courtesy of British pressure, and a place on the Allied Control Council. Yet, militarily and economically weakened by the war France had little leverage and could do no more than obstruct agreements among the others. With the exception of those few, small states which had escaped entanglement in the war, the French predicament was in some senses a familiar one. Economic devastation, military weakness and awareness of impotence in the event of a resurgence of German power were the common denominators of European states. Of the three victors, one, Britain, had been financially drained by the war and, despite pretensions to be one of the big three, was heavily dependent upon the United States. Even the Soviet Union looked to the United States for aid in its reconstruction programme.

Allied preparation for reconstruction, which meant essentially American preparation, was, however, woefully inadequate. As one American official, Penrose, complained in April 1944: 'Little provision has been made so far for the transition period between relief and the early stages of "rehabilitation" on the one hand and the application of long-term economic measures on the other.'[2] The latter were embodied in the Bretton Woods institutions, the International Monetary Fund, the World Bank and the planned World Trade Organization, but these were not in operation, and were in any case not designed to deal with the phase of reconstruction between emergency relief operations and the operation of a restored and liberal world economic order. The United States actually compounded the problems of the Europeans by ending Lend-Lease aid as soon as the war with Japan was won.

As European industry laboured under shortages of fuel and raw materials, especially coal, Europe began to build up a massive deficit with the dollar bloc. In 1946 western Europe had a trading deficit of US$2356 million with the United States. In that year, the lion's share of the deficit came from Britain ($764 million) and France ($649 million), but in 1947, as the total western European deficit rose to $4742 million, others acquired substantial deficits.[3] Both Britain and France had negotiated loans from the United States. The British loan, of $3750 million, had been made conditional upon a return to the convertibility of sterling. When Britain attempted to fulfil, this condition, a massive outflow of gold and dollars forced a sudden and dramatic retreat. Underlying structural weakness, and not convertibility itself, was the main cause of the problem.[4] Yet the summer 1947 crisis in Britain did graphically illustrate the inability of west Europe to move to the multilateral free trading system which the Americans saw as the basis of the post-war world. By then, American policy-makers had begun to grasp, and even exaggerate, the extent of Europe's plight. On 27 May 1947 Under Secretary of State Will Clayton wrote that 'It is now obvious that we grossly underestimated the destruction to the European economy by the war. We understood the physical destruction, but we failed to take fully into account the effects of economic dislocation on production ... Europe is steadily deteriorating ... Millions of people in the cities are slowly starving.'[5]

The first two years of peace confronted Europe's federalists with the harsh realities of the post-war world. Hopes for a political movement drawing on the resistance quickly faded. Only in Italy did a resistance-based political party, the

Action Party, have any success, and it soon lost ground to the more traditional parties. The Italian Christian Democratic Party, especially Alcide de Gasperi, showed interest in the idea of European integration, but de Gasperi represented a defeated enemy state and had little leverage. There were still federalists who believed in the idea of a popular movement forcing reluctant governments to convene a constituent assembly for Europe. In October 1946, Umberto Campagnola was able to persuade a majority of the Italian Movimento Federalista Europeo to support the idea. With less success, Denis de Rougement argued, at the Montreux Conference of the European Union of Federalists (UEF) in August 1947, that militant federalist movements should seek to push governments towards full-scale political federation.[6] Montreux, the first full conference of the UEF, marked the beginning of a reluctant compromise with the emerging post-war international order. At the Hertenstein Conference of federalists in September 1946, the delegates still hoped to avoid a division of Europe into competing blocks. They even rejected the suggestion that they formally congratulate Churchill for his Zürich speech, made at the same time as the Hertenstein Conference, lest they appear to support the formation of a western bloc. Although the committed federalists were wary of Churchill's speech, the status of the ex-prime minister and his rhetoric fostered illusions about British interest in European union. Closer attention to his words, however, leaves little doubt that he did not intend Britain to be part of the proposed union: 'The first step is to form a Council of Europe ... In all this urgent work, France and Germany must take the lead together. Great Britain, the British Commonwealth of Nations, mighty America, and I trust Soviet Russia ... must be the friends and sponsors of the new Europe and must champion its right to live and shine.'[7] As the division of Europe became more and more imminent, the UEF was forced to adapt. The Montreux conference reasserted its opposition to the division of Europe, but acknowledged that a start would have to be made with only part of Europe (Document 2.3).

During 1946 the division of Europe was crystallizing in the heart of Europe: Germany. Amidst the Paris Council of Foreign Ministers, General Lucius Clay suspended deliveries of reparations from the American zone on 3 May 1946, citing failure to introduce the agreed central economic administration of occupied Germany as justification. It was, as Clay knew only too well, not only the Soviets who were the obstacle here. The French sought to extract concessions to their demands for security as a precondition of agreeing to central administration.[8] The Paris Council also saw an American offer to merge its zone with any others willing to cooperate. That offer formed the basis of the Anglo-American decision at the end of the year to merge their two zones. It was the first step towards the formation of a west German state. A new consensus was forming in the foreign policy establishment of the United States, a consensus which saw the Soviet Union as expansionist and unreliable, though no final decisions had been taken. The Moscow Council of Foreign Ministers held in March and April 1947 saw a last effort by the new American Secretary of State, George C. Marshall, to find a four-power agreement. The failure of the conference pleased the British Foreign Minister Ernest Bevin, who was already committed to a west German state but needed American backing.[9] It was symbolic of the deteriorating climate that, during the Moscow Council, the American President announced what became known as the Truman Doctrine. Intending to win Congressional support for American aid to Greece and Turkey, Truman painted a picture of manichean divide 'between alternative ways of life'. Anti-communism was being deliberately used to persuade Congress to relax the purse strings.[10]

The combination of the aid programme for Greece and Turkey and the deteriorating situation in Europe induced a wide-ranging review of American aid policy. One of the main contributors to that review was the newly established Policy Planning Staff under George Kennan. Kennan's so-called 'long telegram' of 1946 had done much to promote the new consensus about the Soviet Union. Kennan, however, was more discriminating than many converts to the principles of his long telegram. He worried about the misunderstanding of 'what the press has unfortunately come to identify as the "Truman Doctrine" ', and argued that American 'aid to Europe should be directed not to the combating of communism as such . . . but the economic maladjustment which makes European society vulnerable to exploitation by any and all totalitarian movements and which Russian communism is now exploiting'.[11] Kennan also recommended that the formal initiative for this aid programme should come from the Europeans themselves, to avoid the impression of America imposing its way of life upon Europe. Kennan's sensitivity on this issue was not shared by all (Document 2.1). Among the other issues raised was the extent of the proposed aid programme and, specifically, whether the United States should offer to extend it to east Europe. Here, Kennan recommended that it should, but only in a form calculated to induce Soviet opposition. Earlier, on 17 January 1947, John Foster Dulles had publicly called for the unification of west Europe, both to act as a bulwark against the Soviet Union and to provide a framework for solving the German problem.[12]

In contrast to Dulles's explicit advocacy of political federation, the American offer to Europe, announced in a speech by Secretary of State George Marshall on 5 June 1947, required only that the Europeans develop a joint programme. It was also formally open to all European states. When Bevin met the French Foreign Minster, Georges Bidault, on 18 June, he was disappointed to find French insistence on consultation with the Soviet Union before calling a Europe-wide conference. At the tripartite meeting which began on 27 June, the Russians had come prepared to negotiate in good faith, though with clear instructions to avoid commitment to a joint programme and to keep Germany off the agenda.[13] Bevin's insistence upon a coordinated programme, together with reports from Moscow about Anglo-American agreement to German involvement in the programme, hardened the Soviet stand, and on 2 July they rejected the Marshall Plan. Despite this, Moscow did not immediately discourage the east Europeans from attending the conference which Bevin and Bidault had set for 12 July. Within days, however, Moscow advised them not to attend. The Czechoslovaks, who had accepted the invitation, argued in favour of attending, citing their economic ties with the west, to no avail (Document 2.2).

When the conference assembled it duly established a Committee of European

Economic Cooperation (CEEC). That did not mean that the Europeans were willing to cooperate to the extent that the Americans wanted. More ambitious Americans, including Will Clayton, wanted firm commitment to free trade principles, along with the establishment of a customs union and a currency union. In August Clayton had to be restrained by Under Secretary of State Lovett, who advised that 'While in many respects the long-run gains of European economic integration in terms of specialization of production and economic location – achieved ideally through both a customs and a currency union – would be the most beneficial consequences of a recovery program, these goals must be put in perspective in relation to more urgent short-term needs.'[14] That still left plenty for the Europeans and Americans to disagree about. One point of dispute, which was to plague the history of Marshall Plan aid, was the existence and nature of a continuing organization to oversee the programme. Britain led opposition to American demands for a strong supranational body, denouncing them as a threat to national sovereignty. So strident was the dispute that it delayed publication of the Committee's report until 22 September (Document 2.5).

American advocacy of a strong supranational body reflected both a genuine belief that this was in Europe's interest and an awareness of the need to make the whole project attractive to the United States Congress. There was strong support in Congress for more radical solutions, although the suggestion from Senator J. William Fulbright that the goal of political unification be included in the American Act was successfully resisted. Instead Congress satisfied itself with holding up the American model and referring to a 'joint organization'. There was a reference to 'unification', of an unspecified kind, in the 1949 Act, and to 'further integration' in the 1950 Act, but Congress held back from trying to force the Europeans to federate.[15] Congress had insisted that American aid should be managed by an Economic Cooperation Administration separate from the State Department and headed by a businessman, Paul Hoffman, rather than a career diplomat. This opened up the way for men who were convinced that Europe's ills arose not just from its political and economic fragmentation but also from a divisive class structure, conflictual labour relations and outmoded management and production techniques. In brief, not only should Europe become more like America, Europeans should become more like Americans. The Europeans were often receptive to this message, though sensitivities were easily injured. The message of increased productivity, in which the United States enjoyed a considerable lead, appealed to the British Chancellor Stafford Cripps, who agreed with Hoffman in July 1948 on the desirability of establishing an Anglo-American Council on Productivity (AACP). On the other hand, wounded pride was behind the assertion at the 1948 Trades Union Congress that, 'If American practice is held up to us as a pattern for us to follow, and when the mechanical equipment of our factories is contrasted with those of America, we are not being conservative or obstructive in saying that the productive techniques which have been carried further in other countries, we invented.'[16] As analogous productivity councils were established in the other Marshall Plan countries, responses to the productivity message varied according to the local socio-economic traditions, but in all cases the response was ambiguous.[17]

The role of the CEEC and its successor, the Organization for European Economic Cooperation (OEEC), continued to be a source of tension between Britain and the United States (Document 2.10). The United States special representative in Europe, W. Averell Harriman, complained on 31 July 1948 that in the OEEC, 'each representative is inclined to consider first the interests of his own country and there is no one to initiate or advocate matters requiring top level consideration'. To remedy this deficiency, he argued that the 'OEEC must be led by a man of international political position as a type of director general'.[18] The man upon whom Americans' hopes rode was Paul Henri Spaak, then Prime Minister of Belgium. Spaak himself was reluctant, but more importantly, Britain, backed by the Scandinavians, was vigorously opposed to the whole idea. The Americans did not give up and returned to their proposal in August 1949, when Spaak had ceased to be Prime Minister. Again, however, British opposition blocked the proposal. Eventually, in January 1950 the British accepted a compromise brokered by Norway, and Dirk Stikker became Political Conciliator of the OEEC. The post itself was far weaker than the original American suggestion envisaged, and Stikker himself less radical than the federally minded Spaak.

Whereas in west Europe the dominant superpower was the predominant advocate of integration and, indeed, federation, in the east the dominant superpower was a major obstacle. At first this was not clear, despite Stalin's veto of the wartime Polish–Czechoslovak confederation (see Chapter 1). Discussions about unification had taken place between the Yugoslav communists, led by Josip Tito, and the Bulgarians, led by Georgi Dimitrov, towards the end of the war. There was in fact a long record of communist support for some form of federation. As early as January 1920, the Balkan Communist Conference advocated a Balkan Socialist Soviet Republic.[19] With Soviet approval, the Yugoslavs and Bulgarians worked towards an agreement which was substantially in place by the beginning of 1945. At the Yalta Conference, however, the British and the Americans questioned an agreement to which one of the parties, Bulgaria, was still officially an enemy state. Britain also objected to the exclusion of Greece from the proposed union.[20]

There were periodic references to the idea in the following year, but little happened until after the peace treaty with Bulgaria was signed in February 1947. After this there was a flurry of diplomatic activity with numerous bilateral treaties being signed. A Yugoslav–Bulgarian agreement at Bled in August 1947 included reference to preparations for a customs union and, according to some participants, federation was discussed.[21] At this point Stalin raised objections, but not to the principle of unification. He objected only to the lack of consultation with Moscow. Tito and Dimitrov took care to consult Moscow about the next step, which was a treaty signed on 27 November. Again this included reference to preparing for a customs union. After November there were signs of increasing Soviet dissatisfaction with the independent line being taken by Yugoslavia, especially with respect to Albania. Yet Moscow's policy still seems to have been undecided, for on 17 January *Pravda* published a statement by Dimitrov in which he held out the prospect of an east European federation (Document 2.7). Days later, *Pravda*'s editors distanced themselves from Dimitrov's statement. At meetings with the Bulgarians and Yugoslavs in January and February, Stalin lashed out, accusing them of a failure to consult and dismissing ideas of a wider federation as ridiculous, only to speculate upon federation himself. The Yugoslavs were humiliated by being ordered to sign a treaty promising consultation. Although accounts of the meetings vary, Stalin's hostility was clear enough. The projected federation was dead.[22]

Soon afterwards, the communists moved to consolidate their position in Czechoslovakia. The Prague coup, as it became known, was another symbol of the hardening of the east–west divide. Czechoslovakia was the last of the east European states where the communists had seemed to be prepared to share power. The Prague coup, by brutally dashing any prospects of power sharing, was a heavy blow for those in the west who believed that Europe should seek to find a 'third way' between the 'alternative ways of life' of the Truman doctrine. The rhetoric of a third way was very widespread in the early post-war years. It was a British Conservative, Robert Boothby, who opined, in February 1946, that 'I feel that in Western Europe we have a separate, different contribution to make, based upon our long history, our traditions, and our culture, which might combine the best elements both of Soviet Russia and the United States.'[23] The rhetoric of the third way did transcend the usual party political divisions, although it was stronger on the non-communist left than elsewhere. There were also geographic limits to its appeal. Indeed, association of the idea of European integration with the idea of a third force encouraged scepticism within the Dutch Labour Party, which shared the Atlanticist sentiment common in the Netherlands.[24] Much, of course, depended upon the exact connotations of the idea of a third way. It could invoke, as in Boothby's statement, the idea of drawing upon elements of the socio-economic systems of the two superpowers. It could suggest the possibility of Europe, or west Europe, as an independent political and strategic force, able to resist either of the two superpowers. In some versions there was a claim that Europeans, understanding both the 'alternative ways of life', would be able to mediate between the Americans and the Russians, whose antagonism was supposedly aggravated by mutual incomprehension.

All these notions were evident among advocates of a third way in Britain, along with a strong anti-American sentiment. Within the British Labour Party, critics of Bevin's foreign policy argued that he was too subservient to the United States and that European failure to steer a middle course between the two superpowers actually increased the prospects of another war. In October 1946 several Labour members of parliament wrote to the Prime Minister voicing these arguments and asking Clement Attlee to find 'a genuine middle way between the extreme alternatives of American "free enterprise" economics and Russian socio-political life'.[25] The highpoint of third force sentiment in Britain came with the signing of the Dunkirk Treaty in March 1947. A Franco-British alliance was seen as the basis of Europe as a third force. The French government which negotiated the treaty did not see it in this way at all.[26] The treaty did not solve any of the underlying problems. It had been possible only because France had dropped its insistence upon British assent to French policy on Germany. On the British side the treaty was intended to provide a boost to the beleaguered French Premier, Leon Blum, and as an alternative to what the French really wanted at that moment – increased coal supplies.

Despite the criticism of Bevin, he too was interested in the idea of Europe as a third force. Uncertain of the extent of American commitment to Europe, and often resentful of what he saw as the high-handed style of the Americans, Bevin looked to Anglo-French cooperation as the basis for a more independent Europe. There were, however, recurrent obstacles. Bevin's idea of using British and French colonies in Africa as a starting point ran into opposition from the Colonial Office. The possibility of a customs union with west Europe was criticized by the economic ministers in the Cabinet. Bevin himself was critical of the repeated pleas by French socialists for Britain to take the lead in uniting Europe along federal lines. At the end of 1947 and beginning of 1948, while Bevin was still speculating on the third force option, an alternative came into view.

On 17 December 1947 Bevin discussed with Marshall the possibility of 'some western democratic system comprising the Americans, ourselves, France, Italy etc.', adding that this 'would not be a formal alliance, but an understanding backed by power, money and resolute action'.[27] A memorandum of 13 January reiterated that there was no need for a formal alliance with the Americans, though Bevin was thinking of formal treaties, modelled on the Dunkirk Treaty between the Europeans. On 21 January the Americans were still 'not clear whether Mr. Bevin envisages the direct participation of the United States in the security treaty arrangements'.[28] Bevin's speech on 22 January was similarly vague, invoking the need for some kind of spiritual federation of the west (Documents 2.8 and 2.9). There is no agreement on whether Bevin did have a clear conception of what he wanted at this stage. By March, however, Bevin had clarified his intentions and exploited the worsening climate to prod the United States into entering into discussions. The Prague coup had already caused alarm. When there were rumours that the Soviet Union might suggest a treaty with Norway, Bevin conveyed an alarmist message to the Americans on 11 March. The Norwegians, he argued, could be offered reassurance, but

> Mr Bevin fears that such language may not suffice to induce the Norwegian government to hold out and he considers that all possible steps should be taken to forestall a Norwegian defection at this time, which would involve the appearance of the Russians on the Atlantic and the collapse of the whole Scandinavian system. This would in turn prejudice the chance of calling any halt to the relentless advance of Russia into Western Europe.[29]

More specifically he suggested three systems – one involving France, Britain and the Benelux states, an Atlantic security system, and one for the Mediterranean. On the following day, Marshall agreed to immediate discussions. Even before these discussions began, one element of Bevin's tripartite system was already in place. The Brussels Pact of 17 March 1948 committed Britain, France and the Benelux states to assist any member of the Pact who was attacked. The Pact was a vital step. As with the Marshall Plan, the Americans had made it clear that the prospects of American assistance would be enhanced if the Europeans first demonstrated their willingness to cooperate. The Pact itself had been negotiated rapidly, but not without difficulty. France wanted an enlarged Dunkirk Treaty firmly focused on guarantees against

German aggression. The Benelux states favoured a mutual defence pact of a style known to be favoured by the Americans. The argument for a Dunkirk-style treaty was that an anti-German alliance would seem less threatening to the Soviet Union. Again the Prague coup served as a catalyst. In the light of the coup the French concluded that there was no longer any point in taking Soviet sensitivities into consideration.[30]

Continuing tension between France and the Anglo-Saxons over Germany meant that France was excluded from the discussion between Britain and America and Canada which opened on 22 March 1948. On 1 April the final draft recommended a North Atlantic Defence Agreement. It also specified that 'when circumstances permit' Germany should be invited to join, though this 'objective ... *should not be publicly disclosed*' (emphasis in the original).[31] France was already being pushed to consent to the establishment of a west German state. The French fought hard for a weak central authority and the retention of Allied controls, especially over the Ruhr. They sought to link agreement on Germany to a security guarantee. They obtained some satisfaction over the Ruhr, in the shape of an International Ruhr Authority, but no security guarantee. Even the Ruhr Authority was deemed to be too weak and the French later sought to renegotiate its provisions, without success. The German reaction to the Allied offer, communicated to them on 1 July 1948, was equivocal. They naturally welcomed greater control over their own destiny, but equally naturally they did not welcome the prospect of consolidating the division of Germany. The tight link between the division of Europe and the division of Germany had endowed the idea of Europe as a third force with special significance in Germany. As the German socialist Carlo Schmid had argued in 1947, a united Europe could constitute an alternative to its division between the superpowers. It could also form a framework within which Germany could regain equality with the other European states. Until that framework was established, he recommended that Germany should remain in 'its present interim state' (Document 2.4). Schmid was influential in shaping the response of the German ministers when they met at Koblenz on 8–10 July 1948. To the surprise and irritation of the military governors, the Germans stated that 'nothing should be done to give the character of a state to the organisation which is to be formed notwithstanding the granting of the fullest possible autonomy to the population of this territory'.[32] In the same month Soviet pressure, in the form of the Berlin blockade (which had begun on 24 June), forced the Germans to move closer to the western powers. Residues of their earlier hesitancy were evident in the Basic Law which eventually emerged, but there was going to be a German state in the west.

The strength of French fears about German revival was evident in the French response to the Hague Congress of May 1948. The Congress had been called by a coalition of European movements which formed in December 1947 under the name of the International Committee of the Movements for European Unity. French socialists saw this as an opportunity to seize the initiative and develop Europe as a third force on the basis of an Anglo-French, and socialist, alliance. However, at the Selsdon Park socialist conference of March 1948, British Labour Party representatives made clear their opposition to participation in the Hague Congress. At a further meeting in Paris, on 24–25 April, they even refused to allow individual members of the Labour Party to decide for themselves whether they wished to attend. The French socialists, in an attempt to preserve at least the facade of unity, reluctantly went along with most of Labour's demands. It was yet another blow to the idea of a third force.[33]

The Hague Congress duly met and issued a resolution calling for the creation of a European Assembly, as well as the integration of Germany into a federal Europe. Later, on 19 July, Foreign Minister Georges Bidault proposed to the Consultative Council of the Brussels Pact that it should set up a committee to study the idea of an assembly. France had specific reasons for wanting an assembly. According to the French Foreign Ministry, it was 'essential to present to the German political imagination a continental system in which Germany has a part and a role'.[34] Moreover, the French believed that it would be more difficult for Germany to withdraw a delegation from an assembly than from a council of ministers.[35] The new Foreign Minister, Robert Schuman, won over Spaak and they launched a joint initiative on 2 September. The British response was to raise numerous obstacles and to suggest purely intergovernmental cooperation instead. In October Britain was pushed into agreeing to establish a study committee, but sought to prevent the creation of an assembly. Some progress was made in December, when it was suggested that the conflict between the British and French views could be resolved by having both a council of ministers and an assembly. That left the difficult issue of the status of each and their relation to each other. The French unsuccessfully resisted British demands that the council should have control of the assembly's agenda. British efforts to constrain the assembly continued in January, when Hugh Dalton objected to the proposals that the assembly be composed of delegates elected by national parliaments and that the assembly's members should be allowed to vote individually. The French President, Paul Reynaud, expressed his surprise that Britain, 'the symbol and champion of democracy' was proposing a system which was authoritarian and, in its detail, totalitarian.[36] The British gave way on the issue of voting, but the dispute over the method of selecting members of the assembly was settled only by the expedient of allowing each state to determine for itself how to select its members. On that basis, the Statute of the Council of Europe was signed on 5 May 1949. Britain had succeeded in undermining the French vision of an assembly which might provide a basis for resolving the German problem, but it had failed to muzzle the assembly. Bevin was wrong to claim that the majority of governments favoured the British view of the Council of Europe, but he was right to state that it was the product of 'conflicting views' of its 'nature and purpose' (Document 2.13).

The negotiations on the North Atlantic Treaty also reflected conflicting views (Document 2.11). As with the Marshall Plan, a key factor was the need to secure congressional support for any treaty. Advocates of an alliance won a major victory when they persuaded Senator Arthur Vandenburg to introduce a resolution sanctioning 'Association of the United States by constitutional process, with such regional and other collective arrangements as are based on continuous and effective self-help and mutual aid, and as affect its national security.'[37] The Vandenberg resolution had been carefully worded to accept the principle of an alliance, while at the same time setting limits to the commitments which the United States would enter into. The Europeans wanted tight obligations, especially in the event of an attack upon a member state, while the Americans sought a looser formulation. The demand for strict obligations was led by France; at the end of December the negotiators settled on a compromise which was very close to the French position. That, however, proved to be unacceptable to the senators and had to be rewritten.[38] Accordingly, Article 5 of the North Atlantic Treaty obligated each member state to take 'such action as it deems necessary' in response to an attack upon a member of the alliance (Document 4.1).

When the North Atlantic Treaty was signed on 4 April 1949 the Americans had committed themselves to more than they intended but less than the Europeans wanted. All that existed in April 1949 was a treaty. There was no North Atlantic Treaty *Organization* (NATO). That emerged only over the following years in response to unresolved problems, notably the role of Germany in the Atlantic security system. The fact that the Europeans had got less than they wanted was symbolized the very day after the treaty was signed, when the Brussels Pact states submitted a request for military aid. France, much to the irritation of the Americans, had been clamouring for this throughout the negotiations. Now that the treaty was signed, the other Europeans joined the queue. The contrast between Marshall Plan aid and military aid within the North Atlantic Treaty framework was a contrast between two distinct perceptions of the threat faced by western Europe. The Marshall Plan was based on the assumption elaborated by Kennan, that economic stagnation and the associated despondency were the real threat. The militarization of aid rested on the assumption that the threat was external.

The Soviet response to the North Atlantic Treaty was predictably hostile, but there was no move at this point to form a counter alliance. Nor did the treaty stop Soviet agreement to end the blockade of Berlin in May 1949. The measured Soviet response was a reflection of the fact that the treaty did nothing to resolve the German question. When German rearmament appeared on the agenda the Soviet response would be different. The Soviet Union had not sought to imitate western efforts at integration in the economic field either. The Marshall Plan had been followed by a series of bilateral economic treaties, which became know as the Molotov Plan. Bilateralism had been the dominant strategy of the Soviet Union towards the states of the eastern bloc since the end of the war. In January 1949 the announcement of the Council for Mutual Economic Assistance (CMEA) did not signal a significant move towards multilateralism. The announcement was brief and limited. It stressed the sovereignty of member states and promised little more than 'exchanging economic experience, extending technical aid . . . and rendering mutual assistance with respect to raw materials, foodstuffs, machines, equipment, etc.'[39] Although little is known about the discussions surrounding the creation of the CMEA, there are suggestions that it was a pale reflection of more ambitious schemes. One document obtained by an American Embassy indicates provisional agreement upon a form of supranational planning (Document 2.12) which the Soviet Union would later strive to achieve, without success. In 1949 integration within the Soviet bloc, whether in the economic or military field, was characterized by bilateralism and the use of party channels rather than inter-state agreements to coordinate policy.

By the end of the 1940s, all realistic hope of a united Europe as a third force equal to the two superpowers had vanished. Such integration as had been achieved had taken place under the aegis of the superpowers. In the east, Soviet disinterest in the idea meant that this amounted to very little. In the west, intense American interest had not sufficed to overcome the hesitations of the Europeans themselves. The main, but not the only, obstacle was that the state best situated to lead the Europeans towards integration – Britain – was unwilling to do so. France looked in vain for British leadership and was still seeking to control its inherently more powerful German neighbour. The west German state, whose creation embodied the failure of Europe as a third force, still stood on the sidelines of the process of integration. Its formal integration into the structure of post-war Europe had begun when the Germans took up a seat in the OEEC in October 1949. On the other hand, it was not a member of the Brussels Pact, the North Atlantic Treaty or the Council of Europe.

The mere proliferation of forums of integration – the Brussels Pact, OEEC, the North American Atlantic Treaty, the Council of Europe – was a defeat for those with more ambitious hopes of a federal Europe, above all for the Americans. In December 1948 the State Department summarized the position: ' "Integration" will thus proceed at a different pace in the various fields of interest and with somewhat different participants in each case. This is desirable if the pace is not to be set by the slowest.' It was a good prediction. So too was the fact that 'we must recognize that the possibilities for the organization of Western Europe are definitely limited by the great area of uncertainty and disagreement surrounding the future of Germany'.[40]

NOTES

1. Quoted in Walther Lipgens, 'Innerfranzösische Kritik an der Aussenpolitik De Gaulles 1944–1946', *Vierteljahreshefte für Zeitgeschichte*, Vol. 26 (1976), p. 145.
2. E. Penrose, *Economic Planning for Peace* (Princeton, 1953), p. 187.
3. A.S. Milward, *The Reconstruction of Western Europe* (London, 1984), pp. 26–7.
4. On this see Alex Cairncross, *Years of Recovery* (London, 1985), pp. 121–64.
5. *Foreign Relations of the United States* (hereafter *FRUS*), 1947, Vol. 3, p. 230. For a useful brief survey of the food situation see David Ellwod, *Rebuilding Europe* (London, 1992), pp. 32–5.
6. Walther Lipgens, *A History of European Integration, Vol. 1, 1945–1947* (Oxford, 1982), pp. 277 and 665.
7. A. Boyd and F. Boyd, *Western Union* (London, n.d.), p. 112.
8. In his *Decision in Germany* (London, 1950) Clay claimed that French obstruction 'seemed of less importance as the intransigent Soviet position made it appear unlikely that these central agencies could operate successfully', p. 124.
9. British resolve is emphasized by Anne Deighton, *The Impossible Peace* (Oxford, 1990).
10. Daniel Yergin, *Shattered Peace* (Harmondsworth, 1980), p. 283.
11. *FRUS*, 1947, Vol. 3, pp. 229 and 225.

12. Klaus Schwabe, 'Die Rolle der USA', in Wilfried Loth (ed.), *Die Anfänge der europäischen Integration* (Bonn, 1990), p. 174.
13. Geoffrey Roberts, 'Moscow and the Marshall Plan', *Europe-Asia Studies*, Vol. 46 (1994), pp. 1371–86.
14. *FRUS*, 1947, Vol. 3, p. 386.
15. On the various formulations see I. Wexler, *The Marshall Plan Revisited* (Greenwood, IL, 1983), pp. 20–7.
16. Quoted in Peter M.R. Stirk, 'Americanism and anti-Americanism in British and German responses to the Marshall Plan', in Peter M.R. Stirk and David Willis (eds), *Shaping Postwar Europe* (London, 1991), p. 30.
17. While historians now express caution about the impact of these programmes they still have their advocates. See James M. Silberman and Charles Weiss, *Restructuring for Productivity: The Technical Assistance Program of the Marshall Plan as a Precedent for the Former Soviet Union* (World Bank, 1992).
18. *FRUS*, 1948, Vol. 3, p. 473.
19. The resolution is in L. S. Stavrianos, *Balkan Federation* (Hamden, 1964), pp. 303–6.
20. P.S. Wandycz, 'Recent traditions of the quest for unity', in J. Lukaszewski (ed.), *The Peoples' Democracies after Prague* (Bruges, 1970), pp. 75–7.
21. Vladimir Dedijer, *Tito Speaks* (London, 1953), p. 314.
22. For differing accounts of the motives see Gavril D. Ra'anan, *International Policy Formation in the USSR* (Hamden, 1983) and Leonid Gibianski, 'The 1948 Soviet-Yugoslav conflict and the formation of the "socialist camp" model', in A. Westad *et al.* (eds), *The Soviet Union in Eastern Europe 1945–89* (Basingstoke, 1994), pp. 26ff.
23. Robert Boothby in *Documents on the History of European Integration*, Vol. 2, doc. 192.
24. W. Asbeek Brusse, *The Dutch Social Democrats and Europe*, EUI Colloquium Papers 306/88, pp. 5–6.
25. Quoted in Jonathon Schneer, 'Hopes deferred or shattered: the British Labour left in the third force movement, 1945–49', *Journal of Modern History*, Vol. 56 (1984), p. 205.
26. G.H. Soutou, 'Georges Bidault et la construction européene 1944–1954', *Revue d'histoire diplomatique*, no. 105 (1991), pp. 269–72.
27. *FRUS* 1948, Vol. 3, p. 1 (22 December 1947).
28. ibid., p. 10 (21 January 1948).
29. ibid., pp. 46–7 (11 March 1948).
30. John W. Young, *France, the Cold War and the Western Alliance* (Leicester, 1990), p. 179.
31. *FRUS* 1948, Vol. 3, p. 75.
32. Quoted in Peter H. Merkl, *The Origin of the West German Republic* (New York, 1963), p. 53. On Schmid's influence see Hans-Peter Schwarz, *Vom Reich zur Bundesrepublik* (Stuttgart, 1980), pp. 574–88.
33. Wilfried Loth, *The SFIO and the Beginnings of European Integration, 1947–54*, EUI Colloquium Papers 301/88, p. 9.
34. Quoted in Marie-Thérese Bitsch, 'Le role de la France dans la naisance du conseil de l'Europe', in Raymond Poidevin (ed.), *Histoire des debuts de la construction européene* (Brussels, 1986), p. 170.
35. ibid., p. 171.
36. ibid., p. 190.
37. *The Private Papers of Senator Vandenberg*, p. 407.

38. Timothy P. Ireland, *Creating the Entangling Alliance* (Westport, CT, 1981), pp. 110–11.
39. Quoted in Giuseppe Schiavone, *The Institutions of Comecon*, (London, 1981), p. 15.
40. *FRUS* 1948, Vol. 3, p. 303.

FURTHER READING

D. Ellwood, *Rebuilding Europe* (Harlow, 1992).

M. Hogan, *The Marshall Plan* (Cambridge, 1987).

W. Lipgens, *A History of European Integration*, Vol. 1 (Oxford, 1982).

W. Loth, *The Division of the World* (London, 1988).

C. Maier (ed.), *Germany and the Marshall Plan* (New York, 1991).

A.S. Milward, *The Reconstruction of Western Europe* (London, 1984).

M. Newman, *Socialism and European Unity* (London, 1983).

H. Pelling, *Britain and the Marshall Plan* (London, 1988).

G. Roberts, 'Moscow and the Marshall Plan', in *Europe-Asia Studies*, Vol. 46 (1994), pp. 1371–86.

A. H. Robertson, *The Council of Europe* (London, 1956).

P.M.R. Stirk and D. Willis (eds), *Shaping Postwar Europe* (London, 1991).

O. A. Westad *et al.* (eds), *The Soviet Union and Eastern Europe* (Basingstoke, 1994).

—————————————— 2.1 ——————————————

SUMMARY OF DISCUSSION ON PROBLEMS OF RELIEF, REHABILITATION AND RECONSTRUCTION OF EUROPE, US DEPARTMENT OF STATE, 29 MAY 1947

Foreign Relations of the United States 1947, Vol. 3, pp. 234–5.

These discussions form part of the background to the Marshall Plan. Will Clayton was Under Secretary of State for Economic Affairs.

Some system for closer European economic cooperation must be devised to break down existing economic barriers.

The last point which parallels the recommendation in the Policy Planning Staff paper was elaborated in the ensuing discussion. Three major problems presented themselves:

1. The inclusion or exclusion of Soviet-dominated Eastern Europe.
2. US vs European responsibility and intiative.
3. The timing and machinery to be utilized in developing the plan.

As to point 1, Mr. Clayton expressed the strong view that, while Western Europe is essential to Eastern Europe, the reverse is not true. Coal and grains from Eastern Europe are important to Western Europe, but these products will be exported westward in any event because the necessity of obtaining vital foreign exchange for necessary products from the west creates a suction which the USSR is incapable of counteracting, and there can only be absolute and final domination of Eastern Europe by force of arms. It was concluded, therefore, that a European economic federation is feasible even without the participation of Eastern European countries
. . .

Regarding the problem of European vs US initiative in the plan . . . Messrs Cohen and Thorp emphasized the importance of substantial US responsibility and initiative because (a) experience has demonstrated the lack of ability of European nations to agree on such matters, (b) if agreement is reached, the scheme may not be a sound one and (c) the problem is so complex that no one can plot a definite, final plan now. It should, therefore, be approached functionally rather than by country, concentrating on the essentials, and this is an approach which the US is in a better position than Europe to take.

Balancing the dangers of appearing to force 'the American way' on Europe and the danger of failure if the major responsibility is left to Europe, Mr Bohlen suggested that an alternative is to place strong pressure on the European nations to plan by underscoring their situation and making clear that the only politically feasible basis on which the US would be willing to make the aid available is substantial evidence of a developing overall plan for economic cooperation by the Europeans themselves, perhaps an economic federation to be worked out over 3 or 4 years.

_____ 2.2 _____

STALIN, CZECHOSLOVAKIA AND THE MARSHALL PLAN, 9 JULY 1947

Karel Kaplan, 'Stalin, Czechoslovakia and the Marshall Plan', *Bohemia*, Vol. 32 (1991), pp. 135–7.

At this meeting Stalin forced the Czechoslovaks to retract their previous decision to participate in the Paris Conference on the Marshall Plan.

Generalissimo Stalin said:

After Molotov's return from Paris, the Government of the USSR received news of Yugoslavia's attitude … Initially, the Soviet Government did not answer and concluded that it would be correcter to go to the Conference and then, if it should turn out necessary, to leave the Conference. However, after the reports from the Ambassadors of the USSR had arrived, a different opinion had formed: The credits which are referred to in the Marshall Plan are very uncertain and it turned out that 'using the pretext of credits the Great Powers are attempting to form a Western bloc and isolate the Soviet Union'. (Generalissimo Stalin said this verbatim) …

Generalissimo Stalin continued: 'For us, this matter is a "question of friendship." You would not have any direct advantages from attendance at the Conference. Surely you do not want "kulbany je kredity" (i.e. credits which would endanger our economic and political sovereignty). 'The terms of credit will certainly be bad', said Generalissimo Stalin and added:

'We consider this matter to be a fundamental question on which our friendship with the USSR depends. If you go to Paris, you will show that you want to cooperate in an action aimed at isolating the Soviet Union' …

Minister Masaryk points out that in our country at the time of the decision on attending the Paris Conference the situation was determined by the general knowledge that with respect to raw materials we are 60–80% dependent on the West. The managers of state enterprises keep saying to Minister Masaryk that it is necessary to go to Paris in order not to miss the opportunity of obtaining some credits …

In conclusion, Minister Masaryk emphasized that all political parties are agreed that Czechoslovakia may not undertake anything which would be against the interests of the Soviet Union. The delegation will promptly notify Prague that the Soviet Government considers acceptance of the Anglo-French invitation to be an act directed against it, and Minister Masaryk does not doubt in the least that the Czechoslovak Government will act accordingly without delay. But Minister

Masaryk here requests that the Soviet Government help us in our delicate situation. We do not have any great illusions; perhaps the matter could be fixed in such a manner that one would go to the Conference on one day and leave it on the next.

Then Generalissimo Stalin returned to our participation in Paris and said: 'Participation at the Conference puts you in a false light.' It is 'a break in the front,' it would be a success for the Western Great Powers. Switzerland and Sweden are still wavering. Your acceptance would certainly also affect their decision ...

But Minister Dr Drtina asks that Generalissimo Stalin and Minister Molotov consider one point: The economic situation of the CSR is different from that of the other Slav states, except, of course, the Soviet Union, i.e the living standard of the CSR is dependent above all on foreign trade; and here, unfortunately, the situation is such that 60–80% of our trade depends on the West.

Generalissimo Stalin remarks that our trading balance with the West has been passive.

Minister Dr Drtina says that this is possible, but that the turnover of our trade with the West is large.

Generalissimo Stalin remarks that our exports to the West are not great enough to cover our imports if we have to pay in foreign currency.

Prime Minister Gottwald said that we have to pay in foreign currency and that we only have a little.

Generalissimo Stalin laughed and said: 'We know that you have foreign currency' and, turning to Minister Molotov, he said with a smile: 'They were telling themselves that they could obtain credits and therefore they did not want to miss this chance.' ...

Minister Masaryk asks Generalissimo Stalin to forgive him for speaking openly and says that in our present situation we need a kind of consolation prize, a gesture of the Soviet side ...

In this connection, Prime Minister Gottwald remarked: 'We export light industry products, glass, china, footwear, textiles, etc. to the West. But the USSR has not purchased such products up to now.'

Generalissimo Stalin: 'We can buy these products as well.' Generalissimo Stalin added: 'Our harvest is good this year. The size of our country leads to the fact that only now can we see the situation clearly. The agricultural plan has been fulfilled, indeed exceeded. We can help our friends: Bulgaria, Yugoslavia, Poland, and also you.'

_____ 2.3 _____

EUROPEAN UNION OF FEDERALISTS: RESOLUTIONS OF THE MONTREUX CONFERENCE, AUGUST 1947

A. Boyd and F. Boyd, *Western Union* (London: Hutchinson, 1948), pp. 141–2.

The European Union of Federalists was established in Paris in December 1946. The Montreux Conference was its first full conference.

Having in mind the anxieties and hopes of our time, this Conference of the European Union of Federalists affirms that no national government is any longer capable of assuring to its people liberty, prosperity and peace ...

For the first time in history, all the European federalist movements have come together in a single association to make their voice heard – the voice of Europe itself ...

European federalism, which alone can provide our peoples with the prospect of salvation, is based on the following foundations:

(1) The federal idea constitutes a dynamic principle which transforms all human activities. It brings with it not only a new political framework, but also new social, economic and cultural structures. Federalism is a synthesis, and it is made up of two elements indissolubly linked: of organic solidarity and of liberty, or, put differently, the expansion of the human personality in every sphere of daily life ...

(2) Federalism can be born only from renunciation of all idea of a dictatorial 'New Order' imposed by one of its constituent elements, and of any ideological system ... Each of the nations, each of the elements of which Europe is composed, has its own proper function, its own irreplaceable quality. It follows that, regarded from that angle, a minority has the same human value as a majority. That is why federalism is based on respect for qualities. For example, it is concerned not only with the method of election to a Council of States, but also and above all, with the value of customs, traditions, and the way in which people order their lives ... even if a European Federation can at the beginning unite only some of the States of Europe, the European Union of Federalists will never accept as a fait accompli the division of Europe into two hostile blocs.

To start our efforts at unification in the west of Europe means for the West escaping the risk of becoming the victim of power politics, restoring to Europe, at any rate partially, her pride in her legitimate independence, and holding out a hand to the peoples of the East to help them to rejoin the other peoples in a free and peaceful community.

... federalists must declare firmly and without compromise that it is absolute national sovereignty that must be abated, that a part of that sovereignty must be entrusted to a federal authority assisted by all the functional bodies necessary to the accomplishment, on the federal plane, of its economic and cultural tasks, whether in whole or in part. In particular this authority must possess:

(a) a government responsible to the peoples and groups and not to the federated states;
(b) a Supreme Court capable of resolving possible disputes between state members of the Federation;
(c) an armed police force under its own control ...

_____ 2.4 _____

CARLO SCHMID: 'FRANCO-GERMAN RELATIONS AND THE THIRD PARTNER', 1947

'Das deutsch-französische Verhältnis und der Dritte Partner', _Die Wandlung,_ Vol. 2 (1947), pp. 792–805; in W. Lipgens and W. Loth (eds), _Documents on the History of European Integration,_ Vol. 3 (Berlin: de Gruyter, 1988), pp. 503–6.

The Social Democrat Carlo Schmid played a leading role in drafting the Basic Law of the Federal Republic of Germany, although he had initially opposed the creation of a separate western state.

On the basis of this experience confirmed by history, Franco-German relations will necessarily appear as part of the European problem, or rather perhaps a problem of the political world situated between the two fields of force based on the US and the Soviet Union. But, given the interdependence of all questions that depend on the gravitational force of political bodies of supercontinental size, we are obliged to see the problem of the intermediate area as itself part of the problem of the political structure of our present-day world.

A third power is necessary to prevent the world from being torn apart, but Europe can only become that power if it puts its house in order: in other words, its component states must abandon the principle of sovereignty, on which politics have essentially been based in modern times, in favour of a supranational community. All forms of activity involved in the external relations of a state must be transferred to that community, including foreign relations, defence, major communications, the supply of energy, economic planning and the management of key industries. Only thus will the individuality of individual states cease to be a disturbing and disruptive factor ... In all other spheres, countries may remain as autonomous as they will: the vitality of the union can only be increased by the diversity of its members ...

The following stages might be envisaged, bearing in mind that a scheme of this kind is not a blueprint but merely serves to illustrate the complexity of relationships and the processes that may be required.

(1) As the pressure on the 'middle zone' of Europe becomes stronger, so the centripetal forces within the British family of nations will intensify and extend by way of Britain herself, to Europe ... We should not be deceived by certain superficial phenomena which in Germany, to our misfortune, we have so often interpreted as proofs to the contrary: the behaviour of the Dominions in the United Nations tells its own story. These tendencies should be coordinated, given institutional effect and constitutional order, perhaps by transforming the British Commonwealth into a confederation or union with the same kind of powers as those proposed above for the United States of Europe.

(2) Concurrently one might envisage a federal union of the Scandinavian countries, and an extension of the Benelux system to France and Italy. In a short time this latter would necessarily evolve into a system of unified economic policy, which – given the dynamics inherent in all major economic conceptions, especially nowadays – would soon have political and no doubt constitutional consequences ...

(3) When the two systems have achieved inner equilibrium and have proved to be valuable instruments for increasing the potential of all their members it will be possible for them, with the necessary modifications, to form a union, the attractive power of which will certainly be sufficient to attract other countries of the 'middle zone' ...

(4) What should happen to Germany in the meantime? ... It seems to me preferable for Germany to remain in its present interim state from the foreign policy point of view until some progress has been made towards creating the unions described above. The latter will then have provided Europe, apart from Germany, with a secure economic and political superiority such as to dispel much of the fear that at present acts as a bad counsellor, suggesting to foreign statesmen the discriminatory plans of which we hear from time to time. It will then be easy for the rulers of European states to convince their peoples that a Germany enjoying equal rights need not necessarily be presumed to be an aggressor, and that a United States of Europe can only fulfil its purpose if Germany is granted such equality.

_____ 2.5 _____

COMMITTEE OF EUROPEAN ECONOMIC CO-OPERATION: *GENERAL REPORT,* JULY–SEPTEMBER 1947

Committee of European Economic Co-operation, *General Report,* Vol. 1 (London: HMSO, 1947), pp. 18–20.

The Report was produced at the insistence of the United States as a precondition for the receipt of Marshall Aid. It was intended by the Americans to provide the basis for the coordinated use of aid across Europe. The Study Group and the Franco-Italian negotiations on a customs union did not lead to concrete results.

The Committee has considered the question of Customs Unions as a means of achieving the speedier reduction and eventual elimination of tariffs betwen a group of countries. The advantages which the United States has enjoyed through the existence of a large domestic market with no internal trade barriers are manifest ...

No Customs Union can be brought into full and effective operation by a stroke of the pen. A Customs Union, particularly between several large and highly industrialised countries, involves complex technical negotiations and adjustments which can only be achieved by progressive stages over a period of years. Special problems also arise for countries with a high proportion of their trade outside any proposed Customs Union, or as between countries at widely differing stages of economic development.

Nevertheless, the idea of a Customs Union including as many European countries as possible is one which contains important possibilities for the economic future of Europe, and it is in the general interest that the problems involved should receive careful and detailed study by governments. Several steps have been taken in this connection.

The Governments of Belgium, Luxemburg and the Netherlands signed a Customs Convention in London on 5th Spetember, 1944 ... The convention has been approved by the Parliaments of the three countries and will enter into force by 1st January, 1948. The three countries propose thereafter to conclude an economic union ...

The four Scandinavian countries, namely Denmark, Iceland, Norway and Sweden, have announced after a meeting of their Foreign Ministers which took place in Copenhagen on 27th and 28th August, 1947, that they were taking steps to examine immediately the possibility of an extension of the economic cooperation between their countries, including the question of the elimination, wholly or partly, of the customs frontier between the four countries ...

The Governments of Austria, Belgium, Denmark, France, Greece, Ireland,

Iceland, Italy, Luxemburg, the Netherlands, Portugal and the United Kingdom and Turkey have ... decided to create a Study Group for the purpose of examining the problems involved and the steps to be taken, in the formation of a Customs Union ...

In this connection the French Government has made the following declaration:-

The French Government being of the opinion that the barriers which now exist in the way of a freer exchange of goods and capital, and of a freer movement of persons between the various European countries, constitute one of the most important obstacles to the economic recovery of these countries;

that in the present state of the world only economic units sufficiently large to have at their disposal an important home market are able to lower the price of industrial and agricultural production sufficiently to ensure, thanks to better technique, an improved standard of living for their people and to allow the countries concerned to withstand world-wide competition;

that the present division of Europe into small economic units does not correspond to the needs of modern competition and that it will be possible with the help of a Customs Union to construct larger units on the strictly economic plane;

that these units must not be in any way 'autarchic' in character but on the contrary should increase their trade to the utmost with all other countries or economic groups of countries to the maximuum degree;

that the formation of such Customs Unions is foreseen in the Draft Charter for an International Trade Organisation;

declares that it is ready to enter into negotiations with all European Governments sharing these views who wish to enter a Customs Union with France and whose national economies are capable of being combined with the French economy in such a way as to make a viable unit; ...

The Italian Government ... wishes to associate itself with the above declaration by the French Government ...

2.6

ANDREI VYSHINSKY: A CRITICISM OF THE TRUMAN DOCTRINE AND MARSHALL PLAN, 18 SEPTEMBER 1947

'A criticism of the Truman Doctrine and the Marshall Plan', in United Nations, General Assembly, *Official Records*, Plenary Meetings, 18 September 1947, pp. 86–8.

The Soviet Union, represented by Molotov had intially joined in the preliminary discussions about the Marshall Plan. On 2 July 1947, after receiving instructions from Moscow, Molotov rejected Anglo-French proposals for participation in the plan.

The so-called Truman Doctrine and the Marshall Plan are particularly glaring examples of the way in which the principles of the United Nations are violated, of the way in which the Organisation is ignored ...

As is now clear, the Marshall Plan constitutes in essence merely a variant of the Truman Doctrine adapted to the conditions of postwar Europe. In bringing forward this plan, the United States Government apparently counted on the cooperation of the Governments of the United Kingdom and France to confront the European countries in need of relief with the necessity of renouncing their inalienable right to dispose of their economic resources and to plan their national economy in their own way. The United States also counted on making all these countries directly dependent on the interests of American monopolies, which are striving to avert the approaching depression by an accelerated export of commodities and capital to Europe ...

It is becoming more and more evident to everyone that the implementation of the Marshall Plan will mean placing European countries under the economic and political control of the United States and direct interference by the latter in the internal affairs of those countries.

Moreover, this plan is an attempt to split Europe into two camps and, with the help of the United Kingdom and France, to complete the formation of a *bloc* of several European countries hostile to the interests of the democratic countries of Eastern Europe and most particularly to the interests of the Soviet Union.

An important feature of this Plan is the attempt to confront the countries of Eastern Europe with a *bloc* of Western European States including Western Germany. The intention is to make use of Western Germany and German heavy industry (the Ruhr) as one of the most important economic bases for American expansion in Europe, in disregard of the national interests of the countries which suffered from German aggression ...

_____ 2.7 _____

STATEMENT BY G. DIMITROV ON FEDERATION OF EASTERN EUROPE, 17 JANUARY 1948

Documents on International Affairs 1947–8 (London, 1952), p. 98.

This statement by the Bulgarian communist leader was published in *Pravda*, although in its later editorial of 28 January, *Pravda* distanced itself from Dimitrov's views. This reflected a hardening of the Soviet attitude to federation in the east.

If and when this problem becomes ripe for discussion, the democratic countries – Bulgaria, Yugoslavia, Albania, Rumania, Hungary, Czechoslovakia, Poland, and perhaps Greece – will decide how and when such a federation should come about. What the people are doing now is, in fact, to prepare for such a federation in the future ... If and when a federation was to be created, the people would not listen to imperialists; they would decide this question for themselves, considering only their own interests and those of international cooperation ... We are convinced that only a Customs union can really contribute to the development of our peoples, and therefore we conscientiously and courageously go ahead, preparing this Customs union with all countries who wish to join it ...

_____ 2.8 _____

ERNEST BEVIN: SPEECH ON WESTERN UNION, 22 JANUARY 1948

A. Boyd and F. Boyd, *Western Union*
(London: Hutchinson, 1948), pp. 117, 123, 125, 131.

This speech was an important stage in Bevin's campaign for a western defence alliance. Negotiations began on 4 March, and on 17 March Britain, France, the Netherlands, Belgium and Luxemburg signed a mutual defence treaty, the Brussels Treaty.

The conception of the unity of Europe and the preservation of Europe as the heart of Western civilization is accepted by most people ...

We did not press the Western Union – and I know that some of our neighbours were not desirous of pressing it – in the hope that when we got the German and

Austrian peace settlements, agreement between the Four Powers would close the breach between East and West, and thus avoid the necessity of crystallising Europe into separate *blocs*. We have always wanted the widest conception of Europe, including, of course, Russia. It is not a new idea. The idea of a close relationship between the countries of Western Europe first arose during the war, and in the days of the Coalition it was discussed. Already in 1944 there was talk between my predecessor and the Russian Government about a Western association ... the free nations of Western Europe must now draw closely together ...

First in this context we think of the people of France. Like all old friends, we have our differences from time to time, but I doubt whether ever before in our history there has been so much underlying goodwill and respect between the two peoples as now. We have a firm basis of co-operation in the Treaty of Dunkirk, we are partners in the European Recovery Programme ...

The time has come to find ways and means of developing our relations with the Benelux countries. I mean to begin talks with those countries in close accord with our French Allies ...

Perhaps I may return to the subject of the organisation in respect of a Western Union. That is its right description. I would emphasise that I am not concerned only with Europe as a geographical conception. Europe has extended its influence throughout the world, and we have to look further afield ... The organisation of Western Europe must be economically supported. That involves the closest possible collaboration with the Commonwealth and with overseas territories, not only British, but French, Dutch, Belgian and Portuguese ...

To conclude, His Majesty's Government have striven for the closer consolidation and economic development, and eventually for the spiritual unity, of Europe as a whole; but, as I have said, in Eastern Europe we are presented with a *fait accompli*. No one there is free to speak or think or to enter into trade or other arrangements of his own free will ... Neither we, the United States nor France is going to approach Western Europe on that basis. It is not in keeping with the spirit of Western civilization, and if we are to have an organisation in the West it must be a spiritual union. While no doubt there must be treaties or, at least, understandings, the union must primarily be a fusion derived from the basic freedoms and ethical principles for which we all stand. That is the goal we are trying to reach. It cannot be written down in a rigid thesis or in a directive. It is more a brotherhood and less of a rigid system.

—————————————— 2.9 ——————————————

THE US SECRETARY OF STATE GEORGE C. MARSHALL TO THE POLITICAL ADVISER FOR GERMANY, 6 MARCH 1948

Foreign Relations of the United States 1948, Vol. 3, p. 389.

The European Recovery Programme was the official designation of the Marshall Plan.

Purpose and scope of ERP [European Recovery Programme] and CEEC [Committee for European Economic Cooperation] are far beyond trade relations. Economic cooperation sought under ERP, and of which CEEC is a vehicle, has as its ultimate objective the closer integration of Western Europe. In this way it is a correlative of and parallel to the political and security arrangements sought under Bevin's proposals for Western Union. Full cooperation of the British is necessary if larger objectives are to be achieved.

—————————————— 2.10 ——————————————

THE US AMBASSADOR IN FRANCE, JEFFERSON CAFFERY, TO THE SECRETARY OF STATE, 23 MARCH 1948

Foreign Relations of the United States 1948, Vol. 3, pp. 401–2.

The role of the CEEC and its successor, the Organization for European Economic Cooperation (OEEC), continued to be a source of tension between the United States and the United Kingdom.

In summary, the first week of the CEEC meeting has been characterized by a rapid organization of the working party and by adoption of a tight time schedule ... While this activity is encouraging, there is little evidence that a majority of the delegates have instructions from their home governments which will permit them to come up with the type of continuing organization we have in mind.

The closest approach to the US concept has been the original French proposals which are also receiving support from the Italian delegation ...

British approach ... appears to us to lead to creation of weak organization with primary responsibility for programming the other principal decisions centred in Washington. British have never stated this to be their objective but, on the contrary, state that only way to get strong organization in Europe is to have nations' representatives of high rank assigned full time at seat of organization. They argue that their proposal for placing principal emphasis on role of national representatives insure governmental support. British also argue that given uncertainties as to form of act and wishes of administrator, there must be great flexibility, and that consequent statement of functions of organization should be limited to broad generalities. Although we recognize value of flexibility, we are concerned at vagueness of generalities and are not persuaded that British argument in favour of vagueness is genuine desire to create organization which can adjust itself to meet responsiblities placed upon it, but may be desire to create organization too weak to assume responsibility.

_____2.11_____

CONSIDERATIONS AFFECTING THE CONCLUSION OF A NORTH ATLANTIC SECURITY PACT, 23 NOVEMBER 1948

Foreign Relations of the United States 1948, Vol. 3, pp. 284–5.

The following is an extract from US Policy Planning Staff Paper PPS 43, dated 23 November 1948. It is addressed by the Director of the Policy Planning Staff George F. Kennan to the Secretary and Under-Secretary of State, George C. Marshall and Robert Lovett.

The Policy Planning Staff wishes to invite attention to certain considerations which it feels should be borne in mind in connection with the forthcoming negotiations for a North Atlantic Security Pact, and to advance certain recommendations which flow therefrom:

1. *Misconceptions as to the Significance of the Pact*

There is danger that we will deceive ourselves, and permit misconceptions to exist among our own public and in Europe, concerning the significance of the conclusion of such a pact at this time.

It is particularly difficult to assess the role of such a pact in our foreign policy for the reason that there *is* valid long-term justification for a formalization, by international agreement, of the natural defense relationship among the countries of the North Atlantic community. Such a formalization could contribute to the general sense of security in the area; facilitate the development of defensive power throughout the area; and act as a deterrent to outside aggressive forces.

It is therefore desirable, quite aside from the situation of the moment in Europe, that we proceed deliberately, and with careful study to the elaboration and negotiation of such an agreement.

On the other hand, it is important to understand that the conclusion of such a pact is not the main answer to the present Soviet effort to dominate the European continent, and will not appreciably modify the nature or danger of Soviet policies.

A military danger, arising from possible incidents or from the prestige engagement of the Russians and the western powers in the Berlin situation, does exist, and is probably increasing rather than otherwise. But basic Russian intent still runs to the conquest of western Europe by political means. In this program, military force plays a major role only as a means of intimidation.

The danger of political conquest is still greater than the military danger. If a war comes in the foreseeable future, it will probably be one which Moscow did not desire but did not know how to avoid. The political war, on the other hand, is now in progress; and, if there should not be a shooting war, it is this political war which will be decisive.

A North Atlantic Security Pact will affect the political war only insofar as it operates to stiffen the self-confidence of the western Europeans in the face of Soviet pressures. Such a stiffening is needed and desirable, but goes hand in hand with the danger of a general preoccupation with military affairs, to the detriment of economic recovery and of the necessity for seeking a peaceful solution to Europe's difficulties.

This preoccupation is already widespread, both in Europe and in this country. It is regrettable; because it addresses itself to what is not the main danger. We have to deal with it as a reality; and to a certain extent we have to indulge it, for to neglect it would be to encourage panic and uncertainty in western Europe and to play into the hands of the communists. But in doing so, we should have clearly in mind that the need for military alliances and rearmament on the part of the western Europeans is primarily a *subjective* one, arising in their own minds as a result of their failure to understand correctly their own position. Their best and most hopeful course of action, if they are to save themselves from communist pressures, remains the struggle for economic recovery and for internal political stability.

Compared to this, intensive rearmament constitutes an uneconomic and regrettable diversion of effort. A certain amount of rearmament can be subjectively beneficial to western Europe. But if this rearmament proceeds at any appreciable cost to European recovery, it can do more harm than good. The same will be true if concentration on the rearmament effort gradually encourages the assumption that war is inevitable and that therefore no further efforts are necessary toward the political weakening and defeat of the communist power in central and eastern Europe.

2.12

DRAFT PROTOCOL CONCERNING THE CREATION OF A COUNCIL FOR MUTUAL ECONOMIC ASSISTANCE, 18 JANUARY 1949

Draft Protocol Concerning the Creation of a Council for Mutual Economic Assistance, in Jozef M. van Brabant, 'Another look at the origins of east European economic cooperation', *Osteuropa Wirtschaft*, Vol. 24 (1979), pp. 263–4.

The precise status and authenticity of this document is uncertain.* It may have been one of a number of preliminary drafts for a statute of the Council for Mutual Economic Assistance. If its authenticity is confirmed it will demonstrate the existence of some interest in a much more ambitious form of economic integration than that proposed in the announcement of the creation of the Council for Mutual Economic Assistance.

The representatives of the Governments of the USSR, Rep. of Poland, etc., assembled today, 18 January 1949, in Moscow have resolved as follows.

Art. 1: A multilateral economic organization named the Council for Mutual Economic Assistance composed of all the countries represented and named above is created for a period of 20 years from the signing of the present Protocol.

Art. 2: The purposes of this organization are:

(a) To coordinate the economies of the signatory countries within a general economic plan developed by the Council ...

Art. 3: A Permanent Secretariat General of the Council will he created with its seat in Moscow which will have at its disposal a fund of 100.000.000 rubles obtained as follows: 50.000.000 from the USSR and 10.000.000 each from the other signatory countries – sums which must be deposited either in free currency, rubles or gold by 1 April 1949.

Art. 4: The Council will be convened whenever it may be necessary, each time in a different country under the presidency of the delegate of the host country, but not less frequently than once every three months. At these meetings the economic situation of each country individually will be discussed and analyzed.

* For an assessment, see Jozef M. van Brabant, 'Another look at the origins of east European economic cooperation', *Osteuropa Wirtschaft*, 24 (1979), pp. 243–66.

Art. 5: Beginning with the year 1950 the economic plans of all member countries will be drawn up in conformity with the advice of the Council, but for the present year each signatory country will endeavor to adapt its own economic plan to the provision of the present Protocol and the advice of the Secretariat General in so far as any investment of funds in the execution of predetermined parts of the economic plans of each member country has not taken place up to the signing of the present Protocol . . .

Art. 8: Each signatory country is obligated to make available to the Council all information and documentary material necessary to permit and facilitate the task of the observers which the Council may find necessary to send into any of the signatory countries upon the proposal of the Secretariat General, which has the authority to make any decisions, subject to ratification by the Council at its first meeting. Each signatory country is also obligated to accept and follow the advice of any counsellors and technicians which the Council may find necessary to send, directly or upon request, to any of the signatory countries.

Art. 9: The Governments of the signatory countries obligate themselves to send to the Secretariat General within the first 5 days of each month a detailed statistical situation report concerning production and any other documentary material pertinent to the economic and financial situation of the country concerned for the preceding month . . .

2.13

MEMORANDUM FOR THE SECRETARY OF STATE FOR FOREIGN AFFAIRS, ERNEST BEVIN, 19 OCTOBER 1950

Documents on British Policy Overseas,
Series 2, Vol. 1, pp. 315–18.

The memorandum for Ernest Bevin was drafted in the context of pressure from the Assembly of the Council of Europe for reform of the Statute in a federalist direction. The memorandum was discussed by the Cabinet on 23 and 24 October where its suspicion of the Assembly was shared.

There have always been two conflicting views of the nature and purposes of the Council of Europe. To the majority of the Governments which set it up the Council of Europe was not an instrument for the immediate politicial unification of Europe, but part of the general material and moral build up of which other parts are represented by the OEEC, the Brussels Treaty and the North Atlantic Pact . . .

From the outset this conception has broken down. The idea of a European Assembly has been launched by the European Movement and the Assembly has from the first been dominated by that organisation ... the Consultative Assembly has tended naturally to consist largely of enthusiasts for European federation. It is therefore biased in favour of federal solutions to an extent which wholly invalidates its claim to represent European opinion as a whole ...

The line which I will have to take in Rome must clearly conform to the basic policy which his Majesty's Government have accepted hitherto and to which we must stick, of avoiding commitments in Europe which would affect our position as the leading member of the Commonwealth, our special relationship with the United States and our reponsibilities as the centre of the Sterling Area ...

On the other hand, it would be very wrong, in the present state of morale in Europe, for His Majesty's Government to take up a position which obstructs the endeavours of other European Powers to achieve closer unity. There has always been a certain danger that a refusal by Great Britain to take full part in the movement towards European unity might lead to the creation of a bloc of European Powers inimical to our interests, especially if Germany were to get control of such a bloc. Traditionally, British policy has always been to prevent the formation of any such grouping in the Continent, but the emergence of the Soviet Union as an overriding threat to Europe has altered the basis on which this policy was founded. Subject to careful watch on the revival of German influence and power, I do not think it need any longer be regarded as necessary for His Majesty's Government to work against the creation of close groupings, even of a federal character, between Western European countries. Furthermore, such is the present material and moral weakness of countries such as France and Italy that they are in danger of losing the will to survive as separate independent nations: and it might be fatal to the preservation of democracy in Western Europe if we were openly to discourage the conception of European unity which is reflected in the Council of Europe.

CHAPTER 3

THE SCHUMAN PLAN AND THE EUROPEAN COAL AND STEEL COMMUNITY IN THE 1950s

INTRODUCTION

The European Coal and Steel Community (ECSC) was the first of the European Communities and is probably the least well known. Part of the reason for this is the decline in the economic significance of coal and steel. Even as early as 1963 the German Chancellor Konrad Adenauer felt it necessary to remind his audience that 'coal still meant something at that time' (Document 3.16). Coal and steel meant a great deal at the beginning of the 1950s. Coal and steel bound France and Germany together at the same time as making them direct competitors. France needed German coal in order to fire the furnaces of its steel industry, for which it had ambitious development plans. Those plans and the continued recovery of the

German steel industry raised the prospect of increased Franco-German competition. In addition to their economic importance coal and steel were seen as the sinews of any potential war machine. Hence, when Foreign Minister Robert Schuman suggested that 'Franco-German production of coal and steel as a whole be placed under a common High Authority', he presented his offer as a direct contribution to ensuring peace between the two nations (Document 3.2)

The Schuman Declaration of 9 May 1950 can be seen as the end product of a reconsideration of French policy in 1948 as the Allies moved towards the construction of a west German state.[1] Yet this was not a smooth and unequivocal process. When the same Robert Schuman made the first official state visit to the newly established Federal Republic of Germany, on 1 January 1950, he was received by the French High Commissioner in a ceremony which, according to the historian W. Loth, would not have been out of place in a French colony. The visit was overshadowed by discussions between the government of the Saar and France which threatened to exclude the option of a return of the Saar to Germany. It was indicative of the sensitivity of this issue that Adenauer recalled Schuman's response to the suggestion that they issue a joint communiqué on the Saar issue: 'He answered, that this was not possible, he had not come to negotiate but in order to inform me.'[2]

France's position was not as strong as Schuman's attitude in January suggested. Allied control over the German economy had been relaxed in the Petersberg Agreement of November 1949. On that occasion the Allies had declined to raise the existing limit on German steel output of 11.2 million tons. By the beginning of 1950 Germany was still well below that limit, but in the third quarter of 1949 German steel output crept above France's.[3] As Jean Monnet pointed out to Schuman, the Americans would not support the existing limit indefinitely and France would be able to do no more than delay raising the limit (Document 3.1).[4]

Monnet argued that this could have a disastrous effect upon France's modernization programme, and that increased German competition would result in a revival of pleas for protection and the organization of cartels. Support for cartels was widespread within French industry, the government itself and even the French section of the European Movement. Cartels, it was claimed, much as in the 1920s (see Chapter 1), would facilitate the management of structural change as well as provide the basis for European integration.[5] Monnet was not alone in casting doubt upon this benign view of cartels. The socialist André Philip pointed out that the record of cartels was not to increase production but to 'maintain profits and limit production'.[6] For Philip as for Monnet, integration of the coal and steel sectors was to provide a platform for a Europe-wide control of cartels, the most developed of which were in Germany.

The issue of cartels was important in winning the support of the United States for the project. The fact that the Schuman Plan looked like the kind of initiative which Secretary of State Dean Acheson had told the French in November 1949 that he was looking for, did much to mobilize American support. The Americans were well aware of the risk that the plan could develop into a covert super-cartel, but the potential political rewards were very promising (Documents 3.5, 3.6, 3.7 and 3.14).

Monnet's close links with the Americans also helped to win them over. According to the American Ambassador to France, David Bruce, 'Monnet is leading advocate real anti-cartel legislation and policy of expansion in production.'[7] Monnet was well aware of the suspicions which the project would meet, and had prepared a memorandum, forwarded by Bruce to the State Department, in which he distinguished it from a cartel. It was different, he explained, in its objectives, mode of operation, means of action, management and scope. Of special importance to Monnet himself was its management. He explained that 'Cartel is run by delegates of industry charged with serving interests of principals. Projected organization will be confided to independent personalities who will possess, besides technical capacity, a concern for general interest.'[8] Monnet made the same point in a letter to the British official Edwin Plowden, adding there that government delegates were also a threat to the autonomy of the proposed High Authority (Document 3.3).

Even before the announcement of the Schuman Plan an unofficial emissary had been sent to determine Adenauer's reaction. Adenauer immediately expressed his warm support for the idea. As he later explained, his prompt response was facilitated by the fact that he recalled discussing the integration of heavy industry as the basis for Franco-German reconciliation in the 1920s.[9] For the German government the attractions were self-evident. Germany would be an equal partner in the negotiations and could hardly be expected to consent to an organization which left Allied controls in place. Other responses to the declaration were varied. The Italian Foreign Minister, Count Sforza, was enthusiastic, and expressed the hope that it might also revive interest in a Franco-Italian customs union.[10] The Netherlands and Belgium were much more guarded. In Belgium there was general support for British participation.[11]

From the British point of view Schuman's declaration was not an auspicious start. Britain resented the lack of consultation and was uncertain about its implications. Schuman sought to reassure Bevin that the plan was not a *fait accompli* and that it was a 'European and not purely a Franco-German one'.[12] Despite considerable study of its implications, in which the long-term disadvantages of non-participation were frequently noted, Britain declined to join the negotiations. The official reason was that the French were asking for a prior commitment to establish a High Authority and that this was not acceptable. This also led to accusations that the French, and more specifically Monnet, had deliberately sought to exclude Britain. In fact Monnet made repeated efforts to win over the British, and the French government rephrased the commitment to meet British concerns. The new communiqué, of 1 June 1950, no longer stated that the participants in the negotiations had 'resolved' to establish a High Authority but only that they had it as their 'immediate aim'. The French Ambassador even suggested that 'if the word "immediate" in the phrase "immediate aim" 'should cause us difficulty, the inclusion of this word would not be regarded as essential'.[13] He had also suggested that the British government should follow the example of the Netherlands which had accepted the original communiqué as a basis for negotiation, but pointed out that they reserved the right not to sign any ensuing treaty. That too was rejected by the British. Underlying the quibbling over the precise form of the communiqué was a fundamental difference. As the French Ambassador put it, the British counter draft 'gave no indication that [the British] ... should be willing even to enter into discussions ... within the framework of the French proposals'.[14] Britain had no intention of making the sacrifice of sovereignty which was at the heart of the project (Document 3.8).

The atmosphere was soured only a few days later when the Labour Party National Executive Committee issued a statement, *European Unity*. The document was riddled with sentiments of superiority. It asserted that 'In every respect except distance we in Britain are closer to our kinsmen in Australia and New Zealand on the far side of the world, than we are to Europe', and that 'Civic and administrative traditions would prevent some countries from applying the methods of democratic socialism as practised in Britain and Scandinavia, even if their parliaments had a Socialist majority.'[15] Although Prime Minister Clement Attlee denied that it represented government policy, *European Unity* caused considerable dismay (Document 3.4). It also confirmed the suspicions of those who already felt that Britain had never been prepared to give serious consideration to European unity. Yet so strong was the desire for British commitment to Europe that many on the continent continued to grasp at any hint of British interest. As late as the autumn of 1951 Paul-Henri Spaak, then President of the Council of Europe, still hoped that the British Conservatives, who had gained power in October 1951, might be more amenable. He recalled that the 'disillusionment was cruel'.[16] For all the socialist rhetoric of the Labour government, there was really little difference between the two British parties on the question of Europe.

By the time Spaak finally despaired of Britain, the Paris Treaty of April 1951 establishing the European Coal and Steel Community (ECSC) had been signed. Although this was less than a year after Schuman's declaration, the negotiations had lasted far longer than Monnet had desired. His fears that protracted negotiations would endanger the autonomy of the High Authority had proved well founded. Even before negotiations formally opened on 20 June 1950, Monnet had learned of Dutch and Belgian concerns about the power of the proposed High Authority. The two states sought to coordinate their policy at meetings on 7 and 14 June. The Netherlands was apparently in a weak position.[17] Its coal industry accounted for only 5.6 per cent of the total output of the negotiating states, and its iron and steel industry was even less significant. Belgium was a more significant producer of both commodities, but suffered from high production costs and was burdened with inefficient coal mines. Despite this, Monnet later recalled that Dirk Spierenburg, 'the living incarnation of Dutch stubbornness', 'would be the toughest negotiator, and that his Benelux colleagues were relying on him and on his stubborn temperament to limit the power of the new institutions'.[18] Spierenburg had been instructed to press for some kind of council of ministers to restrain the High Authority. His Belgian counterpart Maximilien Suetens was more interested in a court of arbitrage and the involvement of producers and unions in a consultative role.

When Monnet revealed the French draft treaty on 24 June, he had made some concessions to Benelux concerns (Document 3.9). There was provision for 'an *ad hoc* court of arbitration', though its status did not suggest that Monnet thought it would play a significant role. There was also provision for 'a common assembly', though again its powers were limited. As a colleague of Monnet, Françoise Duchêne, later put it: 'it was to meet like an annual shareholders' meeting once a year, to debate the High Authority's Report; and it had only the shareholders' power to throw out the management'.[19] Monnet suggested that there should be 'regional associations of producers'. He also specified that the regions should be defined 'without taking account of existing frontiers'. Moreover, the associations were to be instruments of the High Authority. He did not intend that cartels, in the guise of producers' associations, should be introduced by the back door. Later, when the Belgians called for national associations of producers, Monnet suspected that this was precisely what the Belgians were seeking.[20] Of Spierenburg's council of ministers there was no mention.

Underlying the disputes were basic differences about the nature of international organizations and, indeed, the structure of the state. One difference concerned the legitimacy of the High Authority. For Monnet this would be derived from a treaty ratified by national parliaments. For Spierenburg, anxious to limit its power, the High Authority was to receive its mandate from the governments which concluded the treaty.[21] The German negotiators, Walter Hallstein and Carl Ophüls, sought to lay the foundations for a federal system. In this scheme there would be a bicameral legislature modelled on the American system, with a council of ministers forming one chamber and parliament the second chamber. Although this would have weakened the intergovernmentalism of Spierenburg's proposal, it met with little sympathy from the French, who preferred a more centralized structure.[22]

Spierenburg argued for a council of ministers whose approval would be required before the High Authority could act. Faced with this Monnet sought a compromise, accepting the principle of a council of ministers but insisting that the High Authority should retain power over coal and steel, while the council would be involved only where broader issues of national economic policy were affected. On 18 July the Dutch cabinet consented to this compromise. There then ensued the detailed argument over the relative power of each on specific issues, which Monnet had sought to avoid. On one of these the Council of Ministers acquired powers which would later be used to paralyze the ECSC. This concerned the ECSC's response to a 'manifest crisis' induced by deficient demand. According to Article 58 of the treaty, the High Authority could set production quotas and take other relevant measures, but only 'with the assent of the Council'.

Most of these points had been settled by the beginning of October, but then, on 4 October, to the surprise of the others, Monnet launched an attack on the provisions for the prevention of cartels. These he now deemed to be insufficient. He demanded a new text bluntly prohibiting any agreement intended to limit production, set prices or carve up markets. Agreements on concentration of undertakings or specialization might be permitted, but only with the prior consent of the High Authority. The precise motives for Monnet's dramatic intervention are disputed, but he clearly feared that his attack upon cartels had not been vigorous enough.[23] On 13 October Monnet advised the American High Commissioner, John McCloy, that he was pessimistic about the negotiations.[24] Resistance to his efforts came from the French steel industry and, more broadly, from the Germans. Hallstein sought to side-step Monnet's onslaught at the beginning of January 1951 by suggesting that the treaty should be signed without the disputed anti-cartel laws.[25] Monnet's response to this was to repeatedly threaten to resign unless the relevant clauses were included. On 22 January he justified this to Schuman on the grounds that without these clauses the ECSC would succumb to the 'domination of the monolithic organisation of the Ruhr', adding that 'the maintenance of cartels is not reconcilable with the increase of productivity'.[26]

The dispute over the 'monolithic organisation of the Ruhr' was complicated by the fact that it also concerned the Allied High Commissioners, who had issued a series of laws decreeing deconcentration. There were three specific issues. The first was the relatively high concentration of the German steel industry. The dispute here was about the extent to which the existing firms were to be broken up into smaller ones. The second was the extent to which German steel producers were to be allowed to retain ownership of coal mines. The third was the existence of a German coal sales syndicate (DKV), which the Americans and French wanted to disband.[27] In September 1950 the Americans, working closely with Monnet, began to push harder for a resolution of these issues, provoking vigorous protest from the Germans. The German press made much of the resignation of the industrialist Hermann Reusch from one of the subcommittees of the Schuman plan negotiations on 29 September.[28] Adenauer in turn exploited the opposition of German industrialists in his conversations with the Allied High Commissioners, and warned that their insistence on the proposed measures could threaten ratification of the ECSC (Document 3.10). Clashes with McCloy's economic adviser, and close friend of Monnet, Robert Bowie, were particularly bitter. At one of these Bowie simply invoked allied rights, telling Economic Minister Ludwig Erhard that the allies had responsibility for deconcentration. Erhard's protests that this put the German government in an impossible position made little impression upon Bowie.[29]

While the Germans undoubtedly used such issues in order to try to deflect the Allies and gain time in the hope of protecting their existing economic arrangements, the question of the status of the German government was a genuine one. The Federal Republic of Germany was in reality under a system of dual control at this time, with the Allies retaining extensive powers under the Occupation Statute. Adenauer had already exploited the fears raised by the Korean war, which broke out in June 1950, in order to argue for an end to the Occupation Statute. His memorandum of 29 August called for its replacement by a system of treaties regulating relations between the Allies and the German government.[30] The Korean war had also led to proposals for German rearmament and a European Defence Community (see Chapter 4) which complicated the Schuman plan negotiations. Monnet's fear, expressed to Schuman in September, was that 'if the Germans get what the Schuman Plan offers them, but without the Plan itself, we shall run the risk of them turning their backs on us'.[31]

A resolution of the dispute over deconcentration had become an effective precondition of the finalization of the Schuman Plan negotiations. Yet at the beginning of 1951 they were no closer to a solution. In late February the Americans issued what amounted to a series of ultimatums to Adenauer. By the end of the month the main stumbling block was the coal sales agency. According to the British Foreign Office, Franco-American insistence upon its dissolution was a product of the 'malign influence of Professor Bowie, the mad mullah of decartellisation'.[32] Under intense American pressure, Adenauer finally gave way on 14 March. He conceded that the coal sales agency would be dissolved by October 1952 and that steel concerns could obtain no more than 75 per cent of their coal from their own mines. The Germans also gave up their opposition to the anti-cartel clauses within the ECSC treaty, clauses which had been drafted by Bowie.[33]

The overriding political commitment of France and Germany to reach an agreement had not stopped acrimonious disputes and repeated brinkmanship in the search for solutions which benefited their perceived economic interests. It did make it easier for them to agree on arrangements, transitional measures and exemptions which met the concerns of the smaller states. Of these, Belgium was the most problematic. At the start Belgium fought for the equalization of wage costs as a precondition for the opening of a common market. Monnet himself had suggested that the High Authority should have some control over wages, but this was vigorously opposed by the Netherlands which hoped to benefit from its low wage costs. As the Germans moved to a position of increasing opposition to granting the High Authority power in this area, and the French also moved closer to the Dutch position, the Belgians were isolated. All that remained of their ambitions was the provision that the High Authority could block a lowering of wages intended to improve an industry's competitive position.[34]

With that avenue blocked, the Belgians looked to transitional measures as a means of safeguarding their position. Monnet's draft of 24 June 1950 had envisaged a 'péréquation fund' which 'will serve to provide temporary assistance to enterprises which require a period of time to adapt to the single market'.[35] It was this which provided the answer to Belgium's problem. The details were worked out by Etienne Hirsch and the Belgian civil servant François Vinck in October 1950. A levy was to be imposed upon low-cost producers in order to provide the péréquation fund. In practice this meant imposing a levy upon German coal producers in order to subsidize less efficient Belgian producers. For the Germans the political gains of the treaty were well worth this price. They had, however, insisted upon retaining Monnet's demand that the subsidy should decrease and be limited to a five-year transitional period. The rationale was that there would be a restructuring of the Belgian industry, involving the closure of the least efficient mines, which in turn would open up the Belgian market to German coal. For one Belgian advocate of the ECSC, the attraction was that 'we think that the Schuman plan can serve to remedy certain disorders which we would perhaps be incapable of curing by our own means'.[36] That was an argument which, implicitly or explicitly, would recur throughout the history of the European Communities. During the foreign ministers' conference of 12–18 April 1951, Paul Van Zeeland won an important concession which suggested that Belgium might not have the political will to follow the argument through to its conclusion. Originally subsidies were to be provided only for a certain quantity of production, output above that limit representing the least efficient. Citing the horrendous social implications of widespread closure, Van Zeeland won agreement to provide subsidies beyond the previously agreed limit.[37]

The complex interaction between domestic constraints and international negotiation was also evident in the case of Italy. There the Ministry of Industry backed the claims of the steel industry for a substantial péréquation fund, half of which would come directly from the Italian government. This was opposed not only by the other states but also by the Italian Treasury Minister, Giuseppe Pella, in an attempt to keep the Italian budget under control.[38] Italy also provided another example of a recurrent feature of Community negotiations – the linkage between one set of negotiations and another. Here the link was with the projected European Defence Committee (EDC). Italy was not very enthusiastic about this idea but did want access to Algerian iron ore which the French were seeking to keep outside the single market. At the Santa Margherita conference in February 1951, the Italians obtained an agreement on iron ore and subsequently displayed some enthusiasm for the EDC.

One issue which proved impossible to resolve either by side-payments or by linkage was the future of the Saar. For both Schuman and Adenauer this was something which could be neither resolved nor ignored. For both of them, especially Adenauer, even the appearance of concessions ran the risk of handing their respective domestic opponents a weapon which could be used to block ratification of the treaty. Since both were minded, as Adenauer later put it, to recognize that 'the negotiating partner also has an opposition', they were able to agree on an exchange of letters by which they acknowledged that neither side construed the treaty as determining the status of the Saar.[39]

The fact that the Treaty of Paris (Document 3.12) was signed in April 1951 was due largely to the political will of the major actors. Schuman and Monnet had the vision to take a step away from the unproductive but reassuring Paris–London axis and seek an accommodation with Germany. Adenauer had the commitment to western integration, and the rehabilitation of a west German state, necessary to make the concessions which led to the treaty (Document 3.3). (For dissenting German views see Document 3.11.) Priority of political will and commitment did not mean indifference to economic interests and strategies. Both Monnet, often through the Americans, and Adenauer, often through Walter Hallstein, pushed each other to the very brink in order to defend their respective interests and visions. The Italians, again with a strong political commitment to European integration, pounced on French vulnerability over the EDC in order to extract concessions on iron ore. Most striking of all was Spierenburg's success in diluting the autonomy of Monnet's High Authority.

Quite how far Monnet had failed to implement his vision was unclear when the treaty was signed. One of the first challenges which Monnet faced involved symbolic issues of status which had little bearing on the operation of the ECSC but were of considerable importance to the parties involved. The context for these was set by a British proposal in March 1952, before the ECSC formally came into existence. Having wilfully excluded itself from the ECSC and from the projected EDC, Britain was in danger of being marginalized. Britain, of course, was not the only European state to have such worries. Sweden's Dag Hammerskjöld explained Swedish suspicion about the 'constitution of a politico-military group in the centre of Europe with all the characteristics of a cartel'.[40] He was not convinced that the British answer to this development would suffice. The British answer had been formally submitted by Foreign Minister Anthony Eden in March 1952, and consisted of the proposal that the ECSC and EDC should operate as specialized bodies within the framework of the Council of Europe. While some British ministers clearly sought to use this as a means of subordinating the supranational ECSC and EDC to the intergovernmental EDC, Eden's intent was less devious. It was simply to find a framework within which Britain could escape marginalization without making the sacrifice of sovereignty involved in joining the supranational bodies.

Monnet, however, was not convinced of British good intent. The issue was complicated even more by the ambition of Camille Paris, Secretary-General of the Council of Europe, to provide a combined secretariat for the Council of Europe and the ECSC Assembly, which he himself would head. This was totally unacceptable to Monnet. Even the apparently innocuous suggestion that Britain might send observers to the ECSC Assembly, who would participate in debate but not vote, was seen as an issue of great symbolic importance. This was acknowledged by the British Ambassador to Paris, who compared the British request with the suggestion that observers might speak in the British House of Commons. As the Ambassador went on to explain, the Assembly had no legislative function, and to that extent his own comparison was misleading. He was right to emphasize the symbolic importance to Monnet of the Assembly providing formal and direct legitimation of the High Authority.[41]

Monnet won the symbolic battles, deflecting Eden's plan for the Council of Europe and Camille Paris's bid for a common secretariat. The battle with the cartels, which was central to Monnet's vision, was a different matter. Ironically, Monnet's strategy was contradicted by the Americans almost from the outset. As part of the commitment to the rearmament of the west in response to the Korean war, McCloy asked the Germans to introduce a programme of prioritization and industrial rationing in March 1951. In the same month he asked the German steel producers' association to prepare plans for increasing steel capacity to 16.5 million tons. In the following month, Fritz Berg, head of the German Federation of Industry, launched a proposal for massive private and public aid for investment in energy, coal, water and rail freight capacity. The private part of the investment package came in the form of a compulsory loan from the manufacturing industry, while the government supplied over twice the amount in the form of tax credits. The package, sanctioned by the Investment Aid Law of 1952, mobilized public and private resources behind German heavy industry. The new spirit was reflected in Allied backing for a cartel, the rolled steel group, to allocate scarce resources.[42]

Monnet's battle against the coal sales syndicate (DKV) turned out to be only apparently successful. The DKV was duly dissolved, only to be replaced by a new organization, Georg. Officially a coordinating body for six separate sales agencies, it effectively continued the old practices. It was not until April 1955 that the High Authority managed to persuade Georg to negotiate on a reform package intended to make the six agencies independent. Part of the problem was that the High Authority, especially its French and German members, was inclined to compromise in order to reconcile the conflicting demands of decartellization and the need for regulation of the market. Even Monnet conceded that 'coal needs a certain type of organisation', though he did not specify what type.[43] Reform did little to improve matters. The High Authority reported that 'At the end of September 1957, the three Ruhr coal-selling agencies raised their prices for all types and grade of coal in a manner identical down to the smallest detail.' The agencies had technically followed prescribed procedures, but the High Authority noted that 'it seems clear from the minutes of the different meetings at which these price increases were approved that the three managements had drawn up the price schedules in common'.[44] The situation had not improved by the end of the decade. Desperately seeking to gain some control over the *de facto* cartel and acknowledging the inadequacy of existing treaty provisions, the High Authority suggested treaty revision.[45] The German government lobbied hard for giving the High Authority loose discretion to authorize unified cartels, but had to accept the principle of High Authority control and at least some specification of the conditions under which this could be done. The proposed amendment was, however, struck down by the Court of Justice in December 1961.[46]

Although the Ruhr, with its strong tradition of cartels, received a lot of attention, the problem of cartels in the coal and steel sector was not restricted to Germany. Indeed, the 112 cases examined under Article 65 between the inauguration of the common market and April 1958 came from every member state, with the exception of Luxemburg. Of these, the High Authority prohibited only three.[47]

The end of the decade witnessed another blow to the High Authority and the principles which Monnet had fought for. The problem here was the Belgian coal industry. There were early signs of the underlying problems. In 1953 Belgium, following Germany's lead, sought a community-wide prohibition of imports from the United States. This, however, was opposed by the Netherlands and the Italians, both small coal producers with an interest in cheap imported coal. With this avenue closed off, Belgium sought first ECSC support for stockpiles and then financing for power stations to burn its low-quality coal.[48] Temporary increases in the price of American coal in 1955 encouraged the Belgian government to delay the agreed restructuring, while the boom in demand for coal in the mid-1950s was used as an excuse by the producers for the maintenance of capacity. The Belgians, however, had only delayed the inevitable. Towards the end of 1957 the demand for coal began to slacken, and early in 1958 the first signs of a crisis in the European coal industry appeared. A continuing fall in demand combined with cheap imported coal from the United States and the third world put pressure on the inefficient Belgian mines. After trying a variety of other measures, the High Authority sought to invoke Articles 58 and 74, to declare a 'manifest crisis' and impose production quotas. In order to do this it required the assent of the Council, which twice refused to give its assent in May 1959. Underlying the problem was the simple conflict of interest between the major coal producers and the importers. Faced with the paralysis of the ECSC, individual states took their own protective measures. In Belgium, however, the scale of the crisis was so extensive that the long-delayed restructuring was finally imposed through market forces. Reflecting on the coal crisis, the High Authority announced in its *Eighth General Report* 'its profound and unanimous conviction that it could not possibly fulfil its responsibilities if the only means at its disposal were that of persuasion, and if the operation of the Community were based on the principle of unanimity' (Document 3.15).[49]

In a sense this had been foreseen by Monnet – hence his desire to establish a powerful High Authority free from the influence of national governments. His pragmatism had forced him to compromise in order to get the treaty at all. Despite the compromises he had still hoped that the principle of suprantionality had triumphed. Looking back from the perspective of the 1970s, he was not so sure: 'We were wrong in those days to talk about a power above nations, the High Authority, as a supranational power. What eventually emerged, even in the Coal and Steel Community days, was a dialogue between the independent body, which was the High Authority, and the Ministers representing the Nation States.'[50]

The ECSC was not without its achievements. It had a significant impact upon the provision of housing in the coal and steel regions; it helped to reduce discrimination in freight rates; and it presided over an increase in intra-ECSC trade which far outstripped increased production and trade with other states. More important than this, however, it had begun the process of liberating France from fear of the Ruhr and the counterproductive desire to find security through strategies of dismemberment and the restriction of German production. For this reason alone, whatever the failings of the ECSC in operation, Schuman fully deserved the praise lavished on him by Konrad Adenauer (Document 3.16).

NOTES

1. Hellmuth Auerbach, 'Die europäische Wende der französischen Deutschlandpolitik 1947/48', in L. Herbst *et al.* (eds), *Vom Marshallplan zur EWG* (Munich, 1990), pp. 577–91.
2. Konrad Adenauer, *Erinnerungen 1945–1953* (Stuttgart, 1965), p. 301. For Loth's judgement see *Option für den Westen* (Munich, 1989), p. 7.
3. In the first quarter of 1950 it began to open up a large gap, with 2.849 million tons against France's 1.994. Matthias Kipping, *Zwischen Kartellen und Konkurrenz* (Berlin, 1996), p. 114.
4. According to a British report, Germany entry to the Council of Europe would trigger pressure for raising the limit. *Documents on British Policy Overseas* (hereafter *DBPO*), Series 2, Vol. 1, doc. 18.
5. Kipping, *Zwischen Kartellen und Konkurrenz*, pp. 135–49.
6. ibid., p. 152. The strength of feeling this issue aroused is evident from the fact that Monnet told a leading French industrialist that his policy was 'inconsistent, indeed criminal', ibid., p. 161.
7. *FRUS*, 1950, Vol. 3, p. 699 (12 May 1950).
8. ibid., p. 701 (12 May 1950).
9. Adenauer, *Erinnerungen*, p. 335.
10. A treaty of 26 March 1949, and a subsequent customs union convention of 23 June 1950, were not ratified. *DBPO*, Series 2, Vol. 1, doc. 11.

11. ibid., doc. 38 (27 May 1950).
12. ibid., doc. 19 (12 May 1950).
13. ibid., doc. 73 (1 June 1950). For the whole affair see Edmund Dell, *The Schuman Plan and the British Abdication of Leadership in Europe* (Oxford, 1995).
14. *DBPO*, Series 2, Vol. 1, doc. 69 (1 June 1950).
15. *European Unity* (London, 1950), pp. 4 and 7.
16. Paul-Henri Spaak, *The Continuing Battle* (London, 1971), p. 219.
17. On the Netherlands see Richard T. Griffiths, 'The Schuman Plan', in *The Netherlands and the Integration of Europe 1945–1957* (Amsterdam, 1990).
18. Jean Monnet, *Memoirs* (London, 1978), pp. 324–5.
19. Françoise Duchêne, *Jean Monnet* (New York, 1994), p. 210.
20. ibid., p. 213.
21. Hanns Jürgen Küsters, 'Die Verhandlungen über das Institutionelle System zur Gündung der Europäischen Gemeinschaft für Kohle und Stahl', in Klaus Schwabe (ed.), *Die Anfänge des Schuman-Plans 1950/51* (Baden-Baden, 1988), p. 83.
22. ibid., pp. 83–5.
23. The fullest survey is provided by Kipping, *Zwischen Kartellen und Konkurrenz*, pp. 214–28.
24. *Dir Kabinettsprotokolle der Bundesregierung*, Vol. 3, 1950, doc. 76.
25. John Gillingham, 'Solving the Ruhr problem: German heavy industry and the Schuman Plan', in Schwabe (ed.), *Zwischen Kartellen und Konkurrenz*, p. 429.
26. Quoted in Kipping, *Zwischen Kartellen und Konkurrenz*, n. 3, p. 251.
27. The British did not, and differed from the French and Americans on other issues. See *DBPO*, Series 2, Vol. 1, docs 210–14, 218–23, 227–40.
28. Reusch, however, was not representative of the steel industry. Werner Bührer, *Ruhrstahl und Europe* (Munich, 1986), pp. 186–9.
29. *Dir Kabinettsprotokolle der Bundesregierung*, Vol. 3, 1950, doc. 71 (10 October 1950).
30. Adenauer, *Erinnerungen*, pp. 358–9.
31. Monnet, *Memoirs*, p. 341.
32. *DBPO*, Series 2, Vol. 1, doc. 220 (27 February 1951).
33. On Bowie's role see Monnet, *Memoirs*, pp. 352–3.
34. Richard T. Griffiths, 'The Schuman Plan negotiations: the economic clauses', in Schwabe (ed.), *Die Anfänge des Schuman-Plans, 1950/51*, pp. 40–3.
35. *FRUS*, 1950, Vol. 3, p. 734.
36. Quoted in Alan S. Milward, *The European Rescue of the Nation-State* (London, 1992), p. 76.
37. Griffiths, 'The Schuman Plan', p. 67.
38. Ruggero Ranieri, 'The Italian steel industry and the Schuman Plan negotiations', in Schwabe (ed.), *Zwischen Kartellen und Konkurrenz*, n. 21, p. 353.
39. Adenauer, *Erinnerungen*, pp. 428–30.
40. *DBPO*, Series 2, Vol. 1, doc. 473 (21 July 1952).
41. ibid., doc. 509 (16 October 1952).
42. J. Gillingham, *Coal, Steel and the Rebirth of Europe* (Cambridge, 1991), pp. 284–5, 307.
43. Raymond Poidevin and Dirk Spierenburg, *The History of the High Authority of the European Coal and Steel Community* (London, 1994), pp. 99–100, 91.
44. ECSC, *Sixth General Report 1958 – Volume 2*, pp. 89–90.
45. ECSC, *Ninth General Report 1961*, p. 23.

46. Poidevin and Spierenburg, *The History of the High Authority*, p. 517.
47. ECSC, *Sixth General Report 1958 – Volume 2*, p. 85.
48. Milward, *The European Rescue of the Nation State*, n. 36, p. 97.
49. ECSC, *Eighth General Report 1960*, p. 11.
50. Quoted in Dell, *The Schuman Plan*, pp. 188–9.

FURTHER READING

D. Brinkley and C. Hackett (eds), *Jean Monnet: The Path to European Unity* (London, 1991).

E. Dell, *The Schuman Plan and the British Abdication of Leadership in Europe* (Oxford, 1995).

F. Duchêne, *Jean Monnet* (New York, 1994).

F. Duchêne, 'French motives for European integration', in Robert Bidelux and Richard Taylor (eds), *European Integration and Disintegration: East and West* (London, 1996), pp. 22–35.

J. Gillingham, *Coal, Steel and the Rebirth of Europe* (Cambridge, 1991).

E. Haas, *Beyond the Nation State: Functionalism and International Organization* (Stanford, 1964).

A.S. Milward, *The Reconstruction of Western Europe* (London, 1984).

A.S. Milward, *The European Rescue of the Nation State* (London, 1992).

A.S. Milward et. al., *The Frontier of National Sovereignty* (London, 1993).

J. Monnet, *Memoirs* (London, 1976).

R. Poidevin and D. Spierenburg, *The History of the High Authority of the European Coal and Steel Community* (London, 1994).

K. Schwabe (ed.), *Die Anfänge des Schuman-Plans* (Baden-Baden, 1988).

F.R. Willis, *France, Germany and the New Europe* (Stanford, 1968).

_____ 3.1 _____

JEAN MONNET: MEMORANDUM TO ROBERT SCHUMAN, 4 May 1950

R. Vaughan (ed.), *Postwar Integration in Europe*
(London: Arnold, 1976), pp. 51, 53–5.

Jean Monnet was Planning Commissioner, responsible for plans for the modernization of France. Monnet himself traced his suggestions in the memorandum back to discussions in 1943.

Wherever we look in the present world situation we see nothing but deadlock – whether it be the increasing acceptance of a war that is thought to be inevitable, the problem of Germany, the continuation of French recovery, the organisation of Europe, the very place of France in Europe and in the world.

From such a situation there is only one way of escape: concrete action on a limited but decisive point, bringing about on this point a fundamental change and gradually modifying the very terms of all the problems ...

The continuation of France's recovery will be halted if the question of German industrial production and its competitive capacity is not rapidly solved ...

Already Germany is asking to increase her production from 11 to 14 million tons. We shall refuse, but the Americans will insist. Finally, we shall state our reservations but we shall give in. At the same time, French production is levelling off or even falling.

Merely to state these facts makes it unnecessary to describe in great detail what the consequences will be: Germany expanding, German dumping on export markets; a call for the protection of French industries; the halting or camouflage of trade liberalisation; the re-establishment of pre-war cartels; perhaps an orientation of German expansion towards the East, a prelude to political agreements; France fallen back into the rut of limited, protected production ...

The USA do not want things to take this course. They will accept an alternative solution if it is dynamic and constructive, especially if it is proposed by France ... At the present moment, Europe can be brought to birth only by France. Only France can speak and act.

But if France does not speak and act now, what will happen?

A group will form around the United States, but in order to wage the cold war with greater force. The obvious reason is that the countries of Europe are afraid and are seeking help. Britain will draw closer and closer to the United States; Germany will develop rapidly, and we shall not be able to prevent her being rearmed. France will be trapped again in her former Malthusianism, and this will lead inevitably to her being effaced.

3.2

ROBERT SCHUMAN:DECLARATION OF 9 MAY 1950

Pascal Fontaine, *Europe – a Fresh Start: The Schuman Declaration 1950–90* (Luxembourg: European Commission, 1990), pp. 44–6.

This declaration by the French Foreign Minister led directly to the negotiations for a European Coal and Steel Community.

World peace cannot be safeguarded without the making of creative efforts proportionate to the dangers which threaten it.

The contribution which an organised and living Europe can bring to civilisation is indispensable to the maintenance of peaceful relations. In taking upon herself for more than 20 years the role of champion of a united Europe, France has always had as her essential aim the service of peace. A united Europe was not achieved and we had war.

Europe will not be made all at once or according to a single plan. It will be built through concrete achievements which first create a *de facto* solidarity. The coming together of the nations of Europe requires the elimination of the age-old opposition of France and Germany. Any action to be taken in the first place must concern these two countries.

With this aim in view, the French Government proposes that action be taken immediately in one limited but decisive point. It proposes that Franco-German production of coal and steel as a whole be placed under a common High Authority, within the framework of an organisation open to the participation of the other countries of Europe.

The pooling of coal and steel production should immediately provide for the setting up of common foundations for economic development as a first step in the federation of Europe, and will change the destinies of those regions which have long been devoted to the manufacture of munitions of war, of which they have been the most constant victims.

The solidarity in production thus established will make it plain that any war between France and Germany becomes not merely unthinkable, but materially impossible. The setting up of this powerful productive unit, open to all countries willing to take part and bound ultimately to provide all the member countries with the basic elements of industrial production on the same terms, will lay a true foundation for their economic unification.

_____ 3.3 _____

LETTER FROM JEAN MONNET TO EDWIN PLOWDEN, 25 MAY 1950

Documents on British Policy Overseas, Series 2, Vol. 1, pp. 94–6.

This letter to Plowden, Chief Planning Officer at the Treasury, reveals Monnet's approach to integration.

The independence of the Authority vis-à-vis Governments and the sectional interests concerned is the pre-condition for the emergence of a common point of view which could be taken neither by Governments nor by private interests. It is clear that to entrust the Authority to a Committee of Governmental Delegates or to a Council made up of representatives of Governments, employers and workers, would amount to returning to our present methods, those very methods which do not enable us to settle our problems. It should be possible to find quite a small number of men of real stature able without necessarily being technicians, and capable of rising above particular or national interests in order to work for the accomplishment of common objectives ...

Furthermore the general objective assigned to the High Authority can be summarised by the formula of raising the standard of life by increasing productivity. All tasks entrusted to it derive from this principle, which would justify the establishment of identical price conditions no less than the effort to modernise production and assistance for rationalising enterprises which would in turn facilitate the maintenance of full employment by redistributing labour in more productive occupations. To accomplish this objective, it seems to us that the Authority will usually be able to confine itself to indirect and general means of action without interfering in the management of the enterprises concerned nor directly determining which of them should be eliminated.

3.4

ANDRÉ PHILIP: *SOCIALISM AND EUROPEAN UNITY*, 1950

André Philip, *Der Sozialismus und die europäische Einheit*
(Gelsenkirchen: Ruhr-Verlag, 1950), pp. 10–15
(translation by the authors)

André Philip was one of the most enthusiastically pro-European members of the Section Française de l'Internationale Ouvrière (SFIO). His reaction to a Labour Party document was shared by many socialists on the continent, especially in Italy and France.

On page seven [of *European Unity. A Statement by the National Executive Committee of the British Labour Party*] we read, 'The Labour Party would welcome with pleasure an economic union which was based upon international planning for full employment, social justice and stability'. After, however, this agreeable reassurance has been given, they go on to prove that it is unattainable. This is done by imposing three preconditions:

1. 'The achievement of this goal assumes a degree of uniformity in the internal policies of the member states which does not now exist and is unlikely to exist in the near future.'
2. 'Only public ownership can make such planning possible, control without ownership can be effective only for negative purposes.'
3. 'All industries concerned in European planning should first be subject to government direction in their own country.' ...

These three statements by our Labour friends do not appear immediately persuasive.

1. Can one really say that international planning is impossible because of currently existing divergencies which will, supposedly, exist in the future politics of member states? ... One may not forget that the nationalised sector in France is no smaller than in Great Britain ... Although our government has a preference for liberal economic reforms, the pressure of events has proven so strong that industrial development in the last few years has taken place under the guidance of the state and with public investment ...
2. Can one say without further ado that planning would be unrealisable and would lead to purely negative consequences if it was not preceded by nationalisation? ... It appears [rather] that we have now reached a point in economic development where power and ownership more and more fall away from each other. No

one claims anymore that shareholders in a limited company exercise any kind of power.

3. A more serious question, the decisive one, is: is international planning possible only on the basis of national planning . . . ? Does one begin in a single country by first establishing regional planning before one creates a national plan? To the contrary, if we want European planning would it not be unavoidable to establish planning offices directly superordinate to the enterprises, and if gradations appear necessary, to place European regional institutions over more national associations? . . .

How can a party which disposes of a majority of a mere five votes look down so arrogantly upon the socialist parties of the continent and declare that a European legislative body 'would exhibit a permanent anti-socialist majority' and that, furthermore, 'the civic and administrative traditions would prevent some countries from applying socialist methods even if they had a socialist majority.' With what original sin are the socialist parties of the continent afflicted, from which solely and only the Labour Party is exempted? . . .

How can the Labour Party reject with horror cooperation with a non-socialist Europe and then affirm its unshakeable ties, its community of world views, its untainted solidarity – on the one hand with a Commonwealth whose governments are all currently conservative and on the other hand with an America which, despite its progressive policies, can certainly not be considered as a representative of socialist ideas?

3.5

TELEGRAM FROM US SECRETARY OF STATE DEAN ACHESON, 10 MAY 1950

Foreign Relations of the United States 1950, Vol. 3, p. 695.

Dean Acheson had been convinced of the need for European integration for several years. His hesitation reflected traditional American fears about European cartels.

In commenting on proposal believe it is important that French be given credit for making a conscious and far-reaching effort to advance Franco-German rapprochment and European integration generally. On the other hand, it is too early for us to give proposal our approval because of the possible cartel aspect and known previous French efforts to secure detailed control over investment policies and management of Ruhr coal and steel industry, and certainly until we know about the character and the details of the scheme. British reaction has not yet developed but believe it is apt to be somewhat cautious.

_____ 3.6 _____

THE ACTING SECRETARY OF STATE TO THE US SECRETARY OF STATE, 10 MAY 1950

Foreign Relations of the United States 1950, Vol. 3, pp. 695–6.

The Acting Secretary John Foster Dulles was to become Secretary of State in the new Eisenhower administration. Dean Acheson, the Secretary of State, was in London.

While obviously many details lacking necessary for final judgement, it is my initial impression that the conception is brilliantly creative and could go far to solve the most dangerous problem of our time, namely the relationship of Germany's industrial power to France and the West. The proposal is along lines which Secretary Marshall and I thought about in Moscow in 1947 but which we did not believe the French would ever accept.

_____ 3.7 _____

THE US AMBASSADOR IN THE UNITED KINGDOM, LEWIS DOUGLAS, TO THE SECRETARY OF STATE, 6 JUNE 1950

Foreign Relations of the United States 1950, Vol. 3, pp. 722–3.

Ambassador Douglas reflected a changed emphasis in United States hopes for European integration, relying upon France instead of the United Kingdom.

The political advantages of the plan ...

(a) The plan is the result of French creative leadership ... it should facilitate France's resumption of continental leadership, which hitherto the US has had to look to a latterly somewhat reluctant Britain to carry.
(b) It should abate, if not dispel, fears of recurrent Franco-German war, and thereby encourage France to acquiesce in increased economic strength of Germany and, possibly at a later date, even in German military participation in Western defense ...
(e) It should constitute an important first stage for a possible future European federation ...

As far as political disadvantages are concerned, it is important that the plan not be used as a vehicle:

(a)   To underwrite the economic base of a 'third force' ...
(b)   To permit the resurgence of Germany as the dominant element in Western continental Europe ...

Economic merits, difficulties and potential abuses: ... If plan, in operation, conforms to general principles of an expanding economy, which the French Government has declared to be its purpose, and does not degenerate into a super-cartel with price fixing, licensing, division of markets, restriction or artificial allocation of funds for investment, and suppression of competition and technical improvements, then the positive economic potentialities of scheme should predominate.

3.8

MINUTES OF A MEETING OF THE BRITISH CABINET, 22 JUNE 1950

Documents on British Policy Overseas, Series 2, Vol. 1 (London: HMSO, 1986), pp. 210–13.

The meeting was held after the decision by the Cabinet, on 2 June 1950, not to take part in the negotiations on the terms set by the French government. The report was subsequently considered by a Committee of Ministers and the issue raised again in Cabinet.

The Cabinet had before them a note by the Secretary of the Cabinet ... covering a report by a Committee of officials appointed to advise on the French Foreign Minister's proposal for integrating the coal and steel industries of west Europe.

In a preliminary discussion of the report the following points were raised:

(a)   Some concern was expressed about the attitudes which trade unions might take towards this proposal ...
(b)   The Government had already given ample proof that they were prepared in principle to support all reasonable plans for promoting closer economic co-ordination in Europe. They were not therefore opposed in principle to some integration of the coal and steel industries of west Europe. They must, however, reject any proposal for placing these industries under the control of a supra-national authority whose decisions would be binding on Governments. Equally they could not accept proposals for placing these industries under the control of an industrial cartel on the pre-war restrictionist model ...
(e)   The issues raised by this proposal were complex and far-reaching and it was

essential that Ministers should have full opportunity to consider them in detail. There was no reason to suppose that this opportunity would be lacking; for it was likely to be some time before any detailed scheme emerged from the international discussions now proceeding in Paris. The greatest risk was perhaps that a deadlock would be reached in those discussions and the United Kingdom Government would be asked to assist in resolving it.

_____ 3.9 _____

JEAN MONNET'S DRAFT TREATY, JUNE 1950

Foreign Relations of the United States 1950, Vol. 3, pp. 727ff.

Monnet's draft treaty, presented at the beginning of the negotiations, gave more power to the proposed High Authority than the eventual Paris Treaty of 1951. His draft is also notable for the absence of any reference to a Council of Ministers.

Article 7. The states whose interests are affected by a decision or a recommendation of the high authority may, with [*within?*] (blank) days following the transmittal of such decision or recommendation, request the high authority to re-examine its position.

At the expiration of the period thus *fixed*, or immediately in the case of a confirmatory decision following a second reading, the decision or recommendation shall be made public.

Decisions dealing with the procedure, regulations and other measures of an internal order as well as the suggestions of high authority may be published immediately.

The same right of appeal shall be open to enterprises in case of a decision or a recommendation directed to them individually.

Article 8. Within (blank) days after the publication of a decision or a recommendation of the high authority which has been confirmed on second reading, a state party to the treaty or an individual enterprise to which such decision or recommendation was directed could have the matter referred to an ad hoc court of arbitration. As an example, this court might consist of five members; the International Court of Justice and the International Labor Organization would each designate a member of the court and the states parties to the treaty would by agreement designate the three other members, using the procedure prescribed in Article 3. These three members should, as far as possible, be chosen from nationals of states not parties to the particular cause, or from persons not connected with the affected enterprise. The member designated by the International Court of Justice would be the president of the court.

Appeals would be admissible only if they were founded on the violation of treaty obligations binding on the high authority or, with respect to appeals by states, if the decision or recommendation was of such a nature as to compromise either a policy of full employment in an expanding economy or the equilibrium of the external balance of the interest state.

If the court should decide that there had been a violation of treaty obligations, its decision shall be binding on the parties.

In all other cases where an appeal was admissible, the court would act as a mediator and would address to the high authority a recommendation as defined in Article 6.

In principle, the taking of an appeal would not have the effect of suspending the decision of the high authority pending a determination of the appeal . . .

Article 11. Once a year, the parliament of each of the member states shall elect delegates drawn from its own membership. All of those elected shall convene once each year in a common assembly for the purposes set forth in the following articles . . .

Article 13. If the common assembly censures the report of the high authority by a two-thirds majority, the members of the high authority must resign in a body. They shall continue to carry on current business until they are replaced . . .

Article 15. The high authority shall provide for establishment of three consultative committees of employers, of workers and of consumers. These committees may be convened separately or jointly on the initiative of the high authority . . .

Article 19. The states parties to the present treaty commit themselves:

1. To take all measures necessary to assure the creation of a single market for coal and steel embracing the whole of their territories as well as the pooling of their production; and, specifically, on the request of the high authority, to abolish:

    All import or export duties, or equivalent taxes, and all quantitative restrictions on the movement of coal and steel amongst the states parties to this treaty;

    All subsidies or assistance to the industries in question;

    All types of differentiation between the national and external markets in transport rates on coal and steel;

    All restrictive practices tending to the division and exploitation of national or external markets . . .

Article 20. In order to provide itself with intermediaries for the execution of the missions which are imparted to it, the high authority may accredit regional associations of producers or encourage their creation . . .

Article 24. In order to attain the objectives which are assigned to it, starting from the disparate conditions under which production now takes place in the various member countries, the high authority should institute a temporary mechanism of perequation making it possible to assure that during the period of transition such shifting of production as may occur will be gradual.

The perequation fund will be supplied by contributions levied upon producers on a uniform basis. The fund will serve to provide temporary assistance to enterprises which require a period of time to adapt to the single market. The amount of such perequation shall be constantly reduced during this transition period . . .

Article 25. . . . The high authority shall have the power to determine the methods of establishing prices; it shall be empowered in particular:

To prescribe that enterprises shall quote prices based on the place of production;

To prescribe that each enterprise shall make public price lists applicable to all consumers without discrimination

To establish general or regional maximum and minimum prices between which, unless a special exception is made, prices must be included . . .

Article 30. When the high authority recognizes that certain legal or administrative measures in one of the member states, particularly concerning the basis of assessment and the rate of taxes, the conditions of banking, the financial market, or the rates of transport, or that any other elements of the economic situation which could possibly be corrected through appropriate action are such as to jeopardize conditions of competition in the production of coal or steel, it will make the necessary recommendations to the government concerned.

In case the high authority should deem that these legal or administrative measures or those elements of the economic situation jeopardize competition by providing abnormal facilities for enterprises located within the territory of the state in question, the high authority will have the power to equalize conditions of competition by imposing a levy on the enterprises which benefit from these advantages. This levy may be maintained until such time as the high authority notes that the necessary corrective action has been introduced.

In case the high authority should deem, on the contrary, that such measures or such elements of the economic situation work to the detriment of enterprises located within the territory of the state in question, it may provide or authorize this state to provide temporary assistance to these enterprises; this assistance shall be limited to a period announced at the time it goes into effect. During this period the government concerned must take the corrective action which the circumstances require . . .

Article 34. The institution of the high authority will in no way prejudice the status of ownership of the enterprises.

In the pursuit of its mission, the common high authority will take account of the international commitments of the different member states, including the obligations of every nature imposed on Germany as long as such obligations exist . . .

3.10

KONRAD ADENAUER IN CONVERSATION WITH THE ALLIED HIGH COMMISSIONERS, 1950

Akten zur Auswärtigen Politik der Bundesrepublik Deutschland: Adenauer und die Hohen Kommisare 1949–1951, Vol. 1 (Munich: Oldenbourg, 1989), pp. 309–11.

This was one of several conversations on the Schuman Plan between Chancellor Konrad Adenauer and the Allied High Commissioners. André François-Poncet was French High Commissioner for Germany (1949–53), and John J. McCloy was American Military Governor and High Commissioner for Germany (1949–52).

Adenauer: I see, as you do, the success of the Schuman plan as a political event of the first order. The agreement must of course be approved by the Bundestag. For me, there is no doubt that the Social Democrats will vote against it. Just this morning a committee of industrialists came to see me ... The gentlemen came to see me ... to express to me their great concern about the Schuman plan. The *Verbundwirtschaft* [economic network] is, in the opinion of our people, a vital condition for our industry. If the *Verbundwirtschaft* is destroyed I think it is totally impossible – I ask you not to take this in any way as a means to an end, it is rather my honest conviction – that the Schuman plan will be able to find a majority in the Bundestag ...

François-Poncet: I can only say to you, that French industrialists have taken similar steps. That proves only that the industrialists have little imagination and that they have great difficulty understanding a system which deviates from what they have been accustomed to since childhood ...

McCloy: I want to say one more word about deconcentration ... You will have greater employment in Germany as a result of deconcentration, you will have a better standard of living, you will also have a new economic morality – precisely in the form of free competition.

_____3.11_____

FRITZ BAADE: *PROBLEMS OF THE SCHUMAN PLAN,* 1951

Probleme des Schuman-Plans, Kieler Vorträge, New Series 2 (1951), pp. 21–2.

Fritz Baade was a member of the Sozialdemokratische Partei Deutschlands (SPD). His hostility to the Schuman Plan and strident tone reflect the desire of the SPD to demonstrate its nationalist credentials.

The London Economist writes quite briefly of the Schuman Plan on 10 March: 'The Americans can and should use the Germans' dependence on the grain and raw materials to press for signature; . . . ' Ladies and Gentlemen, for a German who has experienced the times after the First World War and who knows what it means when one is forced to sign a Treaty under the threat that otherwise one will not receive grain, these are scarcely friendly tones. The Economist continues: 'And the western governments should now explain firmly to the Germans that acceptance or rejection of international control of heavy industry will be treated as evidence of their reliability as equal partners in Europe.'

Ladies and Gentlemen, this is the theory of prepayment, the theory that the Germans have to sign whatever is presented to them time and again before they can be trusted and treated as equal partners.

The Economist continues: 'On the other hand let it be recognised that the Germans are being asked to give up a great deal: the fruits of their natural advantage in raw materials, a form of industrial organisation whose efficacy has been proved, and a monopoly selling agency which, they claim, enabled uneconomic mines to be worked and employment to be maintained. These are advantages that no German politician can surrender without misgivings.'

Ladies and Gentlemen, what the Economist writes here appears to me to be the basic truth about the Schuman Plan. We are expressly asked to sign something which the others are convinced we would not sign without duress. And we are asked to give up things which no responsible German politician may give up without very serious misgivings and without very pressing reasons.

_____3.12_____

TREATY ESTABLISHING THE EUROPEAN COAL AND STEEL COMMUNITY, 1951

Treaty Establishing the European Coal and Steel Community, (High Authority of the ECSC, 1951)

The Treaty was signed on 18 April 1951.

Article 1: By this Treaty, the High Contracting Parties establish among themselves a European Coal and Steel Community, founded upon a common market, common objectives and common institutions.

Article 2: The European Coal and Steel Community shall have as its task to contribute, in harmony with the general economy of Member States and through the establishment of a common market as provided in Article 4, to economic expansion, growth of employment and a rising standard of living in the Member States ...

Article 4: The following are recognised as incompatible with the common market for coal and steel and shall accordingly be abolished and prohibited within the Community, as provided in this Treaty:

(a)   import and export duties, or charges having equivalent effect, and quantitative restrictions on the movement of products;

(b)   measures or practices which discriminate between producers, between purchasers or between consumers, especially in prices and delivery terms or transport or transport rates and conditions, and measures or practices which interfere with the purchaser's free choice of supplier;

(c)   subsidies or aids granted by States, or special charges imposed by States, in any form whatever;

(d)   restrictive practices which tend towards the sharing or exploiting of markets.

Article 7: The institutions of the Community shall be:

a High Authority, assisted by a Consultative Committee;
a Common Assembly (hereinafter called the 'Assembly');
a Special Council of Ministers (hereinafter called the 'Council');
a Court of Justice (hereinafter called the 'Court').

Article 9: The High Authority shall consist of nine members appointed for a year and chosen on the grounds of their general competence ...

The members of the High Authority shall, in the general interest of the Community, be completely independent in the performance of their duties. In the performance of these duties, they shall neither seek nor take instructions from any Government or from any other body. They shall refrain from any action incompatible with the supranational character of their duties.

Article 24: The Assembly shall discuss in open session the general report submitted to it by the High Authority.

If a motion of censure is ... carried by a two-thirds majority of the votes cast, representing a majority of the Members of the Assembly, the Members of the High Authority shall resign as a body ...

Article 26: The Council shall exercise its powers in the cases provided for and in the manner set out in this Treaty, in particular in order to harmonise the action of the High Authority and that of the Governments, which are responsible for the general economic policies of their countries ...

Article 57: In the sphere of production, the High Authority shall give preference to the indirect means of action at its disposal, such as:

- co-operation with Governments to regularize or influence general consumption, particularly that of public services;
- intervention in regard to prices and commercial policy as provided for in this Treaty.

Article 58:

In the event of a decline in demand, if the High Authority considers that the Community is confronted with a period of manifest crisis and that the means of action provided for in Article 57 are not sufficient to deal with this, it shall, after consulting the Consultative Committee and with the assent of the Council, establish a system of production quotas ...

Article 65:

1. All agreements between undertakings, decisions by associations of undertakings and concerted practices tending directly or indirectly to prevent, restrict or distort normal competition within the common market shall be prohibited, and in particular those tending:
   (a) to fix or determine prices;
   (b) to restrict or control production, technical development or investment;
   (c) to share markets, products, customers or sources of supply.
2. However, the High Authority shall authorize specialization agreements or joint-buying or joint-selling agreements if respect of particular products if it finds that:
   (a) such specialization or such joint-buying or -selling will make for a substantial improvement in the production or distribution of those products;
   (b) the agreement in question is essential in order to achieve these results and is not more restrictive than is necessary for that purpose; and

(c) the agreement is not liable to give the undertakings concerned the power to determine the prices, or to control or restrict the production or marketing of a substantial part of the products in question within the common market, or to shield them against effective competition from other undertakings within the common market.

3.13

KONRAD ADENAUER, CHANCELLOR OF THE FEDERAL REPUBLIC OF GERMANY, IN THE BUNDESTAG, 12 JULY 1952

C. C. Schweitzer, D. Karsten, R. Spencer, R. Taylor Cole, D. Kommers and A. Nicholls (eds), *Politics and Government in the Federal Republic of Germany: Basic Documents* (Leamington Spa: Berg, 1984), p. 291.

Konrad Adenauer, Chancellor of the Federal Republic of Germany, had been familiar with ideas on the integration of the European coal and steel industries since the 1920s. His prime concern, however, was with the political rehabilitation of Germany and reconciliation with France.

It is my opinion and belief that the parliaments of the six European countries which will have to deal with this European Coal and Steel Community realize exactly what it is all about and that in particular they realize that the political goal, the political meaning of the European Coal and Steel Community, is infinitely larger than its economic purpose ...

Something further has resulted during the negotiations. I believe that for the first time in history, certainly in the history of the last centuries, countries want to renounce part of their sovereignty, voluntarily and without compulsion, in order to transfer the sovereignty to a supranational structure ...

_____3.14_____

REPORT BY THE US DEPARTMENT OF STATE TO THE COUNCIL ON FOREIGN ECONOMIC POLICY, 16 MARCH 1955

Foreign Relations of the United States 1955–1957,
Vol. 4, pp. 266–7.

The Council on Foreign Economic Policy considered issues which cut across departmental boundaries. At its meeting of 20 December the Council agreed with a subsequent State Department text, the conclusions of which are similar to those given below.

The European Coal and Steel Community represents a dramatic development in the direction of European unity, the promotion of which has been established by Congress and the Executive Branch as a basic objective of US policy ... The President has on frequent occasions expressed his support for this objective, and has described the CSC as 'the most hopeful and constructive development so far toward the economic and political integration of Europe.' ...

While the Community's progress in combating restrictive practices has been slow, it has been substantially more active in this sphere than most individual European governments or other international bodies. Further, it should be realized that the CSC cartel problem cannot be considered entirely apart from the same basic cartel problem in other segments of the European economy. Some progress on this problem has been made by Western European governments since the war. Much remains to be done ...

_____3.15_____

THE HIGH AUTHORITY'S ASSESSMENT AT THE END OF THE DECADE, GENERAL REPORT 1960

European Coal and Steel Community, *Eighth General Report* 196, pp. 10-11.

This assessment was made against the background of differences between member states and the High Authority over the response to the coal crisis at the end of the decade.

These various items on the credit side should not, however, obscure the fact that a number of practical difficulties have been encountered in the operation of the Community, and that the means of action at the High Authority's disposal are not always all that they might be. A good deal has been said about the extensive powers vested in the High Authority under the Treaty, but the fact remains that the Treaty does not leave it to the High Authority alone to decide whether some of these powers are to be used. Experience has shown that this is a source of possible disagreement between the High Authority and the Council of Ministers. Thus in 1959 the two institutions took different views of the coal situation. In point of fact, the trouble is not so much these divergences in themselves as the atmosphere they tend to create. For the Community to function smoothly and effectively, it is essential that the terms of reference of the different institutions should be scrupulously respected, and that all parties should work to arrive at constructive decisions in conformity with the rules of the Treaty ...

The High Authority, for its part, is fully alive to the importance of its relations with the member Governments, and will do everything in its power to ensure that these are as close as possible. At the same time, it would emphasize its profound and unanimous conviction that it could not possibly fulfil its responsibilities if the only means at its disposal were that of persuasion, and if the operation of the Community were based on the principle of unanimity ...

It can fairly be said that had it not been for the High Authority's powers of decision not even the very first stage in the introduction of the Common Market would have gone through to schedule. And the High Authority's role as arbiter is still essential today to the ordered functioning of the Community ...

_____3.16_____

RECORD OF A CONVERSATION BETWEEN KONRAD ADENAUER AND GERMAN JOURNALISTS, 2 JULY 1963

Hans Peter Mensing (ed.), *Adenauer: Teegespräche 1961–1963* (Berlin: Siedler Verlag, 1992), p. 388.

In this conversation, Adenauer confirmed the long-term political significance of the European Coal and Steel Community even after the economic significance of coal had declined.

Gentlemen, if we think back to the first years after 1945, after our collapse, then you will remember how Russia and France quite seriously aired the idea not to allow a central power to arise in Germany, to divide up this Germany into a series of pieces. Might I also remind you that, then, the plan to internationalise the industrial region – coal still meant something at that time – was aired, and that precisely Russia and France pushed for this internationalisation. Then you will concede that I am right [to say]: without reconciliation with France, Europe is unthinkable.

That was the thought of Robert Schuman – whom one cannot mention often enough in this context – as he suggested the coal and steel union. At that time he wrote me a private letter, alongside the official one, in which he said: we have great anxiety about and great mistrust towards Germany when it has recovered. Our people fear that Germany will then revenge itself on France. Thus, he wrote in the letter, armament shows itself first of all through coal production and the production of iron and steel, which are indeed connected. Therefore, if we, he continued, create an institution which makes it possible for one people to observe a sudden increase of the production of iron and steel by another, and vice-versa, then that is the best means to set aside mutual mistrust.

I tell you this in such detail, gentlemen, so that you will see what the origins of this co-operation of France and Germany were in general and that then, naturally, great anxiety prevailed in France about what might happen between the Germans and the French as things developed. If you consider that, gentlemen, you will agree with me, I believe, that without this reconciliation between France and Germany, Europe would not have been created.

FROM NATO TO THE WEU

1949–1955

INTRODUCTION

The significance of the signing of the North Atlantic Treaty on 4 April 1949 was far from clear at the time. In a forthright discussion the day before the signing, President Truman asserted that 'none of us are under any illusions that the Atlantic Pact is more than a symbol of our common determination, a contract as it were, under which our new partnership must now proceed to develop the concrete means of first containing, then defeating World Communism'.[1] Among the concrete measures which the President and Secretary of State Dean Acheson had in mind were the rearmament of Japan and Germany, decolonization and concentration of European efforts within the framework of 'closer European political unification'.[2] The protests of the French over German rearmament, of the Dutch against the characterization of their colonial policy as 'reactionary', of Britain against 'entangling commitments', were all brushed aside. For all the forcefulness of Truman and Acheson on 3 April 1949, persuading the Europeans to take concrete measures proved to be a long and difficult process. The major difficulty was, not surprisingly, German rearmament.

In other respects, the Europeans were not slow in coming forward. The day after the Treaty was signed, the Brussels Pact powers lodged their pleas for military aid. The French especially had pushed for military aid even during the negotiations on the Treaty, but these demands had been resisted for fear of inflaming senatorial opposition (see Chapter 2). Although Congressional approval of the Treaty had yet to be secured, the Europeans could wait no longer. The significance of this step was evident to the Italians, who lodged their separate plea on 6 April. The Italian Ambassador noted that he

> has also been instructed to point out that the Italian Government realises that, since Italy is engaged in the effort of achieving economic recovery through the assistance generously granted by the American Government in the framework of the European Recovery Program, it would be harmful to increase military production to such an extent as to endanger the successful pursuance of economic recovery.[3]

Henceforth, the tension between the commitment to economic growth and the provision of welfare, on the one side and the commitment to rearmament on the other dogged efforts to strengthen Atlantic integration.

On 25 July 1949, the day on which the North Atlantic Treaty was ratified by the United States,[4] Truman proposed a military aid programme to Congress. As with the Marshall Plan, it was not easy to gain Congressional support. The influential Senator Arthur Vandenburg, who had recommended ratification of the Treaty only because he saw it as a limited commitment, insisted upon certain preconditions. Essentially his argument followed the American strategy with respect to the Marshall Plan. Aid would be forthcoming only if there was a common, Alliance-wide, plan for rearmament. In terms of the Treaty this meant that implementation of Article 3 providing for 'mutual aid' was dependent upon implementation of Article 9, which provided for the establishment of a Council and other bodies, including a Defence Committee (Document 4.1). The latter was duly established at the first Atlantic Council on 17 September 1949 along with various other organs, among which were five regional planning groups. It was indicative of continuing American hesitation that the United States was a full member of only two of these, the North Atlantic group and the Canada–United States group. Within the three European groups it accepted only the status of 'consulting member'. The September Council paved the way for the Mutual Defence Assistance Program, which was enacted on 6 October, although Dean Acheson recalled that it took the 23 September announcement of the explosion of an atomic bomb to overcome Congressional opposition: 'Once again the Russians had come to the aid of an imperilled nonpartisan foreign policy.'[5]

In the spring of 1950 the United States was still seeking to balance its commitment to the 'entangling alliance' against its fear that that same alliance could become an open-ended commitment. Indeed, part of the argument for the military aid programme was that it would enable the Europeans to rearm and thereby preclude the need for sending American troops to the continent. Similarly, when

President Truman approved the January 1950 'strategic concept' for the new alliance, the primary American responsibility was strategic bombing and collaboration with Britain in securing sea and air lanes. The Europeans were equally reluctant to extend their commitments. They resisted American pressure to increase their defence capacity. They were reluctant to draw up a genuinely integrated defence programme, with the result that at the May 1950 Atlantic Council meeting the allies scarcely got beyond adding up their disparate budgets and force levels.[6] Reluctance to make economic sacrifices even extended to European attitudes towards the restriction of sensitive exports to the eastern bloc, which the United States was pushing within the newly established Co-ordinating Committee (COCOM).[7]

Nevertheless, initially the minimalist American approach to European security was believed in Washington to be working, at least to the extent that Europe appeared to be gaining sufficient strength to defend herself without a substantial commitment of American ground forces. This sentiment prevailed as long as the primary concern of NATO's leaders was 'not a Soviet invasion . . . but the instability of the European partners'.[8] The invasion of South Korea by North Korea in June 1950 changed all that. Following the Berlin blockade, the communist takeover in Czechoslovakia and the Soviet atom test, it raised acute fears of further Soviet pressure on Europe. The North Korean attack, which was seen in the west as Soviet aggression by proxy, gave rise at once to fears that a divided Europe and Germany might also fall victim to a Soviet-backed assault. The German Chancellor, Konrad Adenauer, had already been alarmed by the development of a large armed so-called People's Police in East Germany. In the light of Korea, he told the Allied High Commissioners that he had no doubt that Stalin intended the same fate for Germany.[9]

Although West Germans had more cause for alarm than most, the consternation was widespread. The French socialist deputy André Philip commented at this time: 'Europe cannot organise its defence without America, but even with this help she will expose herself to all kinds of risks, if she remains bound up with national military units, with her old, expensive and useless armies.'[10] On 11 August 1950 Winston Churchill stated that although he thought the American atomic force would dissuade the Soviet Union from invading west Europe, this situation would not endure for ever, and that it would be necessary to create a powerful European force which would be placed under the control of a European defence minister. While Korea induced some to look to a European solution, a more immediate strategy was to strengthen the west by the rearmament of Germany, whether within the framework of a European force or not. French insistence that the western line of defence should be placed as far east as possible between the Rhine and the Elbe only strengthened this argument. Congress was particularly of the view that to defend Europe as far as possible to the east, it was necessary to use the human and economic resources of West Germany.

There was also significant political reasons for rearming the Germans. A west German military connection with the other nations of west Europe would further her integration into the western political system. It would also counter possible German neutralism. By increasing the west's military power with a rearmed

Germany, Acheson believed that the negotiating position of the west *vis-à-vis* the Soviet Union would be enhanced. Economic considerations were also weighed in the balance. Many west Europeans feared that west Germany would have a major trading advantage if all its resources were freed for the production or purchase of non-military goods. In a worst-case scenario, on the other hand, if the absence of an effective west German defence enabled the Soviets to conquer west Germany, all her resources would fall to the Soviet Union.[11] 'The United States had very speedily come to realize that integration was the best means of combating the main danger: a west Europe that was economically impoverished, locked in its old conflicts, and incapable of utilising the economic and military potential of Germany, its most powerful country, in short, a Europe which would not be slow in becoming an easy prey for the Soviet Union.'[12]

The most important initiative for German rearmament came in September 1950 at the Atlantic Council meeting in New York. There the official United States memorandum disavowed any intention of creating a German national army. Instead it proposed 'German divisions [which] would be integrated with non-German units in corps and higher units'.[13] The whole ensemble would constitute 'an integrated force in Europe, within the framework of the North Atlantic Treaty' and would fall under the control of a 'Supreme Commander'.[14] During the Council meeting, the French Foreign Minister, Robert Schuman, raised a host of objections, though he conceded that the French were not 'irrevocably opposed', as long as the other European armies were rebuilt before anything was done about Germany.[15] French fears were expressed more forcefully by the French ambassador to London, who described the whole arrangement as 'disastrous' and claimed that 'the Germans have only one interest and that is the unification; and that they can achieve this end either by going Communist or through a preventive war'.[16] In reality, the virulently anti-communist German Chancellor had no intention of countenancing either alternative, though French fears were understandable (Document 4.8).

The pressure for German rearmament placed the French government in a difficult position, given the recent memories of Nazi occupation. It counted on the institution of a single Atlantic Command. France promised to make a great military effort: ten French divisions in Germany in 1951, fifteen in the following year and twenty in 1953. After rejecting the idea of a national German army, René Pleven, the French Premier, proposed on 24 October 1950 the 'creation for common defence of a European army attached to the political institutions of a united Europe'. The French Foreign Ministry took the view that although the idea of German rearmament would be exceedingly unpopular among the French, France should not challenge the principle of German rearmament as such. Instead, she should prepare means permitting the retention of sufficient control on the part of the French government. This could only be accomplished in the framework of collective organization in which France would participate and play, by the nature of things, a determining role. This army would be placed under the authority of a European Minister of Defence, under the control of a European Assembly with a common military budget. Already in December 1949 Chancellor Konrad Adenauer had declared that if west Germany were to participate in the defence of west Europe, he would be in favour of a German contingent in a European force, rather than a *Wehrmacht*. The Pleven Plan had been designed by Jean Monnet and in its final form was a serious design to further the project of European integration, expanding it into the field of defence. At the same time, Pleven hoped that in this form the unacceptable prospect of German rearmament could be made more tolerable by rearming Germans without rearming Germany. The political battle lines were drawn between those who feared the rearming of Germany and those who felt that Germany could be more effectively monitored from within than outside and who considered the Soviet threat more imminent.

Initially the Pleven Plan received only limited support from the United States and other west European governments. This was because it was presented as an alternative to the 'Atlantic' option of integrating Germany into NATO. Many west Europeans feared that Pleven's proposed European Defence Community (EDC) might encourage the United States to withdraw. The NATO option, furthermore, had no reference to any type of supranationality and did not require European states *de jure* to renounce any aspect of their sovereignty. As an example of an inter-governmental alliance, the NATO proposal contained no commitment to an automatic response to aggression.

The British government viewed the Plan with some suspicions, suspecting that it was 'a manoeuvre in French domestic politics', though the cabinet agreed not to oppose it. This reluctant acceptance did not extend to the idea of British inclusion.[17] On this point there was no difference between the Labour government and the Conservative opposition. This is clearly reflected in Winston Churchill's speech in Strasbourg in August 1950. He called for 'a European army under unified command and in which we should all bear a worthy and honourable part'. This fell short of involvement, for, as he said: 'We are with Europe but not of it, we are interested and associated but not absorbed.' The British government was unwilling during the long EDC debate to promise the kind of troop commitment to the continent which the French wanted. A large part of the British forces was occupied overseas. Britain still saw herself as essentially a global power. There was also, crucially, deeply rooted objection to the supranationalism of the proposal.

Realizing that no progress could be made without French support, the United States moved from the proposal of rearming Germany within NATO to providing concerted support for the EDC option. The conversion was neither quick nor easy. Although Pleven's proposals had found some immediate supporters, the dominant American attitude was one of suspicion that the French proposals were a mere delaying tactic. The Defence Department, which remained committed to the original American proposals, even argued against a European supranational force on the grounds that the Germans would fight only in defence of their nation, not for a European entity.[18] It was not until June 1951 that Eisenhower was won over as a result of patient persuasion by John McCloy, the United States High Commissioner in Germany, and after a highly successful meeting with Monnet. The conversion was important in bringing the full weight of American support behind the plan, and in convincing Adenauer that this was the only option available. As a German military expert put it in August, the Americans were 'resolved to exert massive pressure on anyone who now wanted to break out of the defence community'.[19]

With American support, the Paris conference spent nineteen months devising a framework which attracted enough of a consensus to allow the signing of the EDC Treaty in Paris on 27 May 1952. The Treaty differed in a number of essential points from the original French proposal. In the negotiations the west Germans insisted on the principle of complete equality. Pleven had envisaged a French general being in overall command. Under the EDC, a board of commissioners, including Germans, was to run the army. The basic national unit would be the *groupement*, consisting of 13,000 men instead of the 5000 which the French had in mind. The difference was crucial. France had opposed the creation of German divisions, the smallest military unit capable of independent manoeuvre, and favoured 'combat teams' of 5000 men. Unable to agree, the parties referred the issue to General Eisenhower, who, with considerable dipomatic skill, supported the idea of the *groupement* of 13,000 men. In reality this meant that there would be German divisions, albeit under a different name. The French had also failed to maintain their opposition to the creation of a German ministry of defence.[20]

The institutions of the EDC closely resembled those of the ECSC, but their competences would be different. The guiding body was to be the council of ministers, which had to determine Community policy. The board of commissioners, consisting of nine members, would be charged with the execution of the decisions of the ministers. It also had to prepare a budget to fix the contribution of each member state to it. It would be authorized to procure supplies, establish and direct military schools and determine the territorial deployment of troops under NATO directives. While all these powers involved surrender of national sovereignty, in most matters the council of ministers had to give unanimous approval. As far as its institutional set-up was concerned, the EDC can be better regarded as a forerunner of the EEC than as a replica of the ECSC. Articles 10 and 11 provided limited safeguards for the autonomous use of armed forces by national governments for national purposes. Article 10 stated that forces to be used in overseas territories remained outside its competence, although such forces should not be of a size which would 'compromise the participation of each member state in the European defence force'. Article 11 gave member states the right to keep national police and gendarmerie to ensure domestic order, although again the size of such forces should not 'exceed the limits of their mission'. Article 43 stated that the votes of member states were to be calculated on the basis of the size of the national contributions. This put France at a disadvantage. With her heavy commitment in Indochina, she could only afford ten *groupements*, as against twelve each for Germany and Italy.

By a separate agreement, signed on 26 May 1952, with the three occupying powers, Germany was to regain much of her national sovereignty once the EDC came into operation. This was a crucial part of the process for the Germans, even if the occupying powers balked at the word sovereignty, preferring to concede to Germany 'full authority over its internal and external affairs'.[21] However, to meet fears over German rearmament, a number of restrictions were placed upon west German sovereignty. The Federal Republic was not allowed to have any military force other than those controlled by the EDC or to produce nuclear and other specified types of weapons. In West Germany itself, the Treaty provoked considerable division. Many felt it would be better not to rearm. The Social Democrats were strongly opposed for the same reason that had led them to reject the ECSC. They feared that German rearmament, in whatever framework, would make German reunification impossible. In defending the Treaty the Christian Democratic Chancellor Konrad Adenauer deployed the argument that acceptance would restore sovereignty and rehabilitate West Germany as an equal among other west European states.

Initially Pleven had obtained a majority of 343 to 225 for his plan when he submitted it to the National Assembly in October 1950. Over the next four years opposition in France increased. When the Treaty was signed in May 1952, the Six also concluded an agreement with the United Kingdom in which the British undertook to supply military aid automatically in the event of an attack on one of the EDC members. Simultaneously, an additional protocol to the NATO Treaty was adopted in which the parties agreed that an armed attack against one of the EDC states would be considered as an attack against all NATO members. Even these two agreements did not sufficiently reassure the National Assembly. The French tried to obtain United Kingdom assurance that British troops stationed on the continent would be kept there. The British refusal to integrate (Churchill's 'we are not members of the EDC, nor do we intend to be merged in a Federal Europe system') was one of the main arguments used in France against the ratification of the Treaty. Why should France have to merge her army in a European conglomeration, if Britain did not? At the same time, a large part of the French army was tied up in Indochina and was to be defeated there in 1954. Many in France were afraid that French commitments in Indochina would not allow her to contribute sufficient forces and resources to the European theatre to match the German contribution. As we saw above, German rearmament would mean that Germany would be likely to have a preponderance in any European force. After Stalin's death, too, in March 1953 east–west relations seemed to be improving. The Soviet peace initiative at this time tended to make strong advocacy of rearming Germany look aggressive.

The new government of René Meyer, dependent upon Gaullist support, effectively sought to renegotiate the Treaty at the beginning of 1953. Among the protocols which Meyer put forward were demands to transfer forces unilaterally to France's overseas territories and to freeze the weighted votes to ensure French equality with Germany. In February, however, the others agreed only to regard the protocols as 'interpretative texts' which did not constitute a revision of the Treaty.[22] Furthermore, they insisted that the protocols be rewritten to conform to the spirit of the Treaty. When they were finally agreed in March 1953, many of the original French demands had been whittled away.[23]

To remedy a widely felt concern about the lack of democratic control over the EDC, Article 38 was inserted in the Treaty (Document 4.9). The intitiative here came from the Italian Alcide de Gasperi, who had been prompted by the federalist Altiero Spinelli. Although de Gasperi passed over Spinelli's suggestion of a constituent assembly to draft a European federal constitution, his more modest proposals still met fierce resistance from the Benelux states. Finally, in December 1951, a compromise brokered by Konrad Adenauer was reached.[24] It called on the *ad hoc* EDC Assembly to study 'the constitution of an Assembly of the European Defence Community elected on a democratic basis'. The Assembly began its deliberations in September 1952 and reported six months later. It proposed a European Political Community (EPC) which would transcend sectoral integration, inaugurating a comprehensive political federation to which the ECSC and EDC would be subordinated. A draft treaty was drawn up, but despite its very significant institutional implications it attracted little debate, by contrast with the political battle over the EDC. When it was published none of the Six had yet ratified the EDC Treaty. With the French rejection of the EDC, the EPC proposal was abandoned. Political union along these lines was not to be considered seriously again until the 1980s. Indeed, Monnet had not anticipated such radical proposals at such an early date. As he recalled in his memoirs: 'We could no longer wait, as we had once planned, for political Europe to be the culminating point of a gradual process, since its joint defence was inconceivable without a joint political authority from the start.'[25]

Ironically, the Netherlands was the first state to ratify the EDC treaty, in February 1954. The Netherlands had been the most reluctant of the parties to the treaty, agreeing to become full participants only in the negotiations in October 1951. In the preceeding month, Foreign Minister Dirk Stikker noted that 'Unpleasant as it may be, we have to take account of the development of political events, since the Big Three have promised their support for the creation of a European army.' He promptly added that 'It is hard indeed to accept the loss of independence in the making of our own foreign policy.'[26] Within a matter of months of Dutch ratification, Belgium, Luxembourg and Germany followed. There was, however, little sign of the EDC's proposer, France, following suit. Tired of waiting, Secretary of State John Foster Dulles threatened the French with an 'agonising reappraisal' of American policy towards Europe on 14 December 1953 (see also Document 4.10).

A final attempt was made to break the deadlock at a conference in Brussels in August 1954, shortly before the scheduled debate in the French National Assembly. To the horror of his partners, the French Prime Minister, Mendès-France, formally prosed a new set of protocols which systematically undermined the supranational character of the community. Moreover, he proposed that integration be restricted to the 'forward zones'. In effect, this meant that whereas all German forces would form part of the integrated European force, only those French forces stationed in Germany, together with their support units, would be integrated. It was a blatant attempt to reintroduce the discriminatory character of the original Pleven Plan which had been whittled away during the treaty negotiations. Mendès-France predictably met with firm opposition. Even before the conference, the French had been warned by The Netherlands that the reintroduction of discrimination was a 'grave political error' and that The Netherlands would prefer a solution within NATO to the new French proposals.[27] Mendès-France had to face the National Assembly on the basis of the existing treaty.

The French National Assembly rejected it on a procedural motion by 319 to 264 votes on 30 August 1954. Nationalist Gaullists united with Communists to defeat the plan, in the former case in particular because of the perceived loss of independence. De Gaulle ridiculed the 'so-called "European Army", which, by alchemical mixture, algebraic combination and cabalistic formulae would resolve the problem of security'.[28] In the end, a number of deputies from the centre parties also rejected the plan. In France the refusal to understand the limits of French freedom of action and the international context in which the plan was proposed pervaded the entire course of the debate on the EDC. As Aron and Lerner put it: 'A substantial number of deputies in the National Assembly voted on the EDC as if the choice available to them was: German rearmament or no German rearmament ... but only after the EDC was rejected did it become clear ... that the alternative to no German rearmament had already been foreclosed by the joint Anglo-American decision that, one way or another, Germany would be rearmed. The only choice left open to French policy was which way, EDC or NATO?'[29]

The lesson of the EDC debate was that supranational integration in defence went to the heart of national interest and sovereignty. It showed that 'The impetus for allegiance to a supranational authority must be stronger than simply external pressure or fear, both of which were present in the early 1950s in abundance. Such radical departures from nationally autonomous policy must offer benefits, be they economic or otherwise, that outweigh the political costs of abjuring national autonomy ... The EDC debacle demonstrated that integration is more than either symbolism or efficiency, and security cannot be based solely on either. The legacy of these lessons was to remain long after German rearmament had ceased to be a subject of debate.'[30] At all events, the collapse of the EDC established a seemingly rigid division in European integration. Political integration was shelved and defence integration became subsumed within NATO cooperation. As John Pinder points out, at this time 'many doubted whether the federal idea could recover from this apparently decisive defeat'.[31]

When the rejection was announced John Foster Dulles declared: 'The French negative action, without the provision of any alternative, obviously imposes on the USA the obligation to reappraise its foreign policies, particularly those in relation to Europe.' It was to the alternatives that minds were now turned. It was at this point that Britain, which had refused to give sufficiently satisfying guarantees to France over the EDC, and if given earlier might have saved the project, moved to resolve the situation. It was obvious to Anthony Eden and his colleagues that the US would continue to insist on German rearmament, and that west European defence without Britain would be unacceptable to the French, because of their fear of German domination. From the British perspective, an intergovernmental solution would be acceptable in a way that a supranational one would not. An existing intergovernmental solution already lay at hand in the shape of the Brussels Treaty Organization. The same idea had occured to Mendès-France. Worried by Dulles's repeated threat of an 'agonising reappraisal' and fearful that the Pentagon would push for a rapid and destabilizing rearmament of Germany within a purely NATO framework, Mendès-France grasped at the Brussels Pact as a ready made solution.[32] It also had the advantages that it already included Britain and was primarily intergovernmental, both factors which recommended the project to French public opinion.[33] The French military had even begun to favour this kind of solution as early as 30 June, well before the vote in the French National Assembly.[34] Yet Mendès-France was content to leave the intitiative to Eden, lest a French initiative polarize the debate.

The negotiations which Britain initiated were not without their problems (Document 4.11). The French were anxious to build up the amended Brussels Treaty Organisation in order to avoid the appearance of a predominantly NATO-style solution. Nevertheless, after the protracted negotiations and ratification debates, the new negotiations proceeded quickly and culminated in the protocols and conventions which were signed in Paris on 23 October 1954. In effect, the Paris Accords provided that the 1948 Brussels Treaty Organisation – which had been expanded to include West Germany and Italy, and redesignated as the Western European Union (WEU) – would replace the defunct EDC project. Although Britain was a full participant in the WEU, the latter would not become a supranational organization. Britain committed herself to maintain four divisions and a tactical air force on the continent for fifty years, and agreed not to withdraw these forces if this was against the wishes of the majority of the Brussels Treaty powers.

The Paris Accords also provided that West Germany would become a member of NATO but would remain subject to restrictions on its military activities, including prohibition on the acquisition of biological, chemical and nuclear weapons. The National Assembly finally accepted the Paris Accords on 29 December 1954 by 287 to 260 votes. It did so only after Premier Mendès-France had warned that the agreements were 'the sole means of preserving the Western Alliance' and that the United States had 'come within a millimetre' of deciding on German rearmament without French consent. On 5 May 1955, after ratification by all parties, the Federal Republic became a sovereign state. The new treaty ending the Occupation Statute was a marked improvement over its 1952 predecessor, conceding the Federal Republic of Germany 'the full authority of a sovereign state', although it did specify that the allies retained their rights 'relating to Berlin and to Germany as a whole, including the reunification of Germany and a peace settlement'.[35] Four days later, the Federal Republic also became a member of NATO.

It was not until the mid-1980s, with renewed discussion of a 'European defence identity', that the WEU attracted significant attention, though this is not to say that the WEU did not perform some useful tasks in the intervening years. For example, it played a decisive part in 1955 in the resolution of the vexatious Saar problem, removing a major stumbling block to Franco-German reconciliation, and, it has been argued, easing the way for France to sign the Treaty of Rome.[36] Its major service, however, lay in facilitating German rearmament and membership of NATO. In some respects it resembled the ECSC (see Chapter 3). Whatever their subsequent deficiencies, and they were considerable if measured against the hopes orignally placed on them, their undeniable historical significance lay in their contribution to the western integration of the Federal Republic of Germany.

The NATO which the Federal Republic joined was a much more elaborate and sophisticated organization than it was when Dean Acheson had proposed German rearmament in September 1950. The Ottawa Council of September 1951 had instituted a Temporary Council Committee to scrutinize defence capacities and budgets. According to the historian Charles Maier, this 'collective scrutiny of budgetary data relating to defence' was an unprecedented procedure in time of peace.[37] Yet there were limits to this. The United States exempted itself from the level of scrutiny which the others were subject to on the grounds of its already high defence expenditure. The real reason was that the Defence Department did not want American decision-making to be constrained by the requirements of multilateral procedures.[38] The asymmetry in the Alliance was inevitable given the preponderance of the American military and its possession of the only effective atomic deterrent in the west. That asymmetry was aggravated when NATO in December 1954, agreed to align its strategy with the American 'New Look' policy, which envisaged greater reliance upon nuclear weapons. This led to even greater concern about consultation within NATO. In fact, NATO had implications which reached far beyond the purely military realm, as the title – *The Report on Non-military Co-operation of 1956* – indicates.

The failure of the EDC signified the subordination of a European strategy to an Atlantic one (Document 4.13), which posed problems both for the Alliance itself and for the status of the Europeans within the Alliance.[39] Integration within the Alliance would always run up against the barrier of American reluctance to be constrained by multilateral procedures. Yet the Europeans could not live securely without the Alliance, even if they fretted about, and were occasionally frightened by, their relative subordination. That dilemma would haunt them all, especially France, which had initiated and then turned its back upon the EDC.

NOTES

1. The record of this conversation is reproduced in Cees Wiebes and Bert Zeeman, 'Eine Lehrstunde in Machtpolitik', *Vierteljahreshefte für Zeitgeschichte*, Vol. 40 (1992), pp. 415–23, here p. 415.
2. ibid., p. 422.
3. *Documents on International Affairs 1949–1950*, p. 264.
4. On these developments see Alan Henrikson, 'The creation of the North Atlantic Alliance 1948–1952', *Naval War College Review*, Vol. 32 (1980), pp. 26–7.
5. Quoted in ibid., p. 26.
6. Lawrence Kaplan, *A Community of Interests* (Washington, DC, 1980), p. 89.
7. Vibeke Sorensen, 'Defence without tears', in F. Heller and J. Gillingham (eds), *NATO: the Founding of the Atlantic Alliance and the Integration of Europe* (New York, 1992), p. 263.
8. Lawrence Kaplan, *The US and NATO: the Formative Years* (Lexington, MA, 1984), pp. 143–4.
9. This on 17 August. *Akten zur Auswärtigen Politik der Bundesrepublik Deutschland. Adenauer und die Höhen Kommissare*, Vol. 1, doc. 15.
10. Quoted in Pierre Gerbet, *La Construction de l'Europe* (Paris, 1994), p. 126.
11. See Ronald E. Powaski, *The Entangling Alliance* (Westport, CT, 1994) pp. 6–8.
12. See Pierre Melandri, 'The United States and the process of European integration', in Antonio Varsori (ed.), *Europe 1945–90* (London, 1995), p. 115.

13. *Documents on British Policy Overseas*, Series 2, Vol. 2, doc. 33.
14. ibid.
15. ibid., doc. 32 (17 September 1950).
16. ibid., doc. 38 (21 September 1950).
17. ibid., doc. 92 (30 October 1950).
18. T.A. Schwartz, *America's Germany* (Cambridge, MA, 1991), p. 133.
19. Quoted in Paul Noack, 'EVG und Bonner Europapolitik', in H.-E. Volkmann and W. Schwengler (eds), *Die Europäische Verteidigungsgemeinschaft* (Boppard, 1985), p. 250.
20. For these French concessions see Edward Fursdon, *The European Defence Community* (London, 1980), pp. 123–4; and Wilfried Loth, *Der Weg nach Europa* (Göttingen, 1990), who notes that the concession of a German Defence Ministry induced the resignation of the French Minister of Defence, Jules Moch, p. 96.
21. Article 1, Convention on Relations between the Three Powers and the Federal Republic of Germany. The Three Powers retained certain rights, some of them extensive. See Article 5.
22. Fursdon, *The European Defence Community*, p. 209.
23. Montescue J. Lowry, *The Forge of West German Rearmament* (New York, 1990), p. 213.
24. Walter Lipgens, 'EVG und politische Föderation', in *Vierteljahreshefte für Zeitgeschichte*, Vol. 32 (1984), pp. 637–88.
25. Jean Monnet, *Memoirs* (London, 1978), p. 343.
26. Quoted in Jan van der Harst, 'The Pleven Plan', in R.T. Griffiths (ed.), *The Netherlands and the Integration of Europe* (Amsterdam, 1990), p. 146.
27. *Documents Diplomatiques Français 1954 (21 Juillet–31 Décembre)*, doc. 71 (16 August 1954).
28. See Maurice Vaïsse, 'De Gaulle and the defence of Europe' in Antonio Varsori (ed.) *Europe 1945–1990*, p. 176.
29. Raymond Aron and Daniel Lerner, *La Querelle de la CED* (Paris, 1956), p. ix.
30. See Holly Wyatt-Walter, *The European Community and the Security Dilemma 1979–92* (London, 1997), p. 26.
31. See John Pinder, *European Community* (Oxford, 1995), p. 7.
32. *Documents Diplomatiques Français*, doc. 154, Annexe (8 September 1954).
33. ibid., doc. 193 (18 September 1954).
34. Pierre Guillen, 'Die französische Generalität und die Aufrüstung der Bundesrepublik und die EVG', in Volkmann and Schwengler (eds), *Die Europäische Verteidigungsgemeinschaft*, pp. 155–6.
35. Wolfgang Benz (ed.), *Deutschland seit 1945* (Munich, 1990), pp. 203–4.
36. See M. Clarke and R. Hague (eds.), *European Defence Cooperation: America, Britain and NATO* (Manchester, 1990), p. 56.
37. Charles Maier, 'Finance and defense', in Heller and J. Gillingham (eds), *NATO*, p. 345.
38. Kaplan, *A Community of Interests*, p. 164.
39. For an interesting assessment of these issues see Steve Weber, 'Shaping the postwar balance of power: multilateralism in NATO', *International Organization*, Vol. 46 (1992), pp. 633–80.

FURTHER READING

J. Baylis, *Anglo-American Defence Relations 1939–84* (London, 1984).

A. Cahen, *The Western European Union and NATO: Building a European Defence Identity in the Context of Atlantic Solidarity* (London, 1989).

S. Dockrill, *Britain's Policy for West German Rearmament 1950–55* (Cambridge, 1991).

E. Fursdon, *The European Defence Community* (London, 1980).

A. Grosser, *The Western Alliance* (London, 1980).

F. Heller and J. Gillingham (eds), *NATO: The Founding of the Atlantic Alliance and the Integration of Europe* (New York, 1992).

L. Kaplan, *A Community of Interests* (Washington, DC, 1980).

E. Nolfo (ed.), *The Atlantic Pact Forty Years Later* (Berlin, 1991).

O. Riste (ed.), *Western Security: The Formative Years, European and Atlantic Defence 1947–53* (Oslo, 1985).

P.M.R. Stirk and D. Willis (eds), *Shaping Postwar Europe* (London, 1991).

T. Taylor, *European Defence Cooperation* (London, 1982).

E. van der Beugel, *From Marshall Aid to Atlantic Partnership* (Amsterdam, 1966).

J.W. Young, *Foreign Policy of Churchill's Peacetime Administration 1951–55* (Leicester, 1988).

F.R. Willis, *France, Germany and the New Europe* (London, 1968).

_____ 4.1 _____

THE NORTH ATLANTIC TREATY, 4 APRIL 1949

The North Atlantic Treaty 4 April 1949, *NATO Facts and Figures*
(Brussels, 1971), pp. 270–3.

The following articles were included in this Treaty which was initially signed by
the Foreign Ministers of Belgium, Canada, Denmark, France, Iceland, Italy, the
Netherlands, Norway, Portugal, the United Kingdom and the United States. It was
an important step in the evolution of the policy of western containment of the
Soviet Union.

Article 1: The parties undertake, as set forth in the Charter of United Nations, to
settle any international dispute in which they may be involved by peaceful means in
such a manner that international peace and security and justice are not endangered,
and to refrain in their international relations from the threat or use of force in any
manner inconsistent with the purposes of the United Nations.

Article 2: The parties will contribute towards the further development of peaceful
and friendly international relations by strengthening their free institutions, by
bringing about a better understanding of the principles upon which these institutions are founded, and by promoting conditions of stability and well-being. They
will seek to eliminate conflict in their international economic policies and will
encourage economic collaboration between any or all of them.

Article 3: In order more effectively to achieve the objectives of this Treaty, the
Parties, separately and jointly, by means of continuous and effective self-help and
mutual aid, will maintain and develop their individual and collective capacity to
resist armed attack.

Article 4: The Parties will consult together whenever, in the opinion of any one of
them, the territorial integrity, political independence or security of any of the Parties
is threatened.

Article 5: The Parties agree that an armed attack against any or more of them in
Europe and North America shall be considered an attack against them all and
consequently they agree that, if such an armed attack occurs, each of them, in
exercise of the right of individual or collective self-defence recognised by Article 51
of the Charter of the United Nations, will assist the Party or Parties so attacked by
taking forthwith, individually and in concert with the other Parties, such action as
it deems necessary, including the use of armed force, to restore and maintain the
security of the North Atlantic area. Any such armed attack and all measures taken
as a result thereof shall immediately be reported to the Security Council. Such

measures shall be terminated when the Security Council has taken the measures necessary to restore and maintain international peace and security.

Article 6: For the purpose of Article 5 an armed attack on one or more of the Parties is deemed to include an armed attack on the territory of any of the Parties in Europe or North America ... on the occupation forces of any Party in Europe, on the islands under the jurisdiction of any Party in the North Atlantic area north of the Tropic of Cancer or on the vessels or aircraft in this area of any of the Parties ...

Article 9: The parties hereby establish a Council, on which each of them shall be represented to consider matters concerning the implementation of this Treaty ... The Council shall set up such subsidiary bodies as may be necessary; in particular it shall establish immediately a Defence Committee which shall recommend measures for the implementation of Articles 3 and 5.

———————— 4.2 ————————

THE FOUNDATIONS OF THE NORTH ATLANTIC TREATY ORGANIZATION

Robert Murphy, 'The foundations of the North Atlantic Treaty Organization', *Bulletin*, 34, April 1956 (Washington: Department of State), p. 646.

This speech by the US Deputy Under-Secretary of State Robert Murphy was made on 2 April 1956. Murphy at the time was primarily concerned with Soviet affairs. He had earlier been involved in the implementation of the Marshall Plan.

Stripped to its essence, the justification for NATO is a simple exercise in elementary arithmetic. North America and free Europe combined now produce about 70 per cent of the world's manufactured goods, while the entire Soviet bloc, including China, produces only about 20 per cent. On the other hand, Soviet control of the territory and resources of west Europe would give the Soviet bloc 50 per cent of the total world's industrial production, as against North America's 40 per cent. The Atlantic nations, so long as they are joined together, are in a position to maintain decisive industrial superiority over the Soviet bloc for an indefinite period of years. Soviet domination of west Europe would rapidly shift the industrial balance to the Communist side.

_____ 4.3 _____

THE PLEVEN PLAN FOR A EUROPEAN DEFENCE COMMUNITY (EDC), 1950

D. Patijn (ed.), *Landmarks in European Unity*
(Leiden: Europa Institute, 1970), pp. 73–85.

The following announcement of the Plan was made to the French National Assembly by French Prime Minister René Pleven on 24 October 1950. The proposal was for a European army under a European minister of defence, who would be under the supervision of a European assembly. Supporters saw this as a further integration of West Germany into a western European community.

Germany, which is not a party to the Atlantic Treaty, is nevertheless also destined to enjoy the benefits of the security system resulting therefrom. It is consequently right that it should make its contribution towards setting up a system of defence for west Europe. Consequently, before opening discussions on this important problem in the Assembly, the [French] Government have decided to take the initiative of making the following declaration ...

The setting up of a European Army cannot result from a mere grouping together of national military units, which would in reality only mask a coalition of the old sort. For tasks which are inevitably common ones, only common institutions will do. The army of a united Europe, composed of men coming from different European countries, must, so far as is possible, achieve a complete fusion of the human and material elements which make it up under a single European political and military authority.

A Minister of Defence would be appointed by the participating governments and would be responsible, under conditions to be determined, to those appointing him and to a European Assembly. That assembly might be the Assembly in Strasbourg, or an offshoot thereof, or an assembly composed of specially elected delegates. His powers with respect to the European Army would be those of a national Minister of Defence with respect to the national forces of his own country. He would, in particular, be responsible for implementing such general directives as he might receive from a Council composed of Ministers of the participating countries. He would serve as the normal channel between the European community and outside countries or international organs for everything relating to the carrying out of his task.

The contingents furnished by the participating States would be incorporated in the European Army at the level of the smallest possible unit.

The money for the European Army would be provided by a common budget. The European Minister of Defence would be responsible for the implementation of existing international obligations and for the negotiation and implementation of new international engagements on the basis of directives received from the Council of Ministers. The European armament and equipment programme would be decided and carried out under his authority. The participating States which currently have national forces at their disposal would retain their own authority so far as concerned that part of their existing forces which was not integrated by them into the European Army.

Conversely, the European Minister of Defence might, with the authorisation of the Council of Ministers, place at the disposal of a participating government a part of its national forces comprised in the European force, for the purpose of meeting requirements other than those of common defence. The European force placed at the disposal of the unified Atlantic command would operate in accordance with the obligations assumed in the Atlantic Treaty, both so far as concerns general strategy and so far as concerns organisation and equipment.

4.4

ERNEST BEVIN, LABOUR FOREIGN SECRETARY, TO THE HOUSE OF COMMONS, 29 NOVEMBER 1950

Ernest Bevin, 29 November 1950, House of Commons Debates, *Hansard* Vol. 481, Cols 1172–4.

This speech expressed the British government's initial reaction to the proposal for the EDC.

The French Government have now produced a proposal for a European Army with a European Minister of Defence, subject to a European Council of Ministers and a European Assembly. This European Army would contain German units as well as units from the other European countries. His Majesty's Government do not favour this proposal. To begin with, we fear that it will only delay the building up of Europe's defences. Our first and most urgent need is to set up the integrated Force under the Supreme Commander. The next step is to provide for a German contribution to that force. These are immediate matters of great urgency. We take the view that the proposal for a European Army is also too limited in scope. We cherish our special ties with our old European friends but, in our view, Europe is not enough; it is not big enough, it is not strong enough and it is not able to stand by itself.

I understand the urge towards European unity and sympathise with it and, indeed, I did much to help bring the Council of Europe into being. But I also understand the new paradox that European unity is no longer possible within Europe alone but only within the broader Atlantic community. It is this great conception of an Atlantic community that we want to build up. The union of twelve free, equal and independent nations, organised for the defence of peace and for the growth of prosperity, comprising most of the free nations of Europe and working in harmony with the aims and purposes of the United Nations, is a great new force in the world. It includes two Commonwealth countries, Canada and ourselves, who will always work in the closest association with the other 53 members of the Commonwealth.

We have set our hopes on this conception. We want it to develop far beyond its immediate purpose of defence into a lasting association of like-minded nations. That is why, I am sorry to say, we cannot accept the French proposal. That is why His Majesty's Government, looking at the problem of the future security of the West, are in favour of the Atlantic conception. Nevertheless, if it is the wish of the French Government and of other Governments in Europe to proceed to examine the possibilities of forming a European Army as a part of the integrated force for the defence of Europe, His Majesty's Government would not stand in their way.

We are trying to reconcile the different approach caused by our geographical position, our international responsibilities, our Commonwealth connection and every other factor concerned, and we are not at loggerheads with the French. If the French, with their long tradition and their European view, take one line regarding Europe and if they will not try to force us into an awkward position, we certainly will put no pressure on them with regard to their desire for a European Army. But I repeat what I said, and I appeal to them to let us get on. We are anxious to avoid delay. The situation in the world is very dangerous. All peoples can combine on this problem of security and peace. It is in the interests of all of us in west Europe that the solution should be found promptly, and security assured ...

_____ 4.5 _____

GENERAL EISENHOWER'S ADDRESS TO THE NORTH ATLANTIC COUNCIL ON THE DEFENCE OF WEST EUROPE, ROME, 26 NOVEMBER 1951

Keesings Contemporary Archives,
Vol. 8 (1951), p. 1181.

At the time, Eisenhower was Supreme Allied Commander in Europe. In 1952 he would be elected President of the United States. The following extracts indicate his enthusiasm for European integration and the EDC proposal.

I do not need to recite to such a body as this the great advantages that would come to us through unification of west Europe, unification in its economy, its military systems, finally its political organisms. Under such conditions we would no longer have the job of trying to determine what each nation would have; we would have Mr Monnet's true concept of a single balanced force for the whole. No nation would have to keep, for prestige purposes alone, particular units, officers, organizations, or services. All this you can easily comprehend. But even as we long for such a great advance, I assure you that under the programs now in hand we can, in west Europe, erect a defense that can at least, although expensively and uneasily, produce a stalemate. But that is not good enough. As my chief of staff pointed out to you, we need depth to our defensive position; we need German assistance, both in geography and in military strength, if these can be obtained with justice and respect to them and to ourselves.

It is because of these reasons, of which the ones I have given you are only a few, that I have come to believe that we should have a European Defense Force. But merely because I believe we must have a European Defense Force does not mean that I am stopping for one instant my efforts to co-operate with every one of the chiefs of staff in all our countries to produce, now, what they can as effective national forces.

But if we can go ahead with the European Defense Force, gaining German strength without creating a menace to any others and in such a way that the Germans could co-operate with self-respect, our goals will become much more readily obtainable. Here I must say one word about the German position. We cannot have mere hirelings and expect them to operate efficiently. NATO has no use for soldiers representing second-rate morale or a second-rate country. German help will be tremendously important as it is freely given; and it can be so given, I believe, through a European Defense Force.

This European Force would serve another great purpose – it would stand alongside the Schuman plan – which must be successful – and the two would constitute great steps toward the goal of complete European unity.

Just as European unity is important to all of us, there is nothing more important to the entire NATO organization than an underlying unity among all of us based upon a clear comprehension of the facts at issue. It is not enough that all of our governments agree. The important thing is that the populations standing behind those governments must agree. Our peoples must understand that, for each nation, the concept of collective security by co-operation must be successful or there is no acceptable alternative for any of us. All of us must understand that the task we have set for ourselves can be done because of our great resources and our determination and skill. All of us must understand that this task must take first priority over and above all else except only that of assuring acceptable levels of living in our own countries. Unless this kind of information is gotten out and understood, we are victims first of our own laziness, our own failures as leaders, and secondly, we are victims of Soviet propaganda, because they will, in all cases, assert the contrary. They will assert that we are trying to get together to launch a great invasion, when they well know that the entire aggregate of the forces we are talking about have no power to launch any attack across Europe. All soldiers know that it is an entirely different thing to establish a military stalemate in west Europe on the one hand, and, on the other, to conduct an offensive. The Soviet general staff is completely capable of understanding this ...

_____ 4.6 _____

SIR WINSTON CHURCHILL, CONSERVATIVE PRIME MINISTER, TO THE HOUSE OF COMMONS, 6 DECEMBER 1951

Winston Churchill, 6 December 1951, House of Commons Debates, *Hansard*, Vol. 494, Cols 2594–6.

The following extract from this speech stresses the British position of support for, but refusal to merge with, the proposed EDC.

At Strasbourg in 1950 the Germans did not press for a national party. On the contrary, they declared themselves ready to join a European Army without having a national army. Dr Adenauer has renewed to us this assurance, and that is still the German position and their preference – no national army. This is a very great and helpful fact which we must all take into consideration. The size and strength of any German army, whether contingent or otherwise, and its manufacture of weapons, would in any case have to be agreed between the Allied Powers concerned. There, in short, is the policy which I have always advocated and which I am very glad to find is steadily going forward.

Difficulties have, however, arisen about the texture of the European Army. Should it be an amalgam of the European nations divested of all national character- istics and traditions, or should it be composed of elements essentially national but woven together by alliance, common organisation and unified command? On this point the discussions have at times assumed an almost metaphysical character, and the logic of continental minds has produced a scheme for what is called the European Defence Community. That is, at least, an enlightened if not an inspiring title.

The European Defence Community has not yet taken its final shape. The Paris Conference has been sitting for nine months, and it is now on the point of producing its Report. I am sorry the late Government did not send a delegation to this Conference instead of only an observer. The technical discussions have proceeded smoothly and in great detail, and at last the far-reaching political issues which have been raised and which surround the military questions have been reached. We do not know how these will be settled, and we have had no voice or share in the long argument. As soon as the Conference reaches its final conclusions we shall consider the way to establish the most effective form of association with the resultant organisations. In this way a European Army, containing a German contribution of agreed size and strength, will stand alongside the British and United States Armies in a common defensive front. That, after all, is what really matters to the life or death of the free world.

As far as Britain is concerned, we do not propose to merge in the European Army but we are already joined to it. Our troops are on the spot, and we all do our utmost to make a worthy and effective contribution to the deterrents against aggression and to the causes of freedom and democracy, which we seek to serve. These matters will, of course, require to be further discussed as the weeks pass by, and we shall probably know much more about what is the decision taken on the Continent than we can attempt to anticipate and imagine at this moment.

————————————— 4.7 —————————————

ARTICLE 38 OF THE TREATY ESTABLISHING THE EUROPEAN DEFENCE COMMUNITY, 27 MAY 1952

European Parliament, *Selection of Texts Concerning Institutional Matters of the Community from 1950 to 1982 (Luxembourg, n.d.), p. 53.*

Following this article it was proposed that the ECSC Assembly be turned into an ad hoc EDC Assembly to consider a more wide-ranging political integration. Early in 1953 it reported in favour of a European Political Community (EPC) which would go beyond the sector-by-sector approach to integration. This would be the beginning of a comprehensive political federation to which the ECSC and EDC would be subordinated. The EPC was abandoned with the collapse of the EDC.

Article 38:

1. Within the period laid down in the second paragraph of this Article, the Assembly shall study:

   (a) the constitution of an Assembly of the European Defence Community, elected on a democratic basis;
   (b) the powers which would devolve on such an Assembly;
   (c) any changes which might have eventually to be made to the provisions of the present Treaty concerning the other institutions of the Community, particularly with a view to safeguarding an appropriate representation of States.

   The Assembly will be particularly guided in its study by the following principles: The final organisation which will replace the present provisional organisation should be so conceived as to be able to constitute one of the elements in a subsequent federal or confederal structure, based on the principle of the separation of powers and having, in particular, a two-chamber system of representation. The Assembly shall also examine problems arising from the co-existence of different agencies for European co-operation already established or which might be established, with a view to ensuring co-ordination within the framework of the federal or confederal structure.

2. The proposals of the Assembly shall be submitted to the Council within six months from the assumption of duties by the Assembly. On the advice of the Council, these proposals will thereafter be transmitted by the Chairman of the Assembly to the Governments of the Member States who will, within three months from the date on which the matter has been brought to their notice, convene a conference to consider the proposals.

───────────────── 4.8 ─────────────────

KONRAD ADENAUER: *MEMOIRS 1945–53*

Konrad Adenauer, *Memoirs 1945–53* (London: Weidenfeld & Nicolson, 1966), pp. 416–17.

Adenauer was the first Chancellor of the German Federal Republic. He regarded integration with the west as essential for his country's security, prosperity and political rehabilitation.

In my opinion the European nation states had a past but no future. This applied in the political and economic as well as in the social sphere. No single European country could guarantee a secure future to its people by its own strength. I regarded the Schuman Plan and the European Defence Community as preliminary steps to a political unification of Europe. In the EDC Treaty there was a specific provision for a controlling body, the so-called Parliamentary Assembly – incidentally the same assembly that exercised the parliamentary controlling function in the Coal and Steel Community – to examine the questions arising from the parallelism of diverse existing or future organisations for European cooperation, with a view to securing their coordination in the framework of a federal or confederate structure.

The military aspect was only one dimension of a nascent Europe, or, more rightly at first, west Europe. If a perfect partnership was to be achieved within west Europe, one could not stop with defence ...

After twelve years of National Socialism there simply were no perfect solutions for Germany and certainly none for a divided Germany. There was very often only the policy of the lesser evil.

We were a small and very exposed country. By our own strength we could achieve nothing. We must not be a no-man's-land between East and West for then we would have friends nowhere and a dangerous neighbour in the East. Any refusal by the Federal Republic to make common cause with Europe would have been German isolationism, a dangerous escape into inactivity. There was a cherished political illusion in the Federal Republic in those years: many people believed that

America was in any case tied to Europe or even to the Elbe. American patience, however, had its limits. My motto was 'Help yourself and the United States will help you' ...

There were those in Germany who thought that for us the choice was either a policy for Europe or a policy for German unity. I considered this 'either/or' a fatal error. Nobody could explain how German unity in freedom was to be achieved without a strong and united Europe. When I say 'in freedom' I mean freedom before, during and above all after all-German elections. No policy is made with wishes alone and even less from weakness. Only when the West was strong might there be a genuine point of departure for peace negotiations to free not only the Soviet zone but all of enslaved Europe east of the Iron Curtain, and free it peacefully. To take the road that led into the European Community appeared to me the best service we could render the Germans in the Soviet zone ...

4.9

THE DEBATE IN THE FRENCH NATIONAL ASSEMBLY, 29–30 AUGUST 1954

W. Rossenberger and H. Tobin (eds), *Keesing's Contemporary Archives 1954*, Vol. 9 (London: Longman Group, 1957), pp. 13751–5.

After this debate the EDC plan was defeated by 319 to 264 votes.

M. Mendès-France (Prime Minister): I wish to speak of the situation that will arise if you accept or if you reject the Treaty. If you ratify the Treaty, the proposals made by our five colleagues at Brussels will be maintained ... The most important advantage, in my opinion, is that the EDC links the German Federal Republic politically to the Western World ... The entry of the Treaty into force will mark an important step on the road to Franco-German reconciliation, which is one of the conditions of peace ... Should you decide to refuse ratification, the problem of west Europe, and of Germany and her rearmament will still arise in one form or another and will again come before you ...

Our British and American Allies have already made it known that, in the event of the French Parliament rejecting the Treaty, they would be ready to take important international decisions – notably to restore full sovereignty to the Federal Republic. That country [West Germany] would receive all the attributes of sovereignty except in the military field. The decision of our allies seems to me inevitable, whether the Treaty is ratified or not ... If we do not ratify the Treaty our allies will not renounce their attempt to obtain a German contribution to Western defence. That means that we would soon be faced with proposals for the rearming of Germany, on which you would be called upon to pronounce ...

We have been speaking about tomorrow and we must look facts in the face. What is the basis on which the Government's foreign policy rests? It is the Atlantic Alliance. To avoid any misunderstanding, I solemnly affirm that my Government will accept no measure, proposal or suggestion contrary to that alliance. Voices have been heard in our country which speak of the isolation in France, of the reversal of alliances, of French neutralism, of German neutralisation. The Government's views have not changed; our foreign policy remains one of faithfulness to the alliance which gives us our security, an alliance based on the friendly cooperation of associates enjoying equal rights, debating their common problems, and remaining judge of their own vital interests.

As regards our relations with Great Britain it is an axiom of French policy that nothing should ever separate us. Whether or not we are members of the same grouping, our two peoples are united by an alliance which does not need to be defined in writing because it is vital. There remains the last problem – Germany's place in Europe. Our constant aim is to bring about a definite reconciliation between the two countries within a European framework . . . and I have already indicated our intention of giving back to Germany her full sovereignty in agreement with our allies.

General Aumeran (Independent Republican): Ratification [of the EDC Treaty] will put us in the same ranks as two vanquished peoples and three small nations [the other members of the Six] . . . We should have no illusions about the fact that Germany has been chosen as the pivot of European defence. As the Atlantic Pact can be revised in 1959, a good opportunity will arise to substitute Germany for France, who in the meantime would have been deprived of her army and perhaps of her empire . . . The EDC with its forty divisions will never frighten the Soviet Union. What is frightening is the prospect of a sovereign Germany entering this organisation, a Germany admitted to atomic secrets and bent on revenge . . . A catastrophe would rapidly result. It is the task of France to create a climate of peace and prevent the rearming of Germany . . . The rejection of the Treaty will not only permit the reconciliation of Frenchmen, but will bring about conditions in which we can seek a defensive system that will take into account the great changes that have come about in recent years.

M. Herriot (Radical, Président d'Honneur of the Assembly): I say with my fullest conviction that no international negotiations aimed at securing liberty and peace can be carried out without the mutual support of France and Britain . . . I have read the [EDC] texts with anguish. There is nothing in them to show that Britain would be at our side to resist the strength and any eventual manoeuvres of Germany. Britain must be at the side of France in this matter to act with equal responsibility in the face of a new German threat, should it arise. The absence of solidarity between Britain and France is, in itself, sufficient to make me reject EDC.

But we have other reasons for opposing the Treaty, the chief of which is the loss of our country's sovereignty and independence. The EDC Treaty aims at restoring

Germany's sovereignty but represents a backward step for France with regard to her sovereignty ...

I say that the EDC means the end of France ... I shall be told 'If you do not believe in the EDC you do not believe in Europe'. I protest against such a conclusion ... We do not want a solution through rearmament ... We want a solution for Europe as a whole, for United Europe, not for the 'Europe of the Five or Six'. We want peace for its own sake, not the rearmament of certain countries. I do not want the EDC – I want a *rapprochement* with Germany and with all the countries of Europe based on other principles.

4.10

STATEMENT BY THE US SECRETARY OF STATE, JOHN FOSTER DULLES, TO THE PRESS, 31 AUGUST 1954

Department of State, *Bulletin*, 13, Washington, DC, September 1954.

This reflects the anger and disappointment of the United States at the failure of the French National Assembly to ratify the EDC.

The French rejection of the European Defense Community is a saddening event. France thus turns away from her own historic proposal made nearly four years ago. That proposal sought a unification of the military strength of continental Europe into a single European Army so as to end the era of recurrent European wars, the last two of which became world wars.

The French action does not change certain basic and stubborn facts:

(a) The effective defense of continental Europe calls for a substantial military contribution from the Germans; yet all, including the Germans themselves, would avoid national rearmament in a form which could be misused by resurgent militarism.

(b) Germany cannot be subjected indefinitely to neutrality or otherwise be discriminated against in terms of her sovereignty, including the inherent right of individual and collective self-defense. Limitations on German sovereignty to be permanently acceptable must be shared by others as part of a collective international order.

(c) The prevention of war between neighbouring nations which have a long record of fighting cannot be dependably achieved merely by national promises or threats but only by merging certain functions of their government into supranational institutions.

To deal with these facts was the lofty purpose of EDC. Four of the six prospective members of the EDC had ratified that treaty – Belgium, Germany, Luxembourg and the Netherlands. A fifth, Italy, was on the point of ratifying it. The United Kingdom and the United States had made far–reaching commitments of association with EDC. France thus disassociates herself not only from her own proposal but from her prospective partners who had stood united at the recent Brussels conference . . .

The French negative action, without the provision of any alternative, obviously imposes on the United States the obligation to reappraise its foreign policies, particularly those in relation to Europe. The need for such a review can scarcely be questioned since the North Atlantic Council of Ministers has itself twice declared with unanimity that the EDC was of paramount importance to the European defense it planned. Furthermore, such review is required by conditions which the Congress attached this year and last year to authorizations for military contributions to Europe.

The Western nations now owe it to the Federal Republic of Germany to do quickly all that lies in their power to restore sovereignty to that Republic and to enable it to contribute to international peace and security. The existing treaty to restore sovereignty is by its terms contingent upon the coming into force of EDC. It would be unconscionable if the failure to realize EDC, through no fault of Germany's, should now be used as an excuse for penalizing Germany. The Federal German Republic should take its place as a free and equal member of the society of nations. That was the purport of the resolution which the US Senate adopted unanimously last July, and the United States will act accordingly.

The United States stands ready to support the many in west Europe who despite their valiant efforts are left in grave anxiety.

It is a tragedy that in one country nationalism, abetted by communism, has asserted itself so as to endanger the whole of Europe.

4.11

STATEMENT OF FOREIGN SECRETARY, SIR ANTHONY EDEN, TO THE BRITISH CABINET, 30 SEPTEMBER 1954

PRO, London – CAB 128/27 pt 2 CC 62 (54) 1 Secret,
1 October 1954.

The following commitment to continental defence was intended to reassure both the United States and France. It led to the resolution of the German rearmament question and German membership of NATO in 1955.

The Foreign Secretary reported to the Cabinet on the position reached in the discussions at the Nine-Power Conference now proceeding in London.

The Foreign Secretary said that at the present stage of the Conference it was most important that we should do everything we could to make it easier for Dr Adenauer to secure the support of German public opinion for any settlement on which agreement might be reached. It was possible that the French Government would try to insist that their participation in a general settlement must be conditional on a prior solution of the problem of the Saar. He, therefore, proposed to tell M. Mendès-France privately that, if the French Government were to do this, we should feel unable to adhere to the offer we had made about the maintenance of British forces on the Continent of Europe. It would, of course, remain open to the French Government to try to reach agreement with the Federal German Government about the Saar separately from any general European settlement.

4.12

PARIS TREATY, 23 OCTOBER 1954

The Paris Treaty, 23 October 1954, James Bellini, *French Defence Policy* (London: RUSI, 1974), pp. 79–85.

With the collapse of the EDC, Anthony Eden, then British Prime Minister, proposed that Germany sign the Brussels Treaty of 1948. The 1954 protocols modified the Brussels Treaty to establish the Western European Union (WEU). This enabled Germany to join NATO and stressed the WEU's role in promoting European integration. Germany joined NATO on 5 May 1955.

Article I: The Federal Republic of Germany and the Italian Republic hereby accede to the Treaty as modified and completed by the present Protocol.

Protocol no. 2 on forces of western European union.

Article VI: Her Majesty the Queen of the United Kingdom of Great Britain and Northern Ireland will continue to maintain on the mainland of Europe, including Germany, the effective strength of the United Kingdom forces which are now assigned to the Supreme Allied Commander, Europe, that is to say four divisions and the Second Tactical Air Force, or such other forces as the Supreme Allied Commander, Europe, regards as having equivalent fighting capacity. She undertakes not to withdraw these forces against the wishes of the majority of the High Contracting Parties who should take their decision in the knowledge of the views of the Supreme Allied Commander, Europe. This undertaking shall not, however, bind her in the event of an acute overseas emergency. If the maintenance of the United Kingdom forces on the mainland of Europe throws at any time too great a strain on the external finances of the United Kingdom, she will, through Her Government in the United Kingdom of Great Britain and Northern Ireland, invite the North Atlantic Council to review the financial conditions on which the United Kingdom formations are maintained.

Protocol no. 3 on the control of armaments.

Part I: Armaments not to be manufactured

Article I: The High Contracting Parties, members of Western European Union, take note of and record their agreement with the Declaration of the Chancellor of the Federal Republic of Germany (made in London on 3rd October 1954), in which the Federal Republic of Germany undertook not to manufacture in its territory atomic, biological and chemical weapons.

_____4.13_____

RELATIONS BETWEEN NATO AND THE WEU, 1955

Foreign Relations of the United States 1955–57, Vol. 4, pp. 19–20.

This telegram from the US Delegation at the NATO Council Ministerial Meeting is dated 11 May 1955, and sheds interesting light on perceptions of the relationship.

Spaak (Belgium) led off discussion re NATO–WEU relationships by saying early doubts he had had as to which forum political questions should be discussed had, as result present meetings, been resolved in favour NATO. Emphasized following points in support this view: (1) there was no such thing as 'European' defense; effective Atlantic defense required participation US and Canada; (2) only NATO could take decisions as important for example as that taken by NAC Ministerial meeting last December re MC-48 concept [this was 'The most effective pattern of military strength for the next few years', a NATO planning document]; (3) European idea necessarily limited concept. Even small European powers affected by great power decisions re world problems and NATO forum was place where small powers could be informed and consulted as to what might affect them. Concluded by suggesting NATO political consultation during current meetings could lead toward sort of Atlantic Commonwealth analogous to British Commonwealth in which, without voting procedure and without specific commitments, Ministers could exchange views and then return home to work toward broad common policy. Expressed hope these ideas would find place in communiqué.

Pinay (France), Martino (Italy), and Steel (UK) associated themselves fully with views expressed by Spaak. Adenauer also agreed with Spaak that NAC was place in which major political problems should be discussed but pointed out WEU 'must have life of its own' and free discuss whatever problems it saw fit. Lange (Norway), speaking as representative of European country not member of WEU, pointed out it especially important from Norway's viewpoint that NATO remain principal forum for political discussion and for working out common Western policy. Said Norwegian public had evidence some worry that WEU might lead to inner circle within NATO which could limit opportunities countries such as Norway make full contribution to NATO. Cunha (Portugal) associated himself with Spaak and Lange. Beyen (Netherlands) asked Adenauer elaborate what he meant by WEU's having 'life of its own' and also asked whether Chancellor's statement had been intended qualify views expressed by Spaak. Adenauer replied by saying functions of WEU and NATO were different; said it was WEU's job and not NATO's undertake control of armaments, etc. Also pointed out some of those who had helped establish WEU believed it would grow and lead toward greater cohesiveness its members in certain fields. At same time, Chancellor was in full agreement with Spaak that NATO rather than WEU was proper place discuss major problems international policy. Pinay supported foregoing views expressed by Chancellor and emphasized there no real question of competition between NATO and WEU. Zorlu (Turkey) recalled that last January Turkish Delegation had submitted memo to NAC on question NATO relations with WEU which thought pertinent to present discussion. Said obviously desirable insure closest collaboration between two organizations. Way to avoid duplication whenever new agency was proposed for WEU was to find out first whether any existing NATO agency could do job. Suggested this concept be incorporated in minutes of meeting. Spaak said there was no contradiction between what he had said earlier and full activity on part of WEU in field of tasks laid down in protocols. Also agreed with Chancellor that there considerable area potential development for WEU especially in economic and social fields. Pearson (Canada) agreed with Chancellor that WEU had important role to play and with Spaak that NAC must continue to be forum for working out common policy for West.

CHAPTER 5

THE ROME TREATIES AND THE DEBATE ON A FREE TRADE AREA

1955–1958

INTRODUCTION

The defeat of the EDC proposals by the French National Assembly came as a disappointment to many supporters of west European integration, not least since it also involved the rejection of the ambitious draft statute for the European Political Community (EPC). Others had been unhappy about the association of such integration (which they conceived as a guarantee of peace among the nations of west Europe) with rearmament. While the protracted EDC debate had been in progress, it was hardly practicable to pursue other plans for integration. Now that the question of German rearmament was resolved by NATO membership with guarantees, a block to further integration was removed. The chief problem with the EDC proposals, from the point of view of the supporters of further integration, had been that it was the army which had been chosen as the next target for integration. The essentially intergovernmental Western European Union (WEU) had enabled the conflict over German rearmament to be resolved, but it was unable to provide much unity among its members in defence or other areas. Despite some speculation about expanding the WEU's role, Britain soon realized it could not afford the defence commitments it had made, and the Six sought a further basis for integration.

What subsequently happened has often been presented as the great *rélance*, a revival of European initiative spurred by the challenge of earlier defeat.[1] Seen from another perspective, the meeting at Messina (see below) was a further stage in efforts towards integration that had never really stopped. The subsequent founding of the European Economic Community (EEC) and Euratom (European Atomic Energy Community) in 1957 was the result of detailed negotiations and the combination of and coincidence of different national interests, at the same time as the recognition of common interests. The hope of many of those involved was that political unity would ultimately evolve out of economic integration. The drafters of the Treaties of Rome fought shy, though, of any instant constitutional blueprint for a fully fledged federation.

International circumstances had not favoured the EDC. The French Army was tied up in Indochina. The Korean war was brought to an end and the new Soviet leaders seemed to hold out some prospect of *détente*. The need for German rearmament no longer appeared so pressing. By contrast, the formulation and ratification of the Rome Treaties was markedly aided by the international situation. The Soviet suppression of the Hungarian uprising in 1956 coincided with the Suez Crisis, in which the British and French were forced by international, particularly US, pressure to call off their invasion of Egypt when it repossessed the Suez Canal. These events were reminders of the vulnerability of west Europe and the decline of French and British power. Both Britain and France were forced dramatically to reappraise their role in the world. Guy Mollet, the French Prime Minister, humiliated by his involvement in Suez, was the more determined to push through the EEC and Euratom. Suez increased French distrust of the United States and of Britain, who had led the retreat. The advantages of further cohesion with the other five seemed very evident. At the same time, the question of the rich mining area of the Saar (which had been separated from Germany in 1946 at French insistence, and had been a very contentious issue in Franco-German relations) was resolved when the Saar was integrated with the Federal Republic on 1 January 1957. These facts help to explain why a France that rejected the EDC in 1954 was willing to sign the Treaties of Rome in 1957.

In addition, there was the impact of African and Asian nationalism. This, as David Arter points out,

> suggested a covert goal of integration – to compensate for the loss of empire while also seeking to provide the means for preserving colonial advantages. Regional integration would enable west Europe to be more independent of colonial raw materials and markets, but also create a power bloc capable of exerting more effective control over colonial territories. It was significant that, during the setting up of a Common Market, France persuaded the other members of the Six to assume joint responsibility for maintaining a flow of capital to her colonial possessions and to initiate steps to establish the framework of a customs union between these colonies and the metropolitan states.[2]

Indeed it was France's colonies, especially Morocco, Tunisia and Algeria which dominated the French press and newsreels during the years 1955 to 1957.[3] Economically, France was caught between fear of losing the protected markets of the overseas territories and recognition that France alone could no longer provide the necessary investment funds. So pressing was the latter that officials had begun to speculate on European integration as a solution even before the Benelux initiative which led to the EEC.[4] Yet it was not until the end of the negotiations that France secured an acceptable deal. Even then, during a meeting of heads of government in Paris on 19–20 February 1957, Mollet had to appeal to German goodwill in order to persuade Konrad Adenauer to override the objections of his own officials and to effectively subsidize French investment in her overseas territories. From the resulting fund of 581 million (US dollars), of which France and Germany provided 200 million each, France drew no less than 511 million.[5]

In late 1954, the governments of the Six had begun to consider a new economic initiative which would complement the European Coal and Steel Community. The Belgian Government argued that the Six should extend the Community to cover specific sectors of the economy – particularly transport and further sources of energy. This received some support from French ministers in the centre-right Movement Republican Populaire (MRP), already known as the 'Party of Europe' in French politics, from Jean Monnet, from the German Vice-President at the High Authority of the ECSC, Franz Etzel, and from the ECSC Common Assembly. Monnet's priority in continuing with a sectoral approach to integration at this time was to develop a European atomic energy industry. A general common market was of far less interest to him.

The Dutch, especially Foreign Minster Jan Willem Beyen, were initially the most ardent opponents of this sectoral approach, pressing instead for a general economic common market, as they had during the negotiations over the European Political Community in 1953. This would include the agricultural exports which were a mainstay of the Dutch economy, also an attractive aspect of the common market to the French. Similarly, the German government favoured wider trade liberalization over a sectoral approach, although the Germans were bitterly divided over the geographic extent of liberalization and over whether or not strong supranational institutions were desirable (Document 5.1). Economics Minister Ludwig Erhard stressed the need for freeing trade with the Americans and, in view of their important trade with Europeans outside the Six, urged that economic integration not be confined to those countries willing to participate in elaborate institutional arrangements. Erhard was opposed by Franz Etzel and Walter Hallstein, State Secretary of the Foreign Office, among others. Even his closest advisers were divided.[6]

On 20 May 1955, the Benelux countries presented joint proposals, combining the sectoral and common market approaches, to be considered at a special meeting of the ECSC Council of Ministers at Messina in June. As an example of how the small Benelux countries could influence European integration, it was strikingly similar to the Benelux initiative which produced the Maastricht Treaty in 1991. The Benelux memorandum provided the basis for the agreement made at Messina, although it was initially criticized by the Germans for being too ambitious and too focused on trade among the Six. The Germans had managed to agree on a negotiating position on 22 May, but only at the expense of compromises on both sides. On learning of the German position a disillusioned Monnet wrote to Adenauer: 'The German proposals aim simply at turning back to the economic co-operation of sovereign states: such a procedure cannot bring about the changes which are necessary for Europe's future'.[7]

The world's media almost overlooked the Messina Conference of 2–3 June 1955. Initially, 'Messina produced no sharp electric shock signalling a new determination to resume the process of uniting Europe.'[8] The success of the weekend took everyone by surprise, not least the foreign ministers of the Six who took part. The ministers appointed the Belgian Foreign Minister Paul-Henri Spaak to head an intergovernmental committee charged with the preparation of a report into the viability of both a common market unifying customs policy by setting a common external tariff rate and an atomic energy agency, to coordinate nuclear research and development and establish a common market for fissionable materials. The ministers agreed on a resolution which adopted the objectives of the Benelux programme but set out different procedures for, and a more gradual approach to, their implementation. It had been difficult to persuade the French to agree to this. France feared a repetition of the EDC debacle and was not really interested in the idea of a common market, preferring sectoral integration in the field of atomic energy.[9]

The British reaction to the Messina initiative also contributed to the determination of the Six to proceed alone. The reaction was, from the outset, sceptical. The United Kingdom sent Russell Bretherton, a Board of Trade official, as an 'observer' to the Spaak committee. On instruction, he opposed the customs union plan and soon left the committee. His parting words epitomized the British underestimation of the commitment of the Six:

> The future treaty which you are discussing has no chance of being agreed; if it was agreed, it would have no chance of being ratified; and if it were ratified, it would have no chance of being applied. And if it was applied, it would be totally unacceptable to Britain. You speak of agriculture, which we don't like, of power over customs, which we take exception to and of institutions which frighten us . . . au revoir and bonne chance.[10]

The committee established at Messina went to work with great speed, meeting for long sessions at the Chateau de Val Duchesse outside Brussels. After eight months it produced the Spaak Report, which led to the EEC and Euratom. 'The object of a European common market', it stated, 'should be to create a vast area with a common political economy which will form a powerful productive unit and permit a steady expansion, an increase in stability, a more rapid rise in the standard of living, and the development of harmonious relations between the Member States.'[11] This report was accepted by the foreign ministers of the Six in May 1956 in Venice, and the committee was asked to draw up formal treaties. Again this was not a foregone conclusion. It was only with Adenauer's backing that the German Foreign Office was able to gain a mandate from the Cabinet on 9 May to begin to enter into formal negotiations. When the ministers met in Venice, the Germans were surprised by French Foreign Minister Christian Pineau's ready acceptance of entering into negotiations.

While Pineau and Prime Minister Mollet were 'favourably disposed' towards the common market, the French establishment was hostile. Robert Marjòlin recalled a meeting about the Spaak report: 'I said that the Spaak report could serve as a basis for discussion, but that it would need amending here and there. My words met with an icy reception. Verret then asked all the officials present to state their views in turn. All were against, except Bernard Clappier, former *directeur de cabinet* of Robert Schuman ... and myself.'[12] French officialdom was convinced that the French economy, burdened by higher social costs was at a disadvantage *vis-à-vis* the German economy, hence the demand for the harmonization of social costs as a precondition of a customs union. Nor did France want to accept the automatic commitment to enter a customs union envisaged by Beyen, preferring to retain the option to review progress after the initial round of tariff reductions. There were also concerns about Beyen's intention that there would be a low external tariff which, France feared, would expose her to global competition.[13]

Atomic energy on the other hand was a different matter. This was the project favoured by Jean Monnet (Document 5.8). He and his staff had worked out a plan for extending integration to atomic energy and placing it under the High Authority of the ECSC. After resigning the Presidency of the ECSC, Monnet had founded his own pressure group, the Action Committee for the United States of Europe. This body came into existence in October 1955, bringing together representatives of the Socialist, Christian Democratic and Liberal parties, and the non-communist trade unions of the Six. To achieve their objectives, it was necessary, the first annual memorandum of the movement stated, 'to put aside all specious solutions. Mere co-operation between governments will not suffice. It is indispensable for states to delegate certain of their powers to European federal institutions, mandated by all the participating countries taken as a whole.'[14] On one crucial point, however, Monnet's strategy for atomic energy deviated from that of the French government. To the embarrassment of the latter, Monnet's committee put the issue of the purely peaceful development of atomic energy on the public agenda (Document 5.2). In fact the government of Mendès-France had already committed France to a secret atomic weapons programme.[15] The French view was quite simple. As a French memorandum put it in 1955: 'The possession of such weapons now appears to be the right of entry into the club of great powers'.[16] It was hoped that the proposed European Atomic Energy Community (Euratom) would actually aid the French programme by reducing European dependence upon the United States for supplies of uranium and especially by providing for joint financing of an isotope separator for enriching uranium. Support for France's right to develop atomic weapons was crucial to winning over the National Assembly in the vote of July 1956, which allowed the French government to proceed not only with the Euratom negotiations but also with those on the common market.[17] Euratom had another attraction for France. It would allow France to monitor the development of the German atomic industry (Document 5.4). It was for this reason that France insisted upon Euratom's ownership of fissile material. The two French goals proved, however, to be inconsistent. As Spaak explained to the Americans in February 1957, 'he has not supported the French in their desire to provide for complete ownership by Euratom of all fissionable material. Mr Spaak maintained that the French themselves had created the dilemma when they insisted on the right to engage in military uses. This had created a practical difficulty, as it was hard to conceive of Euratom's holding title to material which had been fabricated into a bomb.'[18] The dilemma was not entirely of French making. Germany, especially as represented by the Minister for Atomic Power, Franz Josef Strauss, fought vigorously for private ownership of fissile material, fearing an attempt to control German industry. When the French invoked the British and American precedent of public ownership and control, Strauss dismissed this as irrelevant since it was only justified by the priority given in those countries to military uses, uses which Germany had renounced.[19] It was not until the February 1957 Brussels meeting that the parties accepted a Belgian proposal which, in the words of the Treaty, gave Euratom ownership of special fissile materials but conceded that 'member states, persons or undertakings shall have unlimited right of use and consumption subject only to safety considerations'.[20] Towards the end of 1956 it also became clear to the French that there was no interest among the other five in building the isotope separator. The attractions of Euratom for the French were evaporating before their eyes.

Nevertheless, it was Euratom which kept the French in the negotiations. It had been Euratom, not the common market, which the French had initially wanted. There were in fact repeated French attempts to secure a Euratom treaty prior to a treaty on the common market. In June 1956, the French told Spaak that 'The signature of Euratom is the only means of then bringing about ratification of the common market by the parliament.'[21] This option was strongly resisted by the Germans, and indeed the others, who insisted upon linkage between the two treaties, suspecting that if France obtained agreement on Euratom it would allow the negotiations on the common market to stagnate. Adenauer was tempted to drop the linkage in September at the behest of Monnet, and it was only with difficulty that Hallstein and Etzel held the Chancellor to the German negotiating position.[22]

The Euratom negotiations had also benefited from the support of the United States (Documents 5.5, 5.6), although differences between the State Department and the powerful Atomic Energy Commission complicated matters. It is testimony to the strength of American support for the idea of European integration that the head of the Atomic Energy Commission, Admiral Lewis Strauss, finally gave his blessing to the enterprise. In March 1957 he still insisted that material supplied by the United States should be used for purely peaceful purposes, but added, 'Accordingly, if co-operation with Euratom under these circumstances is, as we understand it to be, important in achieving this Government's foreign policy objective in west Europe, the Commission would be willing to cooperate with Euratom, notwithstanding the weapons feature.'[23]

By the time the treaties were signed, it was becoming increasingly clear that the European Economic Community would be more important than Euratom. During the negotiations Spaak's impact on the committee was of decisive importance for the direction of the European *rélance*. His committee shifted the government's agenda firmly in the direction of a common market, rejecting suggestions that the atomic energy project be given greater priority. There were, though, numerous hurdles to overcome.

A prime obstacle remained French concerns about social harmonization, despite the fact that their own studies of French industry, intended to substantiate their concerns, were inconclusive.[24] They were also opposed to automatic progression of tariff reductions leading to a full customs union. The Germans were still divided, with Erhard repeatedly questioning the wisdom of the whole enterprise. Erhard's criticism was so persistent that Adenauer wrote to his ministers on 19 January 1956 formally invoking his constitutional authority to set the guidelines of government policy.[25] Erhard did not give up. He was encouraged in the summer of 1956 when Britain used the OEEC to launch the idea of a Free Trade Area which would embrace the Six as well as other European states. In Germany Erhard's critics cast doubt on his credentials as a 'good European', a charge which he bitterly resented.[26]

The deadlock on harmonization was broken when Mollet and Adenauer met in November 1956 against the background of the Suez crisis. There is little doubt that the fact that Adenauer made this planned visit despite the Suez Crisis was greatly appreciated by the French, though whether that contributed to the agreement is disputed.[27] The Germans did make some concessions to the French on harmonization, although these subsequently proved to be of little consequence.

Even after the Mollet–Adenauer meeting, a host of problems remained when the heads of government met in February 1957, including the issue of France's overseas territories. Disagreements over agriculture were not resolved until after this meeting, at the end of February.[28] The chief agricultural differences were not, as is often believed, between a Germany anxious to liberalize industrial trade and a protectionist France determined to make the Germans accept an agricultural agreement on their terms. On the contrary, the chief conflicts over agriculture were between France and The Netherlands, the latter pressing for a greater degree of free trade in agricultural goods and eager that the mechanisms for determining prices be based on those used to such good effect in Holland's post-war agricultural system. Indeed, the most difficult parliamentary scenes in the ratification procedures were in Holland, although fear of Germany was still evident in the ratification debate in France (Document 5.9).

The Treaty Establishing a European Economic Community prescribed a customs union, the free movement of capital and labour, fair competition and common policies in transport. It was a complex document, close enough in spirit to the ideas of Beyen (Document 5.7). It also gave powers to the institutions to achieve a balance in the development of the Community, to prohibit monopolies and assist the less well-off regions through a Social Fund and Investment Bank. In agriculture it called for 'reasonable prices' and a stable market in food. The economic benefits of an enlarged and unified market, it was hoped, would increase the standard of living in the countries of the Six and enable west Europe to compete more effectively in world markets. The further consolidation of West Germany with the other five would also reduce even more the possibility of her orientating herself towards east Europe or playing a neutral role.

The EEC created a 'new legal order' independent of the member states whose acts, however, had direct legal effect in those states. The broad aims of the Treaty are listed in Article 2. The Treaty also set down timetables for the reduction of external tariffs, for the removal of quotas internally and for the creation of an external common tariff. These objectives would be achieved a year and a half before schedule. Behind the arrangements on trade there was an implicit political agenda. With the customs union and, more far-reaching, the creation of common policies or the progressive coordination of national policies, the Community would produce 'closer relations between the Member States'. The removal of barriers to trade in agricultural produce, a sector where all member states had managed and protected markets, was to become possible only with the formulation of the Common Agricultural Policy (CAP), something that was to produce more difficulties than anything else in the history of the Community.

The preamble to the EEC Treaty expressed the will to 'establish the foundation of an ever closer union of the peoples of Europe'. The goal of 'political union' was relegated to a vaguely worded reference to the foreign policy cooperation which would grow naturally in the context of increasing coordination of trade and other economic policies. But the very title 'Community' – signifying a community of interest – was an assertion of the intention to commit participating states to more than a loose association. Behind the customs union and, more importantly, the creation of common or progressively coordinated policies, the Community aimed more generally to secure 'closer relations between the Member States'. The subsequent evolution of the European Community owes a great deal to the Treaty of Rome, allowing pragmatic adjustment to circumstances. As Paul Taylor points out:

> It was not tied to a particular prescription: its purpose was not made wholly explicit and it enunciated principles rather than details. It was like the American Constitution in that its level of generality was precisely pitched to allow it to be a focus of the hopes and expectations of a wide variety of different groups, and for these to be adjusted and to find a new reconciliation with each other at various points in the Union's history. Had it been detailed and precise, it would probably have been broken long since, as any formal commitment to federalism would have

lost the states and any firm enunciation of intergovernmentalism would have lost those who wished to transcend the existing political forms. Beyond that it conveyed a vague optimism about a better future which anti-federalists could not explicitly renounce.[29]

The main decision-making body of the Community was the Council of Ministers, drawn from the governments of the individual member states. The European Commission, on the other hand, was to represent the common European interest. This reflected the mixture of the intergovernmental and the supranational in the Community. On the one hand, the member states wanted to retain ultimate powers of decision and legislation. On the other, the Treaty, to be workable, had to be applied at the supranational level. Further progress towards integration was constrained by the member states. On the other hand, if the governments of the Six had the political will to advance further, the Community would be able to do so. This explains the uncertain pace of future integration. The Assembly, later to be renamed the European Parliament, was not comparable, for instance, with the British Houses of Parliament. Its powers are described in the Treaty of Rome as being 'advisory and supervisory'. To begin with it was given the power only to debate the work of the Commission and to adopt, if there were very good reasons, a motion of censure by a two-thirds majority which would force the Commissioners to resign. This was, to all intents and purposes, an unusable power, since it had no powers to replace the Commissioners. The Treaties also provided for the European Assembly to be consulted on certain categories of draft legislation. From 1970, the role of the Assembly was to increase, though it still falls far short of being a plenary legislative assembly.

The formation of the European Community put pressure on those who had excluded themselves. Britain proposed a Free Trade Area (FTA) which was presented as a 'complement' to the Messina plan. This project – Plan G – was initially welcomed by many leading figures in the Six, but during intergovernmental negotiations, again at Val de Duchesse, soon ran up against opposition (Documents 5.11, 5.12, 5.13). The FTA was to be an industrial area, excluding agriculture, with tariffs progressively limited over a ten-year period. In contrast to the members of the emergent EEC, FTA members would retain their existing freedom of action with regard to tariffs affecting the rest of the world, subject to GATT commitments. For France, the FTA was too liberal and had a number of disadvantages compared with the EEC, since agricultural exports would have been excluded from it and the impact of trade liberalization was not balanced by the safeguards and promises of social and economic policy harmonization which the French had secured in the EEC Treaty. By mid-1958, 'Europeans' throughout the Six, notably the first Commission President, Walter Hallstein and Monnet's Action Committee, had turned against the proposals, fearing that without these additional measures the FTA would destroy the cohesion of the common market. In addition, it appeared that the United Kingdom wanted to secure the economic benefits of EEC membership without any sacrifice of its advantageous Commonwealth and agricultural trading position.

At the beginning of March 1958, France tabled two substantial amendments which were wholly unacceptable to the United Kingdom. First, agreement between the Common Market and other OEEC countries was to be reached on an industry-by-industry basis; ailing sectors would have to wait until conditions and competition had been harmonized before entering the FTA. Second, Britain's preferential tariffs for Commonwealth countries were to be extended to a quota of continental European goods. It was clear that France was opposed to the whole FTA concept. The French Foreign Minister, Couve de Murville, summed it up in the following words:

> We believed that the good direction was the Common Market and not the Free Trade Area. France has never been a free-trade country, and it believes more in organisation. The Common Market was not only a free trade for industrial production but also a future agricultural common policy; and that's a thing to which we were very much attached, for the reason simply that agricultural production is important in our country. So we could not accept the British idea. We accepted the Common Market and inevitably a sort of conflict was to appear between Britain and the Common Market countries.[30]

In November 1958, the French announced that there was no point in continuing negotiations with the OEEC and soon after President de Gaulle secured Chancellor Adenauer's backing for suspending the negotiations in return for forthright French support over Russian threats to west Berlin, which was a focus of intense international tension in the years 1958–62 thus reversing the German policy in favour of the FTA which Ludwig Erhard had pressed enthusiastically.

Following the collapse of its plans for a Free Trade Area encompassing all of west Europe, Britain narrowed its objectives. The industrial representatives of the prospective FTA members outside the Six – principally the Scandinavians, the United Kingdom, Switzerland and Austria – had proposed a smaller industrial FTA in April 1958, largely in the hope that it would show the OEEC governments that the plan was feasible. This was to lead to the European Free Trade Association (EFTA), incorporating the Scandinavian states, Britain, Austria, Portugal and Switzerland, which envisaged complete abolition of industrial tariffs by 1970 (Documents 5.14, 5.16). Iceland joined later and Finland became an associate member. By the end of the 1950s west Europe was divided into two trade blocs, the Six and the Seven, and relations between them remained strained throughout the 1960s. The United States was unhappy with this arrangement, and this was reflected in growing Washington pressure for Britain to enter the Community. EFTA significantly failed to force the Community into a wider free trade area. At the same time, the Common Market rapidly proved economically successful (Document 5.15). Within two years the British government had performed a volte-face and submitted the first application to join.

Reflecting on the signature of the Treaties of Rome on 25 March 1957, Marjòlin wrote that 'I do not believe it is an exaggeration to say that this date represents one of the greatest moments of Europe's history.'[31] Yet it was a date which had passed by many of his countrymen. In responses to opinion polls, only 64 per cent had heard of the Common Market and only 49 per cent knew that France was a member. Among those who were correctly informed, support for membership was very high, but the level of disinterest or sheer ignorance confirms that the EEC was the product of a bargain between elites. It was also a bargain whose consequences were uncertain. Much that had agitated the negotiators would seem unimportant in retrospect, while other aspects of the bargain later took on unanticipated importance.

NOTES

1. The most vigorous critic of this view is A.S. Milward, according to whom 'Most of this is myth, nurtured by federalists and other advocates of political unification as an end in itself,' *The European Rescue of the Nation-State* (London, 1992), p. 119.
2. David Arter, *The Politics of European Integration in the Twentieth Century* (Aldershot, 1993), p. 135.
3. According to the assessment of René Girault, 'Everything else is secondary'. 'La France entre l'Europe et l'Afrique', in Enrico Serra (ed.), *The Relaunching of the Treaties of Rome* (Baden-Baden, 1989), p. 352.
4. Frances M.B. Lynch, 'Restoring France: the road to integration', in Alan S. Milward *et al.*, *The Frontier of National Sovereignty* (London, 1993), p. 72.
5. Hanns Jürgen Küsters, *Fondaments de la Communauté économique européenne*, (Brussels, 1990), pp. 265-7.
6. Milward, *The European Rescue*, p. 198.
7. This on 31 May 1955. Quoted in Ulrich Enders, 'Integration oder Kooperation?', *Vierteljahreshefte für Zeitgeschichte*, Vol. 45 (1997), p. 131.
8. William Diebold Jr, *The Schuman Plan* (New York, 1959), p. 664.
9. Hanns Jürgen Küsters, 'Walter Hallstein und die Verhandlungen über die Römischen Verträge 1955-1957', in Wilfried Loth *et al.* (eds), *Walter Hallstein – Ein vergessene Europäer* (Bonn, 1995), p. 91.
10. Quoted in Percy Cradock, *In Pursuit of British Interests*, (London, 1997), p. 122.
11. Walter Lipgens (ed.), *45 Jahre Ringen um die Europäische Verfassung* (Bonn, 1986), p. 391.
12. Robert Marjòlin, *Architect of European Unity: Memoirs 1911-1986* (London, 1989), p. 285.
13. *Documents Diplomatique Française* (hereafter *DDF*), Vol. 1 (1955), doc. 308.
14. Action Committee for the United States of Europe, *Statements and Declarations 1955-67* (London, 1969), p. 11.
15. In December 1954. Peter Weilemann, *Die Anfänge der europäischen Atomgemeinschaft* (Baden-Baden, 1983), p. 39.
16. *DDF*, 1955, Vol. 1, doc. 239.
17. Küsters, 'Walter Hallstein und die Verhandlungen', p. 97.
18. *Foreign Relations of the United States 1955-1957*, Vol. 4, doc. 220.
19. *DDF*, 1956, Vol. 2, doc. 192 (18 September 1956).
20. Article 87.
21. Quoted in Pierre Guillen, 'La France et la négociation des Traités de Rome: l'Euratom', in Serra (ed.), *The Relaunching of the Treaties of Rome*, p. 518.
22. Küsters, 'Wlater Hallstein und die Verhandlungen über die Römischen Verträge', p. 98.
23. *FRUS*, 1955-1957, Vol. 4, doc. 228 (7 March 1957).
24. Lynch, 'Restoring France', pp. 77-84.
25. Hanns Jürgen Küsters, 'Adenauer's Europapolitik in der Gründungsphase der

Europäischen Wirtschaftsgemeinschaft', *Vierteljahreshefte für Zeitgeschichte*, Vol. 31 (1983), p. 660.
26. See his letter to Etzel of 16 November 1956 in Enders, 'Integration oder Kooperation?', pp. 160–4.
27. Milward, *The European Rescue of the Nation-State*, pp. 214–15.
28. Küsters, *Fondaments de la Communauté économique européenne*, p. 237.
29. Paul Taylor, *The European Union in the 1990s* (Oxford 1996), pp. 11–12.
30. Michael Charlton, *The Price of Victory* (London, 1983), p. 226.
31. Marjolin, *Architect of European Unity*, p. 306.

FURTHER READING

W. Hallstein, *Europe in the Making* (London, 1972)
R. Marjòlin, *Architect of European Unity: Memoirs 1911–1986* (London, 1989)
A.S. Milward, *The European Rescue of the Nation-State* (London, 1992)
A.S. Milward *et al.*, *The Frontier of National Sovereignty* (London, 1993)
J. Monnet, *Memoirs* (London, 1978)
J. Pinder, *European Community: The Building of a Union* (Oxford, 1991)
R. Pryce (ed.), *The Dynamics of European Union* (London, 1987)
B. Rudden and D. Wyatt (eds), *Basic Community Laws* (Oxford, 1986)
E. Serra (ed.), *The Relaunching of the Treaties of Rome* (Baden-Baden, 1989)
P.-H. Spaak, *The Continuing Battle: Memoirs of a European 1933–66* (London, 1971)
D.W. Urwin, *The Community of Europe* (London, 1991)
F.R. Willis, *France, Germany and the New Europe 1945–67* (New York, 1968)

_____ 5.1 _____

LUDWIG ERHARD ON THE CONSEQUENCES OF THE BREAKDOWN OF THE EUROPEAN DEFENCE COMMUNITY, 1954

Ludwig Erhard, _The Economics of Success_ (London: Thames & Hudson, 1963), pp. 155–6.

The following was published in September 1954. The author Ludwig Erhard was Vice-Chancellor and Minister for Economic Affairs in the German Federal Republic.

The European Defence Community has broken down in the face of French opposition, the integration tide is no longer running high, and we may well ask ourselves whether we shall have to put away any thoughts of European collaboration and consider the spirit of togetherness as dead. I myself have been one of the few who in the midst of all the clamour for drawing political frontiers have pointed out not once but dozens of times that political and military integration are on a par with economic integration, but that to try to press on too zealously would have dangerous consequences, and might well be doomed to failure or even lead to a reign of _dirigisme_. I have repeatedly pointed out that European states are so sensitive where their nationhood is concerned, and the meaning of sovereignty is so widely misinterpreted, that any proposal whatever involving a limitation of national freedom of action is held to be suspect, and that it is therefore essential to establish principles which are embodied in an accepted order and which exert so to speak an anonymous pressure on nation states.

I have always been of the opinion that European integration must be based less on institutions than on functions. It is here that the degree of economic co-operation already attained is an excellent starting-point and one which deserves more attention by statesmen. For these first steps towards European integration have come about organically, are based on insight and understanding and have been so successful that no country can any longer hold out against this trend. I refer to the efforts of OEEC, EPU, GATT and the World Bank to do away with trade barriers and discriminatory practices; to the efforts to achieve progressive liberalization and especially free convertibility of currencies. Any progress in this direction must in the nature of things strengthen the feeling for political solidarity, and it is surprising that the connection between the two has been so little realized. The irresistible progress of economic integration gives hope to all those who are aware that peace and freedom can be preserved only if all free peoples stand together. In this, France is shoulder-to-shoulder with us and I am confident that the French Prime Minister,

Mendès-France, has grasped this inter-relationship between the political and economic spheres.

_____ 5.2 _____

RESOLUTION AND JOINT DECLARATION OF THE ACTION COMMITTEE FOR THE UNITED STATES OF EUROPE, 19 JANUARY 1956

Action Committee for the United States of Europe: Statements and Declarations 1955–67 (London: RIIA, 1969), pp. 12–16.

The Action Committee, founded by Jean Monnet in October 1955, issued the following as their first major declaration, emphasizing the extension of European integration to atomic energy.

Just as the six Foreign Ministers declared in their Resolution at Messina on 1–2 June 1955, so too do our organisations believe that the establishment of a united Europe must be pursued by the development of common institutions, the progressive merger of national economies, the creation of a common market, and the progressive harmonisation of social policies.

In Brussels, experts of the 'Intergovernmental Committee created by the Messina Conference' have studied the technical problems posed by that Resolution. They have submitted their reports. In the near future the Governments will have to make the necessary decisions to translate the experts' conclusions into actual achievements.

Among these achievements that our Committee wants to be realised, the one that could and should be most rapidly carried out concerns atomic energy ... The development of atomic energy for peaceful uses opens the prospect of a new industrial revolution and the possibility of a profound change in living and working conditions.

Together, our countries are capable of themselves developing a nuclear industry. They form the only region in the world that can attain the same level as the great world powers. Yet separately they will not be able to overcome their time-lag which is a consequence of European disunity.

Action is urgently needed if Europe is not to let her opportunity pass by. An atomic industry producing atomic energy will inevitably be able to produce bombs. For that reason the political aspects and the economic aspects of atomic energy are inseparable. The European Community must develop atomic energy exclusively for peaceful purposes. This choice requires a water-tight system of control. It opens the way to general control on a world-wide scale. It in no way affects the implementation of international agreements already in force.

Mere cooperation among Governments will not suffice to achieve these objectives. It is indispensable that our Senate delegate the necessary powers and give the necessary common mandate to European institutions ...

_____ 5.3 _____

A TELEGRAM FROM THE US SECRETARY OF STATE JOHN FOSTER DULLES TO THE US EMBASSY IN BELGIUM, 26 JANUARY 1956

Foreign Relations of the United States 1955–57,
Vol. 4, pp. 399–40.

After the debacle of the European Defence Community, the United States adopted a lower profile. Nevertheless, American support was still important.

_____

For your information and guidance following represents position US will take on European Integration, Euratom and common market in forthcoming talks with Prime Minister Eden.

1. We welcome strong support UK has been giving to closer international cooperation among countries of Europe and Atlantic Community in NATO and OEEC framework. We do same.
2. But merely cooperative arrangements are not enough to meet three most serious problems in Europe.
   (a) Problem of tying Germany organically into Western Community so as to diminish danger that over time a resurgent German nationalism might trade neutrality for reunification with view seizing controlling position between East and West.
   (b) The weakness of France and need to provide positive alternative to neutralism and 'defeatism' in that country.
   (c) The solidifying of new relationship between France and Germany which has been developing since 1950 through integration movement.
3. Therefore we are concerned about British coolness to six-country integration. We believe this movement is important because it is best hope for solving three foregoing problems. Its success would justify some sacrifice of traditional US and UK interests to achieve it.
4. Six-country supranational Euratom would be a powerful means of binding Germany to West and may be most feasible means for achieving effective control over weapons-quality material. If genuinely supranational, Euratom program would be compatible with national cooperation in OEEC.
5. United States does not attach to common market proposals same immediate security and political significance as we do to Euratom. However we believe that

a common market which results in a general reduction of international trade barriers could contribute constructively to European integration. We therefore look forward with interest to concrete six-country proposals and would welcome staff talks this subject.

_____ 5.4 _____

A FRENCH VIEW OF EURATOM, 5 APRIL 1956

Documents Diplomatiques Français 1956, Vol. 1, doc. 227.

In this document the French Foreign Office listed some of the considerations behind French support for the Euratom project. The fear of German technological progress is especially notable.

Collaboration with the United States – very useful, if not indispensable – will be facilitated without doubt by the organisation of European atomic co-operation. It will permit Belgium to escape more easily from the quasi-monopoly of the United States over the uranium of the Belgian Congo. Isolated, Belgium undoubtedly will have an interest in remaining in the current situation which promises to provide atomic equipment on the cheap, in exchange for the mineral. The other European countries, presently isolated in the face of the United States, will be pitted against each other and the competition will benefit the one or those amongst us who will show the greatest aptitude for supporting extensive controls and contributing worthwhile aid to American industry.

The German situation is invoked in the same way. At first glance it might seem that if projects for European atomic co-operation do not succeed, Germany will be marked ... by a definite backwardness *vis-à-vis* France, arising from starting later than ourselves. This argument takes the short view because, first of all, Germany has a scientific and industrial potential which will allow it to develop rapidly. Besides, the French advantage, though undeniable, is very relative. Bilateral German–American or German–British co-operation will enable Germany to make up for lost time quickly. Now, this co-operation is found not only in German industrial circles but amongst American and English industrialists who are clearly interested in the power of German industry and chemical science.

5.5

A TELEGRAM FROM THE US AMBASSADOR IN FRANCE (DILLON) TO THE US DEPARTMENT OF STATE, 19 NOVEMBER 1956

Foreign Relations of the United States 1955–1957, Vol. 4, pp. 488–9.

The following casts an interesting light on the United States' response to Jean Monnet's enthusiasm for Euratom. At this time, United States' relations with Britain and France were severely strained as a consequence of the Franco-British-Israeli invasion of Egypt after Nasser's nationalization of the Suez Canal.

I had long and interesting conversation Saturday with Monnet. Theme of his thought was that unusual opportunity has been created for US to reap large dividends of goodwill from close and generous association with EURATOM. He believes that EURATOM treaty will probably be successfully completed and signed by end of year.

Monnet feels that Middle East events, i.e., closing of Suez Canal and sabotage of pipelines, have amply demonstrated unhealthy dependence of European economy on Middle East oil and necessity for development of alternate source of energy. The only substantial alternative seems to him to be atomic energy, and he feels time is ripe for very far-reaching development of atomic power in Europe, which, because of higher cost of fuel here, could develop much more rapidly than will be the case in continental US.

Monnet feels that public opinion throughout Europe would be captured by a broad scale and generous program of US support for EURATOM, both in the supply of materials and in technical cooperation. This would breathe substantial new life into President's program 'Atoms for Peace', which so far has been considered primarily as fine theory and as propaganda effort and so has failed to make any very solid impression on European public opinion.

Monnet recognizes that Middle East crisis has caused strain on Atlantic solidarity and does not feel that this can be very satisfactorily patched up, except by diverting the attention of public opinion to some other field. He feels that concrete US support of EURATOM would capture European imagination in the same way as the Marshall Plan, and could not be objected to by the Arab states. He feels that such support by the US should meet the US objective of finding some way to tighten our relationships with Europe without at the same time doing damage to our position in the Middle East.

Monnet feels that to obtain maximum of goodwill for US, it is of great importance that US accept principle that control by EURATOM organization will be adequate for US purposes, thus avoiding necessity for US inspectors in Europe.

He realizes that no firm decision by US can be taken prior to finalization of EURATOM treaty, but emphasized importance of this aspect of matter both as means of gaining goodwill for US and as important element in promoting rapid ratification of treaty.

Monnet recognizes that what he has in mind will probably require amendments to US legislation and will require relatively prompt and very high level support in the US Government if it is to be successful.

I think Monnet's idea is of real importance and I agree with his views. The US has always favored EURATOM as a means of strengthening European unity. Now, however, I think Monnet is right in feeling that EURATOM presents us with a remarkable new opportunity of improving America's position with European public opinion. I would recommend that Monnet's concept be given high level consideration in order that we can be prepared to give prompt and practical support to EURATOM as soon as it comes into being.

_____ 5.6 _____

MEMORANDUM FROM THE US STATE DEPARTMENT: THE STATE OF NEGOTIATIONS OVER EURATOM, 3 DECEMBER 1956

Foreign Relations of the United States 1955–57, Vol. 4, pp. 494–5.

In this assessment, the State Department reflected the need to balance the American desire to control the development of atomic energy and the desire to encourage the Euratom project.

While the Euratom negotiators are unanimous in their intent to develop a comprehensive and effective control system covering all aspects of atomic energy development, the supporters are equally unanimous in their view that some special arrangement must be worked out between the US and Euratom which will require inspection neither by the US along the lines of existing power bilateral arrangements, nor by the International Atomic Energy Agency. The Europeans insist that a subordinate status implicit in US inspection would make the Community politically unacceptable to the participating countries. Inspection by the Agency, when neither the US nor the UK are prepared to accept similar inspection, would be equally unacceptable and be subject to the further fundamental objection of permitting inspection of their facilities by Soviet and satellite personnel.

In recent weeks there has been a sharpening of European interest and hope in Euratom which has led to a sense of urgency on the part of its supporters in Europe. This new optimism and interest arises from the following factors:

The immediate oil crisis arising from the debacle in the Middle East has brought home to the man in the street and the politician the fact known to economists and industrialists that Europe faced a desperate long-range energy situation;

There has been increased awareness by leaders in the Six Nations that their individual national programs for developing the peaceful use of atomic energy were too modest;

Current arguments by the French military that the Middle East demonstrated the facts that no modern state can have an effective military organization without nuclear capability has intensified the feeling that Community development of atomic energy is indispensable in order to avoid or at least to minimize national competition in nuclear weapons development;

The disaster in the Middle East appears to have had on balance the effect of driving the Six Nations closer together and underscoring the need for closer economic and political integration; a further political incentive has been the surprising progress that has been made in negotiating a Common Market treaty, the tacit acceptance by the French of a 'link' between Euratom and the Common Market treaty;

And finally, the political impetus given both of these projects by the willingness of the UK to become associated with the Common Market through a free trade area.

5.7

A FRENCH ASSESSMENT OF THE EEC TREATY, 5 DECEMBER 1956

Documents Diplomatiques Français 1956, Vol. 3, doc. 262.

The French Ministry of Foreign Affairs drew up this assessment of the EEC Treaty. It reveals the persistence of doubts about the form of economic integration and about the institutional compromises which had been necessary to gain agreement between the prospective member states.

The common market has been conceived from a strictly liberal perspective. It could have equally been envisaged according to an essentially organic plan: the convergence of national policies in the economic and financial fields, and not only the commercial; envisaging common interventions and orientations within the framework of a certain supple planning, and with a view to a better European division of labour.

In the plan of the treaty, free exchange is at the base of the common market. But it is a case of free exchange corrected by negative elements – and only by those – of a more organic conception.

The precautions taken envisage nothing to manage the necessary transitions to the integral execution of a common and considered economic policy. What competition loses in liberty is nowhere compensated by a greater organic unity of the economies ...

The diversity of the safeguard clauses will not compensate for the absence of a harmonisation of the conditions of production. Partial harmonisation of social charges, far from sufficing to eliminate disparities between national economies, will create new distortions between industries of the same country ...

If the treaty had been composed of simple but complete mechanisms, its implementation would have depended upon respect by each government for engagements undertaken, with, eventually, arbitration of disputes by a common magistrature ...

The system, as presently envisaged, is at once complex and partial. In numerous areas, the definition of measures to be taken is consigned to common organs ... When, however, automatic procedures have been fixed, they are accompanied with multiple derogations. Each measure of the treaty incorporates, in itself, the possibility for future discussion.

Now, a supranational authority of a technical character cannot pretend to arbitrate every divergence of view, to impose its interpretation of treaty-framework and to impart a communal orientation to the economies of the member states. In its more limited field of action, the High Authority, little by little, has had to limit itself to the role of a guardian of the letter of the treaty and to renounce that of a promoter of common policy. Admittedly, relatively important powers have been accorded, in the market of the six, to the Council of Ministers of the member states, but this is a question of politics, designed to appease the doubts in certain quarters about an excessively supranational Community. It is nor certain that it will suffice to give all the required authority to the institutions of the common market, as this is presently conceived.

In effect, insofar as the treaty leads to the establishment of the intended institutions, economic integration is not a stage towards political integration; on the contrary it seems to be conditioned by the latter.

In summary, the compromise elaborated at Brussels without doubt increases chances of the ratification of the treaty; but it cannot be excluded that it will compromise the success of its future application.

5.8

PASCAL FONTAINE: 'LE COMITÉ D'ACTION POUR LES ETATS-UNIS D'EUROPE DE JEAN MONNET', 1957

Pascal Fontaine, quoted in Robert Marjòlin, *Memoirs 1911–1986* (London: Weidenfeld & Nicolson, 1989), pp. 298–9.

For a while in 1955–56, a number of the supporters of European integration were not conspicuously enthusiastic about the proposal for a Common Market. Jean Monnet, for one, felt that to work simultaneously for Euratom and the Common Market was to overload the agenda.

What was the reason for this omission? Could it have been a miscalculation on the part of Jean Monnet and the members of the Committee? In fact, it was a deliberate choice and a gamble. To choose the domain of atomic energy, to propose a supranational community, this was inherently inconsistent with the principles and the method that had brought the ECSC into being: namely, the delegation of sovereignty in a circumscribed but decisive area. A new, specialized community would do more for European construction than the scheme, too vague and too general, for economic unification. Jean Monnet was not unaware that this economic Community was receiving as much attention from the experts and politicians as the atomic Community. The conclusion of the Spaak Committee's report was that two treaties were necessary. Did Jean Monnet think that only the Euratom treaty would be fortunate enough to see the light of day, being more realistic, more limited in its scope and in the sacrifices it would impose on the signatory states? Be that as it may, there is no doubt that he visualised the atomic Community the more clearly of the two, the economic union being only a hazy image in his mind.

Furthermore, it seemed to him more effective to concentrate the Committee's efforts on one goal, and here he had the members' agreement. The gamble was lost, as we know, for the future of Euratom would soon be compromised both by France's nuclear policy and by the massive exploitation of oil deposits.

_____ 5.9 _____

RESUMÉ OF THE DEBATE IN THE FRENCH NATIONAL ASSEMBLY ON THE RATIFICATION OF THE ROME TREATIES FOR THE EEC AND EURATOM, 2–9 JULY 1957

W. Rossenberger and H. Tobin (eds), *Keesing's Contemporary Archives, 1957*, Vol. 2 (London, Longman Group, 1957), p. 15957.

In contrast to the EDC (see Chapter 4), these treaties were passed by the Assembly by 342 to 239 votes.

M. Pineau [Foreign Minister] refuted the argument that the creation of a 'Little Europe' would impede the creation of a 'Big Europe'. He declared that the interest of other countries (and more especially Great Britain) in Europe would be all the greater once 'solid and dynamic' European organisations were in existence. On the question of the participation of overseas territories in the Common Market M. Pineau maintained that the treaty, in fact, dealt more favourably with the 'territoires d'outre mer' than with metropolitan France, for the following reasons: a) the territories would receive an ever-increasing flow of cheaply-priced goods; b) they would have big new markets for their own products; c) they would be entitled to set up customs barriers to protect their own industries; d) the Community countries would provide them with funds for investment.

Turning to the situation which would arise if Germany were reunified, M. Pineau said that if a reunified Germany decided to withdraw from the European Communities, that, in the French Government's opinion, would entail their dissolution. On the other hand, if a reunified Germany were to take the Federal Republic's place as a Community member, any of the other member-countries would be entitled to withdraw on that account. However, it was impossible to say exactly what would happen in the event of German reunification, since no one knew what the terms of a reunification agreement would be, or, more specifically, whether a reunified Germany would assume the existing commitments of the Federal-Republic.

M. Mendès-France [formerly Prime Minister] attacked the Treaties on several grounds. He asserted, first, that the main beneficiary of the Common Market would be the Rhineland and that it would be the fate of French underdeveloped regions, such as Brittany, to provide labour for Germany. Secondly ... there were really seven members in the two communities, the seventh being East Germany, which would enjoy all the benefits of the system but would be under no obligation towards it. Moreover, the products of the east European and Scandinavian countries would have unimpeded entry to the Common Market zone across the customs-free German zonal boundary. Thirdly, as regards the overseas territories, he criticised the fact that while France's five partners were committed for no more than five years to assist financially in their development, the overseas territories themselves would be open indefinitely to the products of other member-countries.

[He] ... went on to declare that while European economic integration was greatly to be desired, France was not really ready to embark upon such an experiment at that particular moment. It was very doubtful whether the French economy would be out of difficulties within 18 months when the first tariff reductions were due to be made. Moreover, the Algerian campaign, with its attendant effects on the national economy, was likely to continue for another two or three years ...

M. Maurice Faure [Secretary of State for Foreign Affairs and chief representative for France on the Intergovernmental Committee which worked out the two treaties] had previously emphasised that, far from impeding the recovery of the French economy, the Common Market would actually help to bring it about. Replying to those critics who had expressed concern lest France would be compelled to implement decisions of the Council of Ministers of the Community in the event of a balance-of-payments crisis, M. Faure declared that these decisions would certainly not be in the form of a 'Diktat' but would be the result of free deliberations. He asked in this connection what interest the five other member countries could have in ruining the sixth at the price of being unable to sell their own goods to it any longer.

Replying to critics who had expressed concern about the situation of French farmers, M. Faure declared that France 'with the richest and most varied land in the Community' would now get the 'industrial masses of the North of Europe' as buyers without any barriers or limitations – an opportunity which she should seize by conducting an 'active, and at the same time, reasonable agricultural policy, charging fair prices'. French farm production would be protected against non-Community countries by the common customs tariff, while, as regards cereals, farmers would be protected by the system of long-term contracts between member-countries.

M. Bourgès-Manoury [Prime Minister] speaking on the last day of the debate, emphasised that if France refused to ratify the treaties she would run the risk of 'political and economic isolation'. Moreover, the other five countries might go ahead to create the Community without French participation, in which case France would be without the guarantees now accorded to her. Referring particularly to French relations with Western Germany, [he] declared 'Our wish has been always to set up a democratic and stable framework firm enough to guide the expansion of German industrial power in the direction of the common interests of the European countries, and sufficiently flexible to guarantee respect of our own fundamental interests ... Those who fear the weight of Germany at our side should think about the weight of a Germany not linked with us, or even ranged against us.' In conclusion he emphasised that the Government would neglect no effort to bring about a wider trade association including, above all, Great Britain.

M. Robert Schuman (MRP), M. Paul Reynaud (Independent) and M. René Pleven [all former Prime Ministers and protagonists of European unification] warmly supported the ratification. M. Duclos for the Communists denounced the treaties as 'an economic-military enterprise of a syndicate of capitalist exploiters serving German imperialism'.

5.10

THE TREATY OF ROME ESTABLISHING THE EUROPEAN ECONOMIC COMMUNITY, 25 MARCH 1957

Common Market Law: Text and Commentaries (London: Stevens and Sons, 1962), pp. 206–303.

The following is only a selection of the 248 articles which made up the Treaty. It outlined the Community institutional framework and sphere of competence.

Article 8

1. The Common Market shall be progressively established in the course of a transitional period of twelve years.

The transitional period shall be divided into three stages of four years each; the length of each stage may be modified in accordance with the provisions set out below.

2. To each stage there shall be allotted a group of actions which shall be undertaken and pursued concurrently.

3. Transition from the first to the second stage shall be conditional upon a confirmatory statement to the effect that the essence of the objectives specifically laid down in this Treaty for the first stage has been in fact achieved and that, subject to the exception and procedures provided for in this Treaty, the obligations have been observed.

This statement shall be made at the end of the fourth year by the Council acting by means of a unanimous vote on a report of the Commission. The invocation by a Member State of the non-fulfilment of its own obligations shall not, however, be an obstacle to a unanimous vote. Failing a unanimous vote, the first stage shall automatically be extended for a period of one year.

At the end of the fifth year, the Council shall make such confirmatory statement under the same conditions. Failing a unanimous vote, the first stage shall automatically be extended for a further period of one year.

At the end of the sixth year, the Council shall make such a statement acting by means of a qualified minority vote on a report of the Commission ...

Article 9

1. The Community shall be based upon a customs union covering the exchange of all goods and comprising both the prohibition, as between Member States, of customs duties on importation and exportation and all charges with equivalent effect and the adoption of a common customs tariff in their relations with third countries ...

Article 12

Member states shall refrain from introducing as between themselves, any new customs duties on importation or exportation or charges with equivalent effect and from increasing such duties or charges as they apply in their commercial relations with each other.

Article 38

1. The Common Market shall extend to agriculture and trade in agricultural products. Agricultural products shall mean the products of the soil, of stock-breeding and of fisheries as well as products after the first processing stage which are directly connected with such products ...

4. The functioning and development of the Common Market in respect of agricultural products shall be accompanied by the establishment of a common agricultural policy among the Member States ...

Article 39

1. The common agricultural policy shall have as its objectives:

(a) to increase agricultural productivity by developing technical progress and by ensuring the rational development of agricultural production and the optimum utilisation of the factors of production, particularly labour;
(b) to ensure thereby a fair standard of living for the agricultural population, particularly by the increasing of the individual earnings of persons engaged in agriculture;
(c) to stabilise markets;
(d) to guarantee regular supplies; and
(e) to ensure reasonable prices in supplies to consumers.

2. In working out the common agricultural policy and the special methods which it may involve, due account shall be taken of:

(a) the particular character of agricultural activities, arising from the social structure of agriculture and from structural and natural disparities between the various agricultural regions;
(b) the need to make the appropriate adjustments gradually; and
(c) the fact that in Member States agriculture constitutes a sector which is closely linked with the economy as a whole.

_____5.11_____

BRITISH MEMORANDUM TO THE ORGANIZATION FOR EUROPEAN ECONOMIC CO-OPERATION REGARDING A EUROPEAN FREE TRADE AREA, 7 FEBRUARY 1957

Cmnd 72 (London: HMSO, 1957), pp. 433–4, 436.

The British proposal of a Free Trade Area met with a mixed response. While Ludwig Erhard supported it (see Introduction), Paul-Henri Spaak preferred the Common Market to this 'much more modest enterprise which offered no prospect of a European political union'.*

Her Majesty's Government are glad that the negotiations which were set in train in June 1955 for the establishment of a Customs and Economic Union consisting of France, Germany, Italy, Belgium, Holland and Luxembourg are now approaching a successful conclusion. There are, however, substantial reasons why the United Kingdom could not become a member of such a Union. These arise in particular from the United Kingdom's interests and responsibilities in the Commonwealth. If the United Kingdom were to join the Customs and Economic Union, the United Kingdom tariff would be replaced by a single common tariff with the other member countries against the rest of the world. This would mean that goods entering the United Kingdom from the Commonwealth would have to pay duty at the same rate as goods coming from any other third country not a member of the Customs and Economic Union, while goods from the Union would be admitted free of duty. Her Majesty's Government could not contemplate entering arrangements which would in principle make it impossible for the United Kingdom to treat imports from the Commonwealth at least as favourably as those from Europe.

... At the same time it is of great importance in the view of Her Majesty's Government to establish free trade over as wide an area as possible within west Europe. It was for this reason that Her Majesty's Government strongly supported the decision taken by the Council of OEEC in July 1956 that a study should be made urgently to discover whether other member countries of the Organisation could be associated with the Customs and Economic Union ...

Her Majesty's Government's concept of the Free Trade Area differs in some important respects from that of the Customs and Economic Union now contem- plated by the Messina Powers. The arrangements proposed for the Customs and Economic Union involve far-reaching provisions for economic integration and harmonisation of financial and social policies, and for mutual assistance in the financing of investment. These arrangements are to be effected within an

* Paul-Henri Spaak, *The Continuing Battle* (London, 1971), p. 236.

appropriate institutional framework. Her Majesty's Government envisage the Free Trade Area, on the other hand, as a concept related primarily to the removal of restrictions on trade such as tariffs and quotas. Nevertheless, Her Majesty's Government recognise that co-operation in the field of economic policy is of great and continuing importance. In practice an appreciable movement towards closer economic co-operation may be expected to take place among the members of a Free Trade Area over a period of years, either as a matter of deliberate policy or as a spontaneous development.

5.12

A STATEMENT BY WALTER HALLSTEIN, PRESIDENT OF THE COMMISSION, TO THE EUROPEAN PARLIAMENTARY ASSEMBLY, 20 MARCH 1958

Miriam Camps, *Britain and the European Community 1955–1963* (Oxford, Oxford University Press, 1964), p. 149.

Hallstein had served as State Secretary in the German Foreign Office and had worked closely with Jean Monnet in bringing about the European Coal and Steel Community before becoming the first President of the Commission.

We should state clearly that we reject this charge of discrimination and that therefore the argument about division which has been built up on it is invalid ... it is indeed true that the consequence of setting up the Community is that transactions within the Community are treated differently from transactions between the Community or its Members and the outside world. There is therefore differentiation. But differentiation is not always discrimination ... Discrimination may be said to exist only when the same situation is handled differently without justification. This, however, is not the case. The situations are not the same.

The European Economic Community represents one situation. That, we all know, does not mean only the abolition of customs barriers and of innumerable restrictions on trade between the six Member States; nor is it only a customs union with a uniform external tariff. It is the harmonization, co-ordination, even unification, of major aspects of economic policy and profoundly modifies the economic policy of the six States ... Thus there can only be discrimination, in other words an unwarranted differentiation in the treatment of other European States, if the Six deny to other European States the treatment which they accord one another, that is, if they refuse admission to a State which is willing to pay the same price as the Six for the advantages of membership of the customs union. Obviously that has not happened. Quite the opposite: the Treaty embodies the principle of the open door.

5.13

A STATEMENT BY THE PRESIDENT OF THE UK BOARD OF TRADE REGINALD MAUDLING TO THE CONSULTATIVE ASSEMBLY AT THE COUNCIL OF EUROPE, 27 APRIL 1959

Council of Europe, *Report of Debates*, 27 April 1959, pp. 273–4.

This was a direct criticism of the views of the European Commission. Maudling's defence of 'European discrimination' was strikingly similar to the Hallstein argument for 'Community discrimination', however.

The first question we must ask ourselves is whether there is a need for a European solution. I am myself confident that the answer of the Assembly will be 'Yes'. I say 'a' European solution meaning to emphasise that it must be one solution for all the seventeen members of the OEEC, a multilateral solution and not a bilateral agreement . . . There must be one solution, and it must be a European solution, in the sense that it is a system for Europe whereby we do not discriminate against one another but we do discriminate against the rest of the world; we treat one another, as Europeans, differently from the way in which we treat other countries, but we treat one another as Europeans in the same way as we treat all other Europeans.

There are some people who say the opposite of that. They say that the Community must find its place in the world as a whole and not merely in Europe. They say that while it is true that the Community has problems in its relations with Scandinavia and Switzerland, it equally has problems of relations with the United States, Japan and Costa Rica. I do not accept that point of view, and I do not think that any of us who support the ideal of Europe as a unity can support that idea. If we have before us this ideal of Europe as the home of our civilisation and as a cultural, social and political entity, surely we must believe in Europe as an economic entity. Unless we all regard ourselves as Europeans and as members of a European system in solving our economic problems, we shall soon find it impossible to do so in solving some of the great political problems. I conclude that we must seek a single multilateral system for Europe, meaning by Europe all seventeen members of the OEEC.

5.14

PRESS RELEASE: STOCKHOLM DRAFT PLAN FOR A EUROPEAN FREE TRADE ASSOCIATION, 21 JULY 1959

Cmnd 823 (London: HMSO, 1959), pp. 3–5.

Having failed to persuade the six members of the EEC to join a free trade area, seven other European states formed EFTA. The importance of their relations with the EEC is evident in the press release.

Ministers from Austria, Denmark, Norway, Portugal, Sweden, Switzerland and the United Kingdom met at Stockholm on 20th and 21st July, 1959.

Ministers decided to recommend to their Governments that a European Free Trade Association among the Seven countries should be established. The object of this association would be to strengthen the economies of its members by promoting expansion of economic activity, full employment, a rising standard of living and financial stability. Ministers affirmed that in establishing a European Free Trade Association it would be their purpose to facilitate early negotiations both with the European Economic Community and also with the other members of the OEEC who have particular problems calling for special solutions. These negotiations would have as their object to remove trade barriers and establish a multilateral association embracing all members of the OEEC. Governments would thus be able to reinforce European economic co-operation within the OEEC and to promote the expansion of world trade. Ministers approved the draft plan for a European Free Trade Association, which they decided should be published, and instructed officials to draft a Convention, using the draft plan as a basis in the light of discussions at the ministerial meeting and to present a text for submission to Ministers by 31 October 1959.

_____5.15_____

COMPARATIVE TRADE GROWTH, 1953–1963

OECD, *General Statistics* (Paris, 1963).

The figures below illustrate the high rate of growth of intra-EEC trade.

Comparative trade growth, 1953–63 (millions of US dollars or index 1953 = 100)

Year	Intra-EEC	Intra-EFTA	Intra-OECD* (excluding EEC)	Intra-European OECD (excluding EEC)	Intra-North America	World (Index)
1953	334	190	1,302	847	455	100
1954	388	201	1,307	879	428	106
1955	471	213	1,499	1,016	483	118
1956	536	227	1,661	1,091	570	127
1957	597	243	2,644	1,188	576	135
1958	566	233	2,480	1,143	530	133
1959	674	299	2,715	1,225	584	144
1960	845	288	3,049	1,425	565	161
1961	975	315	3,190	1,582	563	169
1962	1,116	335	3,388	1,710	605	181
1963	1,311	356	3,290	1,690	640	193

* Non-EEC OECD comprises Canada, United States, Austria, Denmark, Greece, Ireland, Norway, Portugal, Sweden, United Kingdom and Yugoslavia.

_____5.16_____

FOREIGN TRADE OF EFTA STATES, 1958

'Sieben und EWG', PA AA 353/Ref. 200-1 A2 (18 June 1959), in Wolfram Kaiser, 'Challenge to the Community', *Journal of European Integration History*, Vol. 3 (1997), p. 12.

The figures below indicate the importance of the EEC to many EFTA states.

Exports of EFTA states as a percentage of total exports (1958)

	To EFTA	To EEC	To OEEC
Austria	10.5	49.7	62.6
Denmark	40.3	31.7	73.4
Norway	37.5	27.3	66.2
Portugal	17.5	24.7	43.1
Sweden	34.9	31.0	67.3
Switzerland	15.5	39.2	55.8
United Kingdom	10.1	13.1	27.4

Imports of EFTA states as a percentage of total imports (1958)

	From EFTA	From EEC	From OEEC
Austria	11.2	55.6	66.8
Denmark	39.6	36.1	76.0
Norway	37.8	35.3	73.5
Portugal	21.6	39.2	61.5
Sweden	24.5	41.8	66.7
Switzerland	10.8	58.8	70.0
United Kingdom	9.7	14.1	27.2

CHAPTER 6

THE CONSOLIDATION OF INTEGRATION AND ITS LIMITS IN THE WEST

1959–1968

INTRODUCTION

The Community developed with conspicuous economic success in the 1960s. Politically, too, it started to assert a new presence on the international stage. The establishment of association agreements with the former colonies of the Six gave preferential treatment for a range of imports from (mainly African) developing countries to the common market, and established a development fund which increased the European aid effort considerably. Moreover, even before the common external tariffs were fully established, the Community began to agree common positions in international economic negotiations, notably in the embattled all-European negotiations over tariff reductions with the OEEC and its successor organizations – the Committee of the Twenty, then reformed as the OECD – and in the Kennedy Round of the GATT for tariff reductions with the other industrialized countries.

As observers watched Community policies develop, they saw in them a new way of looking at international relations based on the natural interest of nations in cooperation rather than the classical 'realist' view of international relations as an inevitably anarchic contest over power and resources. The increasing confidence of the Community's founders, however, contrasted with the disharmony within the Community between 1962 and 1966. Economic success was combined with significant political difficulties, which exposed very differing perceptions of the future of the Community (Documents 6.1, 6.2).

In the event, progress towards a customs union was faster than had been planned in the EEC Treaty. The first step was taken on 1 January 1959, when tariffs between member states were cut by 10 per cent. The protocol to the Treaty which provided safeguards for France did not need to be invoked. Erhard had been right all along. France's problem had been an overvalued franc. Devaluation and other financial reforms under de Gaulle's new government solved the problem.[1] The Commission, backed by Germany, then proposed the acceleration of further tariff cuts, which on 12 May 1960 the Council of Ministers agreed. By 1 July 1962 customs duties among the Six had been reduced by half and the third and final stage of the establishment of free trade within the customs union was concluded in 1968, a year and a half before schedule. There had been fears that progress towards the customs union would lead to the outbreak of a trade war with the EFTA states. So severe were these fears that the British Prime Minister Harold Macmillan speculated upon a retreat to 'fortress Britain', though a junior minister noted that this was impossible save at the cost of 'a reduced (and electorally unsaleable) standard of living'.[2] The EEC's acceleration of tariff reductions further demonstrated the wider interdependencies in Europe as it forced EFTA to try, unsuccessfully, to match the EEC's progress.[3]

The success of the EEC was soon proven. Trade in industrial products between the Community member states doubled in four years and the average growth among the economies of the Six in the 1960s reached between 5 and 6 per cent. Predictions that the weaker economies – France and Italy – would lose from increased competition within the common market proved groundless, since France and Italy in fact increased their trade far more than the other member states, and their economies appeared to be converging with that of West Germany. Germany, on the other hand, also made gains of her own, particularly in catching up with French manufacturers in the private car market. The smaller Benelux states had a far greater proportion of their imports and exports staked on the common market, but their gains from the new competitive conditions had less effect on them because they had already begun to adjust to a lower tariff regime ten or more years before.

Tariff reductions for agricultural trade proved far more difficult. Intermittent discussions on the subject during the first stage of the common market were concluded by marathon sessions in December 1961 and January 1962, after the French and Dutch governments had insisted on reaching agreement on the foundations of a Common Agricultural Policy (CAP) before the second stage of the common market. The French added that there could be no discussions over British membership of the Community before the establishment of the CAP.

The partial removal of barriers to trade in agricultural produce was a matter of broad consensus among member states. They all had managed and protected markets and intended to keep them so. Tensions focused now more on the level of agricultural prices within the Community, which the Benelux countries believed should be kept low by means of low duties on agricultural imports, while Germany, France and Italy argued that a higher proportion of the agricultural population could be sustained with less cost to the governments if import levies and consumer prices were higher. The result was a compromise that leaned further to the Franco-German position than most observers expected. In the event, hopes that the higher level would facilitate the modernization of French, Italian and, to a lesser extent, German agriculture and at the same time the liberalization of world agricultural trade proved over-optimistic – all the member states could do was stave off open revolt from European farmers by increasing their financial support. By the 1980s, a mass migration from the countryside had decimated the rural population, yet still the CAP was taking up nearly 70 per cent of the EC budget.[4]

As part of the package of compromises leading to the breakthrough on agri-culture, France accepted the implementation of Articles 85 and 86 covering competition rules. As Hans von der Groeben, a Commissioner at the time, later argued, this was important not only because of its contribution towards the creation of the common market but also because the Council accepted that 'Articles 85 and 86 of the Treaty were matters of European law, to be interpreted and applied by the Commission and the Court of Justice, i.e. the two supranational institutions which are independent of the member states.'[5]

In these as in other issues, the fortunes of the Community now depended heavily on the policies and personality of the new French President Charles de Gaulle, who had come to power in France in 1958 in the severe national crisis over Algeria. Since de Gaulle had attacked both the ECSC and the EDC, it was a reasonable supposition that he might attempt to reverse the decision to ratify the EEC and Euratom treaties. This was not to be. He was quick to see the potential economic benefits of the EEC to France, provided her agricultural interests were protected, and the potential political benefits of a stronger European Community – and provided, again, the Community did not develop along supranational lines, encroaching upon French sovereignty. Indeed, for de Gaulle the cohesion of the Six offered the prospect of French political leadership in Europe, a platform for the revival of France's fortunes as a power on the international stage.

The Community was set to become an important force in the global economy – an economic giant. But the Community's strengths did not, at this stage, extend to foreign or defence policy. It was not a political giant and in particular could not form a distinctive common policy on the Cold War. The Europeans proved unable to agree on how to coordinate their foreign policies, although at the end of the 1950s there seemed to be increasing consensus in favour of an intergovernmental structure to balance the developing supranationalism in the Community.

De Gaulle's interest in European cooperation was increased when President Eisenhower rejected his 1958 proposal for a triumvirate (consisting of France, Britain and the United States) to coordinate policy within NATO. His tentative suggestions for the coordination of foreign policy met with a mixed response. Germany was sufficiently interested to make its own proposals for regular consultation in October 1959, proposals which were substantially adopted in the following month. German willingness to cooperate did not signify total agreement. At the beginning of 1960, the Foreign Office noted that 'We have to expect from de Gaulle's France certain requests for French leadership over continental Europe which we cannot accept because of our situation and our interests. We therefore have to reject carefully these requests without hurting French sensitivity.'[6] Chancellor Adenauer, however, was more sympathetic to de Gaulle both because of the importance of Franco-German reconciliation and because of his increasing suspicions of a lack of Anglo-American resolve over Berlin. The Netherlands and Belgium distrusted de Gaulle, not least because of his 1958 proposals for NATO, which would have relegated them to second-class status within the Alliance.[7] Yet it was only the strongly Atlanticist Netherlands which held to a course of consistent opposition to de Gaulle. Isolated, The Netherlands found it difficult to resist the evolving compromises between the others. The compromise was further elaborated by the main statesmen of the Community in the course of 1960, and was embodied in the Bonn Declaration of July 1961 and the French government's draft treaty of November 1961, known as the Fouchet Plan. This envisaged an intergovernmental arrangement with little parliamentary supervision and promised a review of what further integration might be possible after three years.

The French proposals considered by the Fouchet Commission envisaged that major political decisions on foreign and defence policy matters, as well as cultural and scientific matters, were to be taken unanimously by the heads of government at state summit meetings. The other five feared that the proposals anticipated the amendment of the Treaty of Rome to create a political union with a new agenda and agenda-setting mechanism. There would be a separate European Political Commission comprising officials of the foreign ministries of the Six, who would reside in Paris and coordinate agendas for meetings of foreign ministers and of the heads of state. De Gaulle aggravated the disagreements by revising a tentative compromise. One of his own ambassadors conceded that de Gaulle 'could not resist the temptation to add two or three little touches'.[8] De Gaulle's 'little touches' inflamed suspicions that he intended to weaken NATO and to undermine the supranational structure of the existing Communities. As Belgian Foreign Minister Paul-Henri Spaak recalled, 'everything we wanted had been left out and all those measures we most disliked had been included'.[9]

There was here a potential link between these proposals and the issue of British entry to the Community, which The Netherlands, backed by Belgium, insisted on as a precondition for agreement in the Fouchet talks. There was a certain irony in French opposition to British entry, in that the intergovernmental mode of decision-making favoured by Fouchet was much more congenial to the British government than the mode envisaged in the Rome Treaty, which provided for the staged introduction of majority voting. If Britain and the other applicant states were to enter the EEC they would have to accept majority decisions taken on the ordinary agenda. But the Fouchet Plan would ensure that any extraordinary agenda items, especially those involving matters of political significance that would threaten British sovereign interests, could be vetoed by Britain. At least on this narrow basis, de Gaulle and the British government shared an intergovernmentalist view of the Community's future. (For de Gaulle's view see Document 6.4.)

De Gaulle, however, was not convinced of British commitment to Europe, and saw her as a Trojan horse for American influence. Adenauer also had doubts about British entry. He was ambivalent about the economic implications of British membership, but the prime issue was Germany's relationship with France, as he made clear to his own cabinet in June 1962: 'I judge the situation from a political perspective and not from a trade-political viewpoint ... I say that tariff agreements have to remain behind political questions and the question which decides our history is not our relationship to England, but that between us and France.'[10] Yet, as John Pinder explained, 'The Fouchet Plan foundered because it provoked sharp opposition among France's five partners: partly because of a cleavage between de Gaulle's policy towards the United States and theirs; partly because federalists objected to the stress on intergovernmental at the expense of federalist institutions'.[11] It was in particular opposed by the three smaller states in the EEC who wanted the applications from the United Kingdom, Denmark and Ireland to be settled before political union was considered. With France unable to persuade its EEC partners, the Plan was abandoned in 1962.[12] All that was left of the Fouchet Plan was the Franco-German Treaty of January 1963. This bilateral agreement was later to be seen as the culmination of efforts towards Franco-German reconciliation and the framework for subsequent cooperation. At the time its reception was ambivalent. The German parliament added a preamble to its ratification, stressing its contribution to the Atlantic community and the integration of Europe, including Britain.[13] Neither corresponded to de Gaulle's vision of the Treaty. The atmosphere was not helped by the lapidary observation of Ludgwig Erhard: 'Bilateralism is dead.'[14]

The rejection of the Fouchet Plan contributed to the growing divide between France and the other member states, which culminated in the 'empty chair crisis' of 1965. The failure of the project for a Union of States meant that there was to be no political cooperation in the Communities throughout the whole of the 1960s. There were no more summits, apart from a very formal one in Rome in 1967, and the periodic meetings of foreign ministers begun in 1960 were no longer held after the first veto against British entry (January 1963).[15] New possibilities of political cooperation emerged only after de Gaulle's departure. But the affair of the Fouchet Plan had left its mark, and useful lessons were learnt for the future.[16]

The failure of Fouchet was followed, in January 1963, by de Gaulle's veto of British entry (Document 6.5). The British decision to apply had not been an easy one. As the late Professor Northedge commented, there were distinctive perceptions about European integration on either side of the Channel:

For continental Europeans who had looked forward to the opportunity to build a united Europe during the long years of Nazi occupation, bodies like the Council of Europe, the Coal and Steel Community, the Economic Community were the fulfilment. For Britain, joining organisations such as these represented the disappointment of expectations of hopes of better things. In their inmost thoughts the

British were never really convinced about the merits of European unity. Unity was all right as a slogan ... but it was not a programme for practical action.[17]

Nevertheless, by 1961 Britain had reversed her position, and on 31 July Prime Minister Harold Macmillan announced an application to join. He had been left in no doubt by President Kennedy of the continuing enthusiasm and encouragement of the United States in general for European integration and in particular for Britain to become a member too (Document 6.3). Macmillan's wish further to strengthen the Anglo-American relationship was one of the considerations which led the Prime Minister to open negotiations. Others were the transparent economic success of the common market, the very evident decline of Commonwealth trade with Britain by contrast with the increase of trade with Europe, the relative failure of the European Free Trade Association (EFTA) to offer comparable advantages to those of the Community, fear of exclusion from the new trading bloc, and the desire to reassert British influence in the world.

With decolonization and the decline of empire (particularly the 'Wind of Change' in Africa), Britain at last, and belatedly, started to reorientate her policy towards a more, though not exclusively, regional role. Macmillan was, perhaps, primarily concerned with the additional diplomatic leverage which Britain would gain with its American ally once it was inside the Community. A string of diplomatic failures and problems financing Britain's military position as a global power convinced Macmillan that Britain would soon be superseded by the Community as America's closest partner. He persuaded the cabinet and Conservative Party that there was no alternative. Dubious of the declining value of the American alliance, unable to fashion a French alliance and foiled in the attempt to create a kind of west European organization most appropriate to British interests, the British Government embarked on a course, as Peter Calvocoressi has pointed out, 'which was a long way from the top of its list of priorities'.[18] The decision to apply was taken against a background of public indifference. There was no great pressure from the governing Conservative Party or from business interests. Advocates of integration had even been hesitant about putting the real issues before Cabinet.[19]

While the Community formally welcomed Britain's application, it soon became evident that the French were doing everything possible in the negotiations to ensure that the British could enter only at a very heavy price. Britain's opposition to the Community had earlier strengthened the resolve of the Six to forge ahead without her. Now Britain's application had exactly the same effect – France insisting that progress had to be made in agreements over the CAP, overseas territories and political union before Britain might enter. The particularly difficult economic issue was Commonwealth produce. For Britain, the formation of the CAP before she entered was the worst element in this, since the United Kingdom had hoped that its influence would prevent price levels from being as high as they proved to be. Indeed, this was one of the reasons why Macmillan made the application at a relatively early stage.

The negotiations over Britain joining the CAP after its ground rules had been established proved, therefore, to be the toughest obstacle to British membership, prompting opposition from British farmers and, in a less uncompromising fashion, from most Commonwealth leaders. The British adopted, too, a somewhat uncompromising line in the negotiations, mainly for tactical reasons, but this had a negative effect on the Six. Nor did Macmillan seriously attempt to mobilize British public opinion in favour of the application. By the end of 1962 de Gaulle was looking for pretexts to end the negotiations, and he found one in the Nassau agreement between Macmillan and Kennedy, by which Britain had made its defence strategy dependent on the American supply of Polaris nuclear missiles. At a televised press conference on 14 January 1963, de Gaulle rejected a similar offer from the US and accused Macmillan (unfairly, it seems) of having misled him. Britain had proved, he argued, that it was not truly 'European' in its commitment, and the deadlock in negotiations in October–November 1962 was a further reason for breaking off the negotiations.

De Gaulle's veto came as a very considerable shock. It made a mockery of the promised consultation in the Franco-German Treaty, which was signed only days after de Gaulle's veto. The anger of the other five was clearly expressed by Spaak at the final session in Brussels. The negotiators for the other five even discussed the option of ignoring de Gaulle and forming a new grouping, though enthusiasm for such a radical option dissipated overnight.[20] De Gaulle's reason for rejection was largely political, as Edward Heath, the chief British negotiator, noted in his statement at the meeting: de Gaulle had one view of Europe, the British Government had another. Macmillan thought that the French President's opposition was more fundamental: the British would be a competitor for influence over the Community, and de Gaulle had terminated the negotiations just when it seemed they might succeed. The Polaris arrangement had conflicted with de Gaulle's proclaimed mission to free Europe from the 'double hegemony' of the superpowers in the cold war. The rejection of Britain was part and parcel of his campaign against 'Anglo-Saxon' influence and for a 'European Europe' – one in which French influence might be paramount. Humiliating as it was for the British, de Gaulle's speech was also a reminder to all potential applicants that full membership demanded not only technical and policy adjustments to the Treaties, but also a more profound reorientation of political attitudes.

In 1962, the British Labour Party decided to oppose the Macmillan application. The Labour parliamentary leader Hugh Gaitskell invoked Commonwealth ties and warned against the end of 'one thousand years of history' since the Anglo-Saxons established an English kingdom.[21] When Labour came to power in 1964 there was little enthusiasm for a new application. Only as it became clear that there was little alternative did senior members of the cabinet gradually move towards a new bid. Other EFTA governments supported this, since Britain's pivotal trading position was critical in bringing about the wider open market to which both groups aspired. French reservations were again voiced, this time compounded by concerns over the British economic position, leading to the devaluation crisis of November 1967.

At a press conference in that month, de Gaulle restated his doubts about Britain's ability to make the necessary adjustments, concluding that 'in order that the British Isles can really make fast to the Continent, there is still a very vast and deep mutation to be effected'.[22] The other five announced their support for the British application, but to no avail. Until 1969, his final year in office, de Gaulle continued to play with the possibility of British EC membership in exchange for the establishment of political union. By then, the British Government was tired of waiting. It leaked a suggestion that the French President had made to the British Ambassador in Paris, Sir Christopher Soames, offering a close political and military alliance excluding the smaller states in the Community. The motives for this diplomatic indiscretion are disputed. The British distrusted de Gaulle's motives. There was a lack of coordination which served to aggravate the situation.[23] Whatever the motives, British entry, together with that of Denmark and Ireland, had now to wait for de Gaulle's successor, Georges Pompidou.

The momentum of the Community derived from three main sources: the implementation of the Rome Treaties; the need for the Community to negotiate as an entity with other countries and blocs; and the development of the institutions. France had set the pace of European integration with the Schuman and Pleven Plans, but now, it seemed, her role was to obstruct further political development with her 'empty chair' boycott of the institutions in 1965, which was only brought to an end with the Luxembourg Agreement of 1966. The 1965 crisis concerned several issues: agriculture, the method of financing the Community, the budgetary powers of the Assembly. Already some decisions in the Council of Ministers were being taken by simple majority. The Treaty of Rome indicated that this would be true of most Council decisions by 1966. The refusal of de Gaulle to allow enlargement left France in an organization most of whose other members were more enthusiastic that the Community should evolve in a supranational direction.

The initial significance of 30 June 1965, when the crisis began, was that the system for financing CAP had to be put in place by that time or the farm programme could not operate. The proposals relating to CAP financing involved the collection of levies on imports of farm produce from the non-EEC countries into the EEC, and their disbursement to farmers in the member countries to compensate for the lower prices they were getting worldwide for their products. The President of the Commission, Walter Hallstein, also proposed to direct the proceeds of these levies to the Commission for it to administer as the EC's 'own resources'. Although no amendment to the Treaty of Rome was required by this proposal, it would have meant a very substantial increase in the funds available to the Commission above what had been expected by the member states. It was also suggested that the European Assembly should be able to amend the Commission's annual draft budget by simple majority vote. If the Commission approved such an amendment, the Council of Ministers could turn it down only if five out of the six members voted to do so.

Although this appeared to increase the Assembly's budgetary powers, more significantly it would also enhance the ability of the Commission to control the whole process, because it was also proposed that the Commission could table amendments to the Assembly's amendments which could be accepted by a four-sixths majority of the Council. If accepted, these proposed procedures would mean that France and West Germany could be outvoted in the Council by the less powerful member states, and the will of the supranational bodies could prevail over that of the two dominant states in the Community. Accordingly, the French Foreign Minister brought to an end the Council of Ministers meeting deliberating on the Hallstein package, and de Gaulle withdrew French participation from the main committees of the EC.

The quarrel about agriculture provided the French President with an opportunity to attempt to impose his agenda of a more intergovernmental Community. The transition from a conflict over agriculture and Commission prerogatives into a clash over the basis of common policy-making in the Council of Ministers can be seen in the shifting position of Spaak and the Belgian government, initially supporting the French until it became clear that there was no prospect of French compromise over institutional progress in the Community. The Dutch Government and Parliament, by contrast, were consistent in hard-line opposition to French positions across the board during this crisis, and played an important part in whipping up the European Assembly against the French position. Within France, the 'empty chair crisis' came to dominate the presidential election campaign in 1965. The French election of December was the last within the original Six members in which membership of the Community was a contested issue.

The crisis was only brought to an end with this Luxembourg Compromise – or 'Disagreement', as it was more accurately labelled (Document 6.9). Advocates of integration like State Secretary Lahr initially presented it as a triumph, representing the defeat of French ambitions for treaty revision.[24] That much was true. Nevertheless, the 'legend' of the Luxembourg Compromise had a stultifying effect on the Community for as long as there was a lack of political will to enforce treaty provisions.[25] This left an accumulating backlog of proposals and, effectively, political paralysis in the Community. The widespread recognition that the Luxembourg Agreement was impeding the development of the Community did not lead to a breakthrough until the Community introduced qualified majority voting for a number of policy areas in the Single European Act which came into effect on 1 July 1987 (see Chapter 9).

De Gaulle also sought to reduce significantly the importance of the Commission. As part of the Luxembourg Compromise, the ability of the Commission to put items on the agenda of the Council of Ministers was restricted by the requirement that they must first be shown to the representatives of the Six permanently residing in Brussels. It would be wrong, however, to present the French position as simply one of obstruction.[26] It was, after all, the French who insisted most firmly, whatever its subsequent shortcomings (Document 6.12), on the need for a coherent agricultural policy for the Community. Agreement on agriculture followed in fact in May 1966, albeit through a procedure which left the original budgetary procedures in place. The French were also quite content with the passage of a new treaty providing for the merger of the three Communities in 1964 (signed by the governments in April 1965 and entering into force in 1967). By this merger, the three separate Councils of Ministers of the ECSC, EEC and Euratom and the executive agencies of the three Communities were combined into a single Council and a single 'European Commission'. Nevertheless, legally, the three Communities continued to exist, governed by separate treaties.

As Paul Taylor points out,

> there was a sense in which [de Gaulle] won the argument ... he headed off the
> further development of the first image of European cooperation that involved a
> fairly straightforward shift of power and authority to Brussels ... But there was
> also a sense in which he lost. The Community proved to have acquired strength
> enough to withstand his attack, in terms of the effectiveness of the institutions, the
> status of its leadership, and the level of more general support. It had begun to
> emerge as a political system with resources of its own.[27]

The Community had also significantly entrenched itself as a legal system with
important implications for the concept of national sovereignty. The *Costa* v. *ENEL*
case established the legal status of the Community as a system with its own Court of
Justice overriding national systems. The other very important *van Gend en Loos*
case established the principle of direct effect. Individuals could sue and be sued
under Community law and they had now acquired the right to sue their own
governments (Documents 6.8, 6.9).

A dominant leitmotif in the struggle between France and the other five was also
evident in the debate between supporters of a 'European Europe' and 'Atlanticist'
defenders of the NATO Alliance (and British inclusion in the Community). While the
United States hoped to press its European partners into a combined nuclear effort, the
'Multilateral Force', only the Germans really welcomed the opportunity of participat-
ing in a European nuclear deterrent. The whole idea had been to reassure the
Germans by offering them some form of participation in nuclear decision-making.
France was bitterly opposed to the plan and warned that 'If the multilateral force
were to lead to the creation of a German–American military alliance, we would not
consider that as being fully consistent with the relations we have with the Federal
Republic which are based on the Franco-German Treaty.'[28] Although the United
States backed away from its own proposals, the debate around the multilateral force
did much to sour the atmosphere and increase de Gaulle's hostility to NATO.

De Gaulle opposed any transnational interference in the French nuclear programme and in its military affairs in general. His reference to Europe 'from the
Atlantic to the Urals' heralded increasing attempts to strike an independent line in
discussions with the Soviets. In March 1966 de Gaulle announced that France was
withdrawing its armed forces from the integrated NATO command structure
although France retained its seat on the NATO council (Documents 6.10, 6.11).
NATO, which had been discussing reform for a decade, was now forced into
seriously considering a new role for itself, a task entrusted to the Belgian Foreign
Minister Pierre Harmel. It was not without irony that the Council which met to
approve the Harmel Report in December 1967 was presided over by de Gaulle's
Foreign Minister Couve de Murville.

Looking back over the 1960s, observers noted that the two main characteristics
of the new Communities were, paradoxically, crisis management at an institutional
level and steady progress in detailed policy-making. This conundrum lay at the heart
of much theorizing about the nature of the EC. There was much debate as to
whether the Europeans had transcended the 'obsolete' nation state or merely
created institutions for resolving international conflicts.[29] The formation of the

Community had provoked many theoretical interpretations of the integration process, particularly among American political scientists. Most notable was the so-called 'neo-functionalist' argument that Community actions in the economy would have a 'spill-over' effect into other sectors, and also on the process of institutional integration.[30] The crisis in the Community shook such optimism severely.

The crisis demonstrated that integration was not an automatic process. Indeed, steps towards integration could provoke a backlash. This was not to be the last time the Community was to be painfully reminded of this simple truth (see Chapter 10). The crisis also demonstrated more than this. It had arisen not only because of a conflict between advocates and opponents of further integration – it had arisen because of a clash between different visions of what integration ought to mean. The fact that de Gaulle sneered at the word 'integration' and that he was often infuriatingly vague in articulating his vision do not detract from the fact that he had a vision of Europe which was more than the sum of its sovereign states. As the debate in Britain shows, there were political risks involved in clearly stating the motives and consequences of integration. There were also political risks involved in concealing motives and glossing over consequences. Finding the balance between formulations all could live with, because their significance was ambivalent, and facing up to the divergence of vision and interest within the Community, was a difficulty which would continue to plague both the Community and the Atlantic Alliance.

NOTES

1. Robert Marjolin, *Architect of European Unity: Memoirs 1911–1986* (London, 1989), p. 300.
2. W. Kaiser, 'Challenge to the Community', *Journal of European Integration History*, Vol. 3 (1997), p. 11.
3. ibid., p. 20.
4. For the fateful consequences of the early decisions see Hans von der Groeben, *The European Community: The Formative Years* (Brussels, 1987), pp. 70–8.
5. ibid., p. 110.
6. Quoted in Hartmut Meyer, 'Germany's role in the Fouchet negotiations', *Journal of European Intergration History*, Vol. 2 (1996), p. 43.
7. Yves Stelandre, 'Le pays du Benelux, l'Europe politique et les négociations Fouchet', *Journal of European Intergration History*, Vol. 2 (1996), p. 23.
8. Quoted in Jean Lacouture, *De Gaulle: The Ruler 1945–1970* (New York, 1991), p. 349.
9. Paul-Henri Spaak, *The Continuing Battle* (London, 1971), p. 440.
10. Oliver Bange, 'Grand designs and the diplomatic breakdown', in George Wilkes (ed.), *Britain's Failure to Enter the European Community 1961–63* (London, 1997), p. 205.
11. John Pinder, *European Community* (Oxford, 1991), p. 192.
12. The opposition of The Netherlands was central to this. See Bernard Bouwman, 'Longing for London', in Anne Deighton (ed.), *Building Postwar Europe* (Basingstoke, 1995), pp. 141–58.
13. Ludolf Herbst, *Option für den Westen* (Munich, 1989), p. 204.
14. Ulrich Lappenküpper, 'Ich bin wirklich ein güter Europäer', *Francia*, Vol. 18, no. 3 (1991), p. 99.

15. George Wilkes, 'Eye-witness views of the breakdown', in Wilkes (ed.), *Britain's Failure*, p. 248.
16. Roy Pryce (ed.), *The Dynamics of European Union* (London, 1987), pp. 126–7.
17. Roy Jenkins (ed.), *Britain and the EEC* (London, 1983), p. 26.
18. Peter Calvocoressi, *The British Experience 1945–75* (London, 1978), pp. 221–2.
19. Jacqueline Tratt, *The Macmillan Government and Europe* (Basingstoke, 1996), pp. 168–85, 189–90.
20. George Wilkes, 'Eye-witness views of the breakdown', in Wilkes (ed.), *Britain's Failure*, p. 247.
21. John W. Young, *Britain and European Unity, 1945–1992* (Basingstoke, 1993), p. 81.
22. Quoted in F. Nicholson and R. East, *From the Six to the Twelve* (Harlow, 1987), p. 54
23. See Young, *Britain and European Unity*, pp. 103–4.
24. *Akten zur Auswärtigen Politik der Bundesrepublik Deutschland*, 1966, Vol. 1, doc. 25 (31 January 1966).
25. The phrase is that of Rolf Lahr, 'Die Legende vom *Luxembourg Kompromiss*', *Europa-Archiv*, Vol. 38 (1983), pp. 223–32.
26. For a sympathetic assessment of de Gaulle's policy see Wilfried Loth, 'De Gaulle und Europa: Eine Revision', *Historische Zeitschrift*, Vol. 253 (1991), pp. 629–60.
27. Paul Taylor, *The European Union in the 1990s* (Oxford, 1996), p. 17.
28. Quoted in John Newhouse, *Collision in Brussels* (New York, 1967), p. 40.
29. See Stanley Hoffmann, 'Obstinate or obsolete: the fate of the nation state and the cases of west Europe', *Daedalus*, Vol. 95 (1966), pp. 862–915.
30. The jargon of integration theory is not easy to penetrate. Charles Pentland, *International Theory and European Integration* (London, 1973) is still helpful.

FURTHER READING

B. Balassa, *The Theory of Economic Integration* (London, 1962)
S. Bodenheimer, *Political Union: A Microcosm of European Politics 1960–66* (Leiden, 1967)
M. Camps, *Britain and the European Community 1955–63* (London, 1964)
M. Camps, *European Unification in the Sixties: From the Veto to the Crisis* (New York, 1966)
A. Deighton and A.S. Milward (eds), *Accelerating, Deepening, Enlarging* (Baden-Baden, 1998)
S. George, *Awkward Partner* (Oxford, 1990)
R. Griffiths and S. Ward (eds), *Courting the common market* (London, 1996)
H. von der Groeben, *The European Community. The Formative Years* (Brussels, 1987)
A.J.R. Groom and P. Taylor, *Functionalism* (London, 1975)
R.J. Harrison, *Europe in Question* (London, 1974)
W. Kaiser, 'Challenge to the Community', *Journal of European Intergration History*, Vol. 3 (1997), pp. 7–33
L. Lindberg, *The Political Dynamics of European Economic Integration* (Stanford, CA, 1963)
J. Lodge (ed.), *The European Community: Bibliographical Excursions* (London, 1983)
N.P. Ludlow, *Dealing with Britain* (London, 1997)
J. Newhouse, *De Gaulle and the Anglo-Saxons* (London, 1970)
C.C. Pentland, *International Theory and European Integration* (New York, 1973)
R. Pryce (ed.), *The Dynamics of European Union* (London, 1987)

H. Spaak, *The Continuing Battle* (London, 1971)

D.W. Urwin, *The Community of Europe* (London, 1991)

G. Wilkes (ed.), *Britain's Failure to Enter the European Community 1961–63* (London, 1997)

F.R. Willis, *France, Germany and the New Europe 1945–67* (New York, 1968)

---------------------------------- 6.1 ----------------------------------

JEAN MONNET: 'PROSPECT FOR A NEW EUROPE', 1959

Bull. EC, Supplement 2, 1959, pp. 3–4.

The following is an extract from an interview given by Monnet in 1959.

The Community and the Free Trade Area

M. Monnet, you have been pointing out that a big market is the essential basis for further economic expansion. Why does the six-nation Community oppose British proposals for an even bigger market in the form of a 17-nation European Free Trade Area or customs union?

The European Economic Community is much more than a customs union. The Free Trade Area proposed by Britain is much less than a cutoms union. The Free Trade Area would exclude agriculture, from which 18 million persons and their children in the six-nation area earn their livelihood. It does not provide, as a customs union would, for a common external tariff. Each of the member nations would be free to maintain its own external tariffs. The Free Trade Area would be a market in which you exchange goods but do not build a common policy. Each nation would have its own economic policy.

The six-nation common market, on the other hand, is not just a customs union or a big market. It is a Community with common rules and common institutions which can gradually build a common policy to foster rapid economic growth.

Towards Majority Voting

How can the Community arrive at a common economic policy if each nation, in the Community's Council of Ministers, has a veto over the actions of the executive?

The unanimity rule only applies during a transition period. Subsequently, almost all decisions will be made by majority vote. In fact, some decisions are made by majority vote right from the start.

The Community's institutions consist of a Council of Ministers, a European Economic Commission, an Assembly, which is a kind of Parliament, and a Court of

Justice, which is an embryo Supreme Court. What we have is a system of checks and balances similar to that in most constitutions.

The Council of Ministers is designed to bring together national views, the views of the six governments. It meets at intervals. Each government is represented in the Council by its Foreign Minister or by one or more other Ministers, such as the Finance, Transport or Agricultural Ministers, as the subject matter requires.

The continuing, day-to-day executive work of the Community is handled by the nine-member European Economic commission. The Commission is responsible to the Assembly of the Community. It defends the common interests of the Community and represents the Community viewpoint, rather than national views. It acts by majority vote in all things.

The Commission has numerous real powers, specified in the Treaty, which it exercises on its own authority. Where general rules have to be set, the Council of Ministers makes the decisions. But it must do so on the proposals of the Commission. It cannot amend the Commission's proposals except by unanimous vote.

The British have proposed a majority vote in the Council of Ministers of the proposed Free Trade Area. Why wouldn't this work as well?

There would be no independent Commission in the Free Trade Area representing the Community-wide viewpoint. Under such circumstances, a majority in this Council of Ministers may just represent a coalition of interests. In difficulties arising between one nation and another, there would be arbitration by coalition, instead of the creation of common policies to solve common problems.

6.2

LUDWIG ERHARD: 'WHAT WILL BECOME OF EUROPE?', 1960

The Economics of Success (London: Thames & Hudson, 1963), pp. 317–18.

The following is an extract from an article by the Vice-Chancellor and Minister for Economic Affairs of the German Federal Republic, published in *Handelsblatt* in December 1960. He was a strong advocate of a non-protectionist Europe.

Starting from the integration of the Six in the framework of the common market, a highly praiseworthy and sober move was made back to the foundations of the Treaty, i.e. to its economic objectives, and if not a stop at least a brake has been put on political speculation. This clear definition of duties clears the way for realistic decisions, and one is no longer branded as a 'bad European' if one rejects the highly subjective fantasies of those who will only think in terms of the Six. Although it has become abundantly clear in the meantime that, without prejudice to the proper application of the Treaty and to the solidarity of the Six, this integration of Little Europe, particularly in its political implications, is not sufficient to solve either the European problem as a whole or that of the Atlantic Community, I would like to point out once more that no such limitations were envisaged when the Rome Treaties were born. In fact, a formal and officially inspired announcement was made by the then President of the European Commission that a widespread European free trade zone would be set up as a defence against destructive influences and any disturbances created by them. The responsible statesmen in the EEC countries have accepted the principle of a multilateral association with regard to their economic relations with the other free countries of Europe, and the EEC Council of Ministers passed resolutions to the same effect. Every citizen has a right to know what has come of these good intentions and he will want to know what has stood, or is still standing, in the way of their realization.

6.3

'THE DEVELOPING ATLANTIC PARTNERSHIP', SPEECH BY US UNDER-SECRETARY GEORGE W. BALL, 2 APRIL 1962

American Foreign Policy: Current Documents 1962
(Washington: Department of State, 1966), pp. 582–7.

This extract offers a further clear illustration of the rationale behind the United States' support for west European integration. George Ball was a firm believer in the Atlantic partnership, a close adviser of President Kennedy and a friend of Jean Monnet.

... Through the whole of the postwar period we Americans have taken no comfort from the disparity between our own resources and those of any other nations of the free world. We have been proud that the United States is a world leader isolated by the possession of an overwhelming proportion of the total wealth, power, and resources. In our minds – and I am sure to your minds as well – a strong partnership must almost mean a collaboration of equals. When one partner possesses over 50 per cent of the resources of so great an enterprise and the balance is distributed among 16 or 17 others, the relationship is unlikely to work with full effectiveness. And so long as Europe remained fragmented, so long as it consisted merely of nations small by modern standards, the potentials for true partnership were always limited.

But a Europe united and strong can be an equal partner in the achievement of our common endeavours – an equal partner committed to the same basic objectives as we ourselves. For, after all, you and we alike believe in the presentation and extension of freedom and in the values that distinguish free men from slaves.

I cannot overstate the enthusiasm with which Americans have welcomed the burgeoning strength and cohesion of Europe. But why is it that one sometimes hears in Europe – almost never in America – timid voices ominously complaining that a united Europe might become a neutralist 'third force'.

Let me say emphatically that we Americans have no fear that the new Europe will be neutralist any more than we fear that America will return to isolationism. The neutralism of which we heard a fair amount a decade ago was an expression of weakness, not strength. It sprang from a belief that Europe could no longer play a significant role in the power contest between the United States and the Communist bloc. Persuaded that they could not influence the outcome by taking sides, its advocates assumed a role of Olympian detachment from the battle, measuring out equal amounts of criticism for each side. As the nations of west Europe have grown more united, the voices of neutralism that produced such a frightful cacophony 10 years ago have been largely stilled.

6.4

PRESIDENT CHARLES DE GAULLE ON EUROPEAN INTEGRATION, PRESS CONFERENCE, 15 MAY 1962

R. Vaughan (ed.), *Post-War Integration in Europe* (London: Edward Arnold, 1976), pp. 158–61.

The President offered the following comments on west European integration in this press conference on Europe. His objection to the Jean Monnet approach is clear, as is his fear of the extension of American influence in Europe.

I should like to speak particularly about the objection to integration. People counter this by saying: 'Why not merge the six states together into a single supranational entity? That would be very simple and practical.' But such an entity is impossible to achieve in the absence of Europe today of a federator who has the necessary power, reputation and ability. Thus one has to fall back on a sort of hybrid arrangement under which the six states agree to submit to the decisions of a qualified majority. At the same time, although there are already six national Parliaments as well as the European Parliament and, in addition, the Consultative Assembly of the Council of Europe ... it would be necessary to elect over and above this, yet a further Parliament, described as European, which would lay down the law to the six states.

These are ideas that might appeal to certain minds but I entirely fail to see how they could be put into practice, even with six signatures at the foot of a document. Can we imagine France, Germany, Italy, The Netherlands, Belgium, Luxembourg being prepared on a matter of importance to them in the national or international sphere, to do something that appeared wrong to them, merely because others had ordered them to do so? Would the peoples of France, of Germany, of Italy, of The Netherlands, of Belgium or of Luxembourg ever dream of submitting to laws passed by foreign parliamentarians if such laws ran counter to their deepest convictions? Clearly not. It is impossible nowadays for a foreign majority to impose their will on reluctant nations. It is true, perhaps, that in this 'integrated' Europe as it is called there might be no policy at all. This would simplify a great many things. Indeed, once there was no France, no Europe; once there was no policy – since one could not be imposed on each of the six states, attempts to formulate a policy would cease. But then, perhaps these peoples would follow in the wake of some outsider who had a policy. There would, perhaps, be a federator, but he would not be European. And Europe would not be an integrated Europe but something vaster by far and, I repeat, with a federator. Perhaps to some extent it is this that at times inspires the utterances of certain advocates of European integration. If so, then it would be better to say so.

6.5

PRESIDENT CHARLES DE GAULLE, PRESS CONFERENCE, 14 JANUARY 1963

A Retrospective View of the Political Year in Europe (Paris: WEU, 1964), pp. 20–2.

This extract offers de Gaulle's justification for his rejection of Britain's application to join the Community. He was also subsequently to veto the attempt by the Labour Government under Harold Wilson in 1967. On 22 January the President signed the Treaty of Friendship with the German Federal Republic, providing for institutional cooperation in foreign policy, defence, culture and education. This rapprochement contrasted sharply with the veto.

Can you define explicitly France's position towards Britain's entry into the common market and the political evolution of Europe?

A very clear question, to which I shall endeavour to reply clearly ... the means by which the people of Great Britain are fed and which are in fact the importation of foodstuffs bought cheaply in the two Americas and in the former dominions while, at the same time giving, granting considerable subsidies to English farmers. These means are obviously incompatible with the system which the Six have established quite naturally for themselves.

The system of the Six – this constitutes making a whole of the agricultural produce of the whole Community, in strictly fixing their prices, in prohibiting subsidies, in organising their consumption between all the participants, and in imposing on each of its participants payment to the Community of any saving they would achieve in fetching their food from outside instead of eating what the common market has to offer.

Once again, what is to be done to bring England, as she is, into this system? One might sometimes have believed that our English friends, in posing their candidature to the common market, were agreeing to transform themselves to the point of applying all the conditions which are accepted and practised by the Six. But the question, to know whether Great Britain can now place herself like the Continent and with it inside a tariff which is genuinely common, to renounce all Commonwealth preferences, to cease any pretence that her agriculture be privileged, and, more than that, to treat her engagements with other countries of the free trade area as null and void – that question is the whole question. It cannot be said that is yet resolved. Will it be so one day? Obviously only England can answer.

The question is even further posed since after England other States which are, I repeat, linked to her through the free trade area, for the same reasons as Britain, would like or wish to enter the common market.

It must be agreed that first the entry of Great Britain, and then these States, will completely change the whole of the actions, the agreements, the compensations, the rules which have already been established between the Six, because all these States, like Britain, have very important peculiarities. Then it will be another common market whose constructions ought to be envisaged; but one which would be taken to 11 and then 13 and then perhaps 18 would no longer resemble, without any doubt, the one which the Six built.

Further, this community, increasing in such fashion, would see itself faced with problems of economic relations with all kinds of other States, and first with the United States. It is to be foreseen that the cohesion of its members, who would be very numerous and diverse, would not endure for long, and that ultimately it would appear as a colossal Atlantic community under American dependence and direction, and which would quickly have absorbed the community of Europe.

Thus, it was psychologically and materially possible to make an economic community of the Six, though not without difficulties. When the Treaty of Rome was signed in 1957, it was after long discussions; and when it was concluded, it was necessary in order to achieve something that we French put in order our economic, financial, and monetary affairs . . . and that was done in 1959.

From that moment the community was in principle viable, but then the treaty had to be applied. However, this treaty, which was precise and complete enough concerning industry, was not at all so on the subject of agriculture. However, for our country this had to be settled.

Indeed, it is obvious that agriculture is an essential element in the whole of our national activity. We cannot conceive, and will not conceive, of a common market in which French agriculture would not find outlets in keeping with its production. And we agree, further, that of the Six we are the country on which this necessity is imposed in the most imperative manner.

This is why when, last January, thought was given to the setting in motion of the second phase of the treaty – in other words a practical start in application – we were led to pose the entry of agriculture into the common market as a formal condition.

This was finally accepted by our partners but very difficult and very complex arrangements were needed – and some rulings are still outstanding. I note in passing that in this vast undertaking it was the governments that took all the decisions, because authority and responsibility are not to be found elsewhere. But I must say that in preparing and untangling these matters, the Commission in Brussels did some very objective and fitting work.

Thereupon Great Britain posed her candidature to the common market. She did it after having earlier refused to participate in the communities we are now building, as well as after creating a free trade area with six other States, and, finally, after having – I may well say it, the negotiations held at such length on this subject will be recalled – after having put some pressure on the Six to prevent a real beginning being made in the application of the common market. If England asks in turn to enter, but on her own conditions, this poses without doubt to each of the six States, and poses to England, problems of a very great dimension.

England in effect is insular, she is maritime, she is linked through her exchanges, her markets, her supply lines to the most diverse and often the most distant countries; she pursues essentially industrial and commercial activities, and only slight agricultural ones. She has in all her doings very marked and very original habits and traditions. In short, the nature, the structure, the very situation ('conjuncture') that are England's differ profoundly from those of the continentals. What is to be done in order that England, as she lives, produces and trades, can be incorporated into the common market, as it has been conceived and as it functions? It is a hypothesis which in the eyes of some can be perfectly justified, but it is not at all what France is doing or wanted to do – and which is a properly European construction.

6.6

PAUL-HENRI SPAAK ON THE DE GAULLE VETO, AS RECORDED IN HIS MEMOIRS, *THE CONTINUING BATTLE*, 1971

Paul-Henri Spaak, *The Continuing Battle: Memories of a European, 1936–66* (London: Weidenfeld & Nicolson, 1971), pp. 476–7.

Spaak was Foreign Minster of Belgium at the time of de Gaulle's veto. His outrage at de Gaulle's behaviour was shared by many other participants in the negotiations.

During the afternoon of the 14th of January 1963, while we were in session, the official messengers brought us news flashes of the press conference General de Gaulle was just holding in Paris. Once we had seen these despatches we could no longer keep our minds on the technical issues before us. A new political event of extreme importance was in the making: General de Gaulle had torpedoed our negotiations without having warned either his partners or the British. He had acted with a lack of consideration unexampled in the history of the EEC, showing utter contempt for his negotiating partners, allies and opponents alike. He had brought to a halt negotiations which he himself put in train in full agreement with his partners, and had done so on the flimsiest of pretexts.

What had happened? There is every reason to believe that it was the attitude adopted by Macmillan at his meeting with Kennedy in Bermuda which so upset the President of the French Republic. Macmillan's crime was to have reached agreement with the President of the United States on Britain's nuclear weaponry. He had in fact arranged for the purchase of Polaris missiles from the United States. In General de Gaulle's eyes the cooperation with the Americans was tantamount to treason against Europe's interests and justified his refusal to allow Britain into the common market. The General's resentment was all the greater because a few days before the Bermuda meeting he had received Macmillan at Rambouillet. The British Prime Minister, he claimed, had told him nothing of his nuclear plans. On the other hand, de Gaulle gave Macmillan no warning that he was about to torpedo the negotiations in Brussels. I think the full truth about these events still remains to be told. The French and British versions which have been circulating in the chancelleries differ, but what is certain is that France, without consulting her partners, unilaterally withdrew from negotiations to which she had earlier agreed and that she did so, moreover, after first insisting that the Six must present a united front.

We were faced with a complete volte-face. Stunned and angry, our first reaction was to ignore what had been said in Paris and to continue the negotiation as if nothing had happened. The British showed extraordinary sang-froid. Though, deep down, they were greatly shocked, they gave no outward sign of this and continued to present their arguments at the negotiating table with imperturbable calm.

_____ 6.7 _____

VAN GEND EN LOOS, 1963

ECR 1 (1963) Case 26/62

This was a crucial judgment in Community history, arising from the case of a transport company with the above name against the Dutch taxation authority. The European Court of Justice ruled that EC law was a new legal order directly applicable in member states. The judgment was rendered on 5 February 1963.

The objective of the EEC Treaty, which is to establish a common market, the functioning of which is of direct concern to interested parties in the Community, implies that this Treaty is more than an agreement which merely creates mutual obligations between the contracting States. This view is confirmed by the preamble to the Treaty which refers not only to governments but to peoples. It is also confirmed more specifically by the establishment of institutions endowed with sovereign rights, the exercise of which affects member states and also their citizens. Furthermore, it must be noted that the nationals of the States brought together in this Community are called upon to cooperate in the functioning of this Community through the intermediary of the European Parliament and the Economic and Social Committee.

In addition the task assigned to the Court of Justice under Article 177, the object of which is to secure uniform interpretation of the Treaty by national courts and tribunals, confirms that the States have acknowledged that Community law has an authority which can be invoked by their nationals before those courts and tribunals.

The conclusion to be drawn from this is that the Community constitutes a new legal order of international law for the benefit of which the States have limited their sovereign rights, albeit within limited fields, and the subjects of which compromise not only member states but also their nationals. Independently of the legislation of member states, Community law therefore not only imposes legislation on individuals but is also intended to confer upon them rights which become part of their legal heritage. These rights arise not only where they are expressly granted by the Treaty, but also by reason of obligations which the Treaty imposes in a clearly defined way upon individuals as well as upon the member states and upon the institutions of the Community ...

6.8

COSTA V. ENEL, 1964

ECR (1964) Case 6/64, pp. 585–600.

The following judgment arose from a case taken by one Signor Costa against the Italian National Electric Energy Company (Ente Nazionale Energia Elettrica Impresa Già della Edison Volta). In it the European Court of Justice confirmed the primacy of EC law. The case was heard in 1964.

By contrast with ordinary international treaties, the EEC Treaty has created its own legal system which, on the entry into force of the Treaty, became an integral part of the legal systems of the member states and which their courts are bound to apply.

By creating a Community of unlimited duration, having it own institutions, its own personality, its own legal capacity and capacity of representation on the international plane and, more particularly, real powers stemming from a limitation of sovereignty or a transfer of powers from the States to the Community, the member states have limited their sovereignty, albeit within limited fields, and have thus created a body of law which binds both their nationals and themselves.

The integration into the laws of each Member State of provisions which derive from the Community and more generally the terms and the spirit of the Treaty, make it impossible for the States, as a corollary, to accord precedence to a unilateral and subsequent measure over a legal system accepted by them on a basis of reciprocity. Such a measure cannot therefore be inconsistent with that legal system. The executive force of Community law cannot vary from one State to another in deference to subsequent domestic laws, without jeopardising the attainment of the objectives of the Treaty set out in Article 5(2) and giving rise to the discrimination prohibited by Article 7.

The obligations undertaken under the Treaty establishing the Community would not be unconditional, but merely contingent, if they could be called in question by subsequent legislative acts of the signatories ...

The precedence of Community law is confirmed by Article 189, whereby a regulation 'shall be binding' and 'directly applicable in all member states'. This provision, which is subject to no reservation, would be quite meaningless if a State could unilaterally nullify its effects by means of a legislative measure which could prevail over Community law.

It follows from all these observations that the law stemming from the Treaty, an independent source of law, could not, because of its special and original nature, be overridden by domestic legal provisions, however framed, without being deprived of its character as Community law and without the legal basis of the Community itself being called into question.

The transfer by the States from their domestic legal system to the Community legal system of the rights and obligations arising under the Treaty carries with it a permanent limitation of their sovereign rights, against which a subsequent unilateral act incompatible with the concept of the Community cannot prevail. Consequently, Article 177 is to be applied regardless of any domestic law, whenever questions relating to the interpretation of the Treaty arise ...

--------------------- 6.9 ---------------------

THE LUXEMBOURG AGREEMENT (COMPROMISE), 29 JANUARY 1966

Bull. EC, 3–1966.

This resolved the 'empty chair crisis' between France and the other five. It also reduced the institutional importance of the Commission and hindered the process of integration until the mid-1980s. It reduced the importance of the Commission and delayed the timetable established by the Treaty of Rome for the completion of the common market. The consequence of the agreement was that the Council of Ministers was very reluctant to proceed with an issue unless unanimity were guaranteed. Subsequent enlargement of the Community made this even more problematic.

Relations between the Commission and the Council

Close co-operation between the Council and the Commission is essential for the functioning and development of the Community. In order to improve and strengthen this co-operation at every level, the Council considers that the following practical methods of co-operation should be applied, these methods to be adopted by joint agreement, on the basis of Article 162 of the EEC Treaty, without compromising the respective competencies and powers of the two Institutions.

1. Before adopting any particular important proposal, it is desirable that the Commission should take up the appropriate contacts with the Governments of the member states, through the Permanent Representatives, without this procedure compromising the right of initiative which the Commission derives from the Treaty ...

Majority voting procedure

1. Where, in the case of decisions which may be taken by majority vote on a proposal of the Commission, very important interests of one or more partners are at stake, the Members of the Council will endeavour, within a reasonable time, to reach solutions which can be adopted by all the Members of the Council while respecting their mutual interests and those of the Community, in accordance with Article 2 of the Treaty.

2. With regard to the preceding paragraph, the French delegation considers that where very important interests are at stake the discussion must be continued until unanimous agreement is reached.
3. The six delegations note that there is a divergence of views on what should be done in the event of a failure to reach complete agreement.
4. The six delegations nevertheless consider that this divergence does not prevent the Community's work being resumed in accordance with the normal procedure.

6.10

FRANCE AND NATO, 1966

French Embassy Press and Information Service, New York, Speeches and Press Conferences, No. 239, 1966.

The following statement was made by President de Gaulle at a news conference on 21 February 1966. In this year he withdrew all French land and air forces from NATO's integrated military command, expelled all American military personnel from French territory and demanded the removal of NATO's headquarters from French territory.

Nothing can make a law enforceable, without amendment, when it no longer agrees with the ways of the times. Nothing can make a treaty wholly valid when its object has changed. Nothing can make an alliance remain as such when the conditions in which it was concluded have changed. It is therefore necessary to adapt the law, the treaty and the alliance to the new factors, failing which the texts, emptied of their substance, will, if circumstances so require, be nothing more than useless papers in the archives, unless there is a harsh break between these obsolete forms and the living realities.

Well! If France considers, today still, that it is useful to her security and to that of the West that she be allied with a certain number of States, particularly with America, for their defence and for hers in the event of aggression against one of them; if the declaration made in common on this subject, in the form of the Atlantic Alliance treaty signed in Washington on April 4, 1949, still remains valid in her eyes, at the same time she recognizes that the measures for implementation taken subsequently no longer correspond to what she deems satisfactory, with respect to herself, in the new conditions.

I say, the new conditions. For it is quite clear that, owing to the internal and external evolution of the countries of the East, the Western world is no longer threatened today as it was at the time when the American protectorate was set up in Europe under the cover of NATO. But, at the same time as the alarms were dying down, there was also a reduction in the guarantee of security – one might say absolute – that the possession of the nuclear weapon by America alone gave to the Old Continent, and in the certainty that America would employ it, without reservation, in the event of aggression. For Soviet Russia has since that time equipped itself with a nuclear power capable of striking the United States directly, which has made the decisions of the Americans as to the eventual use of their bombs at least indeterminate, and which has, by the same token, stripped of justification – I speak for France – not the Alliance, of course, but indeed integration.

On the other hand, while the prospects of a world war breaking out on account of Europe are dissipating, conflicts in which America engages in other parts of the world – as the day before yesterday in Korea, yesterday in Cuba, today in Vietnam – risk, by virtue of that famous escalation, being extended so that the result could be a general conflagration. In that case Europe – whose strategy is, within NATO, that of America – would be automatically involved in the struggle, even when it would not have so desired. It would be so for France, if the intermeshing of her territory, of her communications, of certain of her forces, of several of her air bases, of some of her ports with the military system under American command were to continue much longer. Moreover, our country, having become for its part and by its own means an atomic power, is led to assume itself the very extensive strategic and political responsibilities that this capacity involves and that, by their nature and by their dimensions, are obviously inalienable. Lastly, France's determination to dispose of herself, a determination without which she would soon cease to believe in her own role and be able to be useful to others, is incompatible with a defense organization in which she finds herself subordinate.

Consequently, without going back on her adherence to the Atlantic Alliance, France is going, between now and the final date set for her obligations, which is April 4, 1969, to continue to modify successively the measures currently practised, insofar as they concern her. What she did yesterday in this respect in several domains, she will do tomorrow in others, while taking, of course, the necessary measures so that these changes take place gradually and so that her allies cannot be suddenly, and because of her, inconvenienced. In addition, she will hold herself ready to arrange with one or another of them, and in the same manner in which she has already proceeded on certain points, the practical relations for cooperation that will appear useful on both sides, either in the immediate present or in the eventuality of a conflict. This naturally holds for allied cooperation in Germany. In sum, it means re-establishing a normal situation of sovereignty, in which that which is French as regards soil, sky, sea and forces, and any foreign element that would be in France, will in the future be under French command alone. This is to say that in no way means a rupture, but a necessary adaptation.

6.11

FRANCE AND NATO: THE US RESPONSE, 1966

American Foreign Policy: Current Documents 1986
(Washington, State Department, 1969), p. 337.

The statement below was made in an address by Under-Secretary of State George W. Ball to the American Society of International Law in Washington on 29 April 1966.

The idea of a united Europe linked in equal partnership across the Atlantic had great resonance on both sides of the ocean [in the early 1960s]. But already there were forces working against it, in particular the decision of the government of one European nation-state to separate itself from the others and to seek a special position of primacy in west Europe. The purposes of that government should not be a matter for polemics; they are on the public record, fully expressed or implied in any number of official statements.

That government has sought to half the drive towards European unity in the name of uniting Europe; to transform the European common market into a mere commercial arrangement by hobbling the powers of the executive; to prevent other Western European nations from achieving any participation in the management of nuclear power so as to preserve its own exclusive position as the sole nation with nuclear weapons on the Western European Continent; to reduce the influence and ultimately the presence of the United States in Europe; and, finally, to free itself from obligations to the great postwar system of European and Atlantic institutions in order to achieve freedom of political and diplomatic manoeuvre that could permit it to deal, to its own advantage, with what it has described with a curious impartiality as 'the two great hegemonies'.

_____6.12_____

SICCO MANSHOLT ON THE REFORM OF THE COMMON AGRICULTURAL POLICY, 1970

E.C. Bull, November 1970

Dr Mansholt was Vice-President of the Commission. The plan named after him was the origin of the Common Agricultural Policy (CAP). The following was written in 1970 and describes the difficulties he faced. CAP remains one of the major problems of the Community.

On 10 December 1968, I put before the European Community's Council of Ministers a memorandum on the reform of Community agriculture. Hitherto, the policy followed in the Six had led to an absurd state of affairs. Huge sums were being spent by the member Governments on structural improvements. Yet these did nothing to remedy our real agricultural problem – farms were too small, and farmers' incomes and living standards were lagging further and further behind those of other population groups.

To try to remedy this, I drew up for the Commission a programme entitled 'Agriculture 1980' which provided for:

1. A different price policy, aimed at restoring a more normal relationship between market and price trends.
2. Radical land-reform measures to bring farms up to a viable size and enable farmers to live as comfortably as everybody else.

The plan's basic premise was that the Community's farming population of 10–6 million should be reduced by five million. This exodus was to take place in an orderly manner, accompanied by all the measures necessary to provide financial assistance and create new jobs. The allocation of structural improvement aid among those who did not leave the land would be progressively concentrated on farms large enough to pay their way ...

It shocked the public and brought an avalanche of criticism from politicians ... This memorandum, however, was only a proposal for discussion ... We received many highly favourable reactions, but a great deal of criticism still persists on certain points, which need some clarification ...

Why didn't we present a plan earlier? Mainly because the member Governments would not hear of it. In its first memorandum, the so-called Green Bible of 1960, the Commission proposed a comprehensive policy, covering not only prices and market organisation, but also structural reform – which the Council never tackled. When the common agricultural policy took shape, it covered only prices and market organisation. The Governments had jealously kept the structural side in their own domain, thereby depriving farm policy of an essential element for its success.

The price policy, based on consensus politics rather than economics, has taken us almost to the end of the road, with structural surpluses costing astronomical amounts. Dairies churn out subsidised butter regardless of market needs; no one worries about packing the stuff, because no matter whether it is bought, stored, sold cheaply or destroyed, the producer gets the guaranteed price.

CHAPTER 7

INTEGRATION IN EASTERN EUROPE

1949–1991

INTRODUCTION

From the perspective of the post-Cold War period, integration in east Europe can appear as part of military and economic competition with the capitalist west, which the socialist east ultimately lost. Without the benefit of hindsight, the outcome was not self-evident to observers in the west or in the east. Indeed, American observers invoked the prospect of communist economic superiority as a reason for further integration in the west.[1] Although the outcome of the competition was not always clear, the fact that there was a competition was a key factor for both sides. As each side struggled for moral superiority as well as economic and military superiority, the identity of Europe, its geographic extent and culture, became a bone of contention (Document 7.7). From the west came comments which recalled nineteenth-century doubts about the European character of Russia. With more subtlety, but with no more appeal for the Soviet Union, President de Gaulle accepted Russia's European vocation – as part of a Europe from the Atlantic to the Urals – but only on the assumption that the ideological division of Europe was a transient and alien imposition.

Within the east there had been little theoretical preparation for integration between socialist states. The only model available was the Soviet Union itself. From this perspective relations between the different nations of the Soviet Union could serve as a model for relations between the nations of the wider socialist commonwealth.[2] That, however, would have entailed the incorporation of the states of east Europe into an expanded Soviet Union. Once this option had been rejected, the rulers of the eastern bloc were left with the problem familiar to western leaders: how to reconcile the existence of independent states, with the associated diversity of national identity and conflicts of economic and security interests, and the perceived need for integration. There were, of course, differences between the east and the west. There was a stronger ideological conformity in the east, bolstered by the doctrine of socialist or proletarian internationalism. Second, the Soviet Union enjoyed a privileged position as the first socialist state. Equally important was the fact that the Soviet Union was a member of both the forum for military integration (the Warsaw Treaty Organization, WTO) and the forum for economic integration (the Council for Mutual Economic Assistance, CMEA). In the west the corresponding superpower, the United States, was a member of NATO but not of the European Communities. There were calls for more intensive Atlantic integration but these were never realistic. The asymmetry between the United States and the European states was too great to make Atlantic integration an attractive proposition for either the United States or the Europeans. In the east, Soviet hegemony and ideology were sufficient to overcome the obstacle of asymmetry to the extent that the Soviet Union was included in the forum of economic integration. The eastern European states, cut off from west European markets by the logic of the cold war, really had little alternative but to seek closer integration with the Soviet Union. Nevertheless, the asymmetry between the member states of the CMEA did cause problems. Economically bilateral relations with the Soviet Union distorted the trade of the smaller east European states. Militarily, the ability and willingness of the Soviet Union to enforce conformity operated as a powerful constraint.

Soviet hegemony and ideological conformity were not absolute. The diverse security interests, and even more so the diverse economic interests, as well as differences in ideology, acted as obstacles to deeper integration, even when this was desired by the Soviet Union. Here Romanian opposition to Soviet initiatives stands out. With little exaggeration the Romanians can be described as the eastern bloc's Gaullists, successfully balancing opposition to the Soviet Union with the need to avoid provoking the superpower too far. Those who went further, Hungary and Czechoslovakia, suffered the penalty of military intervention and incidentally exposed the underlying difference between the western bloc and the eastern bloc. Romanian opposition, like the more ill-fated Hungarian and Czechoslovak challenges, arose in part from a historical legacy which predated the socialist regimes. This is especially clear in Romania's opposition to economic integration which can be set in the context of a tradition of protectionism which dates back to the nineteenth century.[3]

The relationship between the contingencies of historical experience and the structural constraints of centrally planned economies is a major factor in explaining the extent and limits of integration in the eastern bloc. It was one of which the socialist leaders were well aware. The reference to 'the substantial differences in the level of development of national productive forces, differences that stem from the historical conditions of capitalist development' in the Basic Principles of the International Socialist Division of Labour was not merely socialist rhetoric (Document 7.3). The broader historical legacy of the region was one of strong protectionist sentiment, of relatively low levels of industrialization (with the exception of the Czech lands and East Germany), of the bilateral organization of trade, and of a strong desire to catch up with more advanced neighbours. On the political front, fear of domination by larger or more advanced neighbours (Germany and Russia), as well as the mutual recriminations and suspicions about territorial borders and the fate of minorities, formed part of the same legacy. The political fears were largely suppressed, partly in the interests of socialist solidarity and partly for fear of provoking the Soviet Union, which, in turn, provided reassurance, at least for Czechoslovakia and Poland, against the prospect of a resurgent Germany.

The structural constraints were evident quite early in the history of the CMEA. Underlying them all was the inherent difficulty of integrating centrally planned socialist economies. Given central planning, every element of integration, from each trade deal to each agreement on product specialization, is an inherently political act.[4] Similarly, the principle of public ownership made it difficult to disentangle sacrifices of sovereignty and processes of integration. Whatever the economic system, these two things are inevitably linked. However, in market-based economies it is possible to distance the state from the process of integration by setting up a framework within which private actors can trade and invest without calling into question the sovereignty of the state. Given the principle of public ownership, each such act is, however, an act of the state. The consequence, as Hungarian commentators frequently pointed out, was that integration presupposed domestic economic reform (Documents 7.10, 7.12). Again, this was true in the west as well, but in the east the required economic reform posed more of a challenge to the dominant economic ideology.

More specific constraints – the minimal amount of multilateral as opposed to bilateral trade, the associated lack of convertible currencies and divergent price levels, the limited extent of labour and capital mobility, the absence of genuinely supranational planning authorities – proved to be no less intractable. Indeed, the striking feature of the CMEA's record is the way in which the organization kept returning to these same problems without making any substantive progress in resolving them. When, on the eve of the CMEA's dissolution, N. I. Ryzhkov, Chairman of the USSR Council of Ministers, lamented its deficiencies, he was listing problems which had been on the agenda since the mid-1950s (Document 7.13).

One of the first problems to be identified was a product of historical contingency but became so deeply entrenched that it acquired all the obduracy of a structural constraint, namely the adoption of the Soviet model of industrialization by the east European countries. This had not been inevitable. In 1946 the Polish leader Wladislaw Gomulka had expressly rejected the Soviet model, with its 'tremendous hardships'.[5] Gomulka, however, fell victim to the Stalinization of the eastern bloc, which brought greater ideological conformity and unrestrained pursuit of the Soviet model. That meant that each of the east European states set out to construct an industrial base characterized by heavy industry and power generation. Consumer goods, agriculture and extractive industries all suffered from neglect. Again the origins of this strategy lay not just in the history of socialism but also in the pre-socialist history of the region. Fear of being kept at a semi-colonial level of development, producing raw material and foodstuffs for more advanced states, drove east Europe's elites to industrialize even when this was not in their comparative advantage. The new socialist rulers, including Poland's, were not immune to these sentiments (Document 7.1).

As early as 1953 the headlong drive for industrialization ran into difficulty as popular resentment at the associated deprivation threatened to spill over into open dissent. The reduction of food exports to the benefit of the domestic market and rapidly changed investment plans disrupted relations between the member states of the CMEA. The economic dislocation induced attempts to breathe life into the CMEA which had been largely moribund since its formation in 1949. Even more important was the death of Stalin in 1953. Stalin had preferred to coordinate policy through inter-party discussions, by-passing intergovernmental organs. His successors showed more sympathy for intergovernmental cooperation, though progress was slow. The CMEA did consider Polish and German suggestions for the creation of Standing Commissions in 1954, but did not agree to their creation until 1956. The year 1954 did see the liquidation of most of the joint-stock companies which had been set up between the Soviet Union and the east European states after the Second World War. These companies, although formally constituted on an equal basis, effectively gave the Soviet general managers substantial control over sectors of the east European states' economies. They also enjoyed exemption from taxes and other privileges and benefits. Their liquidation is generally interpreted as a sign of a new more cooperative attitude on the part of the Soviet Union.

A move to multilateral cooperation has also been cited as a possible motive for the creation of the Warsaw Treaty Organization (WTO) in 1955.[6] This was not the official justification which was, rather, that the WTO had been formed in response to the rearmament of West Germany and its entry into NATO. The official reason should not be discounted. Many member states had suffered severely under the German Occupation in the Second World War. It is notable in this context that the agreement on the formation of a joint command postponed a decision on the participation of the forces of the German Democratic Republic (GDR). According to the French Ambassador to Warsaw, this may have been because of reservations expressed by Poland and Czechoslovakia.[7] If some east Europeans harboured suspicions about their own Germans, they had even more reason to be fearful of the west's Germans. Among the other explanations for the creation of the WTO is the suggestion that the Soviet Union wanted a bargaining counter in the forthcoming

1955 Geneva negotiations with the west. The Warsaw Treaty did indeed expressly provide for its own dissolution in the event of the 'conclusion of a general European treaty of collective security'. Moreover, the Soviet Union continued to make this link right up to the very end of the WTO.

The year after its creation, the WTO was invoked in order to justify the Soviet invasion of Hungary, whose reformers had sought to leave the organization. The WTO itself played no role in the decision to invade. Its Political Consultative Committee did not even meet between January 1956 and May 1958. Ironically, the Moscow declaration – a purely Soviet declaration – justifying the invasion also offered improved economic cooperation 'in order to remove any possibility of the violation of principles of national sovereignty'.[8] In the aftermath of the revolt in Hungary and smaller disturbances in Poland, the Soviet Union did make concessions, concluding agreements sanctioning the stationing of Soviet forces in the east European states. Soviet advisers, including military advisers, were also withdrawn, marking a further step away from the old Stalinist pattern of informal integration. In one case the agreement proved to be of relatively short duration. The April 1957 agreement with Romania was followed just over a year later, in May 1958, by the announcement that the Soviet Union had agreed to withdraw its forces.[9] It is true that Romania did not have the strategic significance of the WTO's front line states or of Poland. Nevertheless the concession was a significant one. Although Soviet motives are not certain, it is probable that the concession was made in order to gain Romanian acquiescence to increased economic integration.

Economic integration, however, brought Romania into increasing conflict with the Soviet Union and the more industrially advanced east European states, the GDR and Czechoslovakia. The underlying problem had been identified by Khrushchev in February 1956. According to Khrushchev, 'There is no need at present for each socialist country to develop all branches of heavy industry, as was necessary for the Soviet Union, which for a long time was the only socialist country in the capitalist encirclement.'[10] Romania, one of the least developed of the CMEA states, was not inclined to alter its strategy and published articles seeking to justify a protectionist strategy in 1957 and 1958. One point of dispute was that of prices. Since there was no free market to set prices, these had to be agreed by the states. The CMEA sought to remedy this problem in 1958 through the Bucharest price clause. The clause contained a set of guidelines by which intra-CMEA foreign trade prices could be derived from world market prices.[11] In reality, prices were still set by time-consuming bilateral bargains.

The first half of the next decade saw a major effort to advance integration, an effort which was defeated by the Romanians. On the eve of the new decade, in December 1959 in Sofia, the CMEA finally agreed upon a Charter. It is revealing that the organization had existed for just over a decade without having a formal charter. Equally striking is the comment of the Polish delegate to Sofia, who proudly proclaimed that the publication of the Charter 'puts an end once and for all to the speculations of certain foreign economic circles about the alleged supranational character of the Council'.[12] The Charter provided for an intergovernmental organization with no supranational authority, no majority decision-making and, equally significantly, no court to oversee and enforce implementation of the Charter (Document 7.2). The publication of the Charter did, however, inaugurate a more intense period of debate. The first concrete product of this was the Basic Principles of the International Socialist Division of Labour (Document 7.3).This had been formulated by the CMEA in December 1961, but had to be ratified by a conference of party leaders in June 1962. The document itself embodied the irreconcilable differences of the Member States. Alongside commitments to specialization stood commitments to balanced development and the reduction of historic disparities in levels of development. Dissatisfaction with this document, at least among the advocates of greater specialization, was evident from the continued Czechoslovak campaign which criticized, among other things, the efforts of some member states to develop steel capacity despite the lack of adequate raw material reserves. More important still was Khrushchev's initiative in August 1962. He repeated his earlier criticism of small states which attempted to develop a wide range of heavy industries, bemoaned the absence of a multilateral payments system, and called for the coordination of investment especially in extractive industries. His offer to reduce production of some items in the Soviet Union in order to allow the expansion of production in other Member States is especially striking. Such concessions did little to appease the Romanians. At the end of 1962 Khrushchev's demand for new initiatives was being buried, and in July 1963 a conference of party leaders praised the virtues of 'bilateral consultations between member states' in order to coordinate plans.[13]

Khrushchev's efforts had not been entirely fruitless. One concrete achievement was agreement on an Executive Committee and new Standing Commissions in June 1961. In July 1963 agreement on an International Bank for Economic Cooperation (IBEC) was reached. Its main task was to facilitate multilateral payments. There had been an earlier attempt to do this, through an agreement to use Moscow as a clearing house for multilateral settlements. That had clearly been a failure and the IBEC proved to be only marginally more successful. In the light of Khrushchev's vision of socialist integration, these successes were very limited. Indeed, the IBEC was indicative more of the persistence of a long recognized and intractable problem.

Despite the effective defeat of Khrushchev's plans, the Romanians still felt under pressure. From the summer of 1958 the Romanians had been relatively restrained, probably in the hope of obtaining credits and equipment for the expansion of the chemical and steel industries. Aid for the construction of the prestigious Galati steel mill became a focus of their efforts. At the end of 1960, however, it was clear that the Soviet Union was not going to provide the level of assistance that Romania desired. Subsequently, Romanian authors adopted a more polemical tone. One striking example of the issues at stake was the argument that the development of heavy industry was essential in building socialism – because it fostered the development of an industrial proletariat.[14] That the issue of integration was bound up not only with arguments about development and underdevelopment but also with arguments about the nature of the socialist state became unequivocally clear in 1964, when the Romanian party mounted a full-scale attack on the advocates of integration (Document 7.6). For the Romanians, supranational integration was simply incompatible with the socialist state.

The Romanians also led the resistance to Soviet attempts to strengthen the WTO. On this issue, the new Romanian leader Nicolae Ceauşescu raised the stakes even higher. Not only did he dismiss the military blocs of the west and east as anachronistic; he also, in a speech of May 1966, threatened to open up the question of east Europe's territorial boundaries. The outcome was a stalemate. At the WTO meeting in Bucharest in July 1966, the Soviet Union did not press the issue of organizational reform and the Romanians joined in signing a declaration whereby the member states renounced any territorial ambitions. Romania had drawn back but was no more inclined to be compliant. The Romanians dissented from criticism of the increasingly liberal line taken by Czechoslovakia at the WTO Sofia meeting in March 1968, and were excluded from the subsequent meetings which coordinated the invasion and suppression of Czechoslovak reforms later in the year. In the wake of the Czechoslovak crisis some institutional reforms were made. The March 1969 WTO meeting agreed on the creation of a Committee of Defence Ministers, a Military Council and a Technical Council. There was also a considerable increase in WTO military exercises during the subsequent four years.[15]

The aftermath of the Czechoslovak crisis also witnessed a revival of interest in integration. As usual, efforts were made to placate the Romanians. This time there was a new bone of contention, the word 'integration' itself. Romanian suspicion kept it out of the communiqué issued at the April 1969 CMEA meeting.[16] There was an additional complication in that the Hungarians, who had embarked on domestic economic reform, seeking to decentralize economic decision-making, were opposed to strengthening centralized decision-making within the CMEA. Despite these obstacles some progress was made. There was agreement in 1970 on an International Investment Bank, whose prime purpose was to promote joint investment in raw material extraction. Since the Bank's charter provided for majority voting, Romania did not join – but it had accepted the principle of a CMEA body employing majority voting. Romania also conceded the use of the term 'integration' in the aptly named Comprehensive Programme of 1971. The Romanian concession was less dramatic than it might appear, for there were sufficient reassurances that national planning was not threatened.

The Comprehensive Programme, despite the use of novel terminology, did not signify a radical change in the form of integration, hence the scepticism of some Hungarian reformers (Document 7.10).[17] There was one new principle in the Programme, that of 'interestedness'. Those countries with a declared interest in a particular form of cooperation would be allowed to proceed without the others being able to veto it. There was also extensive reference to 'international industrial associations'. The absence of socialist multinationals was a notable deficiency of integration in the east. Yet despite the promise of the Comprehensive Programme, the creation of genuine socialist multinationals proved difficult. The legal framework was often lacking, and where it was set up there was a reluctance to use it. Ironically, legislation permitting joint enterprises was more typically used to facilitate joint enterprises with western firms. One study in the mid-1980s could identify only ten joint socialist enterprises. According to the same study, the underlying problem was that each of the partners to a joint enterprise was subject to a different national plan. Consequently, joint enterprises required the coordination of national plans, and this had always been the prime obstacle to integration. The only easy solution was to exempt the joint enterprises from national plans, but there were limits to how often this strategy could be used without calling into question the idea of a centrally planned economy.[18] Once again, the link between domestic reform and international integration was clear.

During the 1970s, however, the east European states were engaged in an increasingly desperate dash for growth and increased productivity, often based upon imported western technology. At the same time, they were beginning to suffer from the effects of changes in the global economy, notably the rise in oil prices in 1973–74. All of them, with the exception of Romania, were highly dependent upon the Soviet Union for fuel. Thus the Soviet decision in 1975 to increase its fuel prices substantially and to link future prices more closely to world market prices was a significant blow. The importance of fuel and raw materials was evident in the 1975 Agreed Plan of Multilateral Integration Measures, which was heavily skewed towards these sectors of the CMEA economies.[19] Although the Agreed Plan did entail greater coordination of national plans, more fundamental reform still proved to be elusive, and suggestions at the 1978 CMEA meeting for changes to voting procedures were rejected.

As the CMEA entered the 1980s, its member states were caught in a vice. Still profligate in their consumption of energy, most were heavily indebted as a result of their acquisition of western technology. Soon Poland was forced to announce that it could not meet its debt payments. The debate on integration resumed in the 1980s, but really focused on the well known problems which the CMEA had failed to solve time and again. The result was the Comprehensive Programme of Scientific and Technical Progress of December 1985. Both technological advance and economic decentralization were central to the Programme (Document 7.11). Despite the commitment of the new Soviet leader, Mikhail Gorbachev, to economic reform, the Soviet Union lagged behind Hungary. Indeed, as Hungary's reforms advanced while others, like the GDR and Romania, clung to the old methods, the discrepancy between the CMEA economies grew (Document 7.12). Integration within the CMEA had always been based upon the assumption of the basic similarity of the domestic economic structures of its members. That assumption was no longer valid. Nor were other assumptions. As Gorbachev recalled, he made it clear to his CMEA partners in November 1986 that 'The usual model for economic relations, which had Soviet raw materials flowing primarily to our allies and their finished products to us, was not going to work any more.'[20]

Gorbachev's blunt message and the inadequacy of the hastily devised Comprehensive Programme of December 1985 heralded a new round of debate, albeit one which proved to be inconclusive. It was indicative of the failure of traditional methods that in July 1988 the CMEA agreed, with the exception of Romania, that the member states would seek to create a 'unified market'. In the same year the CMEA and the EEC finally agreed on a Joint Declaration. There was more than a little irony in this. The EEC had long resisted any agreement on the grounds that the CMEA lacked any authority over the trade policies of its members. The EEC finally relented only as the CMEA was on the point of extinction. The concession was a qualified one and was accompanied by negotiations on the bilateral agreements between the EEC and the separate member states of the CMEA which the EEC had always preferred.

N. I. Ryzhkov's address to the January 1990 CMEA meeting amounted to a confession of the organization's failure, and catalogued those well known and intractable problems: the absence of a multilateral payments system, distorted prices, the link between domestic reform and international integration (Document 7.13). Now that domestic reform was becoming a reality, the CMEA was becoming an obstacle. That had been made clear the week before the meeting by the Czechoslovak Prime Minister Václav Klaus when he declared that he would argue for the dissolution of the CMEA and threatened that Czechoslovakia would abandon the organization if the others did not agree. The Soviet Union still argued for reform rather than dissolution, but also contributed to the CMEA's demise. The Soviet decision to switch to hard currencies in place of the transferable ruble meant abandoning a central mechanism of the CMEA, as well as considerable economic hardship for her CMEA partners.

Dissolution was effectively agreed in January 1991, with the final rites being performed in June. Most members had agreed in January to create a successor organization, but the Czechoslovaks dismissed the idea as irrelevant. As *Pravda* noted, the consequences would be painful. Despite the CMEA's deficiencies, the economic links between the member states were substantial (Document 7.15). The disruption was already evident. Hungary, for example, saw its trade with the Soviet Union shrink from 25 per cent in 1989 to a mere 4 per cent at the beginning of 1991.[21] The importance of the Soviet Union as a trading partner, increased by the pattern of dependence on Soviet energy and raw materials at distorted prices, had been one of the things that had held the CMEA together. The asymmetry between the Soviet Union and its CMEA partners now turned from being a virtue to being a vice.

The WTO did not long survive the CMEA. The Soviet Union had already begun to reform its military doctrine, and the WTO sanctioned a switch to 'non-offensive defence' in May 1987. It became clear, however, that more substantive reform would be required. Yet the Soviet Union was reluctant to abandon the WTO while its old adversary, NATO, survived. The latter showed no interest in the long-established Soviet proposal for a simultaneous dissolution of both alliances. But as *Izvestia* noted, the WTO's 'main opponents proved to be inside rather than outside the organization' (Document 7.14). This time it was the Hungarians who pushed for dissolution. As late as May 1990, the commander of WTO forces conceded that some countries might leave the alliance but not that the alliance itself would disappear. As Hungary, closely followed by Czechoslovakia and Poland, demanded the withdrawal of Soviet troops and adopted policies of strictly national territorial defence, Gorbachev could do little more than delay the inevitable. In February 1991, he conceded that the WTO would have to be dissolved. With the end of the cold war, the WTO had lost part of its rationale, but only part. Simultaneous dissolution of both alliances had also been part of that rationale. Although that option met with sympathy in Czechoslovakia, the new post-communist leaders of east Europe had no interest in the perpetuation of military integration with the Soviet Union, no desire to find a new purpose for the WTO.

While the end of the CMEA aggravated the dislocation associated with economic transformation, the dissolution of the WTO left a security vacuum. Both organizations had provided a form of integration, albeit one with substantial limits. In part those limits were a product of the structural constraints inherent in centrally planned economies, constraints which could be overcome only at the expense of radical centralization, or, perhaps, of coordinated radical economic reform. Neither proved possible. In part those limits were a product of the diversity of historical experience which predated the establishment of the socialist regimes and of the inherent asymmetry of forms of integration incorporating the Soviet Union.

NOTES

1. As early as March 1956. Pascaline Winand, *Eisenhower, Kennedy and the United States of Europe* (New York, 1992), pp. 128–9.
2. Kazimierz Grzybowski, *The Socialist Commonwealth of Nations* (New Haven, CT, 1964), pp. 256–7.
3. See Kenneth Jowitt (ed.), *Social Change in Romania 1860–1940* (Berkeley, CA, 1978).
4. Grzybowski, *The Socialist Commonwealth of Nations*, pp. 36–7.
5. Quoted by Dorothy W. Douglas, *Transitional Economic Systems: The Polish-Czech Example* (London, 1953), pp. 46–48.
6. Andrzej Korbonski, *The Warsaw Pact: International Conciliation*, No. 573 (May 1969), pp. 11–12.
7. *Documents Diplomatiques Français*, 1955, Vol. 1, doc. 287.
8. *Current Digest of the Soviet Press*, Vol. 8, No. 40 (14 November 1956), p. 11.
9. On these developments see R.A. Remington, *The Warsaw Pact* (Cambridge, MA, 1971).
10. Quoted in Grzybowski, *The Socialist Commonwealth of Nations*, p. 75. The best source on Romania is John Michael Montias, *Economic Development in Communist Rumania* (Cambridge, MA, 1967).
11. On this complex issue see Eward E. Hewett, *Foreign Trade Prices in the Council for Mutual Economic Assistance* (Cambridge, 1974). The Bulgarians later expressed their dissatisfaction with reference to world market prices on the grounds that these reflected imperialist exploitation of less developed countiries. ibid., p. 164.
12. Quoted in Giuseppe Schiavone, *The Institutions of Comecon* (London, 1981), p. 25.
13. Quoted in Robert S. Jaster, 'The defeat of Khrushchev's plan to integrate Eastern Europe', *World Today*, Vol. 19 (1963), p. 521.
14. Montias, *Economic Development in Communist Rumania*, p. 206.
15. See Dale R. Herspring, 'The Warsw Pact at 25', *Problems of Communism*, Vol. 29 (March–April 1980), p. 5.
16. Henry Wilcox Schaefer, *Comecon and the Politics of Integration* (New York, 1972), p. 50.
17. The scepticism should not be too stongly emphasized. L. Csaba recalled the general enthusiasm of the Hungarians for the Comprehensive Programme, and their subsequent disappointment: *Eastern Europe in the World Economy* (Cambridge, 1984).

18. Harriet Matejka, 'More joint enterprises within the CMEA', in John P. Hardt and Carl H. McMillan (eds), *Planned Economies: Confronting the Challenges of the 1980s* (Cambridge, 1988), p. 178.
19. Alan H.Smith, 'Plan coordination and joint planning in the CMEA', *Journal of Common Market Studies*, Vol. 18 (1979), p. 12.
20. Mikhail Gorbachev, *Memoirs* (London, 1995), p. 471.
21. Giles Merrit, *Eastern Europe and the USSR* (London, 1991), p. 97.

FURTHER READING

M. Brabant, *Economic Integration in Eastern Europe* (New York, 1989).

N. Fodor, *The Warsaw Treaty Organisation* (Basingstoke, 1990).

K. Grzybowski, *The Socialist Commonwealth of Nations* (New Haven, CT, 1964).

G. Holdon, *The Warsaw Pact* (Oxford, 1989).

M. Kaser, *Comecon* (Oxford, 1965).

J. Michael Montias, *Economic Development in Communist Rumania* (Cambridge, MA, 1967).

R.A. Remington, *The Warsaw Pact* (Cambridge, MA, 1971).

H. W. Schaefer, *Comecon and the Politics of Integration* (New York, 1972).

G. Schiavone, *The Institutions of Comecon* (London, 1981).

_____ 7.1 _____

COMMENT BY A POLISH ECONOMIST ON SOCIALISM AND TRADE, 1957

John Michael Montias, *Central Planning in Poland*
(Westport, CT: Greenwood, 1962), p. 281.

This document illustrates the status of Poland as a developing country.

___

Given the present structure of world prices and domestic costs, our comparative advantage lies – generally speaking – in raw materials rather than in fabricated products ... This testifies to the relative weakness of our transformation industry; it proves that we are still very backward in this sector ... The greater profitability of exporting raw materials arises not only from the fact that it enables us to realize an economic rent but because, in this sector, differences in labour productivity between us and the developed countries are relatively least ... If we were guided strictly by profitability considerations ... we should increase the share of raw materials in our export at the expense of finished products ... This would be contrary to the long-run interests of our economic development.

_____ 7.2 _____

CHARTER OF THE COUNCIL ON MUTUAL ECONOMIC AID, 1959

R. Vaughan (ed.), *Postwar Integration in Europe*
(London: Arnold, 1976), p. 9.

The Charter marked a modest step on the road to integration. It was shaped by both socialist ideology and the desires of several member states to assert their sovereign equality.

___

Art. I. Aims and Principles

1. The Council on Mutual Economic Aid shall have the aim of contributing, through the unification and coordination of the efforts of the member countries of the Council, to the planned development of the national economies and an acceleration of economic and technical progress in these countries; to increasing the level of industrialization of countries with a less developed industry; to an uninterrupted rise in labor productivity; and to a steady advance in the well-being of the peoples of the member countries of the Council.

2. The Council on Mutual Economic Aid shall be based on the principles of the sovereign equality of all the member countries of the Council. The economic and scientific-technical cooperation of the member countries of the Council shall be carried out in accordance with the principles of complete equality of rights, respect for sovereignty and national interests, mutual benefit and comradely mutual aid.

Art. II. Membership ...

3. Any member country of the Council may withdraw from the Council by notifying the depositary of this Charter. This notification shall enter into force six months after its receipt by the depository ...

Art. IV. Functions and Powers

1. In accordance with the aims and principles stipulated in Art. I of this Charter, the Council on Mutual Economic Aid:
   (a) shall organize:
      the comprehensive economic and scientific-technical cooperation of the member countries of the Council with a view to the most rational utilization of their natural resources and to acceleration of the development of production forces;
      the preparation of recommendations on major questions of economic ties stemming from the plans for development of the national economies of the member countries of the Council, with a view to coordinating these plans;
      the study of economic problems of interest to the member countries of the Council.
   (b) shall help the member countries of the Council in working out and implementing joint measures ...
   (c) shall undertake other activities necessary for achievement of the aims of the Council.
2. In the person of its agencies acting within the limits of their competence, the Council on Mutual Economic Aid shall be empowered to adopt recommendations and decisions in accordance with this Charter.

Art. IV. Recommendations and Decisions

1. Recommendations shall be adopted on questions of economic and scientific-technical cooperation. Recommendations shall be communicated to the member countries of the Council for their consideration. The member countries of the Council shall carry out the recommendations adopted by them upon the decisions of the governments or the competent agencies of these countries in accordance with their legislation.
2. Decisions shall be adopted on organizational and procedural questions.

Decisions shall enter into force, if not otherwise stipulated in the decisions themselves, on the day of the signing of the protocol of the meeting of the corresponding agency of the Council.

3. All recommendations and decisions of the Council shall be adopted only with the concurrence of the member countries of the Council concerned, and each country shall have the right to declare its interest in any question being considered in the Council. Recommendations and decisions shall not extend to countries that have expressed their disinterest in the given question. However, any of these countries may subsequently subscribe to the recommendations and decisions adopted by the other member countries of the Council.

Art. V. Agencies

1. In order to carry out the functions and powers stipulated in Art. III of this Charter, the Council on Mutual Economic Aid shall have the following basic agencies:
a Session of the Council,
a Conference of Representatives of Countries in the Council,
Permanent Commissions,
a Secretariat.

———————————— 7.3 ————————————

BASIC PRINCIPLES OF THE INTERNATIONAL SOCIALIST DIVISION OF LABOUR, 1961

R. Vaughan (ed.), *Postwar Integration in Europe* (London: Arnold, 1976), pp. 144–8.

The Basic Principles were the product of Khrushchev's push for greater integration. They were formulated in December 1961 and approved by the Conference of First Secretaries of the Communist and Workers' Parties in Moscow in June 1962.

1. Community of socialist countries and international socialist division of labour

The world socialist system is a social, economic and political community of free, sovereign nations following the path of socialism and communism, united by common interests and goals and by indestructible ties of inter-national socialist solidarity.

The close union of the socialist countries within a single system is necessitated by the objective laws of economic and political development ...

The community of socialist countries achieves its aims through all-round political, economic and cultural co-operation, with all the socialist countries guided by the principles of full equality, mutual respect for each other's independence and sovereignty, fraternal assistance and mutual benefit. No member of the socialist camp has, or can have, any special rights or privileges. Adherence to the principles of Marxism-Leninism and socialist internationalism is an indispensable condition for the successful development of the world socialist system . . .

Each socialist country maps out its own economic development plans based on the concrete conditions in the given country, the political and economic goals set by the Communist and Workers' Parties, and the needs and potentialities of all the socialist countries. The new social system makes it possible organically to combine the development of each national economy with the development and consolidation of the world economic system of socialism as a whole. The progress of the entire world socialist system depends on the contribution of each country.

The socialist countries consider it their internationalist duty to direct their efforts to securing a high rate of development in the industry and agriculture of each country commensurate with available potentialities, progressively equalizing economic development levels, and successfully solving the problem of exceeding the world capitalist system in absolute volume of industrial and agricultural production and subsequently surpassing the economically most developed capitalist countries in per capita production and in living standards of the working people . . .

In contrast to international capitalist division of labour, which reflects the exploitation of the weak by the strong and is formed spontaneously, through sharp monopoly rivalry and expansion, accentuating unequal economic development levels and producing an ugly, one-sided economic structure in underdeveloped countries, international socialist division of labour is carried out consciously, according to plan, in conformity with the vital interests of the peoples and with the aim of ensuring harmonious and all-round development of all the socialist countries, and adding strength to their unity.

Planned international socialist division of labour makes for maximum utilization of the advantages of the world socialist system, for a balanced economy in each country, rational distribution of the productive forces throughout the world socialist system, efficient employment of labour and material resources, and enhancement of the defence potential of the socialist camp. Division of labour must guarantee each country the possibility to market its specialized products and to buy the necessary raw materials, equipment and other goods . . .

2.   Co-ordination of economic plans – the principal means of successfully developing and extending international socialist division of labour

. . . CMEA experience in economic co-operation has shown that co-ordination of plans should seek to implement the following inter-related objective principles of international socialist division of labour:

• adequate assessment of the objectively required proportions in the economic development of each country and the world socialist system as a whole, so as to attain a balanced economy in each country;

- high economic efficiency of international socialist division of labour, i.e. a high rate of growth in production and maximum satisfaction of the needs of the population in each country with minimum expenditure of social labour;
- combination of international specialization in production with all-round, comprehensive development of the economies of the individual socialist countries with a view to the fullest and most rational utilization in all the countries of natural and economic resources, including man-power;
- steady elimination of historical differences in the economic development levels of the individual countries, primarily through industrialization of countries with relatively low economic levels, and through maximum utilization of the internal potentialities of each country and of the advantages inherent in the world socialist system . . .

3. Basic directions in rational division of labour in key branches of the economy

. . . Interstate specialization implies concentrating production of similar products in one or several socialist countries so as to meet the needs of all interested countries, thus improving industrial techniques and management, and establishing stable economic ties and co-operation. International specialization should serve to expand production, reduce costs, raise productivity and improve quality and technical standards . . .

5. International specialization and comprehensive economic development in individual socialist countries

The economic complex in each country should be developed in a way that will continuously raise the country's economic level. This presupposes above all maximum development of each country's socialist industry as the leading branch of the national economy, with priority given to the output of the means of production . . .

  As to industries which exist in all or in the majority of the socialist countries, it is advisable to extend inter-state specialization by product. In furthering specialization, account should be taken not only of the requirements of the socialist countries, but also of possibilities for export outside the world socialist . . .

6. Elimination of historical differences in economic development levels of the socialist countries

When they set out to build a socialist society, the countries of the world socialist system differed in level of development of their productive forces. The very nature of socialism dictates equalization of these levels . . .

  In the course of building socialism and communism there will be eliminated the substantial differences in the level of development of national productive forces, differences that stem from the historical conditions of capitalist development . . .

7.   *Division of labour and trade between socialist countries*

International socialist division of labour is the basis for trade between the socialist countries, which is carried out on the principle of equivalent exchange ...

Multilateral co-ordination of plans and the resultant recommendations for specialization and co-operation should ensure that each socialist country has a balanced payments structure, notably through wider use of multilateral settlements ...

It is necessary continually to perfect the system of price formation on the world socialist market in keeping with the requirements of the planned extension of the international socialist division of labour, steady expansion of trade, and accelerated development of the world socialist economy, while creating conditions for the gradual changeover to an independent price basis ...

_____ 7.4 _____

KHRUSHCHEV'S CALL FOR TIGHTER INTEGRATION, 1962

Current Digest of the Soviet Press, Vol. 14 (1962), no. 35, pp. 6–7 and no. 36, pp. 3–4.

Even after the June 1962 conference, Khrushchev continued to push for greater integration. Many of the problems he identified in this article published in August 1962 continued to haunt the CMEA.

Our common aim is to build a world socialist economy as a single complex. But to do this the countries of socialism have no other resources than the accumulations that are created in each of them. Consequently we cannot do without agreement, if only in general outline, without a policy of formation and utilization of accumulations within the framework of the Council on Mutual Economic Aid. This presupposes, first, allocating funds for construction of common projects, a practice that we have only begun, and, secondly, coordination of national plans of capital investment in such a manner as to take account, insofar as possible, not only of national but also of our common interests ...

The Soviet government, like the leaderships of the other countries belonging to the Council on Mutual Economic Aid, stands for increasing the practice of jointly financing the construction of industrial, transport and other enterprises of international significance. It is important to employ joint financing first of all in the raw materials branches producing for export, since these require the heaviest capital outlays. In our view, the necessary conditions have matured for jointly examining in the Council on Mutual Economic Aid the major capital construction projects of common interest ...

Coordination of plans not only does not restrict the economic initiative of the countries but, on the contrary, facilitates the development of such an initiative, while the possibilities for advancing the economy of each country and also developing the world socialist economy as a whole will be utilized far better and more fully.

In the past the Council on Mutual Economic Aid could not change the system of coordinating plans in general and capital investment plans in particular to the new basis because in the first place, under its former Statutes it did not have the necessary powers, and, in the second place, it was not armed with the necessary planning tools – material balance sheets, comparable national-economic indices, and unified statistics. The decisions of the June conference make it possible to organize the work of the Council on Mutual Economic Aid in this important matter in a new way . . .

It must be said that in the sphere of specialization and cooperation in manufacturing the countries of the Council on Mutual Economic Aid inherited a bad 'legacy' from capitalism. Specific conditions of development of many of the people's democracies in the past, when they were part of the system of the world capitalist economy, encouraged the rise of economically unjustified universalization of industry based on small-quantity production. The lack of a reliable raw material and power base and, in particular, their economic dependence on the imperialist monopolies of the big powers deprived most of these countries of the possibility of developing large-scale production. This circumstance, in turn, prevented them from participating in international division of labor on any kind of advantageous conditions and gave birth to a tendency to set up as many kinds of domestic production as they could. There was no confidence that they could obtain everything necessary in exchange for their own products.

In the course of the development of cooperation among the countries participating in the Council on Mutual Economic Aid it has become more and more obvious that such 'universalization' of the economy is not justified. It is too costly.

In general, the tendency to produce the utmost variety of industrial products in the country on the principle of 'having everything of one's own' without regard for the cost of production can arise in our time either as a result of insufficient development of the economy or for reasons of a noneconomic nature. We are speaking, of course, not of the greatest world powers, which are able to develop a more universal industry because of the possibility of organizing specialization and co-operation within the country and because of a relatively larger home market. But international cooperation of production is advantageous even to these countries . . .

It goes without saying that a country such as the USSR with a big market, is able to erect large enterprises of optimum size exclusively for meeting home needs. But it is advantageous to us, too, to participate in international socialist division of labor. The Soviet Union is prepared even to cut down production of some kinds of manufactures if it proves more expedient to produce them in other countries of the Council on Mutual Economic Aid . . .

The practice of foreign trade ties that has taken shape convinces us that we still do not utilize the wealth of possibilities for increasing mutual trade. There are frequent cases of buying needed goods 'on the side', although with proper organization they could be acquired in the countries of our commonwealth. There is no need to demonstrate that this hampers the course of economic construction.

The international socialist division of labor can develop successfully only if the machinery of foreign trade functions smoothly and without hitch, if trade ensures full and timely sale of what is produced on the basis of division of labor. This is why the countries participating in the Council on Mutual Economic Aid have outlined a number of measures to improve the system of foreign trade. In particular, a big role will be played by shifting to multilateral payments, as well as measures for increasing mutual responsibility for fulfillment of trade obligations.

7.5

ROMANIAN REJECTION OF FURTHER INTEGRATION, APRIL 1964

William E. Griffith (ed.), *Sino-Soviet Relations 1964–1965* (Cambridge, MA: MIT Press, 1967), pp. 282–4.

The Romanian Workers' Party rebutted Soviet pressure for supranational integration in this statement.

The successes obtained by the Rumanian People's Republic and by the other socialist countries show that the successful solution of the tasks of developing the economy depends first and foremost on the utilization of each country's internal possibilities, through an intense mustering of its own forces and the maximum use of its natural resources. Decisive for the development of the countries that inherited economic backwardness from capitalism is socialist industrialization, the only road that ensures the harmonious, balanced, and ever ascending as well as rapid growth of the whole national economy ... At the same time the economic and technical-scientific progress of the socialist countries relies on the relations of cooperation and mutual assistance established among them. These fruitful relations have seen a steady development; they have proved their efficiency, making a particularly important contribution to the successes scored by the socialist countries ...

Cooperation within CMEA is achieved on the basis of the principles of fully equal rights, of observance of national sovereignty and interests, of mutual advantage and comradely assistance.

As concerns the method of economic cooperation, the socialist countries that are members of CMEA have established that the main means of achieving the international socialist division of labor, the main form of cooperation among their national economies, is to coordinate plans on the basis of bilateral and multilateral agreements.

During the development of the relations of cooperation among the socialist countries that are members of CMEA, forms and measures have been projected, such as a joint plan and a single planning body for all member countries, interstate technical-productive branch unions, enterprises jointly owned by several countries, interstate economic complexes, etc.

Our party has very clearly expressed its point of view, declaring that, since the essence of the projected measures lies in shifting some functions of economic management from the competence of the respective state to that of superstate bodies or organisms, these measures are not in keeping with the principles that underlie the relations among the socialist countries.

The idea of a single planning body for all CMEA countries has the most serious economic and political implications. The planned management of the national economy is one of the fundamental, essential, and inalienable attributes of the sovereignty of the socialist state – the state plan being the chief means through which the socialist state achieves its political and socioeconomic objectives, establishes the direction and rates of development of the national economy, its fundamental proportions, the accumulations, the measures for raising the people's living standard and cultural level. The sovereignty of the socialist state requires that it effectively and fully avail itself of the means for the practical implementation of these functions holding in its hands all the levers of managing economic and social life. Transmitting such levers to the competence of superstate or extrastate bodies would turn sovereignty into a meaningless notion.

All these are also fully valid as concerns interstate technical-productive branch unions as well as enterprises commonly owned by two or several states. The state plan is one and indivisible; no parts or sections can be separated from it in order to be transferred outside the state. The management of the national economy as a whole is not possible if the questions of managing some branches or enterprises are taken away from the competence of the party and government of the respective country and transferred to extrastate bodies ...

_____ 7.6 _____

PRAVDA'S COMPARISON OF MILITARY INTEGRATION IN NATO AND THE WARSAW PACT, 14 MAY 1965

Current Digest of the Soviet Press, Vol. 18, no. 19 (1966), pp. 24–5.

In this statement *Pravda* sought to balance advocacy of greater integration within the Warsaw Pact with the claim the that the Pact respected the sovereignty of member states.

In 11 years the Warsaw Pact organization has become unconquerable in its might. The basis of this might is the unity and solidarity of the fraternal countries, advancing under the invincible banner of Marxism-Leninism and proletarian internationalism.

The mechanism of the Warsaw Pact organization is constantly improving and growing stronger. The men in its armies are bound by indestructible bonds of combat fraternity, steeled in the course of joint exercises and maneuvers. The 'October Assault,' which took place in the autumn of 1965 on the soil of the German Democratic Republic, was an impressive demonstration of the unity and combat friendship of the armies of the Warsaw Pact countries. The participating units of the National People's Army of the GDR and of the Polish, Soviet and Czechoslovak armies demonstrated a high degree of training and combat readiness.

The defense organization of the fraternal socialist countries, within which the principles of equality, sovereignty, noninterference in one another's internal affairs and complete mutual respect are strictly observed, is steadily developing and gaining strength. Different processes are under way in the aggressive NATO organization, which is being undermined by the contradictions among its participants. The USA and the FRG are trying to use this bloc for their own ends, trampling the national interests, dignity and sovereignty of the other partners. This has confronted NATO with serious difficulties.

7.7

PRAVDA'S VIEW OF EUROPE, 20 MAY 1966

Current Digest of the Soviet Press, Vol. 18, no. 20 (1966), p. 14.

This statement by *Pravda* reflected the orthodox Soviet position that while the Soviet Union counted as part of Europe, the United States did not.

The Soviet Union – the world's largest power, stretching over the territory of Europe and Asia – consistently and firmly takes the position of the necessity of strengthening peaceful cooperation and the security of all peoples. Our country proceeds from the view that the development of cooperation among the states on the European continent can have a beneficial influence on the situation throughout the world.

Unfortunately, attempts have continued for two decades now in the Western part of our continent to lop off a piece of Europe and set it up in opposition to the East European states, primarily the Soviet Union. How many versions there have been of such a truncated Europe! Many years have passed, and life has finally forced realistic-thinking politicians to return to the obvious truth they learned back in school: Europe is the sum total of *all* the states situated on its territory.

Back on 11 April 1960, President de Gaulle stated officially that the European continent must strive toward 'uniting its two parts, finding peace within itself,' and achieving 'an accommodation from the Atlantic to the Urals.' Since that time a course toward general European cooperation has begun to play an important role in French foreign policy. At the same time, as the American newspaper the Washington Post recently noted with envy, this policy is enjoying more and more support not only in France but also in the other countries of west Europe that are desirous of freeing themselves from American tutelage ...

But in France there are other significant forces that are trying to give another meaning to the word 'Europe'. For example, the director of the newspaper *Le Monde*, in talking with me, defended the idea of creating a 'Europe from San Francisco via Paris to Vladivostok'. He and others like him believe that the old geographical concepts have become antiquated in the modern world and that political reality demands a broader approach to solving problems of international cooperation. But with all due respect to the newspaper *Le Monde*, it must be said that the theory of creating a 'Europe from San Francisco via Paris to Vladivostok' is fraught with highly dangerous consequences.

Finally, some French figures propose a third version of a 'modern Europe' – without the USA, but also without the USSR. Professor Maurice Duverger of the University of Paris, for example, has come forward with such a blueprint. Having rightly noted that 'only the existing Europe can counter American hegemony in the Old World', he nevertheless proceeds to advocate a solution that, if attempts are made to implement it, would destroy at one stroke any hopes for European unity: He called upon the French and Germans together to seek 'a way to create an independent Europe within a framework that would bring the People's Democracies and the Western democracies closer together'.

Thus Europe, as conceived by Prof. Duverger, clearly does not extend to the Urals. It is cut off somewhere on its Eastern borders. But it should be clear that plans for creating such a 'Europe', from which a major state such as the Soviet Union is excluded, are built on sand.

Some French supporters of such a 'middle Europe' tried to convince me that this is only an 'intermediate stage' on the path to genuine all-European cooperation, after which there will allegedly be a second stage – the inclusion of the USSR in Europe. But, in the first place, the USSR has no need for anyone to 'include' it in the family of European peoples. Like it or not, the Soviet Union is already in Europe, and, as they say, there's nothing you can do about it. In the second place, European cooperation can be effective only if it is universal.

No, gentlemen, as realistic-minded figures in France quite rightly pose the question, Europe is Europe and America is America. Europeans can and must put their house in order by ensuring peace on the European continent, strengthening European security and guaranteeing businesslike intra-European economic cooperation. They are far from ruling out cooperation with the United States, as well as with all the other countries of the world. But the time for American tutelage over one state or another in Europe has disappeared irrevocably ...

7.8

THE COMPREHENSIVE PROGRAMME, JULY 1971

The Multilateral Economic Co-operation of Socialist States (Moscow: Progress Publishers, 1977), pp. 52, 62–3, 66–7.

The Programme for enhanced integration was agreed at the 25th Session of the CMEA. It was significant for allowing integration between 'interested' member states without requiring the consent of the others.

Co-ordination of Long Term Plans for Key Branches of the National Economy and Lines of Production

... In co-ordinating their plans the CMEA member-countries proceed from the fact that long-term planning outlines the main development trends of the basic branches of the national economy and lines of production for 10–20 years, reflects the basic goals of the countries' economic policy aimed at promoting socio-economic and scientific-technological progress for longer periods and provides the guidelines for the medium-term national economic planning and defines the part the given country is to play in the international division of labour ...

The long-term co-ordination of plans by the CMEA member-countries shall embrace questions in which all or several countries are interested; it shall be carried out on a multilateral or bilateral basis, in accordance with arrangements made by the countries concerned ...

Interested CMEA member-countries shall jointly plan individual branches of industry and lines of production. This new form of co-operation in the planning field is intended to bend their efforts on the most rapid achievement of advanced scientific and technological results, on raising labour productivity, ensuring competitiveness on the world market, and the fuller satisfaction of their requirements for the products of the selected branches or lines of production ... Joint planning shall not interfere with the autonomy of internal planning. Joint planning shall be carried out with national ownership of the corresponding productive capacities and resources preserved ...

_____ 7.9 _____

PÉTER VÁLYI: A HUNGARIAN ASSESSMENT OF INTEGRATION IN THE 1970s

'Hungary and international economic integration',
New Hungarian Quarterly, Vol. 13 (1972), pp. 25–7.

The difficulties inherent in implementing the Comprehensive Programme (see Document 7.8) were identified by the Hungarian economist Péter Vályi in an article published in 1972.

Last year in June, however, at the 25th Session of CMEA, a resolution placed a new stage on the agenda, that of integration. That was when the term 'integration' was first officially used in reference to the objectives of CMEA; a year later, in July this year, at the 26th Session of CMEA, the first achievements of the integration programme and the co-operation of the member countries found deserved appreciation, bearing in mind also that these grew out of many long years of preparatory work and the successes of earlier years.

The question arises why the stage of economic cooperation which is now in process of being elaborated was given a new name. The term integration as such was known the world over but socialist economists did not use it. It could be said that this new term is meant to document that all the countries participating in CMEA wish to produce a major qualitative change in their cooperation. This qualitative change will not, however, be implemented by a mechanical fusion of individual independent economies, such an objective would be unreal, the changes will have to occur in those areas where major problems occurred so far ...

In what way do we want to extend the proven methods of plan-coordination? There is no wish to replace voluntary coordination by directive planning, with the

CMEA centre acting as a joint Planning Office. Nor would it be right if planning were confined to present methods, since that would inhibit progress. These methods are inadequate in two ways. On the one hand coordination only covers a five-year period and does not possess a long-term character, in foreign trade annual plans and agreements are in fact still the rule. What is more, present methods of coordination are not development-orientated, they are not designed to transform the structure of the economy, their objective is merely to increase the turnover of trade between CMEA countries, within a given structure of production ...

The major obstacle in the way of a faster growth in mutual turnover and a gradual specialization in production is that bilateralism which asserts itself in practice, the exaggeratedly detailed quota system, and the practice of annually balancing units of payment.

The CMEA 'Complex Programme' last year declared international specialization in production, the most effective possible manifestation of economic integration, to be the major common objective. A greater part of the positive results of cooperation can indeed be brought to the surface by specialization. It must be borne in mind though that the extension of specialization and the transformation of the general autarchic character of home production is one of the most complex tasks in international economic activity, even under the conditions of a socialist planned economy.

_____7.10_____

REZSO NYERS: A HUNGARIAN ASSESSMENT OF INTEGRATION IN THE 1980s

'Tendencies of tradition and reform in CMEA cooperation',
Soviet and East European Foreign Trade,
Vol. 20, no. 2 (1984), pp. 27–9.

The persistent obstacles to integration were specified by the Hungarian economist Rezso Nyers just over a decade after agreement on the Comprehensive Programme (see Document 7.8).

In attempting to expand the use of economic mechanisms within the CMEA, one encounters the following systemic obstacles:

Domestic market price and value conditions are in basic disagreement with external (international) market price and value conditions. These two prices need to be in agreement to influence economic agents (manufacturers-users-consumers) toward international cooperation and to make such cooperation a concern not only of the government but also of individual economic units.

The multilaterality of relations lacks one of its prime means – an active and effective monetary system. The role of national currencies is usually passive; their exchange rates are in most cases unrealistic; and internal markets are not linked with the CMEA international market – the Hungarian forint is the only currency advancing toward convertibility. Today the transferable ruble can perform only very limited functions.

Overcentralization of rights of decision in the state administrative organizations. In countries with directive systems of economic control (the Soviet Union, the GDR, Czechoslovakia, Romania, and Bulgaria) enterprises do not have the right to make decisions on issues of production and trade; their role is limited to implementation. This circumstance is an extremely powerful brake on cooperation because only prominent issues (numerically a smaller part of cooperation) can be tackled on the state level.

Low flexibility of foreign trade in the system of physically specified bilateral quotas ...

If we observe CMEA traditions, then we can institute a number of minor measures, leaving the substance itself untouched and the system of economic instruments to lead a shadow life. If we do not want to continue on this path, we have to reform, accepting the difficulties this involves ...

Let us now try to review the opportunities actually provided for the promotion of cooperation.

1. *Stopping the decline of integration in the field of energy and raw materials.* It is a paradoxical state of affairs in the CMEA that when the base world market prices were depressed, supply and turnover were growing; but since they have been excessively high (owing to monopoly positions), offers have been decreasing. And considering that the exchange of 'raw material for finished products' between the Soviet Union and the smaller countries is a basic economic-geographical fact in this area, its further decline would not be a natural but an unnatural process; without it CMEA cooperation could only be realized on a lower level than at present. Most certainly this can be the 'hard nucleus' of cooperation in the Soviet-centered sphere of the CMEA. Lately the 'tendency toward disintegration' has manifested itself in this very field, and thus this is where cooperation has to be rechanelled into its original direction.

2. *Boosting the mutual trade in manufactured industrial products.* This is an important opportunity both in the relationship of 'Soviet economy *vis-à-vis* smaller country' and in that of 'smaller economy *vis-à-vis* smaller economy'. In this respect a new situation has been brought about by the slowdown of the dynamism of investment in member countries as well as by the growing demand for a balanced consumer market. The first factor reduces demand for investment goods, while the latter puts a brake on the supply of consumer goods. This can be resolved by increasing the share of products that are competitive with Western imports with respect to price and technical parameters, terms of delivery, and parts supply.

_____7.11_____

N. I. RYZHKOV: A SOVIET VIEW OF THE PROGRAMME OF SCIENTIFIC AND TECHNICAL PROGRESS, 17 DECEMBER 1985

Current Digest of the Soviet Press, Vol. 37 (1985), no. 52, pp. 11–12.

N. I. Ryzhkov, Chairman of the USSR Council of Ministers from 1985 to 1991, was unusually frank in acknowledging the problems the CMEA faced, but still held out hope in this speech to the 41st Session of the CMEA.

However N. I. Ryzhkov said we must admit in all candor that the socialist countries are by no means making adequate use of opportunities for scientific and technical progress and for the joint solution of emerging scientific and technical problems. Therefore the Comprehensive Program of Scientific and Technical Progress assumes strategic significance for all of us ...

By a decision of the Politburo of the CPSU Central Committee, organizations of a fundamentally new type – interbranch and scientific and technical complexes – are now being created in the Soviet Union. Almost all of these organizations will be head organizations for specific problems covered In the CMEA's Comprehensive Program ...

In thinking about the provision of resources for the Comprehensive Program and organizational measures for its fulfillment we are taking a fresh look at many things in our country. The Soviet government is giving the head organizations the right to conclude contracts with organizations of other CMEA member-countries ...

_____7.12_____

HUNGARIAN EMPHASIS ON THE LINK BETWEEN DOMESTIC AND INTERNATIONAL REFORM, 1990

L. Csaba, *Eastern Europe in the World Economy* (Cambridge: Cambridge University Press, 1990), pp. 326–7.

In his book *Eastern Europe in the World Economy*, L. Csaba stressed the link between domestic and international reform.

What, then, is meant by the proposal accepted by the Council session for the coordination of plans at other than the central levels? The growing role of the sectoral ministries is a typical feature of the new Soviet foreign trade legislation. Understandably, the Soviet position is that issues of investment policy and of technological progress were to be determined at this level ...

From the Hungarian point of view, the growing role of the sectoral ministries is not a very promising proposition for two reasons. First, in Hungary sectoral ministries were instrumental in perverting the first phase of the reform in the mid-seventies. It is, therefore, difficult for Hungarian economists to see the regulations of the Soviet law on the state owned enterprise ... which also stipulates the increased foreign trade involvement of this particular management level by granting the sectoral ministries foreign currency funds and the right to initiate joint ventures with foreign partners – as the strongest element of a promising reform legislation. Second, in a more decentralized economic mechanism, sectoral ministries have an inherent propensity to disequilibrate planned bilateral trade flows, thereby eroding the bargains struck by the central planning organs in coordinating plans ...

The point of the communiqué that calls for a growing role for sectoral ministries is a compromise based on the understanding that branches were to play a relevant role in important member states for quite some time to come ... Since the January 1988 government reorganization further cut back the number of ministries in Hungary, practically no agents have remained that can engage in intermediate level coordinative activities in CMEA fora ...

In the present context, two points should be made. For one thing, as Soviet officials have justly noted ... this form of cooperation continues to be restricted to exchange of experiences rather than the firms' organizing cooperation, which is due primarily to unresolved issues of pricing and material-technical supply and/or company rights. For another, several member states have not provided the firms with rights that would permit them to function more organically and independently on external (Comecon) markets. This has to do with the management concepts of the given countries. Leaving apart the quasi war economies of Cuba and Vietnam, we shall find a recent article of the state secretary of the State Planning Commission of the GDR to illustrate the point. On this analysis, East German combines have had direct relations with socialist partners since the mid-sixties; direct relations have developed successfully, and extend to 35 per cent of all industrial employees and 50 per cent of all industrial fixed assets. Joint analyses, the exchange of information and of experiences, as well as joint technological research are all part of direct interfirm contacts. The GDR did not intend to go beyond that range of these contacts which, however, the Soviets tend to find too narrow. As far as Romania is concerned, the major features of the regulation of interfirm contacts have been made public in a speech by Nicolae Ceauşescu, delivered at his meeting with the Premiers heading the delegations to the 1980 Council Session ... Accordingly, Romanian firms and *centrale* may enter into foreign contact following the detailed priorities of the national programmes and research projects, and through the foreign trade organizations. The priority of the national plans was to be guaranteed, and in intra-CMEA deals, compulsory interstate agreements had to pave the way for company action aimed at implementing central tasks in a creative manner. To put the gist of all this another way, a country that does not even contemplate economic decentralization can't be forced into it by a regional cooperation organ.

―――――――――――――――7.13―――――――――――――――

N. I. RYZHKOV: SPEECH ON THE IMPACT OF DOMESTIC REFORM ON THE CMEA, 9 JANUARY 1990

Current Digest of the Soviet Press, Vol. 42, no. 2 (1990), pp. 12–13.

In this speech, Ryzhkov (compare Document 7.11) acknowledged the deep-rooted problems of the CMEA.

―――――――――――――――――――――――――――――――――――

A profound incompatibility has arisen between the very system of international economic ties and the economic reforms being carried out in most of the countries, an incompatibility that is having an increasingly marked negative impact on reciprocal economic ties. In practical terms, it is confronting us with a choice – either to retain the existing foreign-economic mechanism but refrain from conducting reforms, or to conduct a radical restructuring of the mechanism, making it compatible with the economic reforms being carried out in our countries. One has only to pose the question in this way to conclude that there can be only one solution. Economic reforms, a departure from the directive-distributive system of management and a turn toward economic methods are a historical necessity for our countries ...

The existing system of prices and charges was created at a time when trade was determined at the state-to-state level and the CMEA countries were largely isolated from the world economy. At the present time, this practice has essentially become an impediment to the development of ties. Reciprocal-trade prices, which have been formed for the past five years on the basis of world prices are causing considerable distortions in trade proportions, leading to a disruption of equivalent exchange and mutual benefit, and giving the public wrong ideas about the real relations among the countries.

The system of payments in transferable rubles, which was initially conceived as a multilateral system, has for all practical purposes degenerated into a system of bilateral settlements. The transferable ruble was and remains essentially nothing but an accounting unit unrelated either to the national currencies of the CMEA countries or to freely convertible currency, and therefore cannot serve as a fully valid means of payment. At a time when enterprises in the Soviet Union and other countries have gained the right to enter foreign markets and have begun experiencing a need for real means of payment, the transferable ruble has gone from being an instrument of unification to posing an obstacle to the development of ties. Moreover, for the purposes of settling accounts domestically, within the CMEA countries, rates of exchange between the transferable ruble and the national currencies are being set at discriminatory levels in comparison with dollar exchange rates. . . .

7.14

IZVESTIA ON THE IMPACT OF THE DEMISE OF THE WARSAW PACT, 28 FEBRUARY 1991

Current Digest of the Soviet Press, Vol. 42, no. 9 (1991), p. 18–19.

The demise of the Warsaw pact while NATO remained intact was a major blow for Moscow. This is *Izvestia*'s assessment of the position.

The end of the cold war, provided this turn of events can be consolidated, creates favorable conditions for doing away with the bloc-oriented structure of the political world starting with its military component and creating an all-European security system. It would be a good thing if the change in the blocs' functions and roles affected both the Warsaw Treaty Organization and NATO at the same time. That was always Moscow's position. However, amid the fundamentally new historical conditions, in which the Warsaw Pact's main opponents proved to be inside rather than outside the organization, Moscow had to change its position and accelerate changes in the Warsaw Treaty Organization without regard for the situation in NATO. We 'simply' had no other choice . . .

Certain capitals are pondering whether it might not be possible, after leaving the Warsaw Treaty Organizaton, to become affiliated with NATO in some way. In

Brussels, these ideas are viewed as overly exotic and clearly precipitate. Brussels prefers a neutral east Europe.

Attempts to create regional associations are not outside the realm of possibility. For example, a central European association (Poland, Czechoslovakia and Hungary) or a Danube–Adriatic association (Austria, Hungary, Italy, Czechoslovakia and Yugoslavia). Perhaps a Balkan one. The current picture is this: On one side, a 'full-sized', self-confident and self-satisfied NATO, and on the other, a shrunken remnant of the Warsaw Treaty Organization – and an only temporary remnant at that. What does this mean for the USSR's security? Hasn't our strategic position deteriorated?

If one proceeds from the premise that a conventional (non-nuclear) war is possible in Europe, then our strategic position has obviously worsened. But if one takes the view that the probability of a conventional war in Europe is close to zero, then the level of our security has not declined. The second hypothesis seems more plausible to me.

_____7.15_____

PRAVDA ON THE IMPLICATIONS OF THE DEMISE OF THE CMEA, 18 MARCH 1991

Current Digest of the Soviet Press, Vol. 32 (1991), no. 11, p. 15.

Pravda offered a frank account of the differences between the Soviet Union and her CMEA partners as the organization disintegrated.

Dissolving the CMEA has proven considerably harder than creating it. What accounts for this?

The CMEA is a child of its time. It emerged and operated within the framework of the plan- and directive-oriented, centralized system of economic administration.

But there is another truth about the CMEA that cannot be ignored where practical matters are concerned. In the course of four decades, a real economic space developed within the council framework. The CMEA countries are linked by thousands of ties. These ties include cooperative relations, interlocking energy systems and a great many other concrete results of their many years of cooperation.

The severing of traditional ties would lead to a sharp decline in production, the closing of entire branches of industry and mass unemployment. The first steps toward cooperation on the basis of real market relations have been very difficult for us. The CMEA countries agreed, for example, to switch to settling accounts in freely convertible currency at world prices in their mutual trading as of Jan. 1 of this year. Few would deny the necessity and urgency of this step, for it is the only way to become integrated into world economic ties and to put our relations on a realistic basis. But what is the actual situation? The USSR has no foreign currency, nor do our neighbors. There is nothing with which to pay for purchases. This means that a sudden leap from the old to the new is impossible; a kind of transition period is needed in which the currency clearing method and barter deals could be used ...

The Soviet side is convinced that a new organization for multilateral economic cooperation – a legal successor to the CMEA – could help reconstruct the fabric of such cooperation. This view is also held by Bulgaria, Vietnam, Cuba, Mongolia and Romania.

Hungary, Poland and Czechoslovakia see the solution of their economic problems as linked primarily with the development of bilateral relations with the USSR and the other CMEA partners, the development of cooperation within the framework of the recently formed alliance of those three states,* and inclusion in integration processes occurring in west Europe.

The differences are real. How different all this is from the not so distant era of complete agreement and unanimity that led us to general stagnation! Needless to say, we will work together to bring our positions closer and to search for compromises. Under the new conditions, that is the only way to build good-neighbor, mutually advantageous relations between our country and its neighbors.

* The Visegrad triangle

INTEGRATION IN THE WEST

1969–1979

INTRODUCTION

The EEC completed its liberalization of trade in industrial goods in 1968, eighteen months ahead of schedule. Together with the creation of a common external tariff, this meant that a customs union had been achieved. In the first decade since the Treaty of Rome intra-Community trade had grown twice as fast as world trade. GDP expanded by 5 per cent per year. This was a significant success for the process of 'negative' integration – the abolition of barriers, although numerous non-tariff barriers remained (see Chapter 9). It begged the question, however, as to whether and how far the Community would proceed to 'positive' integration – the harmonization of monetary and economic policies. The scale of the task was evident in the

Commission's celebration of the achievement of the customs union: 'All – or nearly all – still remains to be done' (see Document 8.1).[1]

In 1979 that judgement still stood. There had been more achievements, especially the first enlargement in 1973. The numerous policy initiatives, both before and after 1973, had, however, had limited success. The Community, it seemed, was more adept at producing reports defining the malaise of the 'stagnant decade' which followed 1973 than in resolving its problems.[2] Edward Heath commented of this period: 'After the oil crisis of 1973–74 the Community lost its momentum and, what was worse, lost the philosophy of Jean Monnet that the Community exists to find common solutions to common problems.'[3] The difficulty lay not only in the Community's internal differences and disputes but also in an increasingly unstable international environment which sorely tested the Community's ventures into the fields of European Political Cooperation (EPC) and monetary union. In both areas a complex relationship existed between European initiatives and the policy of the United States. In monetary matters, for instance, President Nixon's decision of August 1971 to abandon the gold-dollar standard gave greater urgency to discussion of European monetary cooperation and divided the Europeans on how to respond to the immediate crisis.[4] Euro-American relations were in turn complicated by diverging attitudes towards the eastern bloc. Even the relaxation of tension in the middle of the 1970s, embodied in the Helsinki Final Act of the Conference on Security and Cooperation in Europe of 1975, divided the west. 'It would', a British ambassador wrote, 'be rash to suggest that Dr Kissinger is wrong on all counts', though he conceded little on which he was right and promptly added, 'It sometimes seems as though Dr Kissinger misunderstands the significance of the CSCE to the West.'[5] Since this was the position at a time of détente, it was hardly surprising that the 'new cold war' which emerged at the end of the 1970s witnessed even greater divergence of perceptions.

Ten years earlier, the path to enlargement had been opened up by a change of leadership in France and Germany. Following President de Gaulle's resignation in April 1969, the Hague Summit in December (Document 8.2) allowed his successor Georges Pompidou to win final financial arrangements for the Common Agricultural Policy. It was agreed that the Community's own resources would be obtained by payment to the Community of the agricultural levies, customs dues and a fraction (not more than 1 per cent) of the receipts from Value Added Tax. It was envisaged that the financing of the Community by its own resources would become fully operational in 1975. This was to create problems for Britain from 1973, since she was more dependent on imports from outside the Community and would have to contribute proportionally more to the budget. This agreement was complemented by the Treaty of Luxembourg, which introduced the distinction between compulsory and non-compulsory expenditure and entrenched the European Parliament (EP) in the budget process. The control of the national parliaments over the national contributions was replaced by the EP's control over a budget financed by the Community's own resources.

This, together with other significant considerations discussed below, encouraged Pompidou to open the door for what was to be British, Danish and Irish accession in 1973. Indeed, Pompidou admitted the trade-off between French financial objectives in the CAP and accession. As he said of the Hague Conference, 'I confronted [the other Member States] with a clear choice and I secured on the one hand that definitive arrangements should be made for the agricultural market in exchange for the opening of negotiations with Great Britain on the other.'[6] At the same time, the accession of the other members would provide new export opportunities for the French.

There were other considerations as well. The German Federal Republic was economically extremely strong and in Pompidou's view it was necessary to counterbalance this. British accession would significantly help in this respect. Europe 'from the Atlantic to the Urals' could be traded for Europe from the Elbe to the Thames. As Christian Franck points out, Britain 'would no longer act as a Trojan Horse for America, but rather as a counterweight to West Germany'.[7] The French Government was also alarmed by the more assertive German foreign policy developed by the SPD Chancellor Willy Brandt. Yet Brandt's new *Ostpolitik*, the search for an accommodation with the east, also pointed in the direction of the revival of integration. As he later recalled, 'In reality *Ostpolitik* was one of our reasons for wanting progress in the West.'[8]

While the Hague Summit had given the amber light to the applicant states, enlargement involved detailed negotiation of the conditions. The obvious European commitment of the new Conservative Prime Minister Edward Heath helped. Of all the British prime ministers to date he was the most consistently pro-European, though this was in marked contrast to the general mood of public opinion in Britain at the time. The main obstacle for Britain was her financial contribution. More than 80 per cent of Community expenditure went to finance the CAP, while fewer than 5 per cent of the British population were in agriculture. To a large extent, the entry bids of the three smaller countries stood or fell with that of Britain because of their involvement with the British market. The Irish saw membership as a means of diversifying their trade partners, the Danes were doubtful in spite of parliamentary approval, and the Norwegian people voted in a referendum by a significant majority not to join. Ireland, despite the constraint of neutrality, had little option but to follow the British (some 70 per cent of Irish exports went to Britain). Equally, for the Danes the economic logic was inescapable. Denmark had a substantial agricultural sector that would clearly benefit from the CAP, and with the main Danish export market being West Germany and the second being Britain, remaining outside would have been economically very difficult. In Norway, concerns about agriculture, fisheries and the developing oil industry helped to swing the balance of opinion against, a rejection which was repeated twenty-three years later.

It was the economic aspects of entry that dominated the debate in Britain. Accession requires a new member to have a democratic form of government and to be prepared to accept not only the provisions of the founding treaties but also the *acquis communautaire*, the secondary legislation adopted by the member states since the creation of the Community. Traditionally, Britain had been sceptical both of the customs union and of supranationalism, as had been evident in her rejection of membership of the ECSC and of the EDC. In August 1947, the Senior Economic

Adviser to the Foreign Secretary, Sir Edmund Hall-Patch, had written as follows: 'There is a well-established prejudice in Whitehall against a European Customs Union. It goes back a long way and is rooted in the old days of Free Trade. It is a relic of a world which has disappeared, probably never to return.'[9] For the first fifteen years after the Second World War Britain had held aloof from the integration process. Her resistance to supranationalism also reflected insularity, the experience of two world wars during which British national sentiment had been enhanced, and complacency about her role in the world. At the time of British accession, these prejudices and perceptions were still very much in evidence.

Despite the fact that the Heath application was formally the revived 1967 application of the then Labour Government, the Labour Opposition – with notable defectors including Roy Jenkins, later President of the Commission – opposed the terms of entry and voted against accession. In its manifesto for the October 1974 general election, which it won, it pledged to renegotiate membership. In the event, this turned out to be a perfunctory re-examination of the main points of contention, and few concessions of real substance were obtained. In particular, the agreement for budget rebates reached at Dublin in 1975 was wholly inadequate, as the subsequent wrangles with Mrs Thatcher in the early 1980s were to show. Yet the issue was divisive (Documents 8.4, 8.5, 8.7, 8.8, 8.9). Prime Minister Wilson effectively abandoned the principle of collective cabinet responsibility, allowing ministers to campaign for opposing outcomes. It was only with difficulty that Wilson finally won cabinet approval, and even then he could not swing the majority of Labour Members of Parliament behind him and had to rely on the votes of the opposition.[10] In the subsequent referendum, 67.2 per cent of those voting were in favour of remaining in the Community. Despite this endorsement, the question of membership remained extremely controversial in British political life, deeply dividing the Labour Party until the 1980s. More recently, open divisions over the scope of European integration in monetary and economic policy significantly contributed to bringing the Conservative Party, in government since 1979, to electoral nemesis in 1997.

When Pompidou had agreed to the principle of enlargement in 1969, he had linked it with the 'completion' and 'deepening' of the Community. 'Completion', the financing of agriculture from the Community's own resources, proved relatively easy. 'Deepening' did not, for it involved extending the Community's remit to the contentious areas of monetary union and the EPC. Economic and monetary union (EMU), which Pompidou grandiloquently described as the 'Royal Route', was expected to bring stability and greater coordination of policy. It was believed that, in turn, monetary stability and the harmonization of economic policies would simultaneously consolidate and reinforce the advantages of the common market. The background to this was the significant currency instability in August 1969. Pompidou had devalued the franc by 11 per cent. Two months later, the Deutschmark was revalued by 9.3 per cent. In the following March, the Council of Ministers set up an *ad hoc* group under the chairmanship of Pierre Werner, the Prime Minister and Finance Minister of Luxembourg, the group submitting its report in October of the same year (Document 8.3). It proposed both centralized decision-making in monetary policy and a harmonization of fiscal and budgetary policies, including a community system of central banks. The Werner Report thus tried to mediate between German insistence upon economic convergence as a precondition of monetary union and French preference for using monetary union as a means of bringing about economic convergence. The result predictably satisfied neither side. Moreover, the supranational elements of the Report upset Pompidou, who, in a speech on 21 January 1971, speculated upon the prospects of a 'European con-federation', adding that 'The idea that it might be achieved by setting up technical bodies and committees has already been swept aside by events.'[11] Faced with French reluctance to proceed with the plan, and anxious to obtain French approval of his *Ostpolitik*, Brandt backed away.[12]

Nixon's suspension of the convertibility of the dollar into gold in August 1971 induced crisis, recriminations between the Europeans and the United States and then efforts to restore some stability to the system. The Smithsonian talks in December sought to regulate the position of the dollar by establishing a range, the so-called 'tunnel', within which the dollar would fluctuate. Subsequently, in 1972, the Europeans arranged the 'snake in the tunnel' (Document 8.6). This allowed for a 2.25 per cent fluctuation between the currencies of the Community. At the same time, it permitted a 4.5 per cent fluctuation *vis-à-vis* the dollar. These convergence criteria were at once confronted with major instability in the currency markets and a wave of inflation. Britain, which joined the 'snake' in anticipation of membership of the Community, was promptly forced to abandon it. Italy followed in 1973 and France in 1974. By early 1974, European leaders had capitulated in the face of international economic disorder and plans for EMU were officially abandoned.

At the Hague summit, the ministers of foreign affairs had been instructed to 'study the best way of achieving progress in the matter of political unification within the context of enlargement'.[13] Besides cooperation in the field of foreign policy, political cooperation was later extended to two other areas: the fight against international terrorism (from 1975 onwards) and a European judicial area (from 1977). In contrast with her economic difficulties with the Community, such as the budget and agriculture, the UK was enthusiastic about taking a prominent role in EPC. The resources of an enlarged Europe would make participation in inter-national affairs that much more effective. Even before enlargement, though, the Six had shown a wish to move beyond the failure of the Fouchet Plan of 1962. In October 1968, the Belgian Foreign Minister Pierre Harmel proposed the institution of cooperation between the Six and Britain in the field of foreign policy coordina-tion, defence and security. The Davignon Report which resulted from the Hague summit was approved in October 1970, and set up the consultation procedure which was reinforced by the reports of Copenhagen (1973) and London (1981), before being legally codified in the Single European Act. Consultation was to involve meetings of the Ministers, a Political Committee (made up of the political directors of the foreign ministries) and working groups specialized by region, or according to specific problems. The first ministerial meeting was held in Munich in November 1970 and the first joint declaration (concerning the Middle East) was issued in May 1971. However, at this stage EPC was 'entirely outside the competence of the Treaties ... It had no secretariat (this was provided for in the London Report of 1981) ... at best tenuous links with existing institutions, no fixed meeting-place' and its aims were 'couched in the cloudiest rhetoric', thinly disguising the underlying disagreement about its purpose and its future development. 'There was no mention of "common policy" even as a distant aim.'[14]

The first substantial test, the oil crisis of 1973, provoked defensive national rather than collective responses. The Community had been moving gradually towards some kind of energy policy with security of supplies before 1973, and the OPEC decision to raise prices late in that year might have been expected to act as a catalyst for the policy. In fact it produced anything but solidarity. The British and French sought bilateral arrangements with Iran and Saudi Arabia respectively, and The Netherlands found its supplies completely cut off by OPEC. The policies of the European countries, faced with the oil price rise, increasingly diverged. For instance, Germany responded with restrictive monetary and fiscal policies aimed at controlling inflation, and the Deutschmark quickly established itself as the strongest currency in the 'snake'. By 1977, the 'snake' had essentially contracted into a Deutschmark bloc. As Richard McAllister put it, the member states 'went their separate ways. This applied not just to aspects of external policy, but also to internal economic policy. This was a period that saw, both in the world at large and in the Community, a resurgence of the tell-tale non-tariff barriers.'[15]

Even before the crisis in the Middle East, Euro-American relations had been strained. Secretary of State Henry Kissinger had called for a new Atlantic Charter in April 1973. In his speech, however, he clumsily underlined the asymmetry of the Atlantic relationship. 'The United States', he said, 'has global interests and responsibilities. Our European allies have regional interests.'[16] European resentment towards this was understandable, all the more so since it was not just the product of clumsy diplomacy. It reflected the disunity among the Europeans on the wider global stage. It did provoke the Community to issue a declaration on European identity at the December 1973 Copenhagen summit. This asserted that 'Europe must unite and speak increasingly with a single voice if it wants to make itself heard and play its proper role in the world.'[17] That was true. It was also difficult. At the February 1974 energy conference called by Nixon, the Europeans spoke with divergent and acrimonious voices.

At the end of 1974, the new French President Valéry Giscard d'Estaing sought to remedy the problem of European disunity. Giscard d'Estaing retained the Gaullist suspicion of supranantionalism which he had earlier equated with an 'antinational Europe', but he had also acknowledged that Europe must be more than 'a Europe of alliances, a Europe of states'.[18] His initial proposals invoked memories of the Fouchet Plan, but agreement was reached on a more ambiguous arrangement whereby heads of government would meet 'to increase the solidarity of the Nine'.[19] The precise status of this European Council was not entirely clear. It was not supposed to impinge on existing institutions and commitments established by the Treaty of Rome, but there were fears that it would become an intergovernmental court of arbitration outside the Treaty framework. Yet it also had the potential, by strengthening the intergovernmental dimension of Community policy-making, to bring together within a single overall conference the many different negotiations under way in the dispersed network of functional councils and subordinate commit-tees. A later assessment found that its effect has also been to make the Community more prominent:

> The drama – symbolic and real confrontations – of meetings of the European Council reported to the attending journalists and television crews by each partici-pating leader and each government spokesman has immensely increased the visibility of community policy making to national publics, at the cost of portraying it most often as a succession of zero-sum games ... But the regular and direct involvement, meeting two or three times a year in Community bargaining has at the same time strengthened the collective character of EC policy making.[20]

Another outcome of the December 1974 Paris summit was the belated decision that 'the time has come for the Nine to agree as soon as possible on an overall concept of the European Union'.[21] The Belgian Prime Minister Leo Tindemans was commis-sioned to produce a report with this in mind. Tindemans took up an idea suggested in November 1974 by Willy Brandt, namely 'graduated integration'.[22] By this Brandt meant that the economically stronger countries with the willingness to embark upon further integration should not be held back by the weaker and less willing. The initial response to Brandt's suggestion was unenthusiastic. Never-theless, the idea was placed firmly on the agenda by Tindemans in the following year. The danger inherent in the concept was quite clear. It could lead to a fragmentation of the Community and to a 'Europe à la carte', where member states individually selected which avenues of integration they would enter. This was not what Brandt had intended and he later made clear that the commitments of the Rome Treaties should be inviolable. Tindemans too ruled out Europe à la carte. He insisted instead that 'each country will be bound by the agreement of all as to the final objective to be achieved in common; it is only the timescales for achievement which vary'.[23] Although the Community was already practising something like Tindemans's recommendation with the monetary 'snake', little came of his report (Document 8.11). The idea of graduated integration would keep returning to the agenda, if only in the form of an implicit threat that if more reluctant member states did not sign up the others would proceed without them.

The 'locust years' of the mid-1970s were not entirely devoid of success.[24] Through the 1960s and 1970s association and cooperation agreements had been signed with large numbers of developing countries. The First Yaoundé Convention, signed on 20 July 1963, extended tariff reductions and development aid to eighteen former French colonies in Africa. This was widened to include several more African states in the Second Yaoundé Convention of 29 July 1969. These were replaced on 28 February 1975 by the First Lomé Convention. This established a privileged relationship between the Community and forty-six states in Africa, the Caribbean and the Pacific, known collectively as ACP states. Under this agreement, 99 per cent of ACP exports entered the Community duty-free. This convention also provided for development aid. It was extended in 1979 and 1984, in the Second and Third Lomé Conventions.

In the same year as the First Lomé Convention, the Helsinki Final Act of the CSCE was signed. It covered three 'baskets' of measures covering security, economic and humanitarian issues. The Community as such did not participate in this conference of states, yet given the remit of the conference, matters affecting it were clearly at stake. Technically the problem was side-stepped in September 1973 by allowing Commission representatives to join the Danish delegation. (Denmark held the Presidency of the Council at the time.)[25] In practice, the Commission's influence was more substantive, at least in the economic field. As the British reported, 'Although the European Commission did not participate as such at the Conference, its representatives played an active role and were in practice recognized by the members of the CMEA as having both competence and the confidence of the Nine.'[26] The CSCE, contrary to Soviet wishes, did not agree on the creation of a new organization, but there was a consensus that there should be follow-up conferences. The CSCE, as a rolling programme, was henceforth a permanent feature of Europe's architecture. The Helsinki Final Act also took the process of détente to a new level. Despite the relapse into the rhetoric of the cold war at the end of the decade, it marked the beginning of the end of the cold war division of Europe (see Chapter 11).

In the late 1970s there was renewed interest among European governments in monetary cooperation. In particular, there was German advocacy of a zone of monetary and economic stability which would shield intra-European economic relations from the disruptive effects of American policies. In addition to this, there was a growing consensus, after the inflationary excesses of the mid-1970s, for low inflation and stability, even at the cost of economic growth. The renewed effort to achieve monetary integration began in October 1977 with proposals by the new President of the Commission, Roy Jenkins. Jenkins did not have a good start to his Presidency. There were disagreements with Giscard d'Estaing over whether Jenkins would be allowed to attend the western economic summit in 1977. According to Jenkins, Giscard d'Estaing argued that 'the French government were not in favour of this ... because in their view the Summit should be a meeting of sovereign governments'.[27] Yet the French President did compromise, allowing the Commission to be 'present for discussions within Community competence at session or sessions'.[28]

When Jenkins took up the issue of monetary union in October 1977, he did not even have the support of his own Vice-President, who cast doubt on the wisdom of raising this 'politically absurd' idea.[29] Jenkins's initiative was rescued from the anticipated failure by Helmut Schmidt in February 1978, much to the surprise of Jenkins himself. Schmidt was frustrated by the persistent fall of the dollar against the Deutschmark, and the equally persistent failure of the Carter administration to do anything to halt the decline. At the same time he was annoyed by Carter's calls for the Germans to reflate their economy and act as a locomotive which would pull the world economy out of recession, not least because this would have brought Schmidt into conflict with the Bundesbank. Schmidt used the European Council of April 1978 to launch what became the European Monetary System (EMS).

Agreement on the EMS was facilitated by renewed Franco-German partnership and the good relations between Helmut Schmidt and Valéry Giscard d'Estaing. However, the primary driving force was the Federal Republic. This was a reflection of her increased economic and political power as well as her growing confidence as a power on the European and international scene. In the words of Peter Ludlow, 'the EMS was arguably the first major act of German leadership in the history of the European Community'.[30] Germany's dominant position was only to be further reinforced by the functioning of the EMS.

In April, Schmidt had extracted British consent to the creation of a small committee, consisting of French, German and British representatives, to draw up a report for the Bremen Council in July (Document 8.14). Something of Schmidt's ambition was diluted when he ran into opposition from the Bundesbank to the idea of using German reserves to back the proposed European Monetary Fund.[31] There were also divisions between the member states over the technical details of the system. These technical details, however, would determine which member states would bear the brunt of maintaining the stability of the EMS. The weaker economies naturally preferred a scheme which would protect them from the deflationary pressure of a strong Deutschmark and would oblige the Germans to reflate in response to a rising mark. The Germans were equally naturally opposed to anything of the kind. At the end, a Belgian suggestion served as the basis of a compromise which was actually closer to the German position.[32] With this compromise in place, the December 1978 European Council sanctioned the EMS. At the core of the EMS was the Exchange Rate Mechanism (ERM). Although all members joined the EMS, not all joined the ERM, Britain was one of the non-participants. Among the main differences of the EMS from the 'snake' was the creation of the European Currency Unit (ECU), though as a result of the concessions made to Germany this did not play the role originally envisioned for it.[33] This is not to say that the agreement was unimportant. In subsequent years the constraints of the EMS played an important part in strengthening the resolve of national policy-makers to achieve low inflation. Although Mrs Thatcher resisted until nearly the end of her prime ministerial career, even she was persuaded in the end to join by the argument that it would bring down inflation.

At the end of the decade, the Community was once again taking stock. There had been mounting concern about the supposed extravagance of the Commission, while Jenkins was concerned about its inflexibility. His response was to call for a report from an external committee. The Spierenburg Report was ready in September 1979 but despite some support from Jenkins had little impact, nor did the Report of the Three Wise Men submitted in the following October. The initiative for this came from Giscard d'Estaing, whom Jenkins suspected of attempting to cripple the Commission: 'No doubt there is a desire in Giscard's mind to cut down the power of the Commission, to reduce or eliminate our political role, our connection with Parliament, and half to amalgamate us with the Council secretariat and with COREPER and thus to make us all servants of the European Council.'[34] If such was Giscard's intent, the Wise Men, among whom was Robert Marjolin, the collabora-tor of Jean Monnet, proved too independent to oblige. Their report was notable more for its sense of despair than for anything else. It did record the achievement of the Community, but lamented the decline in the Commission's authority and the increasingly nationalistic attitudes of member states. In his memoirs, Marjòlin recalled that 'There was little more we could do than hope that the situation would not get any worse.'[35] The report itself counselled against the pursuit of 'futuristic visions' whose prospects it judged to be 'exceedingly slight'.[36]

Despite this pessimism, 1979 did witness some, much belated, progress. After many years of discussion and procrastination, direct elections to the European Parliament were introduced (Documents 8.12, 8.13). Article 138 of the Treaty of Rome had specified: 'The Assembly shall draw up proposals for elections by direct universal suffrage in accordance with a uniform procedure in all Member States . . . The Council shall, acting unanimously, lay down the appropriate provisions, which it shall recommend to Member States for adoption in accordance with their respective constitutional requirements.' Proponents of direct elections had argued that the Parliament would remain an impotent assembly as long as it was indirectly appointed from national parliaments. 'Direct elections were the "sine qua non" of the accretion of its powers. The accretion of its powers was seen as the logical corollary of its aspirations and its being the only directly elected and democratically legitimated EC institution.'[37] There had been considerable pressure for such elections, but a Draft Convention was not adopted until January 1976 and elections were not held until June 1979, over twenty years after the Treaty of Rome. Opponents argued that only a prior increase in the EP's powers would justify the expenditure of time, effort and money on direct elections. Underlying much of the resistance was the belief that the EP would acquire power only at the expense of national parliaments. For instance, only ten days after the ministers signed the act authorizing direct elections, the delegates of the annual Labour Party Conference in Britain voted by two to one to oppose European elections on the grounds that these might result in a 'new superstate'. According to the resolution, this would 'further weaken the British people's democratic control over their own affairs' and make realization of the Labour Party's 'basic programme . . . increasingly remote'.[38]

One of the main stumbling blocks had been the Treaty requirement for a uniform electoral procedure. It proved impossible, however, to reach agreement on either a single day or a single electoral procedure. All the direct elections to date have been fought under divergent systems, with Britain retaining the first-past-the-post system, although the new 1997 Labour government in Britain has promised to introduce proportional representation for 1999 in the European elections. Until 1979, the European Parliament consisted of nominated representatives from the national parliaments. The number of representatives increased from 198 to 410 with direct elections, and it has been subsequently increased with each enlargement of the Community. Britain has consistently displayed the least electoral enthusiasm in these elections. In 1979, for instance, the turnout in Italy was 86 per cent, that in the UK 32 per cent.

The uncertainties of the later 1970s were summed up by the American scholar Stanley Hoffmann in an article published in 1979, entitled 'Fragments of the here and now'. 'Western Europe', he wrote, remains a collection of largely self-encased nation-states. The various governments of west Europe have found it useful to establish common institutions to deal with their common problems ... the basic unit of concern, however, remains the nation state ... There was, to be sure, a collective *'projet'* at the outset; its very ambiguity about ends – federation or confederacy? a strong entity or a contribution to global solutions? free trade or common 'dirigisme'? a new power bloc in the world or an exercise in transcending power politics? – helped it grow in the beginning. But later, when each new step seemed to require clarification of the final goals, its ambiguous nature began to plague it.[39]

At the end of the decade the impending second wave of enlargement was already concentrating minds (Document 8.15), even if it was doing little to dispel the Community's ambiguity. It was, however, that same ambiguity which had allowed the Community to come into existence and allowed it to survive. It was that same ambiguity which bedevilled academic attempts to define it or even to reach a consensus over what drove it forward, periodically paralysed it and then allowed it to revive. It was that same ambiguity which allowed it to coexist with the other elements of Europe's complex, overlapping, architecture.

NOTES

1. Declaration by the European Commission on the Achievement of the Customs Union, 1 July 1968.
2. See the chapter 'The stagnant decade, 1973–1983' in Keith Middlemas, *Orchestrating Europe* (London, 1995).
3. Sir Edward Heath, 'European unity over the next ten years: from Community to Union', *International Affairs*, Vol. 64 (1988), p. 200. At the end of the decade, following the Iranian Revolution, there was a second oil-shock with a doubling of prices.
4. Wolfram F. Hanrieder, *Germany, America, Europe* (New Haven, CT, 1989), pp. 290–5.
5. *Documents on British Policy Overseas*, (hereafter *DBPO*), Series 3, Vol. 1, doc. 94 (29 July 1974).
6. *L'Année Politique* (Paris, 1971) p. 417.
7. Christian Franck in Roy Pryce (ed.) *The Dynamics of European Union* (London, 1987), p. 133.
8. Willy Brandt, *People and Politics* (London, 1978), p. 254.
9. Quoted in Michael Charlton, *The Price of Victory* (London, 1983), pp. 70–71.
10. John W. Young, *Britain and European Unity, 1945–1992* (Basingstoke, 1993), pp. 119–29.
11. European Parliament, *Selection of Texts Concerning Institutional Matters of the Community from 1950 to 1982* (Luxembourg, n.d.), p. 203.
12. Haig Simonian, *The Privileged Partnership* (Oxford, 1985), p. 92.
13. European Parliament, *Selection of Texts*, p. 138.
14. See D. Allen, R. Rummel and W. Wessels, *European Political Cooperation* (London, 1982), p. 21.
15. Richard McAllister, *EC to EU* (London, 1977), p. 99.
16. Quoted in Simonian, *The Privileged Partnership*, p. 165.
17. European Parliament, *Selection of Texts*, p. 264.
18. Quoted in Pierre-Bernard Cousté and François Visine, *Pompidou et l'Europe* (Paris, 1974), p. 33.

19. European Parliament, *Selection of Texts*, p. 276.
20. William Wallace, *Regional Integration: The West European Experience* (Washington, DC, 1994), pp. 37–8.
21. European Parliament, *Selection of Texts*, p. 277.
22. Hanns–Eckart Scharrer, 'Abgestufte Integration. Eine Einführung', in Eberhard Grabitz (ed.), *Abgestufte Integration* (Strasbourg, 1984), pp. 6–8.
23. European Parliament, *Selection of Texts*, p. 377.
24. The phrase is that of Richard McAllister, *From EC to EU* (London, 1997), p. 96.
25. See Keith Middlemas, *Orchestrating Europe* (London, 1995), p. 73.
26. *DBPO*, Series 3, Vol. 1, doc. 137 (28 July 1975).
27. Roy Jenkins, *European Diary* (London, 1989), p. 56.
28. ibid., p. 76.
29. Quoted in E. Dell, 'Britain and the origins of the European monetary system', *Contemporary European History*, Vol. 3 (1995), p. 2.
30. Peter Ludlow, *The Making of the European Monetary System* (London, 1982), p. 290.
31. Dell, 'Britain and the origins of the European monetary system', pp. 9–10.
32. This is explained with admirable clarity in ibid., pp. 24–31.
33. See the *Report on Economic and Monetary Union in the European Community* (Luxembourg, 1989), p. 13.
34. Jenkins, *European Diary*, p. 311.
35. Robert Marjolin, *Architect of European Unity. Memoirs 1911–1986* (London, 1989), p. 369.
36. European Parliament, *Selection of Texts*, p. 436.
37. Juliet Lodge and Valentine Herman, *Direct Elections in the European Parliament*, (London, 1982), p. 1.
38. Paula Scalinga, *The European Parliament* (Westport, CT, 1980), p. 144.
39. Stanley Hoffmann, *The European Sisyphus* (Boulder, CO, 1995), p. 182.

FURTHER READING

D. Butler and U. Kitzinger, *The Referendum* (London, 1976).
M. Charlton, *The Price of Victory* (London, 1983).
S. George, *An Awkward Partner* (Oxford, 1990).
R. Jenkins, *European Diary* (London, 1989).
R. Jowell and G. Hoinville (eds), *Britain into Europe: Public Opinion and the EEC 1961–75* (London, 1976).
U. Kitzinger, *Diplomacy and Persuasion: How Britain Joined the Common Market* (London, 1973).
P. Ludlow, *The Making of the European Monetary System* (London, 1982).
R. McAllister, *EC to EU* (London, 1977).
K. Middlemas, *Orchestrating Europe* (London, 1995).
R. Morgan and C. Bray (eds), *Partners and Rivals in Western Europe: Britain, France and Germany* (London, 1986).
M. Newman, *Socialism and European Unity: The Dilemma of the Left in Britain and France* (London, 1983).
F. Nicholson and R. East, *From the Six to the Twelve* (London, 1987).
H. Simonian, *The Privileged Partnership* (Oxford, 1985).
J. W. Young, *Britain and European Unity, 1945–1992* (Basingstoke, 1993)

8.1

DECLARATION BY THE EUROPEAN COMMISSION ON THE OCCASION OF THE ACHIEVEMENT OF THE CUSTOMS UNION, 1 JULY 1968

Bull. EC, no. 7, 1968, pp. 5–8.

The Treaty of Rome had established a precise timetable for the creation of a customs union. Customs duties within the common market were abolished eighteen months ahead of schedule. This declaration looks ahead to future achievements in European integration.

The Europeans face immense tasks . . .

The Customs Union being complete, work on the achievement of economic union must be continued. This means that the common economic policies designed to transform the customs territory into an economically organized continent must be built up or completed . . .

Lastly, the great social changes in a world dominated by technology and speed raise immense questions for our generation: the transformation of society, the organisation of social life, the environment and the destiny of man, his liberty, his security, his health, his life itself.

None of all this, none of these fundamental political, economic, social and human problems can be solved by our old States imprisoned within their narrow frontiers. It is just as impossible to solve them without breaking through the old structures inherited from the past and without creating the European structures which are vital to the work of renewal as it is necessary to retain the old cultures, traditions, languages, originality, everything which gives the States their personalities and which constitutes the beauty, the diversity, the charm, and the immanent value of Europe, and in place of which nobody could possibly desire to set up colourless and impersonal machinery . . .

We must take a step forward in the field of political union. A single Treaty, enabling a new stage forward to be begun, must take the place of the Treaty of Paris (1951) and the two Treaties of Rome (1957), which created our three European Communities. The Council of Ministers of the Community must be re-established in its normal functioning as a body which can take majority decisions. The out-of-date system of the right of veto, which paralyses action, must be done away with. The single Commission must be given the implementing powers enabling it not only to take the initiative in Community progress but genuinely to manage the Community, with the task of management growing as the new Community policies gradually enter into force.

At the same time, the authority entrusted to European Institutions must be steadily given a wider democratic basis – and this must be done more rapidly. The European Parliament must be given greater budgetary and legislative powers. The European peoples must participate increasingly, through direct elections and all other appropriate methods, in Community life at the European level ...

It would be wrong to wait until the European people as a whole is officially consulted and takes part constitutionally and organically in the political life of the European continent. The major social groups in the Community must be called upon more urgently to help here and now.

_____ 8.2 _____

COMMUNIQUÉ FROM THE MEETING OF THE HEADS OF STATE OR GOVERNMENT AT THE HAGUE, 1–2 DECEMBER 1969

Bull. EC, no. 1, 1970, pp. 11–16.

This summit meeting was convoked by the French President, Georges Pompidou. It was the prelude to the first enlargement of the Community and prefigured other key developments in the 1970s. This extract is from a press release from the Dutch Ministry of Foreign Affairs.

5. As regards the completion of the Communities, the Heads of State or Government reaffirmed the will of their governments to pass from the transitional period to the final stage of the European Community and accordingly to lay down a definitive financial arrangement for the common agricultural policy by the end of 1969.

   They agreed to replace progressively, within the framework of this financial arrangement, the contributions of member countries by their own resources, taking into account all the interests concerned, with the object of achieving in due course the integral financing of the communities' budgets in accordance with the procedure provided for in Article 201 of the Treaty establishing the EEC and of strengthening the budgetary powers of the European Parliament.

   The problem of the method of direct elections is still being studied by the Council of Ministers.

6. They asked the Governments to continue without delay within the Council the efforts already made to ensure a better control of the market by a policy of agricultural production making it possible to limit budgetary charges.

7. The acceptance of a financial arrangement for the final stage does not exclude its adaptation by unanimous vote, in particular in the light of an enlarged community and on condition that the principles of this arrangement are not infringed.

8. They reaffirmed their readiness to further the more rapid progress of the later development needed to strengthen the Community and promote its development into an economic union. They are of the opinion that the integration process should result in a community of stability and growth. To this end they agreed that within the Council, on the basis of the memorandum presented by the Commission on 12 February 1969 and in close collaboration with the latter, a plan in stages should be worked out during 1970 with a view to the creation of an economic and monetary union.

    The development of monetary cooperation should depend on the harmonisation of economic policies.

    They agreed to arrange for the investigation of the possibility of setting up a European reserve fund in which a joint economic and monetary policy would have to result . . .

13. They reaffirmed their agreement on the principle of the enlargement of the Community, as provided by Article 237 of the Treaty of Rome.

    In so far as the applicant States accept the Treaties and their political finality, the decisions taken since the entry into force of the treaties and the options made in the sphere of development, the Heads of State or Government have indicated their agreement to the opening of negotiations between the Community on the one hand and the applicant States on the other.

_____ 8.3 _____

CONCLUSIONS OF THE WERNER REPORT ON ECONOMIC AND MONETARY UNION, 11 OCTOBER 1970

Bull. EC, Supplement 11, 1970, pp. 26–9.

This report followed the decision by the Hague Summit (Document 8.2) which called for Economic and Monetary Union (EMU). It was intended that this should be introduced by 1980. Pierre Werner was Prime Minister of Luxembourg. A modified report was accepted by the Council of Ministers in 1971. Subsequently, the plan was eclipsed by the international economic difficulties of the 1970s. The idea of full European Monetary Union was not properly considered again until the late 1980s.

The Group, recalling that the Council adopted on 8 and 9 June 1970 the conclusions presented by the Group in its interim report, suggests to the Council that it should accept the contents of the present report and approve the following conclusions:

A. Economic and monetary union is an objective realisable in the course of the present decade provided only that the political will of the Member States to realise this objective, as solemnly declared at the Conference at the Hague, is present. The union will make it possible to ensure growth and stability within the Community and reinforce the contribution it can make to economic and monetary equilibrium in the world and make it a pillar of stability.

B. Economic and monetary union means that the principal decisions of economic policy will be taken at Community level and therefore that the necessary powers will be transferred from the national plane to the Community plane. These transfers of responsibility and the creation of the corresponding Community institutions represent a process of fundamental political significance which entails the progressive development of political cooperation. The economic and monetary union thus appears as a leaven for the development of political union which in the long run it will be unable to do without.

C. A monetary union implies, internally, the total and irreversible convertibility of currencies, the elimination of margins of fluctuation in rates of exchange, the irrevocable fixing of parity ratios and the total liberation of movements of capital. It may be accompanied by the maintenance of national monetary symbols, but considerations of a psychological and political order militate in favour of the adoption of a single currency which would guarantee the irreversibility of the undertaking.

D. On the institutional plane, in the final stage, two Community organs are indispensable: a centre of decision for economic policy and a Community system for the central banks. These institutions, while safeguarding their own responsibilities, must be furnished with effective powers of decision and must work together for the realisation of the same objectives. The centre of economic decision will be politically responsible to a European Parliament.

_____ 8.4 _____

A COMPARATIVE POLL ON THE EEC IN SEVEN COUNTRIES, 1970

Uwe Kitzinger, *Diplomacy and Persuasion* (London: Thames and Hudson, 1973), p. 33.

A comparative poll on the EEC 1970, European Commission, Brussels.

The response to the following questions illustrates very clearly the gap between British and continental public opinion on the question of Western European integration.

Are you in favour of, or against, Britain joining the European Common Market?

	Holland	Luxem-bourg	West Germany	France	Belgium	Italy	EEC	Britain
In favour	79	70	69	66	63	51	64	19
Against	8	6	7	11	8	9	6	63
Don't know	13	24	24	23	29	40	28	18

Assuming that Britain did join, would you be for or against the evolution of the Common Market towards the political formation of a United States of Europe?

	Holland	Luxem-bourg	West Germany	France	Belgium	Italy	EEC	Britain
In favour	64	75	69	67	60	60	65	30
Against	17	5	9	11	10	7	9	48
Don't know	19	20	22	22	30	33	26	22

Would you be in favour of or against the election of a European Parliament by direct universal suffrage; that is a parliament elected by all the voters in the member countries?

	Holland	Luxem-bourg	West Germany	France	Belgium	Italy	EEC	Britain
In favour	59	71	66	59	56	55	59	25
Against	21	10	9	15	11	6	11	55
Don't know	20	19	25	26	33	39	30	20

Would you be willing to accept, over and above your own government, a European Government responsible for a common policy in foreign affairs, defence and the economy?

	Holland	Luxem-bourg	West Germany	France	Belgium	Italy	EEC	Britain
Willing	50	47	57	49	51	51	53	22
Not willing	32	35	19	28	19	10	20	60
Don't know	18	18	24	23	30	39	27	18

If a President of a United States of Europe were being elected by popular vote, would you be willing to vote for a candidate not of your own country – if his personality and programme corresponded more closely to your ideas than those of candidates of your own country?

	Holland	Luxem-bourg	West Germany	France	Belgium	Italy	EEC	Britain
Willing	63	67	69	61	52	45	59	39
Not willing	18	20	20	22	24	19	18	41
Don't know	19	13	19	17	24	36	23	20

_____ 8.5 _____

'THE UNITED KINGDOM AND THE EUROPEAN COMMUNITIES', LONDON 1971

Cmnd 4715 (London: HMSO, 1971).

This assessment by the British government of the economic effects of British membership of the Community accompanied Britain's final and successful attempt to join.

Growth and prosperity in any country, including of course each of the six Community countries, depend first and foremost upon the size and effective use of its resources of manpower, plant, equipment and managerial skill. It is essential to deploy these resources to the maximum benefit, and this requires the pursuit of appropriate economic policies. This requirement would be mandatory upon the United Kingdom in any event. However, the general economic and commercial environment within which a country operates is also a vital element in its success in creating wealth and promoting welfare. The environment can be conducive to growth, or it can be unfavourable to growth. It is generally agreed that for advanced industrial countries the most favourable environment is one where markets are large, and are free from barriers to trade. These conditions favour specialisation, the exploitation of economies of scale, the developing and marketing of new products and a high level of investment in the most modern and up-to-date equipment. Through increased competition, they foster the more efficient use of resources over a wide area of industry and help to check the trend to monopoly positions on the part of large-scale organisations.

In particular, the development and exploitation of modern industrial technology, upon which so much of our employment and income increasingly depends, requires greater resources for research and development and wider markets than any one Western European nation can provide. The different national systems of corporate law and taxation in west Europe make it difficult for European firms to combine and co-operate effectively to meet competition from the great firms whose resources are based on the much larger home markets of the United States and, more recently, of Japan. In recent years Western European markets for jet aircraft and aero engines, for computers and advanced electronic equipment, for nuclear fuel and power, for motor vehicles and for many other products have been increasingly dominated or penetrated by the much larger international corporations based outside Europe. Together, the Western European nations can organise themselves to compete with these giants, which are otherwise bound to go on increasing their share of European industrial markets.

If we enter the Communities we shall be able to profit from the general advantages of a larger market and, in particular, to play a full part in the development of industries based on advanced technology. If we do not join, we shall forgo these opportunities which the members of the Communities will increasingly enjoy. Their industries will have a home market of some 190 million people, with preferential markets in other European and overseas countries. Our industries would have a home market of some 55 million people, with perhaps another 45 million in EFTA, as against the home market of some 299 million people we should have if we joined the Communities.

Experience of the Six

The economic growth of the Six countries had already been considerable in the 1950s, as they recovered from the disruptions of war and occupation. The formation of the European Economic Community then created an environment within which they have each made further and striking progress over the past decade. In considering the likely effect upon our economy of membership of an enlarged Community we must first examine the evidence of that decade.

The members of the Community created a common market in industrial goods by steadily eliminating the tariffs on imports from one another over the years 1959–68. The abolition of tariffs provided a strong and growing stimulus of the mutual trade of Community countries. It is estimated that by 1969 the value of this 'intra-trade' in manufactured products was about 50 per cent higher than it would have been, had the Community not been formed; moreover it appears that the stimulus to intra-trade is continuing . . .

_____ 8.6 _____

EUROPEAN MONETARY COOPERATION: 'THE SNAKE', 1972

Bull. EC, 4-1972, pp. 43–4.

In 1972 the Council of Ministers agreed to establish a European system of exchange rates, known as the snake, within the framework of the Smithsonian Agreement of 1971. With persistent financial crises, it was effectively abandoned in the mid-1970s.

As a first step towards the establishment of a distinct monetary zone within the framework of the international system, the Council urges the Central Banks of the Member States to reduce progressively, while making full use of the fluctuation margins allowed by the IMF on a world plane, the gap existing at any given moment between the exchange rates of the strongest and the weakest currencies of the Member States.

To this end, for a first period during which these procedures will be tested, the Central Banks are asked to intervene on their respective foreign-exchange markets in accordance with the following principles:

(a) As from a date to be fixed by the Governors of the Central Banks, interventions shall be effected in Community currencies, on the basis of the margins recorded on the markets at that date.
(b) As these limits converge, the margins mentioned under (a) above shall be narrowed down and shall no longer be widened.
(c) By 1st July 1972 at the latest, the gap existing at any given time between the currencies of two Member States may not exceed 2.25 per cent.

In accordance with the Council Resolution of 22 March 1971, the longer-term objective remains the elimination of any fluctuation margin between the currencies of the Community.

_____ 8.7 _____

LABOUR PARTY CONFERENCE RESOLUTION, OCTOBER 1972

Conference Resolution, October 1972, *Report on the 71st Annual Party Conference of the Labour Party.*

This resolution articulates the view widespread in the Labour Party in Britain that Community policies and the achievement of socialist objectives were not compatible.

This Conference declares its opposition to entry to the Common Market on the terms negotiated by the Tories and calls on a future Labour Government to reverse any decision for Britain to join unless new terms have been negotiated including the abandonment of the Common Agricultural Policy and the Value Added Tax, no limitations on the freedom of a Labour Government to carry out economic plans, regional development, extension of the Public Sector, control of Capital Movements, and the preservation of the power of the British Parliament over its legislation and taxation, and, meanwhile to halt immediately the entry arrangements, including all payments to the European Communities, and participation in their Institutions, in particular the European Parliament, until such terms have been negotiated and the assent of the British electorate has been given.

_____ 8.8 _____

'WHY YOU SHOULD VOTE YES', MAY 1975

'Why You Should Vote Yes' – referendum leaflet from 'Britain in Europe' (London, May 1975).

The following are extracts from the 'Britain in Europe' campaign leaflet issued in May 1975. The British referendum posed the question: 'Do you think the United Kingdom should stay in the European Community?'

Our friends want us to stay in. If we left we would not go back to the world as it was when we joined, still less to an old world of Britain's imperial heyday. The world has been changing fast. And the changes have made things more difficult and more dangerous for this country. It is a time when we need friends. What do our friends think? The old Commonwealth wants us to stay in, Australia does, Canada does, New Zealand does. The new Commonwealth wants us to stay in. Not a single one of their 34 governments wants us to leave. The United States wants us to stay in.

They want a close Atlantic relationship (upon which our whole security depends) with a Europe of which we are part; but not with us alone. The other members of the European Community want us to stay in. That is why they have been flexible in the recent re-negotiations and so made possible the improved terms which have converted many former doubters. Outside, we should be alone in a harsh, cold world, with none of our friends offering to revive old partnerships ...

Why can't we go it alone? To some this sounds attractive. Mind our own business. Make our own decisions. Pull up the drawbridge. In the modern world it just is not practicable ...

Our traditions are safe. We can work together and still stay British. The Community does not mean dull uniformity. It hasn't made the French eat German food or the Dutch drink Italian beer. Nor will it damage our British traditions and way of life. The position of the Queen is not affected. She will remain Sovereign of the United Kingdom and Head of the Commonwealth. Four of the other Community countries have monarchies of their own.

English Common Law is not affected. For a few commercial and industrial purposes there is need for Community Law. But our criminal law, trial by jury, presumption of innocent remains unaltered. So do our civil rights. Scotland, after 250 years of much closer union with England, still keeps its own legal system ...

Staying in protects our jobs. Jobs depend upon our industries investing more and being able to sell in the world. If we came out, our industry would be based on the smallest home market of any major exporting country in the world, instead of on the Community market of 250 million people. It is very doubtful if we could then negotiate a free trade agreement with the Community. Even if we could it would have damaging limitations and we would have to accept many Community rules without having the say we now have in their making. So we could lose free access not only to the Community market itself but to the 60 or more other countries with which the Community has trade agreements. The immediate effect on trade, on industrial confidence, on investment prospects, and hence on jobs, could well be disastrous ...

Secure food at fair prices. Before we joined the Community everyone feared that membership would mean paying more for our food than if we were outside. This fear has proved wrong ...

Britain's choice: the alternatives. The Community is not perfect. Far from it. It makes mistakes and needs improvement. But that's no reason for contracting out. What are the alternatives? Those who want us to come out are deeply divided. Some want an isolationist Britain with a 'siege economy' – controls and rationing. Some want a Communist Britain – part of the Soviet bloc. Some want us even closer to the United States than to Europe – but America itself doesn't want that. Some want us to fall back on the Commonwealth – but the Commonwealth itself doesn't want that. Some want us to be half linked to Europe, as part of a free trade area – but the European Community itself doesn't want that. So when people say we should leave, ask them what positive way ahead they propose for Britain. You will get some very confusing answers.

_____ 8.9 _____

'WHY YOU SHOULD VOTE NO', MAY 1975

'Why You Should Vote No' – leaflet from the
'National Referendum Campaign' (London, May 1975).

The following is extracted from the 'National Referendum Campaign' leaflet, also
issued in May 1975. In the event, 67.2 per cent of the votes cast in the referendum
were in favour of staying in the Community.

Re-negotiation. The present Government, though it tried, has on its own admission
failed to achieve the 'fundamental re-negotiation' it promised at the last two
General Elections. All it has gained are a few concessions for Britain, some of them
only temporary. The real choice before the British peoples has been scarcely altered
by re-negotiation.

What did the pro-Marketers say? Before we joined the Common Market the
Government forecast that we should enjoy – A rapid rise in our living standards; A
trade surplus with the Common Market; Better productivity; Higher investment;
More employment; Faster industrial growth. In every case the opposite is now
happening, according to the Government's figures ...

Our legal right to come out. It was agreed during the debates which took us into
the Common Market that the British Parliament had the absolute right to repeal the
European Communities Act and take us out. There is nothing in the Treaty of Rome
which says a country cannot come out.

The right to rule ourselves. The fundamental question is whether or not we
remain free to rule ourselves in our own way. For the British people, membership of
the Common Market has already been a bad bargain. What is worse, it sets out by
stages to merge Britain with France, Germany, Italy and other countries into a single
nation. This will take away from us the right to rule ourselves which we have
enjoyed for centuries ...

Your food, your jobs, our trade. We cannot afford to remain in the Common
Market because: it must mean still higher food prices. Before we joined, we could
buy our food at the lowest cost from the most efficient producers in the world. Since
we joined, we are no longer allowed to buy all our food where it suits us best ...

Your jobs at risk. If we stay in the Common Market, a British Government can
no longer prevent the drift of industry southwards and increasingly to the Continent. This is already happening ...

Huge trade deficit with Common Market. The Common Market pattern of trade
was never designed to suit Britain ...

Taxes to keep prices up. The Common Market's dear food policy is designed to
prop up inefficient farmers on the Continent by keeping food prices high ...

Agriculture. It would be far better for us if we had our own national agricultural
policy suited to our own country, as we had before we joined ...

Commonwealth links. Our Commonwealth links are bound to be weakened much further if we stay in the Common Market. We are being forced to tax imported Commonwealth goods. And as we lose our national independence, we shall cease, in practice, to be a member of the Commonwealth.

Britain a mere province of the Common Market? The real aim of the Market is, of course, to become one single country in which Britain would be reduced to a mere province. The plan is to have a Common Market Parliament by 1978 or shortly thereafter.

What is the alternative? A far better course is open to us. If we withdraw from the Market, we could and should remain members of the wider Free Trade Area which now exists between the Common Market and the countries of the European Free Trade Association (EFTA) – Norway, Sweden, Finland, Austria, Switzerland, Portugal and Iceland. These countries are now to enjoy free entry for their industrial exports into the Common Market without having to carry the burden of the Market's dear food policy or suffer rule from Brussels. Britain already enjoys industrial free trade with these countries. If we withdrew from the Common Market, we should remain members of the wider group and enjoy, as the EFTA countries do, free or low-tariff entry into the Common Market countries without the burden of dear food or the loss of the British people's democratic rights . . .

8.10

A BRITISH ASSESSMENT OF THE NEGOTIATIONS WITHIN THE CONFERENCE ON SECURITY AND COOPERATION IN EUROPE, JULY 1975

Documents on British Policy Overseas,
Series 3, Vol. 2, doc. 136.

The British ambassador to the UN in Geneva, Dr H. T. Hildyard, sent the following assessment of the negotiations within the CSCE, shortly before the signing of the Final Act which took place in Helsinki on 1 August 1975. A. A. Gromyko was the Soviet Foreign Minister. The Brezhnev doctrine of 1968 asserted the right of the Warsaw Pact to intervene in the internal affairs of states in the wider interests of socialism.

For many years the Soviet Union had wanted the West formally to accept, in Mr Gromyko's words, 'the political and territorial realities' resulting from the Second World War, and at the same time to subscribe to East–West *détente* in the limited sense which the Russians conceived of it. The Helsinki preparatory talks showed that the price of the West's agreement would be the broadening of the concept of *détente* to include a gradual liberalisation of contacts between people and in the fields of information and ideas. The Soviet Union was clearly anxious to limit this price as much as possible when the concrete details came to be worked out ...

The Soviet leadership have achieved political, though not legal, recognition of the *status quo*; the results of the Conference are not legally binding ...

The main Western interests were on the one hand to avoid any commitments which could imply eventual acceptance of a pan-European security system or acceptance of the Brezhnev Doctrine, or which could prejudice the reunification of Germany, the development of the European Communities, or the complicated position in Berlin; on the other to reduce to the maximum extent possible the barriers of suspicion and mistrust between East and West.

_____8.11_____

THE TINDEMANS REPORT ON EUROPEAN UNION 1975–76

European Parliament: Selection of Texts Concerning Institutional Matters of the Community from 1950 to 1982
(Luxembourg, 1983), pp. 376–7.

Leo Tindemans was Prime Minister of Belgium. His report, which was commissioned by the heads of government in 1974, raised issues which were increasingly to be discussed in future assessments of the progress of European integration. It proposed economic and monetary union, a common foreign policy and the development of social, regional and industrial policies. It also anticipated the idea of a 'two-speed' Europe – that the EC might progress more quickly if all members were not expected to advance at the same rate in all policy areas.

It is impossible at the present time to submit a credible programme of action if it is deemed absolutely necessary that in every case all stages should be reached by all the States at the same time. The divergence of their economic and financial situations is such that, were we to insist on this progress would be impossible and Europe would continue to crumble away. It must be possible to allow that:

- within the Community framework of an overall concept of European Union
  ...
- and on the basis of an action programme drawn up in a field decided upon by the common institutions, whose principles are accepted by all,
    (1) those States which are able to progress have a duty to forge ahead,
    (2) those States which have reasons for not progressing which the Council, on a proposal from the Commission, acknowledges as valid do not do so, but will at the same time receive from the other States any aid and

assistance that can be given them to enable them to catch the others up.

_____8.12_____

GIUSEPPE SARAGAT, ITALIAN FOREIGN MINISTER, ON THE QUESTION OF DIRECT ELECTIONS TO THE EUROPEAN PARLIAMENT, APRIL 1964

The Case for Direct Elections to the European Parliament by Direct Universal Suffrage (Luxembourg: Directorate-General for Parliamentary Information and Documentation, September 1969).

Direct elections were not held until 1979. The Council of Ministers declined for a long time to initiate legislation for the purpose. At one stage the European Parliament even threatened to take the Council to the European Court of Justice for failing to honour its treaty obligations. Signor Saragat's proposal envisaged partial European elections in 1966, with a full election to be held before 1 January 1970, the original date proposed for the completion of the common market.

The election of Members of the European Parliament by universal suffrage is provided for ... in the three Community Treaties; in the Treaty setting up the ECSC and in the Treaties setting up the Common Market and Euratom. This election was provided for because it was felt to be an essential condition for achieving that ever-closer political, economic and social union among the European peoples which is the ultimate objective of the three Treaties.

Direct elections will play a decisive part in awakening a real awareness of Europe both among the general public and in leading circles. It will fully justify a substantial widening of the European Parliament's powers of initiative and control and, leading as it would to the establishment of a real European and supranational legislative body, it will encourage and indeed necessitate the setting-up of a political institution of like nature. Any remaining opposition to the political integration of Europe is bound to vanish under the pressure of the democratically expressed will of the European peoples.

_____8.13_____

DAVID MARQUAND: 'DIRECT ELECTIONS AND INTEGRATION' FROM *PARLIAMENT FOR EUROPE*, 1979

David Marquand, *Parliament for Europe* (London: Jonathan Cape, 1979), pp. 77–81.

David Marquand was a Labour politician and adviser to the European Commission before becoming a professor of history. The following extract examines the likely impact of direct elections. These elections were held in the same year.

In Community circles, it has sometimes been suggested – in terms implying that the suggestion is virtually self-evident – that integration is bound to benefit, since the mere holding of direct elections will in some way 'legitimise' the Community and the Community process. The Patijn Report claimed that direct elections to the European Parliament 'would ... lend to the exercise of power by the Communities a legitimacy which has hitherto been lacking'. The Tindemans Report said that direct elections would 'reinforce the democratic legitimacy of the whole European institutional apparatus'. The truth is more disturbing. The suggestion that direct elections are bound to make integration easier founders on the simple fact that the body which is to be elected – namely the Parliament – plays only a trivial role in the integration process. Parliament will indeed gain legitimacy from direct elections. But the institutions which determine what happens in the Community – namely, the Commission and the Council – will not be affected one way or another. Direct elections will make a difference to the process of integration, and to the legitimacy of the Community as such, only if Parliament's new weight can somehow be brought to bear in favour of integration, and against the resistance of the national institutions whose positions are threatened by integration. There is no guarantee that this will happen. Indeed, it cannot happen unless the Community's present institutional structure is radically changed. For the hard fact is that, as things are at present, Parliament cannot bring any significant influence to bear on the national resistance to integration.

Indeed, if the present institutional structure remains intact, direct elections may make it even more difficult to achieve further integration than it is already. For the reasons discussed above, elected members are almost certain to want to prove to their constituents and to themselves that they can influence Community decisions. They will soon discover that their influence is very limited. Though the European Parliament has certain powers over Community spending it has no power over Community revenue-raising. Its role in the legislative process, though not as negligible as is sometimes assumed in the United Kingdom, is merely consultative. Community legislation is proposed by the Commission and decided by the Council;

though the Council consults Parliament, Parliament's opinion is not binding. The elaborate process of consultation in which the Commission engages before it makes proposals is not subject to parliamentary scrutiny. Nor are the weekly meetings of the powerful Committee of Permanent Representatives – normally known as COREPER after its acronym in French – which consists of the nine Ambassadors of the Member States to the Community, acting as a kind of legislative sieve, which sends controversial proposals through to the Council of Ministers, but holds back uncontroversial ones for decision by the Ambassadors themselves. In spheres unconnected with legislation or finance, Parliament's role is even more limited. In spite of the Community's growing importance as a negotiating bloc, Parliament plays no part in foreign-policy co-ordination – though its Political Affairs Committee has regular meetings with the foreign minister who holds the presidency of the Council – and does not have to approve the Community's line in trade negotiations. Direct elections will not change any of this. The elected Members will find that laboriously worked-out reports and eloquent speeches in the hemicycle produce no more results than they do at present. Some may sink back into frustrated apathy, but the ablest, the most energetic and the most ambitious can be expected to look for a scapegoat.

_____8.14_____

THE EUROPEAN MONETARY SYSTEM (EMS), 1978

The EMS (Luxembourg: Office for Official Publications of the European Communities, 1985).

The following is an extract from the resolution of the European Council on the creation of the EMS in July 1978. The EMS was established to secure a zone of financial stability for the Member States of the EC. The core is the Exchange Rate Mechanism (ERM), which links the currencies of the member states and limits the degree to which they should fluctuate. It has been a system of cooperation which supporters of European Monetary Union have seen as a transitional arrangement before a common currency.

The European Economic Council states that in the face of the dangers resulting from the serious disruptions of the world economy, especially since the end of 1973, the Community has come through a very testing time, proved its cohesion and thereby made a decisive contribution to the world economy ...

In terms of exchange rate management the European monetary system (EMS) will be at least as strict as the 'snake'. In the initial stages of its operation and for a limited period of time member countries currently not participating in the snake may opt for somewhat wider margins around central rates ... Non-member countries with particularly strong economic and financial ties with the Community may become associate members of the system. The European currency unit (ECU) will be at the centre of the system; in particular, it will be used as a means of settlement between EEC monetary authorities ...

A system of closer monetary co-operation will only be successful if participating countries pursue policies conducive to greater stability at home and abroad: this applies to both deficit and surplus countries alike.

8.15

ROY JENKINS, PRESIDENT OF THE COMMISSION: 'THE EUROPEAN COMMUNITY FROM THE FIRST ENLARGEMENT TO THE SECOND', 1978

Roy Jenkins, President of the European Commission, 'The European Community from the first enlargement to the second', Montagu Burton Lecture, University of Edinburgh, 1978.

Roy Jenkins was President from 1977 to 1981. The following points were made in a lecture at Edinburgh University. Enlargement means the admission of new states to the EC/EU. Greece became a member in 1981, Spain and Portugal in 1986, and Austria, Finland and Sweden in 1995.

The move towards enlargement is linked to the Commission's approach to economic and monetary union. What would clearly be unacceptable in any such desirable move is that only the strong should benefit and the weak should go further to the wall. This need not and must not be the result. There is as much mutual need between the strong and the weak in Europe as there was between the states of the American Union at the end of the nineteenth century. The strong need the underpinning of the unit of the Community market. The weak need the commitment to monetary discipline and the benefit in resource transfers that a powerful Community, socially-oriented, can provide.

These major issues ... the balance between external strength and internal weakness and the pressing need for a new stimulus to our economies, and acceptable levels of employment, especially as we move towards new enlargement of the Community – are those which both in their political challenge and diversity of detail should dominate European discussion in Member States. They are linked the one to the other and it is our perspective of such major issues that should mould our conception of the Community as an organisation for deliberately acting in common in our mutual interest. We ought to eschew both an obsessive concentration on the largely outdated debate between federalism and the often illusory sovereignty of national institutions, and a myopic obsession with alleged bureaucracy and standardisation.

THE EUROPEAN COMMUNITY IN THE 1980s

INTRODUCTION

Despite the positive initiatives at the end of the 1970s – the European Monetary System (EMS) and the introduction of direct elections to the European Parliament – the Community found itself in the early 1980s burdened by considerable pessimism (Document 9.5). 'Europessimism' and 'Eurosclerosis' defined a malaise which was evident in both the institutional stultification in the EC since the Luxembourg Compromise and recession, and in the growth of unemployment throughout the Community. Contributing to this mood was the widely held view that, in competitive terms, Europe was steadily falling behind the more dynamic economies of the United States, Japan and the new 'Asian Tigers' – especially in high technology (Document 9.2, see also Document 9.13). The negative mood in Europe must be understood against the background of the 'new cold war' tensions of the early 1980s and a climate of distrust in EC–US relations, which was reflected in issues of defence, economics and global risk-taking. These years, whose climate was foreshadowed by the 1979 Soviet invasion of Afghanistan, the declaration of martial law in Poland, the Iran–Iraq War, transatlantic wrangles over sanction against the communist bloc and heightened apprehensions over a dramatically accelerated arms race.[1]

At the beginning of the 1980s there were attempts to invigorate the Community. At German initiative, Foreign Minister Genscher was able to agree on a proposal with his Italian counterpart Colombo, which they presented to their partners in November 1981. It was indicative of the reduced ambitions of the time that the Genscher–Colombo Draft European Act was not in fact a proposed treaty at all. They had considered proposing a treaty but deemed this 'little short of unrealistic'.[2] Even as a policy statement it was marred by the divergence between the German interest in improved European Political Cooperation (EPC) and Italian concern about the economic situation. Its prospects were not helped by French indifference. The new French President François Mitterrand was more interested in his own project, launched in June 1981, of a 'social European space'. The only outcome from the German–Italian efforts was the June 1983 Solemn Declaration on European Union. Solemnity, however, did not signify commitment, or so it seemed to Margaret Thatcher, who recalled that she 'took the view that I could not quarrel with everything, and the document had no legal force. So I went along with it'.[3]

The efforts of the European Parliament were no more successful. Here the initiative was taken by the veteran federalist Altiero Spinelli in 1980. According to Spinelli, the underlying rationale for his initiative was that 'Considering the commitments made and never kept by governments . . . to follow the intergovernmental procedure established by the European Treaties means giving up the idea of reform . . . We must see reality for what it is. Either the reform of the European Community shall pass under national ratification of a Treaty drafted by the European Parliament or it shall not pass.'[4] Although concessions were made to governmental sensitivities in the Draft Treaty on European Union of 1984, there was really little prospect of the member states taking it up. Contrary to Spinelli's claims, there was no alternative to the intergovernmental procedure.

The Commission too tried to revive the Community, though it was hindered by the weak leadership of Gaston Thorn and distracted by disputes with Britain and preparations for the accession of Greece to the Community.[5] Among the Commission's more assertive members was Etienne Davignon, who drew on the experience of government–industry collaboration in one of the Community's economic competitors, Japan, to formulate ESPRIT (European Strategic Program for Research and Development in Information Technology). It was significant that he had carefully cultivated the leaders of Europe's largest firms and had involved them in the elaboration of the programme.[6] The mobilization of business interests helped to smooth the elaboration and implementation of programmes but was no more a substitute for interstate agreement than it had been earlier in the century.[7]

The dispute with Britain centred on the British budgetary contribution which, in turn, was linked to the size and operation of the CAP. The CAP was especially sensitive not only because of the vested interests of the various farming lobbies but also because it was a contentious issue in Euro-American relations (see Document 9.3). In May 1980 the Council could manage no more than a temporary agreement and a mandate to the Commission instructing it to come up with proposals which would avoid recurrent crises. While Britain had a case with which some of her partners sympathized, Thatcher's belligerent negotiating style did not help progress to an agreement. The atmosphere soured further two years later, in May 1982, when Britain sought to block agreement on price levels for the CAP, invoking the Luxembourg Compromise. To the surprise of the British, the majority refused to accept that this was an issue of 'vital national interest' and imposed new levels by a qualified majority. In reality, the Luxembourg Compromise had never been anything more than a statement of disagreement which left the treaty-based commitment to majority voting unrevised. Only the absence of political will had allowed it be such an obstacle to progress.

Nevertheless, compromise was still necessary on the British budgetary question. Mitterrand sought to break the deadlock at the March 1984 Brussels Council, but Thatcher refused to compromise. In the wake of the Brussels Council, both sides threatened to escalate the conflict. Thatcher seriously considered withholding Britain's contribution to the budget and was only deterred from this course of action by the possibility of revolt by her own party.[8] Mitterrand referred to a 'Europe of different speeds or variable geometry', implying that if Britain did not cooperate the others might proceed without her.[9] At the Fontainebleau meeting in June 1984 agreement was reached, though whether this marked any significant improvement on what had previously been offered is disputed. At the same summit, a decision was taken to establish two committees. One, the Adonnino Committee, was instituted to make proposals to project the image of a 'Peoples' Europe' among the general public. The second, variously called the 'Ad Hoc Committee' or the 'Dooge Committee', served as a focus for the evolving debate on institutional reform. The task of the Dooge Committee was to translate a wide range of existing views into politically acceptable terms which would lead to significant institutional reform.

The success of the Fontainebleau summit owed a lot to the then President of the Council, François Mitterrand. Ironically, the initial policies of Mitterrand's government had threatened to undermine integration. It had embarked upon a strategy of reflation and nationalization which ran counter to the dominant trend in Europe and North America. The result was speculation on the devaluation of the franc. Mitterrand was soon faced with the alternative of continuing with his socialist strategy and abandoning the EMS, or turning to a policy of austerity. There were advocates of both options among his ministers. Finally, in March 1983 Mitterrand chose austerity and the EMS. The strongest advocate of this had been Jacques Delors, the future President of the Commission. Delors himself had always been pro-European but the crisis of March 1983 left its mark upon him as well. As he observed in October 1983, 'I've always believed in the European ideal, but today it's no longer a simple question of idealism, it's a matter of necessity.'[10] Mitterrand drew the same conclusion and in May 1984 he surprised everyone, including MEPs from his own party, by speaking out in favour of the Draft Treaty on European Union. In reality his support was guarded. He did advocate a new treaty and institutional reform, but the treaty he had in mind would amend the existing treaties rather than replacing them, as the EP's Draft Treaty was intended to do.[11] Nevertheless, he appointed Maurice Faure, a long-standing pro-European, as France's representative on the Dooge Committee. Faure aimed for the 'minimum which would permit the

Community to advance and the maximum which the governments would be able to accept'.[12]

It was at Fontainebleau that there was agreement on the appointment of Jacques Delors as next President of the Commission. His term of office did not begin until January 1985, but he took care to consult the Member States the previous autumn. Of the ideas he put to them – institutional reform, monetary union, foreign and security cooperation, and the completion of the internal market – he found support only for the last. The choice was not surprising. It was, or so it appeared, the least ambitious of the options.

The fact that efforts to counter the malaise of Eurosclerosis, and to inject new optimism into both the European Community and the idea of regional integration, crystallized around the idea of completing the market through 'Europe 1992' and institutional reform was no accident. As the long-time student and advocate of European integration, John Pinder, observed: 'This diagnosis and prescription was not just the brainchild of economists and officials.'[13] It was shared by manufacturers. Although the removal of formal tariffs on trade between Community partners had been achieved by 1968, a significant number and variety of non-tariff restrictions on trans-border economic activity continued to exist, and had in fact increased since the mid-1970s as a consequence of the protectionist response of the member states to the impact of the oil price rise. These included frontier controls, red tape, technical regulations and business laws. In addition, national public procurement markets were characterized by preferential purchasing. Fiscal barriers existed in different rates of VAT and excise duties and in varying degrees of subsidization. All these were regarded as seriously limiting the efficiency, competitiveness and growth potential of European firms, while at the same time contributing to an overall perception of economic stagnation and decline in the Community.

In the challenging context of the early 1980s, European industry began to adopt an increasingly European strategy and perception. In particular, the fragmentation of the west European economy came to be seen as a real problem, because there were still numerous barriers to the free movement of goods. At this time there was also a growing consensus in the Community in favour of economic deregulation and budgetary discipline. The decision to launch 1992 and the single market resulted from several dominant motivations. The convergence of national economic policies around 'monetarist' market-orientated ideas was assisted, to some extent, by the anti-inflationary discipline of the EMS. A key moment here was when the socialist government of François Mitterrand in France was forced to abandon its growth-orientated policies in order to remain within the Exchange Rate Mechanism. It was a telling confirmation of interdependence.

On the one hand there was the belief that excessive regulation had a considerable amount to do with 'Eurosclerosis'; on the other that national economic objectives could not be achieved in isolation. This argued for greater, not less, regional cooperation and integration. The conversion of the Mitterrand government heralded moves towards further EC integration. From a very different perspective, the West German government also strongly favoured further advance. The 1992 project coincided with the foreign policy goals of Christian Democrat Helmut Kohl – a strong proponent of close Franco-German relations and of a revitalised *Westpolitik*, which he saw as a necessary counterbalance to the *Ostpolitik* initiatives of previous Social Democrat administrations. From a different perspective, the Conservative British government also encouraged further integration, with consequences which went further than it had anticipated. While Mrs Thatcher had alienated and antagonized her partners in the Community in the early 1980s, was anything but *Communautaire* in spirit and was fervently hostile to supranationalism, she was also very attracted to the idea of liberalizing the internal European market with its implications for deregulation and elimination of government controls and economic activity. This appeared to her to point more in the direction of an open free-trading area, which suited the British disposition, than an exclusionary union.[14] So, regarding 'Europe 1992' as an exercise in 'negative' integration and overlooking its 'positive' consequences for further integration, she displayed a supportiveness out of character with her normal intransigence.

Estimation of the relative importance of these varied actors and developments has proved contentious. Some accounts emphasize supranational actors (the Commission) and transnational actors (business elites).[15] Others emphasize the importance of changes in the domestic political agenda and the centrality of national governments, and downgrade the role of the Commission.[16] The influence of business elites is usually diffuse, and it remains true that even when they did call for change 'what needs to be explained is why governments finally listened'.[17] The initiative of the Commission is relevant to answering that question. It is true that the Commission can only propose, it cannot dispose, but government leaders have certainly perceived the Commission and especially its President as significant actors, for good or ill.[18]

The Commission's proposal was published in June 1985 with the title *Completing the Internal Market*, although it soon became identified with the slogan '1992'. The White Paper, which was in essence a competition programme, was drafted in large part by Lord Cockfield, who had previously been a Conservative Minister. It proposed nearly 300 measures aimed at eliminating the remaining barriers to the free movement of goods, services, capital and labour within the Community by the end of 1992. Amidst the detail lay the recurrent principle of mutual recognition. The way for this was cleared by the Cassis de Dijon ruling of the European Court of Justice in 1979. This had upheld the right of a French company to sell its liqueur in Germany. It established categorically the general principle that all goods lawfully produced and marketed in one Member State would be accepted by the others, guaranteeing free circulation.

By the time the White Paper was ready, the Council had already received the Dooge Report. It had proved impossible to reach a consensus in the committee, and the Council was presented with a divided opinion. Britain, supported by Denmark and Greece, was opposed to institutional reform, preferring to give priority to discussion of policies. Ironically, that had been French policy before Mitterrand's conversion to institutional reform. In an effort to divert the pressure for institutional reform, the British Foreign Minister Geoffrey Howe used a meeting at Stresa at the beginning of June 1985 to suggest that a 'gentlemen's agreement' to avoid recourse to the veto would suffice. He also suggested that they should concentrate on political cooperation. On the eve of the Milan Council there was further confusion. The Commission's White Paper was misconstrued and seen as an alternative to institutional reform. Lack of coordination between Mittterrand and Kohl resulted in a communiqué which resembled Howe's proposals. Interviewed much later, Delors recalled, 'I read it and I went to see Mitterrand, furious and told him: "it's the Fouchet plan". Saying that is an insult. So he withdrew it.'[19]

At the Milan Council itself the customary divide emerged. To the horror of the minority, however, the Italian Prime Minister, Bettino Craxi, called for a vote under Article 236 which allowed for the convocation of an intergovernmental conference. This time the unsuccessful attempt to invoke the Luxembourg Compromise was more significant. The conference duly opened on 22 July. Although, as the name suggests, an intergovernmental conference was attended by representatives of member states, Delors joined the meetings of Foreign Ministers. The Commission's contribution, though perhaps less than Delors claimed, was substantial. A major victory came with agreement that there should be a Single European Act instead of several separate treaties (Document 9.6). The latter strategy was opposed by the Commission for fear that it would damage the integrity of the Community. There were several other contentious areas. The German Foreign Minister, Genscher, brokered a compromise over the extension of the powers of the European Parliament, further complicating the legislative procedures of the Community. Delors introduced a draft on monetary union relatively late in the day, only to be met by opposition from Germany as well as the more predictable British hostility. The Anglo-German alliance against Delors proved to be short-lived. To the annoyance of Thatcher, the Germans changed their stance. Isolated, Thatcher strove to limit the damage. She recalled being able to restrict the passages on monetary union 'to what I considered insignificant proportions', but added, with the benefit of hindsight, 'this formulation delayed M. Delors' drive to monetary union only briefly'.[20]

The Single European Act (SEA) was effective from July 1987, committing the member states to complete the internal market by the end of 1992, as

> an area without internal frontiers in which the free movement of goods, persons, services and capital is ensured in accordance with the provisions of the Treaty . . .
> It was the first formal amendment of the Community's constitution and its impact affected four distinct areas of community activity. It modified the decision-making process by introducing majority decisions for a significant number of articles; it created a co-decision procedure with the European Parliament; it set a programme and deadline for the completion of the internal market and it incorporated European Political Co-operation (EPC) within the Treaty framework. It provided an example of 'the central paradox in the history of the European Community.[21]

The objective of European Community is political, yet once again the means chosen were primarily economic. The most immediate consequence of the SEA was the completion of the single market. Those areas where member states retained *de jure* power to veto policy were narrowed to 'fundamental constitutional-type questions within the Community, such as enlargement, any redistribution of power among institutions and any move to new uncharted areas of policy'.[22] The increased involvement of the European Parliament in the legislative procedures via the cooperation system was limited, though, to only those areas where majority decisions were permissible under the SEA. A system of two readings was introduced, but to many the Parliament's new powers were a disappointingly modest accretion and fell far short of what MEPs had lobbied for. The Parliament essentially required support from other Community institutions and member states to be assured of influence. In practice, the extent of European parliamentary involvement and the appropriate institutional procedures first raised in the Tindemans Report remained highly contentious (see Document 9.8).

In material terms, the creation of the single market was widely expected to have significant benefits. With the removal of barriers to cross-border economic activity, European enterprise would enjoy further economies of scale and become much more efficient and profitable, enabling it to compete more effectively with the United States and the Far East. The most well known study of these effects was the Commission's Cecchini Report. This concluded that even without accompanying government measures to stimulate demand, the completion of the internal market should lead in the medium term to a 4.5 per cent increase in Community GDP and the creation of 1.8 million new jobs. With concomitant expansionary measures these gains could be as much as 7.5 per cent on GDP and 5.7 million jobs. This analysis provoked considerable criticism and controversy among economists, particularly the suggestion that the removal of non-tariff barriers would lead to a fundamental reconstruction of the European Community economy.[23] The adoption of the single market programme was, nevertheless, a catalyst for a new phase of European integration which was, together with the collapse of the Soviet Empire, to transform the agenda of the Community and wider Europe.

The March 1985 Brussels Council had set the seal upon the accession of Spain and Portugal, bringing the total number of members to twelve. The Mediterranean enlargement of the Community had begun in the same month (June 1975) as the British referendum had confirmed Britain's continuing membership of the Community, when the Karamanlis government in Greece lodged an application to join. This was followed in 1977, after the introduction of democracy in those countries, by similar applications from Spain and Portugal. In all these cases the motivation was primarily political. In the words of David Arter, 'Having recently emerged from the shadow of authoritarian regimes, Spain, Portugal and Greece craved international recognition and viewed accession to the EC as a springboard to rehabilitation within the international fraternity. All three ... desired to undertake a prominent part on the European stage and shed the role of pariah.'[24] Since democracy was a requisite of membership, membership was also viewed by their governments as a guarantee for the preservation of their democratic institutions. However, these applications were not met with unreserved enthusiasm. First of all, the applicants were relatively poor and resources from the richer members would be needed to promote their economic development. Second, all three Mediterranean states marketed agricultural products – citrus fruit, olive oil, wine – which would compete with French and Italian goods. The only Mediterranean applicant to encounter significant opposition within the EC was Spain, largely because of fears of competition from her agriculture. With a population of 38 million and an area of 505,000 square kilometres, of which 276,000 were devoted to farming (the most vulnerable sector in the Community), it was evident that negotiations would not be easy for Spain. Whereas Britain and Denmark favoured widening the Community, Italy and France dragged their heels, emphasizing the need to 'deepen' the EC and to resolve the deadlock over Britain's budgetary contribution. It was inevitable that the further enlargement would introduce a growing north–south dimension into Community politics.

The enlargement and further integration of the Community put further pressure on non-Community European states. EFTA noted that 1992 posed 'a new challenge not only for the Community, but also for EFTA'.[25] Given the level of EFTA's trade dependence upon the Community, this was inevitable. EFTA had little choice but to seek closer agreement with the Community, largely on the Community's terms. Part of those terms, as the Commissioner for External Affairs made clear, was that relations with EFTA would take second place to internal Community integration. In its relations with the CMEA in the east, the Community also spoke from a position of strength. Thus, while the Community entered into discussions with the CMEA, it insisted upon parallel negotiations with the individual CMEA member states for a 'normalisation of relations'.[26]

While the Community counted as an economic heavyweight, it still had a very limited framework for political cooperation, despite the minor improvements of the Single European Act, and lacked a security and defence profile. As on previous occasions, inability to agree upon a defence role for the Community led to the use of the WEU as a substitute. This, however, required care lest the United States conclude that innovation was intended to weaken the Atlantic Alliance. Precisely such fears accompanied the attempt to revive the WEU through the October 1984 Rome Declaration of the WEU (Document 9.4).[27]

While outsiders were impressed by the magnitude of the achievement represented by the SEA, the European Parliament was predictably disappointed. Its complaint that the Act 'will allow utterly contradictory interpretations' was, however, in some ways highly accurate.[28] On her return to London, Margaret Thatcher, as she later admitted, had not grasped the strength of the new dynamism. She told the House of Commons that 'I am constantly saying that I wish they would talk less about European and political union. The terms are not understood in this country. In so far as they are understood over there, they mean a good deal less than some people over here think they mean.'[29] To Jacques Delors the terms meant a good deal more than Thatcher imagined. Employing what was termed a 'Russian dolls' strategy, Delors revealed one package after another, claiming that they were all implied by the SEA. Whether or not they were implied by the Act, they were contained in his vision of a single market, a vision that was radically different from that of Thatcher. For Delors and his team, it was necessary to balance 'efficiency, stability and equity' (Document 9.7).

The first step towards this goal, the so-called *paquet Delors*, was announced under the title of *Making a Success of the Single Act* in February 1987. The package brought together recommendations for solving three problems: the impending financial crisis, the costs of the CAP, and the persistent regional disparities within the Community. The proposed solution for the first was an increase in the Community's 'own resources' and greater flexibility for the Commission. The recurrent problem of the CAP was to be mitigated by guidelines for controlling its cost. Regional disparities were to be tackled by increasing the various structural funds and by making greater efforts to coordinate them. It was predictable that Thatcher would object, but this time she was joined by Helmut Kohl who feared that Germany would bear much of the cost of increased expenditure and was less than enthusiastic about a reform of the CAP that would antagonize the German farming constituency.[30] The conflicting interests within the Community ensured that 1987 ended with the disastrous Copenhagen Summit in December. With Germany taking over the Presidency in January 1988, Kohl moved to break the deadlock. Agreement was finally reached in February, giving the Commission much if not all it wanted. Thatcher haggled until the last minute, which, according to Lord Cockfield, 'rankled deeply'.[31]

The second step involved proposals for monetary union. To supporters of further European integration, monetary union was a logical sequence to 1992, since the existence of different national currencies and monetary policies was a significant barrier to economic transactions across borders. The need to change currencies incurred costs, and governments and banks recognized that in a united market without exchange and capital controls the conduct of strictly 'national' monetary policy would become difficult, if not impossible. If, to some, it was logical to regard monetary union as the complement to 1992, to others it was a major step towards a federal Europe, something which provoked sharply contrasting views and considerable political controversy. This reflected the fact that, despite the considerable level of economic integration to date and the pooling of sovereignty, the EC remained a grouping of nation states with conventional national interests. It would be these nations, though, that for diverse reasons would be the driving force behind monetary integration.

The initiative was taken by the French Finance Minister Edouard Balladur. In January 1988, he wrote to his counterparts arguing that the present arrangements for EMS put unfair pressure on weaker currencies, a view echoed by the Italians.[32] Even in the previous year, Balladur had argued that there was sufficient convergence of views to 'overcome the historic quarrel between the monetarists, who favour prior monetary discipline, and those who believe that monetary order should be left until the final stages of economic union'.[33] In retrospect, that was slightly optimistic. As we saw in Chapter 8, the EMS had accentuated, or at least made more evident, West German economic and monetary dominance. In the early 1980s, France had been forced to bow to German monetary discipline and to abandon expansionary economic policies in order to keep within the ERM banding. From this time onwards, a key objective of the French government was to undermine German monetary hegemony through the transfer of Bundesbank authority to European institutions, although this intention was in the context of a generally strong Franco-German rapport. At the very least France wanted to ensure that, in future, German monetary authority would be compelled to take European, not simply German, economic needs and interests into consideration when constructing their policies. These views were shared by most other EC countries, though the British government still remained outside the ERM and in general opposed any further moves towards monetary integration as a threat to national sovereignty. The West Germans were ambivalent on the issue. Many objected that EMU would undermine the discipline of the Bundesbank. It was also questionable, in the eyes of many, whether monetary union was workable given the considerable economic divergence across the Community. It was feared that any precipitate move towards union might be inflationary.

Franco-German cooperation was facilitated by the broader international agenda. Helmut Kohl was seeking more bilateral cooperation on foreign and defence policy to counter the instability in east Europe and a feared decline in American commitment to European security. French officials indicated a willingness to discuss greater defence cooperation and a strengthened 'European defence identity' in return for concessions on economic and monetary policy. Agreements were signed on 22 January 1988 establishing two bilateral councils, covering economic and defence/security cooperation. The Bundesbank at once showed its scepticism and claimed that this was another example of the German Federal Government making flawed economic policy decisions in the interests of essentially political objectives.

Despite these tensions, at the Hannover Summit in June 1988 national leaders established a commission to study ideas on monetary union and to make concrete proposals for achieving it. Delors was appointed chairman. The Delors Plan, published in April 1989, envisaged a three-stage evolution. The first, to begin on 1 July 1990, would achieve closer coordination of national monetary policies, and all controls on trans-border capital movements within the Community would be abolished. In the second stage, the margin of fluctuation of currencies within the ERM would be tightened and a European system of central banks would be established. In the final stage, a single currency would be created and managed by the European Central Bank (ECB). A currency area would be created, 'in which policies are managed jointly with a view to attaining common macro-economic objectives'.

The Delors Plan was endorsed by the EC leaders at the Madrid Summit in June 1989, with Thatcher expressing strong reservations. While she was an enthusiastic supporter of the removal of non-tariff barriers, which she regarded as a laudable extension of her own liberal economic principles, she was strongly averse to anything that suggested further inroads upon national sovereignty – although signature of the SEA, with its extension of the principle of majority voting, meant just that. As Paul Taylor put it:

> If the goal of a Europe without frontiers was to be achieved a major extension of the scope of integration would necessarily follow ... To cope with the new competition and use the new opportunities, companies would need to 'European-ise' themselves. In short, what was being contemplated even by the most ardent

intergovernmentalists was something that went far beyond the territorial practice of international co-operation between states: it amounted to the creation of a single economic space. A further range of interdependencies would follow.[34]

According to Delors, one of those interdependencies was the social dimension. He told the May 1988 European Trade Union Confederation that the 'social dimension of building Europe' was 'both a condition and goal' of the single market.[35] It was a condition in that without some measure of harmonization of social policy the market would be distorted, as some states sought to exploit the advantage of the lower costs associated with low levels of social provision. It was a goal in so far as Delors drew on personalism, a doctrine critical of the anomie of the free market, to suggest that it was now time to endow the Community with a 'little more soul'.[36] This involved legislation, a charter of social rights and the process of social dialogue between trade unions and employers' organizations brokered by the Community (Document 9.10). Although most of this was unobjectionable to most of the member states, it was anathema to Thatcher. When Delors presented his vision to the British Trades Union Congress (TUC) in September 1988 and was warmly received, Thatcher was enraged. Echoing de Gaulle's antipathy to activist Presidents of the Commission, she later wrote that in the summer of 1988 Delors 'had altogether slipped his leash as a *fonctionnaire* and become a fully fledged political spokesman for federalism'.[37] (Document 9.11 and, for a response, see Document 9.12). Given the doctrinaire tone, it was inevitable that Britain refused to subscribe to the Social Charter adopted at the December 1989 Strasbourg Summit.

The 1980s demonstrated the increasing pressure for integration, but also that political leaders did not have to bow to that pressure. Much depended on the level and direction of consensus. Where there was general aversion or indifference to further integration, Eurosclerosis prevailed. Where there was a majority for integration, especially if the majority was built around the Franco-German axis, obdurate resistance by others was still possible but increasingly risky. As the majority of the Council signed the Social Charter, the agenda was changing and posing a new test for the Franco-German axis and the Community: German unification was back on the agenda.

NOTES

1. The low point of the diasgreement over sanctions, in 1982, concerned a pipeline stretching from Siberia to west Europe. It was one of the few occasions on which Margaret Thatcher opposed American President Ronald Reagan. See Stephen George, *An Awkward Partner* (Oxford, 1990), pp. 139–40.
2. Quoted in Joseph Weiler, 'The Genscher–Colombo Draft European Act: the politics of indecision', *Journal of European Integration*, Vol. 6 (1983), p. 141.
3. *Downing Street Years* (London, 1993), p. 314. With the benefit of hindsight she added that 'the linguistic skelton on which so much institutional flesh would grow was already evident' (*ibid.*).
4. Quoted in Cinzia Rognoni, 'Spinelli's initiative in the European Parliament', in Andrea Bosco (ed.), *The Federal Idea*, Vol. 2 (London, 1992), pp. 303–4.

5. Michelle Cini, *The European Commission* (Manchester, 1996), pp. 63–6.

6. For an early assessment stressing the limited impact of ESPRIT see L.K. Mytelka and M. Delapierre, 'The alliance strategies of European firms and the role of ESPRIT', *Journal of Common Market Studies*, Vol. 26 (1987), pp. 231–53.

7. For expectations to the contrary see Chapter 1, Document 1.2.

8. George, *An Awkward Partner*, pp. 157–8.

9. *Bull. EC* 5-1984, p. 138.

10. Quoted in Charles Grant, *Delors* (London, 1994), p. 55.

11. E.Z. Haywood, 'The French Socialists and European institutional reform', *Journal of European Integration*, Vol. 12 (1989), pp. 133–4.

12. ibid., p. 138.

13. See John Pinder, *European Community* (London, 1995), p. 76.

14. *The Downing Street Years*, p. 546.

15. Wayne Sandholtz and John Zysman, '1992: recasting the European bargain', *World Politics*, Vol. 42 (1989), pp. 95–128.

16. Andrew Moravcsik, 'Negotiating the Single European Act', in Robert O. Keohane and Stanley Hoffmann (eds), *The New European Community* (Boulder, 1991), pp. 41–84.

17. Moravcsik, 'Negotiating the Single European Act', p. 65. Moravcsik, however, is too dismissive of business elites. A more balanced view is in Keith Middlemas, *Orchestrating Europe* (London, 1995), pp. 136–40.

18. Thatcher described Delors as 'a major player in the game', though she claims this only became apparent at the December 1986 London Council. *The Downing Street Years*, p. 558.

19. Quoted in Grant, *Delors*, p. 73.

20. *The Downing Street Years*, p. 555.

21. See François Duchêne, 'More or less than Europe? European integration in retrospect', in Colin Crouch and David Marquand (eds), *The Politics of 1992* (Oxford, 1993), p. 9.

22. See W. Nicoll and T.C. Salmon, *Understanding the European Communities* (London, 1990), p. 223.

23. See F. McDonald and S. Dearden, *European Economic Integration* (London, 1994), pp. 29–36.

24. See David Arter, *The Politics of European Integration* (Aldershot, 1993), p. 190.

25. Quoted in F. Laurson, 'The Commmunity's policy towards EFTA', *Journal of Common Market Studies*, Vol. 28 (1990), p. 314.

26. *Bull. EC* 2-1986, point 2.2.21.

27. William Cromwell, *The United States and the European Pillar* (New York, 1992), pp. 173–4.

28. *Bull. EC* 1-1986, point 1.2.2. Spinelli was even blunter: 'The Council has produced a mouse, a miserable stillborn mouse'. *Ibid.*

29. *The Downing Street Years*, p. 556.

30. D. Dinan, *Ever Closer Union?* (Basingstoke, 1994), p. 152.

31. Lord Cockfield, *The European Union* (London, 1994), p. 139.

32. Daniel Gros and Niels Thygesen, *European Monetary Integration* (London, 1992), pp. 312–13.

33. *Financial Times* (17 June 1987).

34. See Paul Taylor, *International Organization in the Modern World* (London, 1993), p. 77.

35. *Bull. EC* 5-1988, point 1.1.1.

36. *Bull. EC* 1-1989, point 1.1.1. On personalism see John Loughlin, 'French personalist and federalist movements in the interwar period', in P. Stirk (ed.), *European Unity in Context* (London, 1989), pp. 188–200.
37. *The Downing Street Years*, p. 742.

FURTHER READING

M. Cini, *The European Commission* (Manchester, 1996).

M. Franklin, *Rich Mens' Farming* (London, 1985).

C. Grant, *Delors* (London, 1994).

D. Gros and N. Thygesen, *European Monetary Integration* (London, 1992).

G. C. Hufbauer, *Europe 1992 – An American Perspective* (Washington, DC, 1990).

R. O. Keohane and S. Hoffmann (eds), *The New European Community* (Boulder, CO, 1991).

J. Lodge (ed.), *The European Community and the Challenge of the Future* (London, 1989).

G. Mackenzie and A. Venables, *The Economics of the Single European Act* (London, 1991).

K. Middlemas, *Orchestrating Europe* (London, 1995).

F. Nicholson and R. East, *From the Six to the Twelve* (London, 1987).

T. Padoa-Schioppa, *Financial and Monetary Integration in Europe: 1990, 1992 and Beyond* (Cambridge, 1988).

J. Pinter, *European Community: The Building of a Union* (Oxford, 1991).

G. Ross, *Jacques Delors and European Integration* (Cambridge, 1995).

P. Taylor, *The Limits of European Integration* (London, 1983).

L. Tsoukalis, *The New European Economy: The Politics and Economics of Integration* (Oxford, 1991).

S. Weatherill, *Law and Integration in the European Union* (Oxford, 1995).

_____ 9.1 _____

THE COMMON AGRICULTURAL POLICY, 1980

Bull. EC, Supplement 6, 1980, p. 17.

The following extract contains conclusions from the Commission Report on the CAP and proposals for its reform in 1980. By the 1980s the European Commission had come to accept the need for restraint in agricultural expenditure. It was taking two-thirds of the EC budget and rising faster than the resources of the Community could sustain.

The common agricultural policy has broadly achieved its main goals: free trade in agricultural commodities, security of supply of basic foodstuffs at stable prices for the Community's 260 million consumers, growth in productivity and protection of the incomes of 8 million farmers, fair share of agriculture in world trade and contribution of the agricultural sector to the Community trade balance. The CAP has met with serious difficulties:

(a) the open-ended guarantee system has led to serious imbalances between supply and demand in several major agricultural markets, milk being the major problem;

(b) price guarantees or product subsidies have been worked out in an indiscriminate manner between producers and have been of greater assistance to the richer regions than to the least-favoured areas of the Community;

(c) although the financial impact of the CAP is not excessive in relation to the GDP of the Community, it has tended to increase too rapidly in real terms, and the way in which money is spent, for instance on milk surpluses, has been justifiably criticised.

9.2

GROWTH RATES, 1960–94

L. Tsoukalis, *The New European Economy Revisited* (Oxford: Oxford University Press, 1997), p. 16.

During the 1960s and the first part of the 1970s the majority of west European countries enjoyed high growth rates and low unemployment. The performance of the Six was significantly better than that of the UK and the US. Note the dramatic decline in growth rates after the 1973–74 oil crisis. The figures show the average annual per cent change of real GDP at constant prices.

	1960–67	1968–73	1974–79	1980–85	1986–90	1991–94
Belgium	4.6	5.3	2.2	1.4	3.0	1.1
France	5.5	5.2	2.8	1.5	3.0	0.8
Germany	3.8	5.0	2.4	1.4	2.9	1.7
Italy	5.6	4.9	3.7	1.9	3.0	0.7
Luxembourg	2.8	5.5	1.3	2.2	4.7	2.0
Netherlands	4.6	5.1	2.6	1.3	3.1	1.8
Denmark	4.6	4.0	1.9	2.1	1.4	2.0
Ireland	3.6	5.2	4.9	2.6	4.5	4.0
United Kingdom	2.9	3.5	1.5	1.3	3.3	0.9
Greece	5.8	8.4	3.7	1.4	1.7	1.1
Portugal	6.2	7.6	2.9	1.5	5.1	0.7
Spain	7.8	6.7	2.3	1.5	4.5	1.0
EU-12	4.6	4.9	2.6	1.5	3.1	1.2
Austria	4.2	5.7	2.9	1.6	3.0	2.1
Finland	4.1	5.9	2.1	3.2	3.4	-2.0
Sweden	4.5	3.7	1.8	1.7	2.3	-1.7
OECD-Europe	4.6	4.9	2.5	1.6	3.1	1.1
Japan	9.8	9.3	3.6	3.7	4.5	1.4
United States	4.6	3.2	2.5	2.1	2.8	2.4
Total OECD	5.1	4.9	2.7	2.2	3.2	1.6

Note: The total OECD figure includes all the countries that were members of the OECD before 1994.

9.3

US–EUROPEAN ECONOMIC RELATIONS, 1981

Address by the US Assistant Secretary of State for Economics and Business Affairs, Joseph Hormats, to the Mid-American Committee, Chicago, 16 December 1981, *Current Policy*, no. 361 (Washington, DC: State Department, 1982)

The following points are from an address by the Assistant Secretary of State for Economic and Business Affairs, Joseph Hormats, to the Mid-America Committee, Chicago, 16 December 1981. This extract gives some of the major reasons for the economic tension between the United States and the European Community in what was a difficult decade for Europe–North America relations.

Agriculture. The agricultural policies of the United States and the EC are inspired by different economic philosophies. The US farm program is designed to interfere as little as possible in international agricultural markets. When prices are low, the Commodity Credit Corporation (CAC) takes over, and along with farmers, holds surplus US production; it does not dampen world prices by subsidizing exports. Our farmers hold the world's largest grain reserves, thus contributing to world food security and international price stability.

The EC's Common Agricultural Policy (CAP) is based on high price supports. It has no production controls and protects prices by variable levies at the border. It has created burdensome surpluses and serious budget problems for the Community. By subsidizing exports, it has artificially stimulated large-scale European exports in such products as wheat, sugar, and meat. This limits market opportunities for products of such countries as the United States, which compete without subsidies.

We recognize the importance of the CAP to the origins of the Community and to its continued cohesion. Last week in Brussels, US Cabinet members stressed that we would not challenge the fundamental elements of the policies on which European unity is based. We also understand the political, social, and economic conditions under which European agriculture operates, which are quite different from those in the United States. But, we are seriously concerned about the effects of excesses in the CAP. We fear that the EC is seeking to solve its internal agricultural overproduction and budget problems by converting the CAP into a common export policy based on extensive subsidies. We are also deeply disturbed that the EC from time to time considers measures that would curb exports into the EC of soybeans and feed grain substitutes. This would violate their GATT bindings to us.

Some $9 billion in US exports to the EC and more than $40 billion in US world-wide sales are at issue in this area. Serious friction in our bilateral relations would result, as would increased instability in world markets, if present EC policy trends continue. We have made it clear to the Community that if our legitimate agricultural interests and rights are adversely affected, we will strongly defend them. However difficult Europe's internal situation, it cannot be resolved at the expense of US agricultural interests.

We welcome the effort within the Community to reform the CAP, make it less costly to the Community budget, and give it a greater market orientation. It will not be easy for 10 countries with diverse interests to agree on modifications to achieve greater efficiency and reduce cost. But it is a reasonable and sustainable course of action over the long run.

European Unity. We support the objective of European unity as embodied in the European Community. A strong, prosperous and united Europe is important to the security and the prosperity of the United States and the West.

While we may have difficulties with certain EC policies, the existence of the Community as the policy entity for, and representative of, the Ten on trade and other economic issues is much to be preferred to trying to maintain economic relations on these issues with ten countries, with constant friction among them. The Community makes trade and other economic issues more manageable than would be the case if it did not exist. And, its historical outward looking and constructive approach to the world economy has been essential to the success of the Tokyo Round, the creation of the International Energy Agency, and progress on a variety of international economic issues.

9.4

THE ROME DECLARATION OF THE WESTERN EUROPEAN UNION, 27 OCTOBER 1984

WEU Assembly Proceedings, December 1984, pp. 48–9.

The Rome Declaration emphasized the revival of the quiescent WEU in the mid-1980s as a body which could provide a distinctive west European voice on defence and security matters. In 1987 it was to adopt a programme which called for the creation of a 'cohesive defence identity'. The Maastricht Treaty subsequently identified the WEU as a constituent part of the Common Foreign and Security Policy (CFSP) 'pillar'.

4 The Ministers recalled that the Atlantic Alliance, which remains the foundation of western security, had preserved peace on the continent for thirty-five years. This permitted the construction of Europe. The Ministers are convinced that a better utilisation of WEU would not only contribute to the security of west Europe but also to an improvement in the common defence of all the countries of the Atlantic Alliance and to greater solidarity among its members.

5 The Ministers emphasised the indivisibility of security within the North Atlantic Treaty area. They recalled in particular the vital and substantial contribution of

all the European allies, and underlined the crucial importance of the contribution to common security of their allies who are not members of the WEU. They stressed the necessity, as a complement to their joint efforts, of the closest possible concertation with them.

6 The Ministers are convinced that increased cooperation within WEU will also contribute to the maintenance of adequate military strength and political solidarity and, on that basis, to the pursuit of a more stable relationship between the countries of East and West by fostering dialogue and cooperation.

7 The Ministers called attention to the need to make the best use of existing resources through increased cooperation, and through WEU to provide a political impetus to institutions of cooperation in the field of armaments.

8 The Ministers therefore decided to hold comprehensive discussions and to seek to harmonise their views on the specific conditions of security in Europe, in particular:

- defence questions;
- arms control and disarmament;
- the effects of developments in East–West relations on the security of Europe;
- Europe's contribution to the strengthening of the Atlantic Alliance, bearing in mind the importance of transatlantic relations;
- the development of European cooperation in the field of armaments in respect of which WEU can provide a political impetus.

They may also consider the implications for Europe of crises in other regions of the world.

9 The Ministers recalled the importance of the WEU Assembly, which, as the only European parliamentary body mandated by treaty to discuss defence matters, is called upon to play a growing role.

They stressed the major contribution which the Assembly has already made to the revitalisation of WEU and called upon it to pursue its efforts to strengthen the solidarity among the member states, and to strive to consolidate the consensus among public opinion on their security and defence needs ...

9.5

EMILE NOËL, SECRETARY-GENERAL OF THE EUROPEAN COMMISSION: 'THE EUROPEAN COMMUNITY: WHAT KIND OF FUTURE?', 1984

Emile Noël, 'The European Community: what kind of future?',
Government and Opposition, Vol. 20, no. 2 (Spring 1985), pp.
147–55.

These points about the 'institutional drift' of the Community were contained in a
lecture to the Belgian Royal Institute of International Affairs, 20 November 1984.
From 1967 to 1987 M. Noël was Head of the Secretariat-General of the Commission, its most senior administrator.

I now turn to the Community's 'institutional drift' away from the spirit, and indeed the letter, of the Treaties of Rome. This is not a new development: it started with the so-called 'Luxembourg Compromise' and has of late been getting worse.

Rather oddly, the official admission of failure to agree in Luxembourg in January 1966 has been followed ever since by the systematic pursuit of unanimity on anything and everything, even though five of the six Member States then accepted that the Community had firmly stated that in the event of prolonged failure to agree, the matter was to be put to the vote wherever the Treaty so provided. This approach, which has become a still more regular practice since the first enlargement, has meant that the pursuit of unanimity dominates the proceedings not only of the Council but of the bodies doing the preparatory groundwork, the Permanent Representatives' Committee and the expert working parties. Even though the Council itself started to use voting two years ago, it still gets held up by the endless preparatory proceedings, striving for unanimity.

The European Council was throughout closely involved in dealing with the budget crisis, from the Strasbourg session when the crisis started, in June 1979, to the Fontainebleau session in June 1984. By the end of the process the Council of Ministers proper no longer even had any say in the preparations for the Heads of Government's meetings, it was so taken for granted that any ticklish matter (whatever it might be) could only be handled at the very top. In fact, since the Stuttgart session in June 1983 the European Council has ceased to be the organ of supreme political initiative originally intended: it is now doing the job of the Council of Ministers, and at the same time preventing the latter from doing its job itself. At Fontainebleau too, in spite of the wishes of the then President in office of the European Council, only a minute part of the proceedings was devoted to issues concerning the future – the institutional reactivation of the Community, its rehabilitation in the eyes of its citizens.

The fact that the Community system is gradually degenerating into inter-governmental negotiation must be fully recognised. The concentration on unanimity and the constant intervention of the European Council are to a great extent responsible for this degeneration. The European Council, when dealing with Community matters, acts – unsurprisingly – in its own way instead of 'sitting as the Council of the Community' as provided in the decision of 1973 which set it up.

What is more, at Stuttgart the Heads of Government decided, notwithstanding the Commission's objections, to depart from the prescribed Community procedures in their planned overall negotiations and set up the so-called 'Special Council', which could deliberate not only on Commission proposals but on any proposals from Member States. From then on there were constant bilateral talks between the Council Presidency and individual member governments, at the expense of multi-lateral discussions in the Institutions. I am not denying the admirable devotion of the Presidency of the Community, of the ministers and the Heads of State and Government and the hard work they put into securing the agreement that got the Community out of the rut but habits were formed – bad habits, as I see it – and those practices once again begun tend to go on: multiplication of the compromises made by the Presidency on all sorts of subjects, thus supplanting Commission proposals, undue resort to bilateral talks, national glorification of the 'Presidency of the Community', although this is a new office with no legal basis. Something needs to be done about all this. It can still be done, but time is not on the side of the Institutions.

_____ 9.6 _____

LORD COCKFIELD:
'THE SINGLE EUROPEAN ACT', 1994

The European Union: Creating the Single Market (Chichester: Chancery Law Publishing, 1994), pp. 62–3.

The following extract is from Lord Cockfield's *The European Union: Creating a Single Market*. Cockfield was a British member of the Commission between 1985 and 1989 and was responsible for preparing the implementation of the 1992 proposals.

Acte Unique

It is called the *Acte Unique* or 'Single Act' because in the early stages the possibility of a series of Acts, each covering one or more of the subjects under consideration, seemed the likely outcome. And particularly one Act covering matters of Community competence and a separate Act covering political co-operation in foreign affairs, which is not within the Community 'competence' but takes the form of 'co-operation' between the Member States *qua* Member States and not as members of the Community although in practice it is serviced by the Community institutions and is dealt with in the Foreign Affairs Council. Jacques Delors was adamant that there should be a 'Single Act' and in the end he got his way. There are of course *three*, not one, European Communities – the original Coal and Steel Community, the Economic Community and the Atomic Energy Community. The institutions were merged, finally in 1967, but each legally has its own separate existence and its own Treaty. But since 1967 all three have operated as a single 'European Community' – which the Maastricht Treaty has finally legitimised. So far as the 'Community' as such is concerned, the Maastricht Treaty has taken a step backwards in adopting a 'three pillars' approach. But in 1985 when the Single Act was under negotiation Jacques Delors was determined to ensure that the process of consolidation into a single Community should not be reversed by the new developments now contemplated and a series of new and separate Communities created leading not to 'European Union' but to European *dis*union . . .

If the Internal Market Programme was to succeed it would be essential to move away from unanimity, the source of much of the paralysis in the Community, to majority voting. The tragedy of the past, the primary reason for the stagnation of the Community, lay in the fact that while the Treaties envisaged that after the 'transitional period' which ended in 1967, or at the latest in 1973, the general rule should be majority voting, nevertheless the Council of Ministers virtually insisted on unanimity. This stemmed from the so-called 'Luxembourg Compromise' which was adopted in 1966 after the clash with General de Gaulle.

The exact meaning and scope of the Luxembourg Compromise is much disputed but in effect it enabled a single Member State to 'veto' a proposal if what it regarded as its 'very important interests' were at stake. Had the 'veto' been restricted to what truly were 'very important interests', the harm it would have done would have been limited. Unfortunately the policy which developed on the back of the Luxembourg Compromise was to insist on unanimity virtually everywhere and for the Council of Ministers to continue their discussions in the vain hope that unanimity would emerge although the sanction to encourage or enforce unanimity, namely the threat of majority voting, had been removed. The basic problem of course is that a Minister who loses out in an argument has to justify his position to critics in his national Parliament and it is so much easier to come home reporting 'triumph' in the sense of preserving the 'national interest' by blocking a proposal however valuable the measure might have been in Community terms, than to have to face the criticism of having 'sacrificed' 'national interests' however transient or trivial those national interests were. It is a sad fact that the further you go down the Ministerial ladder, the more attenuated courage becomes and nowhere was this more obvious than in the Council of Ministers. This comes out so very clearly if one looks at the decisions – often bold and far-sighted – taken by the Heads of Government at the Summit (the European Council) compared with all too often the indifference, if not hostility, shown by Ministers when the same proposals reached the Council of Ministers.

Against this background, majority voting on Internal Market proposals was an absolute necessity if the programme was to be completed and completed on time as the Heads of Government at Milan were to demand.

_____ 9.7 _____

THE PADOA-SCHIOPPA REPORT, 1987

T. Padoa-Schioppa, *Efficiency, Stability and Equity: A Strategy for the Evolution of the Economic System of the European Community* (Oxford: Oxford University Press, 1987), pp. 5–6.

The following is an extract from *Efficiency, Stability and Equity: a Strategy for the Evolution of the Economic System of the European Community*. The report was submitted to the Commission on 10 April 1987. The Chairman was Deputy Director of the Banca d'Italia. The Committee had been asked to assess the effect of the accession of Portugal and Spain to the Community and the impact of commitment to the internal market on the economic development of the EC.

The main argument may be summarized under four points:

1. The 1985 White Paper on the internal market implies a very strong action to improve the *efficiency of resource allocation* in the Community. The Group strongly supports the final objective and the 1992 target date for its completion. But the programme is getting behind schedule. The most difficult parts are not yet tackled. There are some aspects of the programme where flexibility will be required to permit changes in method and emphasis.

2. The internal market programme creates both opportunities and needs for complementary action to foster the Community's macroeconomic stability and growth. As regards *monetary stability*, the elimination of capital controls, coupled to the requirements of exchange rate stability, means a qualitative change in the operating environment for monetary policy. It will require moving closer to unification of monetary policy. In a quite fundamental way, capital mobility and exchange rate fixity together leave no room for independent monetary policies. In these conditions, it is pertinent to consider afresh the case for a strengthened organisation of monetary co-ordination or institutional advances in this field. Advantages for stabilisation policy can justify such changes.

3. There are serious risks of aggravated *regional imbalance* in the course of market liberalisation. This is because different economic processes will be at work as markets integrate, some tending towards convergence, others towards divergence. Neither dogmatic optimism nor fatalistic pessimism is warranted in these aspects. Opportunities for convergence will be increased, but adequate accompanying measures are required to speed adjustment in the structurally weak regions and countries, and counter tendencies towards divergence. In addition, reforms and development of Community structural funds are needed for this purpose – alongside other reforms for the Community budget as regards agricultural spending and its financing.

4. As for *growth*, the internal market programme, if successful, must mean a perceptible increase in the rate of macroeconomic expansion. There is no way major benefits could be supposed to accrue without this. Indeed, without generating higher growth, the political cost of negotiation would hardly be worthwhile and the programme would fail. The conversion of better functioning markets into macroeconomic results cannot be taken for granted. This does not mean, however, a call for a burst of short-term demand expansion. On the other hand, something along the lines of the Community's co-operative growth strategy must be translated from declarations of principle into reality.

These four points may be regrouped logically in the following way. In terms of overall strategy, the Community has in recent years adopted a clear-cut economic agenda – characterised by the pursuit of *(a) competitive markets* and *(b) monetary stability*. There is increasing consensus over a fundamental wisdom of these choices. They assure, on the one hand, the efficiency of resource allocation and, on the other hand, a vital sustainability condition for economic policy. This agenda is, however, incomplete. Two further elements must be added: *(c)* an equitable *distribution* of the gains in economic welfare, and *(d)* actual *growth* performance. Neither of them are adequately assured as of now. Without them, the Community's system would be likely to falter. A successful strategy will therefore require also adequate mechanisms to aid structural change in the regions and avoid distributive inequities and a preparedness to support the growth process through macroeconomic policy.

Agreement on these four points together should, in the Group's judgement, be the basis of the long-term 'social contract' between the Community and all its Member States. The essential independence between these features of integrated economic systems is well founded in economic theory (Chapter 3) and supported by historical experiences (Chapter 4).

9.8

ENOCH POWELL: SPEECH TO THE HOUSE OF COMMONS ON THE EUROPEAN PARLIAMENT, 26 JUNE 1986

House of Commons Debates, *Hansard* (London, 26 June 1986), Cols 495–8.

The following is an extract from Powell's speech on the European Communities (Amendment) Bill. He had earlier opposed the introduction of direct elections and Britain's accession to the Community in 1973. He was a prominent critic of the Communities, primarily on grounds of the erosion of national sovereignty.

When in 1978 the House ill-advisedly consented to convert the European Assembly into a directly elected body, it was predicted that a directly elected body, which was already endowed with the power to refuse assent to the budget of the Community and to dismiss the Commission, would soon discover and explore the potential powers which it would exercise, as in past centuries the House has made a similar discovery and exploration. The anxiety which was expressed on that score was strong on both sides of the House. As a result of that, what professed to be a protection was written into the European Assembly Act 1978, which enacted: 'No treaty which provides for any increase in the powers of the Assembly shall be ratified by the United Kingdom unless it has been approved by an Act of Parliament'.

Hon. Members who have looked at clause 3(4) of the Bill will notice that that is precisely what we are invited to do in approving the Bill. We do not need to argue whether the consequences of the Treaty and the Bill are an increase in the powers of the Assembly. The government say that this is so. The government may seek to argue that that increase of the powers of the Assembly is not at the expense of the powers of the Parliament, of the United Kingdom. That proposition rests on an important fallacy about the nature of power. There is no vacuum of power unexercised, unavailable, which is ready to be dished out to new occupiers and exercisers.

At the moment, the power exists and it is shared between this Parliament and the institutions of the Community in accordance with a particular pattern. If the power of any portion of those institutions is increased, as the government tell the House it is increased in respect of the Assembly, by the Treaty and the Bill, it must follow that the effectiveness and real power – the political power – of the other elements, the other possessors, is diminished. Whatever is arrogated to the Assembly by the legislation and the Treaty is deducted from what is available to this Parliament and thus, to the people it represents ...

We are performing a type of solecism in attributing the term 'Parliament' to that Assembly. What we should not do is create implications and hollow assumptions which attach to the word 'Parliament' when applied to the European Assembly. The

European Assembly is not, in our sense of the term, a 'Parliament' and it is not the wish of the people of this country that it should ever be a Parliament in the sense of being the ultimate repository of the legislative and executive powers under which the people of the United Kingdom are to live.

9.9

JACQUES DELORS ON EUROPEAN INTEGRATION, 6 JULY 1988

Debates of the European Parliament, No. 2, 1988, p. 138.

The following extract is from a speech by Delors to the European Parliament. He was President of the European Commission between 1985 and 1995 and strongly in favour of closer economic and political integration. Among other initiatives, he was prominent in his advocacy of the Social Charter (see Document 9.10).

My own feeling is that we are not going to manage to take all the decisions needed between now and 1995 unless we see the beginnings of European government, in one form or another. Otherwise, there will be too many decisions to take, too many complications, too many sources of delay. Quite what form this might take remains a matter for conjecture.

As for the displacement of the centre of decision-making, I find it extraordinary that the national parliaments, with the exception of those in the Federal Republic of Germany and the United Kingdom, should have failed to realise what is going on. Ten years hence, 80 per cent of our economic legislation, and perhaps even our fiscal and social legislation as well, will be of Community origin. In 10 countries, though, there has been no realisation of this, and in these same 10 countries, there is no cooperation between European parliamentarians and national parliaments. What I am afraid of is that some of these national parliaments are going to wake up with a shock one day, and that their outraged reaction will place yet more obstacles in the way of progress towards European Union ...

_____9.10_____

JACQUES DELORS ON THE SOCIAL DIMENSION, 12 MAY 1988

Bull. EC, 5-1998, point 1.1.4.

Extract from a speech to the European Trade Union Confederation in Stockholm. His strong advocacy of the social dimension led to increasing tension with the British Prime Minister, Margaret Thatcher.

The debate concerning the necessary social cohesion of the internal market has begun at several levels. However, if it is to develop and lead to specific results, I propose that three initiatives be taken in the next few months.

For example ... why should the Community not adopt a 'base' of guaranteed social rights which would be derived from the European Social Charter? This 'base' could be negotiated by the two sides of industry and then incorporated into Community legislation. It would serve as the cornerstone for the social dialogue and greater social cohesion in Europe. It would be binding in nature.

The second initiative that we plan to take would be to grant every worker the right to continuing training ...

Third point: European company law. The setting up of powerful and dynamic European undertakings would be an important factor in economic and social cohesion ... This ... would of course include legal provisions guaranteeing employee participation in several optional ways ...

Thus the needs of the economy would be reconciled with the call for greater industrial democracy, giving a clear signal in the direction that European producers should take.

9.11

MARGARET THATCHER: 'THE BRUGES SPEECH', 20 SEPTEMBER 1988

Margaret Thatcher, *The Bruges Speech*, 20 September 1988 (London: Conservative Central Office, 1988).

The speech of the British Prime Minister to the College of Europe on the subject of Britain and Europe stirred up considerable controversy. Although the language in which she presented her case was less diplomatic than the Foreign Office might have liked, its views differed little from that of preceding governments with the exception of Edward Heath's. Her 'guiding principles for the future' were interpreted by many as a response to Jacques Delors, President of the Commission, who had prophesied in July 1988 that within ten years 80 per cent of economic, and possibly also fiscal and social policy would be European rather than national in origin (see Document 9.9).

1) ... willing and active cooperation between independent sovereign States is the best way to build a successful European Community. To try to suppress nationhood and concentrate power at the centre of a European conglomerate would be highly damaging and would jeopardise the objectives we seek to achieve. Europe will be stronger precisely because it has France as France, Spain as Spain, Britain as Britain, each with its own customs, traditions and identity. It would be folly to try to fit them into some sort of Identikit European personality ... I want to see ... [the countries of Europe] work more closely on things we can do better together than alone ... But working more closely together does not require power to be centralised in Brussels or decisions to be taken by an appointed bureaucracy. Indeed, it is ironic that just when these countries such as the Soviet Union which have tried to run everything from the centre are learning that success depends on dispersing power away from the centre, some in the Community want to move in the opposite direction. We have not successfully rolled back the frontiers of the State in Britain only to see them reimposed at a European level with a European superstate exercising a new dominance from Brussels.

2) Community policies must tackle present problems in a practical way, however difficult that may be. If we cannot reform these Community policies which are patently wrong or ineffective and which are rightly causing public disquiet; we shall not get the public's support for the Community's future development ...

3) If Europe is to flourish and create the jobs of the future, enterprise is the key ... The lessons of the economic history of Europe in the 1970s and 1980s is that central planning and detailed control don't work, and that personal endeavour and initiative do, that a state-controlled economy is a recipe for low growth, and that free enterprise within a framework of law brings better results ...

Regarding monetary matters, let me say this. The key issue is not whether there should be a European central bank. The immediate and practical requirements are to implement the Community's commitment to free movement of capital ... to establish a genuinely free market in financial services, in banking, insurance, investment; to make a greater use of the ECU [European Currency Unit]. It is to such basic, practical steps that the Community's attention should be devoted. When these have been achieved and sustained over a period of time, we shall be in a better position to judge the next moves. It is the same with frontiers between our countries. It is a matter of plain common sense that we cannot totally abolish frontier controls if we are also to protect our citizens from crime and stop the movement of drugs, of terrorists, and of illegal immigrants ... We in Britain would fight attempts to introduce collectivism and corporation at the European level, though what people wish to do in their own countries is a matter for them.

4) Europe should not be protectionist. The expansion of the world economy require us to continue the process of removing barriers to trade, and to do so in the multilateral negotiation in the GATT [General Agreement on Tariffs and Trade]. It would be a betrayal if, while breaking down constraints on trade to create the Single Market, the Community were to erect greater external protection. We must ensure that our approach to world trade is consistent with the liberalisation we preach at home.

5) Europe must continue to maintain a sure defence through NATO. There can be no question of relaxing our efforts even though it means taking difficult decisions and meeting heavy costs ... We must strive to maintain the United States' commitment to Europe's defence ... NATO and WEU have long recognised where the problems with Europe's defences lie and have pointed out the solutions ... We shall develop the WEU, not as an alternative to NATO but as a means of strengthening Europe's contribution to the common defence of the West.

9.12

HENDRIK BRUGMANS: 'BRITAIN AND EUROPE: A SURVEY', 1991

Hendrik Brugmans, *Britain and Europe: A Survey*
(Hull: Benedicta Press, 1991), pp. 68–71.

Professor Brugmans, first Rector of the College of Europe, Bruges, comments from a federalist viewpoint on Mrs Thatcher's 'Bruges Speech'.

'My first guideline', we read, 'is this: willing and active cooperation between independent sovereign states is the best way to build a successful European Community. To try to suppress nationhood and concentrate power at the centre of a European conglomerate would be highly damaging and would jeopardise the objectives we seek to achieve.'

First of all, one can only deplore her remark about 'suppressing' nationhood. The fact is that nobody, whether in or outside the EEC, has ever dreamed of such a doomladen scenario. Of course, nationhood will survive. Even at the end of the road. Italians will – thank God – still be Italians and Scots, Scots. To doubt this is gravely to underestimate the vitality of our historically formed nations. We hope that all of them will get rid of their chauvinistic delusions and the prejudices which do so much harm. But the sound essence of nationality itself will surely persist. It is regrettable, therefore, that the Prime Minister, in her carefully worded speech, should have introduced a remark that is so absurd, even as a polemical trick. It reminded us painfully of de Gaulle's remark that Europeans in the Community would be condemned to speak 'an integrated volapuk'. The main point of criticism however is that now we are no longer discussing methods of integration only in theory, as would have been the case in the 1940s, but in practice and with the experience of the 1980s behind us. In addition, Mrs Thatcher's ideas are nothing new. They have been expressed on several occasions and by more than one speaker, most notably de Gaulle. More important, they have been tried, and found wanting, at least four times: in the OEEC, the Council of Europe, the WEU and EFTA. . . .

In the case of Mrs Thatcher she objects both to supranational action and to what she, with horror, calls 'Socialism'. In her remarks she made it plain that she did not want to see the Commission become more influential, or more like a Cabinet with 'limited functions but real powers' (the classical definition of a Federal Cabinet), while, at the same time, she was appalled by what President Jacques Delors said in Strasbourg about his plans for the future. Of course he wants to 'plan'; he is a Socialist after all! Above all, she clashed with him when he declared that, in ten years' time, eighty per cent of the relevant decisions about economic and social policy would be taken in Brussels rather than in the national assemblies. Finally, his proposal about social legislation in Europe, seemed to her unacceptable from both angles; it was too federalistic, but it was also creeping Socialism.

In this connection, a widespread misunderstanding has first to be cleared up. What does the word 'Brussels' mean as used by Mrs Thatcher? The implicit answer seems to be the 'eurocrats', a cosmopolitan bureaucracy, an uncontrolled group of so-called 'experts'. There is no doubt that this is a popular misinterpretation, and not only in Britain.

The reality is quite different. No important decision can be made in the EEC, no new orientation be introduced without the agreement of at least the majority, and in some circumstances even today, through the unanimous vote of all governments concerned. It is true that, with regard to the enormous mass of decisions that have to be taken, the Community administration is called upon to do fundamental preparatory work. But normally, the Commission does not submit proposals without first having weighed the foreseeable objections from this or that country and adapting its documents accordingly. Nor does it infrequently happen that a debate in the Council of Ministers leads to a decision to revise the entire proposal. Moreover, if a country should feel by-passed in the exchange of views, its elected members in Strasbourg have ample opportunity to attack the Commission. Consequently, whoever raises the bogus image of an 'all-powerful eurocracy', is guilty either of ignorance or of demagogy.

This having been said, it is clear that Mrs Thatcher, as a staunch Conservative, wanted to see a Europe where the political authorities interfered as little as possible with the economy. She, naturally, wanted to see her version of the market ideology which her Party had applied in Britain, extrapolated as a model for Europe as a whole. This is not an unpopular position, since we actually live at a time where Right-wing parties have the wind in their sails. But even taking this into account, is it imaginable that all Continental governments would follow the same path? Furthermore, is the process of integration as such, compatible with a policy of non-intervention? Let us first examine the economic aspects of this question.

Whether one likes it or not, we do live in a so-called mixed economy; that is in a world where economic decision-making is ceaselessly guided by 'the public hand'. That is the case within each of our countries and also in the EEC. The Single European Act of 1986, which defined '1992', stressed that areas such as scientific research or problems of the environment had to be brought into the sphere of Community tasks. It was also decided that the Social and the Regional Funds should be strengthened so as to pursue a more effective policy by means of which the less prosperous countries and regions of the Community could receive more generous help. The focus on ecology meant that 'Brussels' would be encouraged to intervene whenever industrial decisions were taken that might endanger our quality of life. In fact, it is unimaginable that the frontiers can be opened without such policies being in place, since the less ecologically-minded countries would then enjoy an unfair advantage over their more socially conscious competitors. Ecology, however, is expensive and the price we pay is that products from cleaner countries will cost more. As a result, once there is no question of any one country in the Community taking protectionist measures, the Commission (and who else could take on this task?) will have to ensure that minimum standards are introduced and applied in all member countries.

In conclusion, it is of the essence in the process of integration that the European authorities interfere more and more in the economic network that links our nations. To open frontiers means to introduce European-wide competition between countries and regions as well as individual firms. Such a development cannot be allowed to degenerate into chaos. There have to be rules for such a gigantic game.

9.13

THE IMPORTANCE OF EUROPE, NORTH AMERICA AND JAPAN IN THE WORLD ECONOMY, 1989

The Importance of Europe, North America and Japan in the World Economy (Washington, DC: World Bank, 1991).

The figures below show the percentage share of world population, GDP and trade.

	Share of world		
	Population	GDP	Trade
Western Europe	7	31	45
Eastern Europe and the former Soviet Union	8	4	6
Sub-total	15	35	51
United States and Canada	5	29	19
Japan	2	14	8

CHAPTER 10

MAASTRICHT AND BEYOND: THE EUROPEAN UNION IN THE 1990s

INTRODUCTION

The institutional structure of the EU as well as the extent of its membership has always reflected the disparities of political and economic power which have characterized the European continent for centuries. During the cold war those disparities were both simplified and managed by superpower hegemony, by the division of Germany and by the self-restraint of the Federal Republic of Germany. Within the EC's institutional structure there were faint reflections of those disparities, in the number of members allocated to each country in the European Parliament, in the weighting of votes within the Council of Ministers, and in the number of Commissioners drawn from each nation. But these were crude reflections of larger and more nuanced disparities. Moreover, the institutional framework had been designed to reassure smaller members that they would not be coerced by larger ones – and here it was not only Germany that had been regarded with suspicion. It was true that qualified majority voting (QMV) had been extended by the SEA. On the other hand, unanimity still prevailed in most areas, above all in treaty revision and the admission of new members. Informally, of course, the disparities still mattered. The Franco-German axis formed the cornerstone of the EC, enshrining the reconciliation of two states whose previous antagonism had laid waste to Europe, as well as being the locomotive which periodically pulled the EC forward.

At the end of 1989, the prospect of German reunification threatened, or so it seemed to many, to undermine the basis upon which west Europe had managed to build a common, if hesitant, endeavour. Officially Germany's western allies were committed to supporting reunification, but as the editor of *Die Zeit* complained, their attitude resembled that of Christians to the prospect of heaven: 'Every pious Christian wishes to get to heaven, but none of them wants it to happen too soon.'[1] The extent, and even more so the tone, of the fears which it induced surprised and puzzled many Germans, including Chancellor Kohl's adviser, Horst Teltschik (Document 10.1). Margaret Thatcher's antipathy to the whole process would later become notorious. Even the more sober-minded Prime Minister of The Netherlands, Ruud Lubbers, had his doubts about reunification.[2] The speed of reunification, complete within less than a year of the fall of the Berlin Wall, along with Kohl's seizure of the initiative through his ten-point plan of 28 November 1989, undoubtedly unsettled many.[3] One of the ways in which Kohl sought to reassure his western neighbours and allies was to stress that a reunited Germany would still be a loyal member of the EC and NATO. In the case of the EC he was assisted by Jacques Delors, who repeatedly offered public support for Kohl. In retrospect, it is easy to see reunification and continued membership of the EC as inevitable. At the time it was the potential difficulties – the complexities of reuniting two states with different socio-economic systems and of integrating the former socialist, East German territories into the EC – that dominated the agenda.

Part of the price which Kohl paid willingly, indeed enthusiastically, for the cooperation of the EC was the linkage between reunification and reform of the EC. More specifically, in conjunction with President Mitterrand, on 20 April 1990 Kohl called for an intergovernmental conference on political union which would run alongside the already agreed conference on economic and monetary union.[4] This was duly approved at the Dublin Council at the end of April. The pressure of German reunification which lay behind the Kohl–Mitterrand initiative had not added anything new to the EC's agenda. 'Political union' was a long-standing subject of debate and there had been a flurry of recent activity. German reunification did, however, give a new sense of impetus and urgency to that debate. This was evident in the Dutch memorandum of 1 May 1990 which noted bluntly that 'While the inclusion in the Community of a unified Germany is already an "acquis", this does not provide future generations with a sufficient guarantee that a united Germany will not pursue a course separate from that of the Community. This can only be ensured by so strengthening the Community that the avenue of national "Alleingang" is closed for good.'[5]

As on previous occasions discussion of 'political union' was fraught with difficulty, the outcome was uncertain and could mean either a strengthening of the EC's supranational structures or of its intergovernmental character. That too was noted in The Netherlands memorandum, which reasserted the Hague's traditional commitment to a 'federal structure as the ultimate objective for Europe'.[6] In the negotiations which opened in December 1990, the ground had been more thoroughly prepared for monetary union. German preferences, and more to the point the preferences of the Bundesbank, had already been enshrined in the Delors Report of 1989, much to the annoyance of Margaret Thatcher. That was inevitable. The Deutschmark was Europe's strongest currency, and commitment to its stability was part of the domestic political consensus in Germany and was guaranteed by the independent Bundesbank. Nevertheless, other states fought for their preferences, largely in vain. British proposals for a radical alternative which left open the possibility of a single currency, but did no more than that, were brushed aside by the head of the Bundesbank, Pöhl, as the 'worst possible recipe for monetary policy'.[7] French efforts to secure an intergovernmental counterweight to the proposed European Central Bank were also unsuccessful. The outcome was a commitment to a single currency, over which an independent central bank would preside. It was claimed later that Pöhl had been surprised at the ease with which a European bank modelled on the Bundesbank had been pushed through.[8] The Bundesbank's influence was also evident in the objective criteria which would be used to determine the fitness of individual member states to make the final transition to a single currency: government deficit at or below 3 per cent of GDP and government debt at or below 60 per cent of GDP.[9] The strain all this involved was evident in the opt-out negotiated by Britain, whereby it would not be obliged to make the final transition 'without a separate decision by its government and Parliament'.[10] British reservations centred largely on considerations of sovereignty (Documents 10.6, 10.7). France was less concerned by these, but had been pressured into accepting a tight link between economic convergence and monetary union which was alien to the dominant economic consensus in France. That consensus was embodied in the description of the link by a former French prime minister as 'an archaic impediment to growth'.[11]

Despite the significance of monetary union, France had agreed to German terms in the hope of gaining some share in the control over its more powerful economic neighbour. Fear of exclusion from the charmed circle of monetary union sufficed to keep most of the others on board. The debate on political union was more open, with Delors fighting hard to prevent the reformed EC fragmenting. The Commission's own proposals included a radical restructuring of EC legislation, introducing a new 'hierarchy of norms' to simplify the legislative process. It was typical of intergovernmental negotiations that this elegant suggestion failed to make any headway. Instead of the Commission's simplification, the Luxembourg Presidency suggested a three-pillared structure, with the existing EC, bolstered by economic and monetary union, forming one pillar, and the two other pillars being a Common Foreign and Security Policy (CFSP) and Justice and Home Affairs (JHA).[12] Instead of a streamlined EC with an extended but legally unified remit, Luxembourg had proposed a Union consisting of three separate elements. The Commission was not alone in feeling dissatisfied with this arrangement (for Commission concern see Document 10.3). The Netherlands, which took over the Presidency in the second half of 1991, countered with a draft, in September 1991, whose opening words embodied its intent: 'By this Treaty, which marks a new stage in a process leading generally to a European Union with a federal goal, the High Contracting Parties establish among themselves a EUROPEAN COMMUNITY.'[13] By then it was too late. The Netherlands had badly misjudged the mood of its partners and found no support, save from Belgium and the Commission. Its negotiators were forced into a humiliating withdrawal which became known as the black Monday of Dutch diplomacy.[14]

Despite this blow, The Netherlands played an important role in the final negotiations at Maastricht, with Ruud Lubbers patiently extracting the final concessions necessary for an agreed text. The Treaty on European Union which emerged was not a self-contained document but took the form of an extended revision of the existing treaties. That did not help to make it digestible for Europe's citizens. It was also accompanied by numerous Protocols and Declarations fleshing out some of the detail, entering reservations, notably for Britain over the single currency, and undertaking commitments. The latter was necessary for the Agreement on Social Policy which Britain had refused to accept as part of the Treaty, leaving the others to proceed without her.[15] It was a 'Europe of bits and pieces'.[16] Nevertheless, it did contain substantial commitments, notably on monetary union, and it had extended the remit of the newly created EU. The European Parliament's power had been increased, primarily by the adoption of a new co-decision procedure.[17] Among the numerous other amendments was the reference to the principle of subsidiarity (Document 10.2).

The concept of subsidiarity has its origins in Catholic social theory. It had been part of the parlance of federalists for some time and had already appeared in the SEA's provisions on the environment. The Maastricht Treaty, however, established it as a general principle, According to Article 3b: 'In areas which do not fall within its exclusive competence, the Community shall take action, in accordance with the principle of subsidiarity, only if and in so far as the objectives of the proposed action cannot be sufficiently achieved by the Member States and can therefore, by reason of the scale or effects of the proposed action, be better achieved by the Community.'[18] The significance of this article was soon to be the subject of bitter controversy. Supporters of intergovernmentalism and the nation state invoked it to try to claw back powers from the EC, while those of a more federalist disposition used it to argue not only for more Community action but also for greater participation by the regions of member states. It was this possibility which underlay the assertion by the British Conservative MP and former Chancellor Nigel Lawson: 'What the Brussels Commission wants to do is to destroy the nation state – both ways. Not just through taking far more powers to the centre, to Brussels. But also by devolving powers, and they decide which powers it will be, to the lowest levels.'[19]

The debate over subsidiarity was fed by what was perceived to be a popular backlash against integration. The focal point of this was the result of the Danish referendum on the Maastricht Treaty on 2 June 1991, which rejected ratification by a narrow majority. Some reassurance came from a 69 per cent vote in favour in Ireland in the same month. Mitterrand, who had no need to call a referendum, still did so to bolster his domestic position, and only just gained a majority in favour, at 51 per cent. In reality, the votes probably had more to do with domestic politics than with the EU itself. Nevertheless, the greater willingness of national political elites to attack the EU in their domestic conflicts was significant, especially since the trend was not restricted to the EU's traditional 'awkward partners'. As part of the attempt to defend the EU against charges of excessive centralization and insufficient democracy, the Edinburgh Council of December 1992 drew up an agreement on subsidiarity (see Document 10.4). This did not really clarify the matter. It did signify the defensive posture which advocates of integration, especially the Commission, were being forced to adopt.

The year 1992 had not been a good one. The EU abjectly failed its first test in the area of CFSP. In 1991, as the crisis in Yugoslavia worsened, the Luxembourg Presidency was still confident enough to boast that 'this is the hour of Europe, not the hour of the Americans'.[20] The EU was, in fact, badly divided. As the aspirant states of the disintegrating Yugoslavia clamoured for recognition, they found an ally in Germany. Many Germans understandably felt that having themselves appealed to the principle of self-determination to legitimate German reunification, they could hardly deny the same right to others. Under the threat of unilateral German action, the EU recognized Slovenia and Croatia on 15 January 1992 and Bosnia on 6 April. If anything, this only inflamed the situation. EU leaders were publicly divided and mutual recrimination abounded.

Another major element of the Maastricht Treaty also suffered, exposing divisions between the member states. Britain had joined the ERM in 1990, after much internal debate and at a rate which the Bundesbank considered too high. Then, on Black Wednesday, 16 September 1992, the pound was forced out of the ERM as a direct result of massive speculation by the markets. Less than enthusiastic support from the Bundesbank led to open accusations from British ministers. The result, in the words of the former German Chancellor, Helmut Schmidt, was that 'the pound's collapse has sent the Anglo-German political barometer plunging'.[21] Britain was not the only member state to have difficulty with the constraints of the ERM. Italy was forced to withdraw as well and, along with several other states, brought back exchange controls. The following summer the speculators turned their attention to the French franc, which survived only by widening the ERM bands to allow for its weakness. Again the crisis was accompanied by recrimination, with the French press accusing the Bundesbank's council of 'acting like provincial managers'.[22]

As the EU struggled to cope with its existing commitments, it agreed, at the June 1992 Lisbon Council, to open negotiations on the admission of four EFTA states – Sweden, Finland, Austria and Norway – as soon as the Maastricht Treaty was ratified. Six months later, at Edinburgh, the Council agreed to negotiate without even waiting for ratification, though the prospects for that had increased with acceptance of a series of opt-outs and other concessions to assuage Danish voters. The concessions sufficed to bring about a referendum result in favour of ratification on 18 May 1993. With the central and east Europeans waiting in the wings, enlargement was becoming a major preoccupation once again. This time, however, enlargement was different, both for the EU as a whole and for the applicants. It was different for the EU because the increase in membership could bring about a paralysis of its institutional mechanisms if there was no radical reform (see Document 10.10). It was also different because increased membership would increase the burden on the EU's limited budgetary resources. This was less of a problem with the wealthy EFTA states, but the prospect of admitting the poorer central Europeans, with larger agricultural sectors, was another matter. It was different for the applicants because the commitments they would be asked to undertake were much greater than on any previous expansion of the EC. Indeed, the commitments to economic and monetary union were such that some existing member states were unwilling even to undertake them (Britain and Denmark) or were such that it was thought unlikely that they would be able to fulfil them (Italy).

One of the prime targets for EC reform was the CAP. Reform of this expensive and often counterproductive programme had been on the agenda almost since its inception. A breakthrough did occur in May 1992, when Commissioner Ray MacSharry pushed through a package which cut export subsidies and began the move to direct subsidies in place of inflated guaranteed price levels.[23] Reform of the CAP was motivated not only by internal budgetary pressures and the prospects of enlargement but also by the wider economic context, and especially negotiations for a new GATT within the Uruguay Round. The continued sensitivity of agriculture was evident in November 1992 when Delors tried to overrule MacSharry's agreement with the United States on oil seeds. Delors himself had an emotional commitment to Europe's farmers. He was also responding to intense pressure from the French government. Delors, however, was outvoted in his own Commission and MacSharry returned to conclude the Blair House agreement with the United States.[24] Although France repeatedly threatened to undermine the whole project, the agreement held well enough to facilitate a successful conclusion of the Uruguay Round in December 1993.

Agricultural reform had been part of the package embodied in the February 1992 Commission document *From the Single European Act to Maastricht and Beyond: the Means to Match Our Ambitions*. After acrimonious wrangling at the December 1992 Edinburgh Council, it was agreed that the 'means' – that is, the EC's 'own resources'[25] – should rise from 1.2 per cent of GDP to 1.27 per cent in 1999. The increase seems niggardly but, despite the justified outcry about the profligacy of the CAP, the EC had never operated primarily as an agency for taxing and spending. That remained the preserve of member states. The EC was, rather, a regulatory state, setting the framework within which other actors, including member states, were allowed to pursue their own goals. Even moves away from the initial focus on 'negative integration' (that is, the removal of barriers to trade and so on) towards positive integration (that is, policy coordination) still followed the regulatory logic and style.[26] This characteristic of the EC, its quality of being above all a legal order, gave the Court of Justice a prominent role. Indeed, as is indicated in earlier chapters, the Court often played an active role in pushing forward the process of integration. Yet the Court was not immune to the more hostile environment of the ratification crisis and its aftermath. It too adopted a more defensive posture, even openly renouncing the precedents of its own case law (Document 10.5).

There were limits to the retreat of the EC's supranational institutions. After securing at least part of the strategy embodied in *From the Single European Act to Maastricht and Beyond*, Delors sought to enlarge the agenda through the White Paper, *Growth, Competitiveness, Employment*. Its preparation was sanctioned by the June 1993 Copenhagen Council. The document itself was in part a response to the post-Maastricht loss of confidence, and a recognition that the EC's popularity, like that of national governments, was linked to levels of prosperity. It was also a concession to the Europe-wide retrenchment of the state, as overburdened public coffers increasingly failed to meet the promises of the post-war welfare state. This restraint even elicited enthusiastic approval from the British Chancellor, Kenneth Clarke: 'It is an impeccable statement.'[27] There were limits to the concessions Delors and his team made. The complaint that 'The organisation of work in a standardised way, frequently in huge production units, has distanced the individual from the result of his work', was vintage Delors.[28] The tension between these two approaches had been most evident in the clashes between Delors and the British Conservatives. They also reflected the disparate political cultures of Britain and France, whose diverse conceptions of the role of the state long predated the existence of the EC.[29] However, they could not be reduced to such disparities. The impact of integration on socio-economic structures, and patterns of work and welfare, were issues which cut across the boundaries of member states. As later criticism of Helmut Kohl demonstrates, neglect of employment and welfare in favour of state retrenchment and reliance on market forces, a neglect which might threaten the legitimacy of the EC itself, was a charge which could be levelled against continental Christian Democrats as well as British Conservatives (Document 10.8).

Welfare, employment and agriculture all figured in the negotiations on the admission of the EFTA states which ran through 1993 and into 1994. Agreement was finally reached without allowing the new members any opt-outs, although concessions were granted to soften the impact of integration on sensitive issues such as Norwegian fisheries and transit transport through Austria. The concessions did not suffice to persuade the Norwegians, who rejected membership in a referendum of 28 November 1994. The others, Austria, Finland and Sweden, all approved membership in referendums held between June and November.[30] One of the obstacles to enlargement concerned the existing members rather than the applicants. With enlargement, the number of votes in the Council would increase and so too would the number required to reject a measure where QMV applied. This further weakened the position of the larger states which were already disadvantaged by an allocation of votes which systematically favoured the smaller states. Britain took exception to the new arrangement, proposing to retain the old blocking majority of 23 votes. Britain was joined by Spain, which wanted to preserve the ability of a combination of southern states to block measures favoured by the northern states, soon to be increased by the forthcoming enlargement. It was, as Spanish ministers confessed, 'an unholy alliance'. It was also an unsuccessful one. The Ioanninian agreement of March 1994 granted Britain and Spain little more than a face-saving compromise, though there was agreement to examine 'the question of the reform of the institutions, including the weighting of votes and the threshold for the qualified majority in the Council' at the 1996 intergovernmental conference.[31]

The strains of the post-Maastricht period were also evident in a discussion paper prepared within the German CDU/CSU. The Schäuble–Lammers paper caused sufficient concern for Foreign Minister Klaus Klinkel promptly to distance himself from the view of his fellow party members.[32] His alacrity arose from the fact that the Schäuble–Lammers paper openly advocated the pursuit of integration within a 'firm core', among which they counted, 'at the moment, five to six countries'.[33] The doubt as to whether it was five or six caused alarm in Italy, which was the sixth. Italy, though, was far from being the focus of the paper, which actually was France. Its authors had been concerned about the divergence between a north-east group and a south-western group within the EU during the negotiations over the Uruguay Round.[34] This split, they feared, might endanger the 'core of the firm core' that is, the Franco-German axis. They found further concern in French apprehension that the 'northern enlargement ... and later eastern enlargement will lead to a looser formation, in which Germany will undergo a decisive increase in power and thereby could take on a central position'.[35] Both the dispute leading to the Ioanninian compromise and the Schäuble–Lammers paper were differing responses to the disparities between the member states of the EU, their different size, geographic position, economic strength and political culture. Schäuble and Lammers had not failed to notice 'political culture', albeit briefly, when they explained the contrast between French rhetorical commitment and practical hesitancy by reference to the fact that 'the conception of unalienable sovereignty of the "Etat Nation" still has importance, although this sovereignty has long since become an empty shell'.[36]

Although issues of national identity and sovereignty are more typically associated with the rhetoric of British politics, Schäuble and Lammers were quite right to point to French concern with these issues. French socialist Jean Pierre Chévènement set it out concisely when he argued that the Germans, who defined German identity in ethnic terms, had less to fear from political federation than the French, who defined French identity in terms of membership of the French state.[37] Without the French state, there would be no French citizenship and hence no French identity. Such conceptions, let alone fears, were hardly universal in France, but Chévènement was pointing to a deeply rooted difference in French and German conceptions.[38]

The other fear to which Schäuble and Lammers pointed, that of the decisive growth in German power, was more widespread. The conflicts over CFSP and the recriminations over monetary policy aggravated the issue. So too did the entire debate over the prospects of a multi-speed Europe, Europe à la carte or core Europe. All were answers to one problem – how to manage the diverse capacity and inclination of member states to pursue the path of integration – which only raised another set of questions: how to avoid a new division of Europe which would disrupt the integrity of the EU and reduce some member states to second-class status. These questions were already being confronted on a wider plane by the next wave of applicants. The central and east European states had made their aspirations clear quite early. The EC's response had been hesitant. True, aid had been forthcoming through Phare and then through the European Bank for Reconstruction and Development.[39] More importantly, the EC had concluded a series of trade and cooperation agreements between September 1988 and May 1990, followed by a round of Europe Agreements between December 1991 and October 1993.[40] The core of these agreements was the progressive establishment of a free trade area between the EU and the relevant state. It was not until June 1993, at the Copenhagen Council, that it was accepted, in principle, that they might become members of the EU. Subsequent progress was slow, painfully slow for the aspirant members. The enormity of the transition which these states would have to make was evident in a Commission White Paper of May 1995. This document enumerated a mass of legislation which they would have to adopt, only then to point out that 'The main challenge for the associated countries lies not in the approximation of their legal texts, but in adapting their administrative machinery and their societies to the conditions necessary to make the legislation work.'[41]

The December 1994 Essen Council had made it clear that any eastern enlargement would not take place until after institutional reform of the EU had been agreed at the scheduled 1996 intergovernmental conference. Formal preparation began in June 1995, with the establishment of a Reflection Group to receive reports from EU institutions and to formulate suggestions. The latter proved difficult, with the Group having to report numerous areas of divergence between the views of the member states. At the same time, monetary union continued to agitate all concerned. Part of the problem was that, having embarked upon so ambitious a project, momentum could only be maintained by strong rhetorical reaffirmation of commitment, thereby constantly raising the apparent costs of failure to achieve monetary union. This was evident in a speech on 19 October by Karl Lammers, who stated that, 'If we do not master the IGC summit, we will not scale the far bigger massif of monetary union. Monetary union is the key project for the entire advance of the European integration process. Its ambition is as far reaching as that of the EDC. Its fate must be different.'[42]

The pressure of preparation for monetary union, along with a mixture of continuing divergence on institutional reform and a reluctance of some states to make their stance clear, led to continued reports of despondency. One issue which received some clarification was the German attitude to flexibility. In a joint letter with French President Jacques Chirac, Kohl warned in December 1995 that 'temporary difficulties of one of the partners in following the march forward should not obstruct the EU's capacity for action'.[43] Such assertions still did more to illuminate the problem than identify the solution. There was, in fact, considerable tension between the German preference for a more federal core and the French desire for a ' "strong Europe" without strong institutions and without a strong political legitimacy'.[44] One of the elements of France's 'strong Europe' was the enhancement of CFSP through the appointment of a 'Mr CFSP', that is, an individual who would be the face and voice of the CFSP. Strengthening the CFSP, albeit not necessarily in the form the French desired, was one of the three main aims agreed at the June 1996 Florence Council. The others were 'bringing the Union closer to its citizens' and 'assuring, in view of enlargement, the good functioning of institutions while respecting their balance, and the efficiency of the decision-making process'.[45] Under those reassuring headings lay the unresolved problems of the extent of the EU commitment to ensuring employment and welfare, the voting procedure in the Council and the number of Commissioners.

The issue of employment and welfare threatened to split the Franco-German axis, which even many other member states saw as essential to the EU. With their eyes fixed firmly on monetary union and strict convergence criteria, the Germans were reluctant to enter into commitments which might endanger that goal (Document 10.11). By then, however, the united German front had cracked, with Edmund Stoiber, Bavarian Prime Minister and member of the governing coalition, joining Social Democrat critics of monetary union.[46] Efforts to reassert Franco-German unity were continually dogged by divergent national economic policies and calls from French politicians, including former President Giscard d'Estaing, that divergence from the strict criteria should not stand in the way of monetary union.[47] At the end of the year, during the Dublin Council of December 1996, Kohl managed to push through a stability pact against an isolated France. Even supporters of the pact acknowledged that it was tough. France, however, had not abandoned the fight. There were repeated suggestions that the envisaged European Central Bank should be subject to political oversight, provoking predictable outrage from the Bundesbank. Germany too was having difficulty meeting the criteria it had insisted upon. This induced Kohl to try to indulge in some creative accounting to improve Germany's position, only to be forced to back down by the Bundesbank.[48]

The December 1996 Dublin Council had been presented with a draft Treaty by the Irish Presidency, or, to be more precise, with elements of a draft treaty interspersed with summaries of options where there was insufficient consensus to even indicate a plausible candidate for agreement (Document 10.9). Notable among the points of contention were the key issues of voting in the Council and the structure of the Commission. Distracted by the dispute over the stability pact, the Council made little progress on these issues, bequeathing them to The Netherlands Presidency. The latter had the unenviable task of overseeing the final stretch of the conference which was due to conclude in June at Amsterdam. The persistent problem of monetary union almost derailed the attempt at the last moment, when the newly elected French socialist government seemed to renege on French commitment to the stability pact. A compromise was only reached just before the Amsterdam summit opened.[49]

The Amsterdam Treaty was in many respects a disappointment. It failed to resolve the crucial issue of institutional reform. Although there were some amendments and, suprisingly, an increase in the European Parliament's power through an extension of the co-decision procedure, there was no agreement on the weighting of votes in the Council or on the composition of the Commission (Document 10.10). Instead a Protocol declared that

> At the date of entry into force of the first enlargement of the Union … the Commission shall comprise one national of each of the Member States, provided that, by that date, the weighting of votes in the Council has been modified, whether by reweighting of the votes or by dual majority … taking into account all relevant elements, notably compensating those Member States which give up the possibility of nominating a second member of the Commission.

This did indicate the narrowing of options. The possibility of controlling the number of Commissioners by depriving smaller states of the automatic right to nominate a Commissioner had been rejected. The smaller states had threatened to block the treaty unless it was rejected. That left the option of redressing the balance by increasing the weight of the larger states.

On other issues compromises emerged. French aspirations for a 'Mr CFSP', as well as the integration of the WEU into the EU, were thwarted. The Treaty provisions for CFSP were modest, backed by agreement for the creation of a policy planning and early warning unit. Germany obtained its stability pact in return for a vague chapter on employment to satisfy France. Flexibility was incorporated into the Treaty, though hedged with numerous preconditions. As on so many previous occasions, some of those compromises and apparent rhetorical exercises will probably turn out to have greater significance than some signatories expected. Nevertheless, failure to resolve the issue of the disparities between the Member States was the most striking feature of the treaty. Part of the problem lay in the domestic constraints to which the governments were subject. Here Kohl was no exception. Indeed, Kohl blocked the extension of QMV to several areas to satisfy domestic critics. The comment of one EU official, that 'Kohl is too weak in Germany but he is too strong in Europe',[50] was an oversimplification in many respects, but it did emphasize the growing link between domestic politics and EU politics, as well as the continued significance of Germany.

Despite the limitations of the Amsterdam Treaty, the Council deemed its reforms sufficient to warrant pressing ahead with eastern enlargement. It seemed to be heeding Jacques Santer's injunction that 'We have only one option: to move on' (Document 10.13). That too was inevitably an oversimplification insofar as it did not indicate in which direction the EU had to progress, whether towards a strong Europe without strong institutions, a strong Europe with strong institutions or a Europe with such flexibility that it defied either categorization. Again, however, the simple injunction did encapsulate the driving force behind the EU: fear of regressing to a situation in which there were no institutionalized mechanisms for dealing with Europe's disparities. That is hardly likely in the sense of the dissolution of the EU. However, both enlargement and expansion of the EU remit, the apparent triumph of the EU, were forcing member states to confront the reality of those disparities. Within the originally limited geographic scope of the EC, the institutional arrangements, supported by the protective umbrella of the Atlantic Alliance and the self-restraint of a divided Germany, had helped to manage those disparities. The unanticipated reunification of Germany and the opening up of central and east Europe were forcing those disparities back on to the agenda.

NOTES

1. Quoted in Renate Fritsch-Bournazel, *Europe and German Reunification* (New York, 1992), p. 19.
2. Steven Everts, 'Coming to terms with Germany: the slow and painful adjustment of Dutch foreign policy after 1989', BISA Conference paper, 16–18 December 1996, p. 11. For

Thatcher's emotive hostility see the record of her adviser, George R. Urban, *Diplomacy and Disillusion at the Court of Margaret Thatcher* (London, 1996), pp. 99–107.

3. On the plan and responses to it see Horst Teltschik, *329 Tage* (Berlin, 1991), pp. 50–61.

4. 'Kohl–Mitterrand letter', in Richard Corbett, *The Treaty of Maastricht* (Harlow, 1993), p. 126.

5. 'Dutch Government 1st Memorandum, May 1990', ibid., p. 127.

6. ibid. German reunification eventually led to a reconsideration of the foreign policy orthodoxies of The Netherlands. On this see Everts, 'Coming to terms with Germany'.

7. *Financial Times* (14 November 1990).

8. Joerg M. Winterberg, 'Central bank independence and monetary stability in the EU', *Aussenpolitik*, Vol. 48 (1997), p. 212.

9. These figures were specified in the Protocol on the Excessive Deficit Procedure attached to the Maastricht Treaty. The wisdom of including precise figures was later questioned.

10. 'Protocol on Certain Provisions Relating to the United Kingdom of Great Britain and Northern Ireland'.

11. Quoted by D.R.R. Dunnett, 'Legal and institutional issues affecting Economic and Monetary Union', in David O'Keefe and Patrick M. Twomey (eds), *Legal Issues of the Maastricht Treaty* (London, 1994), p. 136.

12. We have used the titles as they are formulated in the TEU and ignored minor variations in earlier proposals and drafts. According to Enrico Martial, the three pillars strategy was suggested by a senior offical in the French Foreign Ministry, 'France', in Finn Laursen and Sophie Vanhoonacker (eds), *The Intergovernmental Conference on Political Union* (Maastricht, 1992), p. 124. See also Keith Middlemas, *Orchestrating Europe* (London, 1995), p. 188.

13. 'Dutch Presidency Draft Treaty "Towards European Union" 24 September 1991', in Corbett, *The Treaty of Maastricht*.

14. For the significance of this for The Netherlands see Everts, 'Coming to terms with Germany', pp. 16–17.

15. The legal complexities of this are explored in Erika Szyszczak, 'Social policy: a happy ending or the reworking of a fairy tale?', in O'Keefe and Twomey (eds), *Legal Issues of the Maastricht Treaty*, pp. 313–27.

16. This was the subtitle of an article quoted in ibid., p. 321.

17. At British insistence the term does not appear in the TEU. Reference is made to the Article 189B procedure. Again this hardly aids accessibility. On the positions adopted in relation to legislative procedures see Corbett, *The Treaty of Maastricht*, pp. 56–8.

18. For the SEA see Article 130r(4). The wording of article 3B of the TEU contains a host of legal and constitutional problems. On this see T. Schilling, 'A new dimension of subsidiarity', *Yearbook of European Law*, Vol. 14 (1994), pp. 203–55; and A.G. Toth, 'A legal analysis of subsidiarity', in O'Keefe and Twomey (eds), *Legal Issues of the Maastricht Treaty*, pp. 37–48.

19. Quoted in Lars C. Blichner and Linda Sanglot, 'The concept of subsidiarity and the debate on European cooperation', *Governance*, Vol. 7 (1994), p. 294.

20. Quoted in Dinan, *Ever Closer Union* (Basingstoke, 1994), p. 490.

21. *Financial Times* (9 October 1992).

22. *Financial Times* (2 August 1993).

23. This was sufficient to induce the *Financial Times* to describe it as 'the most radical reform of the Common Agricultural Policy since its inception 30 years ago' (22 May 1992).

24. See George Ross, *Jacques Delors and European Integration* (Cambridge, 1995), pp. 211–12.
25. That is, EC revenue. The term was used to distinguish this from the contributions made by member states prior to the introduction of the EC's own resources as agreed in 1970.
26. On this important characteristic of the EC, see Giandemico Majone (ed.), *Regulating Europe* (London, 1996); Paul Kapeteyn, *The Stateless Market* (London, 1993). Strictly, negative integration involves deregulation. In the EC, however, both negative and positive integration have proceded by means of applying rules rather than by taxing and spending.
27. *Financial Times* (13 December 1993).
28. *Bull. EC* Supplement 6 (1993).
29. On this see Kenneth Dyson, *The State Tradition in Western Europe* (Oxford, 1978).
30. For a survey of the negotiations see Francisco Granell, 'The European Union's enlargement negotiations with Austria, Finland, Norway and Sweden', *Journal of Common Market Studies*, Vol. 33 (1995), pp. 117–41.
31. *Bull. EU* 3-1994, point 1.3.28.
32. Embassy of the Federal Republic of Germany, Press Release 103/94 (7 September 1994).
33. 'Überlegungen zur europäischen Politik', *Blätter fur Deutsche und Internationale Politik*, Vol. 10 (1994), p. 1275.
34. On this see Andrea Sukala and Wolfgang Wessels, 'The Franco-German tandem', in Geoffrey Edwards and Alfred Pijpers (eds), *European Treaty Reform* (London, 1997), p. 83.
35. Überlegungen zur europäischen Politik', p. 1276.
36. ibid., p. 1277.
37. See Sukala and Wessels, 'The Franco-German tandem', p. 88.
38. See Rogers Brubaker, *Citizenship and Nationhood in France and Germany* (Cambridge, MA, 1992).
39. Phare: Pologne–Hongrie: actions pour la reconversion économique.
40. The dates refer to the signing of the relevant treaties. They were not ratified until much later. Agreements with the Baltic states were signed in June 1995.
41. COM(95) 163 final.
42. http://europ.eu.int/en/agenda/igc-home/msspeech/state-de/191095.html.
43. *Financial Times* (8 December 1995).
44. The phrase, which encapsulates the dilemma of French policy, is that of Laurent Cohen-Tanugi, 'The French debate', in RIIA, *The 1996 IGS-National Debates (1)* (London, 1996), p. 23. See also Gerd Langguth, 'Ein starkes Europa mit schwachen Institutionen?', *Aus Politik und Zeitgeschichte*, nos. 1–2 (1996), pp. 35–45.
45. *Bull. EU* 6-1996, point 1.7.
46. *Guardian* (16 January 1996).
47. *European* (1–7 February 1996). As one of the main actors behind the introduction of the EMS, Giscard's intervention drew special attention.
48. Amsterdam Treaty.
49. *Financial Times* (17 June 1997).
50. Quoted in *Financial Times* (19 June 1997).

FURTHER READING

R. Corbett, *The Treaty of Maastricht* (Harlow, 1993).

A. Duff, *Subsidiarity within the European Community* (London, 1993).

A. Duff (ed.), *The Treaty of Amsterdam: Text and Communtary* (London, 1997).

G. Edwards and A. Pijpers (eds), *European Treaty Reform* (London, 1997).

R. Fritsch-Bournazel, *Europe and German Reunification* (New York, 1992).

F. Laursen and S. Vanhoonacker (eds), *The Intergovernmental Conference on Political Union* (Maastricht, 1992).

P. B. Lehning and A. Weale (eds), *Citizenship, Democracy and Justice in the New Europe* (London, 1997).

D. O'Keefe and P. M. Twomey (eds), *Legal Issues of the Maastricht Treaty* (London, 1994).

RIIA, *The 1996 IGC–National Debates (1)* (London, 1996).

RIIA, *The 1996 IGC–National Debates (2)* (London, 1996).

G. Ross, *Jacques Delors and European Integration* (Cambridge, 1995).

_____10.1_____

FRENCH CONCERN ABOUT GERMAN UNIFICATION, 1 DECEMBER 1989

Horst Teltschik, *329 Tage* (Berlin: Siedler, 1991), p. 61.

This recollection of Horst Teltschik, adviser to the Chancellor of the Federal Republic of Germany, illustrates the strength of fears about German unification and its potential impact on European integration.

In a heated conversation about Kohl's Ten Point Plan, the Bonn correspondent of *Le Monde*, Luc Rosenzweig, complained that the speech had not been agreed with Paris. I answered that Kohl and Mitterrand had spoken about the German question less than a month ago, extensively and in agreement. Moreover, it never occurred to Mitterrand to consult the government of a partner state before making a public statement about questions of national importance.

The next reproach ran: now the GDR and German unification would be given precedence before European integration. My answer: to the contrary European integration will accelerate. In other respects, the Federal Government finds itself in the position of practically having to agree to every French initiative on Europe. If I were a Frenchman I would take the Germans in tow.

Rosenzweig answers that now the French will have to return to an earlier constellation. Does that mean: co-operation with the Soviet Union against Germany? Mitterand's forthcoming visits to the GDR and Kiev point in that direction. But I don't ask the question.

The next attack follows: Kohl is endangering Gorbachev. The conversation ends with Rosenzweig's gloomy prediction of an end to Franco-German co-operation. The mistrust towards we Germans is deep seated.

_____10.2_____

JACQUES DELORS ON SUBSIDIARITY, 1991

Subsidiarity: The Challenge of Change (Maastricht: European Institute of Public Administration, 1991), pp. 8–9.

At a colloquium in 1991 the President of the Commission, Jacques Delors, recalled the broader meaning of the idea of subsidiarity.

... I would like to remind you that subsidiarity comes from a moral requirement which makes respect for the dignity and responsibility of the people which make up society the final goal of that society.

Subsidiarity is not simply a limit to intervention by a higher authority _vis-à-vis_ a person or a community in a position to act itself, it is also an obligation for this authority to act _vis-à-vis_ this person or this group to see that it is given the means to achieve its ends.

Subsidiarity, because it assumes that society is organized into groups and not broken down into individuals, rests strictly speaking on a dialectic relationship: the smaller unit's right to act is operative to the extent, and only to the extent (this is forgotten very quickly) that it alone can act better than a large unit in achieving the aims being pursued.

_____10.3_____

DECLARATION OF THE COMMISSION ON THE INTERGOVERNMENTAL CONFERENCES, NOVEMBER 1991

Bull. EC, 11-1991, pp. 11–12.

In this declaration the Commission argued for preserving the unity and integrity of the Community.

On 23, 24 and 27 November the Commission discussed the draft Treaties for Political Union and Economic and Monetary Union, as they stand at the current stage of progress in the Intergovernmental Conferences. The Commission has contributed all that it can in the preparation of these drafts and in the search for a dynamic compromise. It is, after all, keenly aware of their importance and of the promise they hold out for the construction of a United Europe.

The Commission conceives this unity in a perspective which would guarantee the effectiveness of the Community, its democratization and a clear distinction between the powers enjoyed by the Community, its Member States and their regions, in full respect of the principles of subsidiarity and diversity. To qualify this perspective as a federal one reflects the present construction of the Community as well as the conception of future developments.

In this spirit the Commission expresses its concern about the concept of Union, as defined in the current version of the draft Political Union Treaty. As matters stand the Union is to develop alongside the Community without there being an explicit restatement, as there was in the Single Act, of the determination to bring together in a single entity all the powers which the Member States plan to exercise jointly in political and economic matters. Moreover, the Union is not expressly given a legal personality in international law. This raises serious difficulties about the Union's representation and about the coherence between foreign policy as such and external economic relations or development cooperation.

The Commission believes that these difficulties could be overcome by spelling out the fact that all the activities provided for by the Treaties are part of a process leading progressively towards attaining Union or a political Community. To go to the root of the problem, the new Political Union Treaty must make a qualitative leap forward towards a common foreign and security policy, greater democracy in decision-making and a coherent, balanced economic and social area. The planned provisions should also put the 12 Member States in a position to step up the quality and effectiveness of their cooperation in matters of law enforcement and the protection of the individual as this common area is established.

Regarding foreign policy, the proposed new framework of 'common actions' will have little meaning unless the Union has the capacity to take quicker decisions and act more effectively in those areas where the Twelve unanimously decide that they share a common interest which they must defend and promote. Within this framework and taking account of the guidelines decided by the European Council, the Council of Ministers of Foreign Affairs should be able to decide by qualified majority, possibly reinforced.

Injecting greater democracy into Community life should be achieved primarily by giving the European Parliament greater powers. Parliament should be able to confirm the Commission by a vote of investiture. Its ultimate role is to become fully a co-legislator through the establishment of a codecision procedure which, while respecting the rules governing efficiency, should apply generally in respect of competencies where the Council acts by qualified majority. The number of areas where Parliament's assent is required should be extended . . .

Stronger economic and social cohesion would make a vital contribution to the success of economic and monetary union, to the benefit of all Member States. The discussions at the IGC [Intergovernmental Conference] have confirmed that there is absolute opposition to the idea of a two-speed Europe. But some countries might be allowed derogations, if need be, to give them a few extra years to catch up with those which have already reached the final stage of economic and monetary union – the single currency and an independent central bank ranking among its salient features.

At the present stage of development of European construction, it is vital that all the Member States confirm their full acceptance of the objective of economic and monetary union. The Commission therefore alerts the Member States to the risks of a general opting-out clause. There was no question of any such clause, for example, when the Twelve adopted the 1992 programme. That programme has hence attained full credibility and the Community institutions are correspondingly stronger. The Community's dynamism has been strengthened and this is precisely what makes it possible to take new decisive steps towards a stronger economic and social area, towards economic and monetary union.

The Commission obviously understands the problems that this or that Member State might have in accepting the full twofold package. But there are compromise solutions which, while meeting the sensibilities of certain Member States, will avoid the risks referred to above and guarantee the political credibility of the European venture. The Commission will do all it can to help the necessary consensus emerge and make the forthcoming European Council a complete success.

The Community has too many international responsibilities to allow itself the luxury of failing to clear the hurdle that so many convinced Europeans want it to clear.

_____10.4_____

THE EDINBURGH COUNCIL ON SUBSIDIARITY, DECEMBER 1992

Bull. EC, 12-1992, point 1.15.

At this Council the member states sought to elaborate on the brief references to subsidiarity in the Maastricht Treaty.

The implementation of Article 3b should respect the following basic principles:-

Making the principle of subsidiarity and Article 3b work is an obligation for all the Community institutions, without affecting the balance between them. An agreement shall be sought to this effect between the European Parliament, the Council and the Commission, in the framework of the interinstitutional dialogue which is taking place among these institutions.

The principle of subsidiarity does not relate to and cannot call into question the powers conferred on the European Community by the Treaty as interpreted by the Court. It provides a guide as to how those powers are to be exercised at the Community level, including in the application of Article 235. The application of the principle shall respect the general provisions of the Maastricht Treaty, including the 'maintaining in full of the *acquis communautaire*', and it shall not affect the primacy of Community law nor shall it call into question the principle set out in Article F(3) of the Treaty on European Union, according to which the Union shall provide itself with the means necessary to attain its objectives and carry through its policies.

Subsidiarity is a dynamic concept and should be applied in the light of the objectives set out in the Treaty. It allows Community action to be expanded where circumstances so require, and conversely, to he restricted or discontinued where it is no longer justified.

Where the application of the subsidiarity test excludes Community action, Member States would still be required in their action to comply with the general rules laid down in Article 5 of the Treaty, by taking all appropriate measures to ensure fulfilment of their obligations under the Treaty and by abstaining from any measure which could jeopardize the attainment of the objectives of the Treaty.

The principle of subsidiarity cannot be regarded as having direct effect; however, interpretation of this principle, as well as review of compliance with it by the Community institutions are subject to control by the Court of Justice, as far as matters falling within the Treaty establishing the European Community are concerned.

_____10.5_____

THE KECK JUDGMENT OF THE COURT OF JUSTICE, 24 NOVEMBER 1993

Keck judgment. Cases 267/91 and 268/91 ECR I (1994), pp. 6130–1.

This judgment of the European Court concerned a claim that the French law prohibiting the resale of goods at a loss was contrary to article 30 of the EEC Treaty.

11. By virtue of Article 30, quantitative restrictions on imports and all measures having equivalent effect are prohibited between Member States. The Court has consistently held that any measure which is capable of directly or indirectly, actually or potentially hindering trade constitutes a measure having equivalent effect to a quantitative restriction.

12. National legislation imposing a general prohibition on resale at a loss is not designed to regulate trade in goods between Member States.

13. Such legislation may, admittedly, restrict the volume of sales, and hence the volume of sales of products from other Member States, in so far as it deprives traders of a method of sales promotion. But the question remains whether such a possibility is sufficient to characterise the legislation in question as a measure having equivalent effect to a quantitative restriction on imports.

14. In view of the increasing tendency of traders to invoke Article 30 of the Treaty as a means of challenging any rules whose effect is to limit their commercial freedom even where such rules are not aimed at products from other Member States, the Court considers it necessary to re-examine and clarify its case-law on this matter.

15. It is established by the case-law beginning with 'Cassis de Dijon' ... that, in the absence of harmonization of legislation, obstacles to free movement of goods which are the consequence of applying, to goods coming from other Member States where they are lawfully manufactured and marketed, rules that lay down requirements to be met by such goods (such as those relating to designation, form, size, weight, composition, presentation, labelling, packaging) constitute measures of equivalent effect prohibited by Article 30. This is so even if those rules apply without distinction to all products unless their application can be justified by a public-interest objective taking precedence over the free movement of goods.

16. By contrast, contrary to what has previously been decided, the application to products from other Member States of national provisions restricting or prohibiting certain selling arrangements is not such as to hinder directly or indirectly, actually or potentially, trade between Member States ... so long as those provisions apply to all relevant traders operating within the national territory and so long as they affect in the same manner, in law and in fact, the marketing of domestic products and of those from other Member States.

10.6

COMMENT ON SOVEREIGNTY AND MONETARY UNION BY THE HOUSE OF LORDS SELECT COMMITTEE ON THE EUROPEAN COMMUNITIES, 1996

House of Lords Select Committee on the European Communities, Session 1995–6, Eleventh Report, Vol. 1 (1996), pp. 52–4.

In this report the Select Committee repeated an earlier warning against conflating the different meanings of the idea of sovereignty.

12. The word 'sovereignty' has a powerful emotional impact, bound up as it is with people's sense of nationhood. But it may be used in several different senses, and in most cases the sense in which the word is used is not defined – although it may often be inferred from the context. In the context of the current debate three distinct senses are relevant.

13. The first sense uses sovereignty to describe the supreme authority in the internal order of a State ... Although Community membership has required constitutional amendment (in Ireland) and has given rise to constitutional conflicts elsewhere, the difficulty arising from 'parliamentary sovereignty' is specific to the United Kingdom. At the time of United Kingdom accession to the Community, it was stated by the Government that membership did not

endanger parliamentary sovereignty, since a future Parliament was free to repeal the European Communities Act and withdraw from the Community. However, it was also made clear that joining the Community, and therefore accepting directly applicable Community law, meant that part of the law of the United Kingdom would be made by the Community's institutions, not by Parliament. It was stated by the Government that Parliament, in passing the European Communities Act in 1972, 'authorised the application in this country of directly applicable Community law and to that extent has delegated its powers'. This Act was of course in itself an exercise of parliamentary sovereignty.

14. Secondly, the word 'sovereignty' is used in international law to describe the characteristics of a State ...

15. The third sense is political rather than legal. It describes the extent to which a State has a power of effective or unfettered action ... It is only in this third sense of the word that sovereignty can be 'pooled'. Many heated exchanges about the 'loss of sovereignty' or 'threats to sovereignty' take place between those who are using the word in different senses. The arguments can be greatly simplified by defining the sense in which the word 'sovereignty' is used.

16. ... At the present stage the Committee consider it essential to identify and segregate each particular area and subject matter where extension of Community power is proposed, and to ask various questions. First, whether this particular area is likely to be regarded as one in which it is vital for Member States to retain their power of decision. Second, whether surrender – total or qualified – of Member States' power of decision, though by itself possibly disadvantageous or undesirable, is likely to be accompanied by advantages deriving from the fact that a similar surrender will be made by other Member States and/or from the likelihood that Community decisions in this area are likely to be more effective. Third, account must be taken of the state of public opinion. Areas relevant to this debate include control of national foreign policy, economic and monetary policy, citizenship, and environmental policy.

17. The Committee's enquiry has considered how sovereignty might be affected by current proposals for change in two particular areas: monetary union, and foreign policy. In evidence and elsewhere, the Government has expressed its concern that monetary union in the form of a single currency would seriously damage the sovereignty of the United Kingdom. Parliamentary sovereignty would have been exercised in the delegation to a Community monetary authority of the competence to make decisions in an important area now within national control. In theory this delegation could always be reversed; Treaty commitments establishing monetary union would continue to derive their legal force from the European Communities Act 1972. In international law, the United Kingdom and the other Member States of the Community would continue to exist as separate sovereign States. There are precedents for the sharing by several sovereign States of a single currency:

18. Disregarding abstractions, the question which the United Kingdom (and

indeed other Member States) should be asking is whether it is acceptable, and in our national interest, that we should entrust decisions on monetary policy to an outside body. Relevant arguments under the broad heading of 'sovereignty' would be that decisions on such matters, but particularly in relation to currency, are essentially attributes of national States; but that, since other States would be similarly surrendering this power, there could be gains in the way of stability, and of enlarging monetary strength, which would be for our benefit. A relevant consideration would also be that such surrender would be not to another State, but to an independent body. On the other hand, it seems to be agreed that Member States ought to retain control in certain areas affected by economic policy. Member States will have to consider how far the need for a central Community monetary authority can be reconciled with governments' desire to retain an influence over economic policy, and with democratic accountability.

19. A second fear about current changes is that the international sovereignty of the Member States could be jeopardised through further advances in European Political Cooperation (EPC). The Community already has full competence over external relations in the field of commercial policy. The EPC arrangements cover a much wider field, being designed 'jointly to formulate and implement a European foreign policy'. If majority voting were introduced into EPC across the board, Member States would lose their current independence of action in international relations, which has always been accepted as one of the key criteria for a sovereign State. With this would logically go separate membership of the United Nations (based on 'the sovereign equality of all its Members') and of all other international organisations, independent treaty-making power, the right to separate diplomatic and consular representation, and the right of individual self-defence.

_____10.7_____

DEBATE IN THE BRITISH HOUSE OF COMMONS TREASURY COMMITTEE ON MONETARY UNION, MAY 1996

House of Commons, The Treasury Committee, Session 1995–96, Eighth Report, Vol. 2, pp. 209–10.

There was debate about economic convergence and monetary union in all member states. In May 1996, the British Chancellor of the Exchequer put the case for economic convergence as a precondition for monetary union.

If you were convergent sufficiently and you maintained that convergence?

(Mr Clarke)   You have to be genuinely competitive but in the modern world it is necessary to be competitive anyway. What will be necessary is for economic policy to be set so as to ensure competitiveness, flexibility, the ability to change and respond to shocks if they occur, because you would not just be able to respond by dramatic changes in monetary policy or devaluation or anything of that kind. But no country has ever willingly used the devaluation remedy, devaluation has never been an advantage to any country in west Europe, and it tends to be an _in extremis_ way of absorbing shocks as to how shocks are absorbed . . .

Except there is a case for saying that our last devaluation after coming out of ERM has been an exception to the rule?

(Mr Clarke)   It is the first devaluation where we have kept the competitive advantage of the currency devaluation, but as people have noticed that is because of a period of exceptionally tight fiscal and monetary policy to avoid the inflationary consequences flowing through. The British pulled their belt in very tightly after Black Wednesday. Had we not done that, we would have suffered the most severe inflation and rising unemployment; the consequences which the Italians have all too often suffered as a result of their devaluations. By the way, the idea that Black Wednesday was an asset to us is something I regard as one of the great myths of our time.

If you do away with the traditional, however ineffective, ways of countering asymmetric shocks, there are two ways of doing it, one is that real labour costs have to decline, or you end up with substantial transfers of funds across the borders to the countries inside the monetary union?

(Mr Clarke)   Well, you have to respond in some way which restores competitiveness. The kind of thing I think you are worrying about is where you lose competitiveness and therefore go into a period of substantial decline in your industries and people start moving because you are losing employment on a grand scale. The only remedy for that is to do something to restore competitiveness in the area in which the haemorrhage is taking place.

The only way to do that is massive investment from somewhere centrally inside the European Union?

(Mr Clarke)   No. I think all the history of great public investment in deprived regions is not very satisfactory. There is a lot of European policy in the structural funds still based on the belief which has rather weakened in this country that massive government funds being moved into deprived regions in itself remedies economic weakness. I do not think it does.

That is a view which you and I would both share, but it is not sadly a view shared by other countries which are likely to be in the monetary union.

(Mr Clarke)   Yes, but we have in the discussions so far in the Council of Finance Ministers got complete agreement that there will not be budgetary consequences from all this, that we are not constructing a case for potential massive changes to funds from any central organisation or as between Member States as a result of EMU. Because you and I agree, I keep trying to underline it, as I think I said earlier, but there is nobody pressing that case at the moment, and as it will require Treaty changes to put in place there is no prospect of anybody paving the way for big budgetary changes ...

It is worth pointing out here, I think, Chancellor, that the own resources decision, which of course has to be ratified by this House, does put a cap on the amount of the Community budget.

(Mr Clarke)   It can only be changed by unanimity. Actually there are others just as hawkish as I am on own resources.

But the argument against monetary union leading to fiscal union is that there will be no possibility of the European State, if you like, requiring large amounts of funds to be raised through taxes centrally to be redistributed to counter asymmetric shocks?

(Mr Clarke)   That is one argument. I just do not think there is any prospect of Member States agreeing to any tax-raising powers of any kind being transferred to central institutions. Nobody is advocating that and there is nobody arguing that the prospect of EMU gives rise to anybody considering it. One of the things which will come up, no doubt, in the IGC is whether we retain unanimity on tax and whether each Member State has a veto on any tax proposals. I strongly believe tax is a matter for the nation state and we should keep a veto. I think the majority of finance ministers do too but to quote just a few, the German one certainly does, and the advocates of EMU do not think it involves any handing-over of power of taxation. There is nobody in Europe who thinks any Member State will surrender its own powers to tax.

If we assume then no tax transfers and we assume no population transfers, and clearly huge localised levels of unemployment would be unacceptable, as the Governor of the Bank of England has pointed out rather graphically, what we are left with then is that unless the economies which joined monetary union are very closely convergent and retain that convergence, monetary union would blow apart because there would be no mechanism for coping with the shocks within it?

(Mr Clarke)   Emotive language, you use, but fair language, but it is just that it will be picked up so I try to avoid phrasing it quite like that. You are quite right, it would be a mistake for any country which did not have a convergent economy in the fullest sense of the word to go into economic and monetary union. It would be a mistake for the countries which let it in, for exactly the reasons that the Governor gives, you will find unacceptable pressures building up in the ailing Member State which was suddenly facing up to the consequences it could not deal with of being admitted. I agree with that analysis.

So what you are saying then is that the decision to go to monetary union, far from being a political decision, has to be a hard-headed economic decision or it is doomed to failure?

(Mr Clarke)   In the first place, yes, I think the only countries that should be contemplating membership of economic and monetary union are the strong, successful, competitive economies capable of being competitive with each other, capable of being competitive in the modern global economy, capable of responding rapidly to changing economic circumstances. It will be the premier league players only who should contemplate joining economic and monetary union. As far as the British are concerned, firstly, we have to get ourselves into that state before anybody really should seriously advocate we should join, and make sure we are up to the big league, as Britain has not always been since the war, and then take the political decision do we want to. Are we concerned about the consequences of such a decision? I agree, there is a political debate to be had which we have had with more or less vehemence this afternoon.

----------------------------10.8----------------------------

GERMAN CRITICISM OF HELMUT KOHL'S POLICY, OCTOBER 1996

Das Parlament (18 October 1996).

As concern about unemployment and lack of public support for integration grew, criticism of the failure of the member states to deal with unemployment through the EU became increasingly frequent. In this instance the German Social Democrats attacked Helmut Kohl.

The *Süddeutsche Zeitung* writes, I quote: 'The British are not the only obstacle.' I will go a step further and say: despite all the European declarations which were made this morning – to be sure half-heartedly – it is in fact the Federal Government [of Germany] that is the real brake ...

Naturally the behaviour of the Federal Government is partly a product of uncoordinated policies. But the core – and that was clear again this morning – lies deeper. Neoconservative economic policy – this morning Mr Klinkel had only one answer to the problem of employment: deregulation – has led to a downward race in the EU as well ...

That the EU member states and, at the front, the Federal Government accept mass unemployment means that the EU is losing acceptance and support in the minds of the people . . .

With this policy, which alienates people from the EU, Helmut Kohl is putting at stake European integration and his own life-work, which he has bound up with Europe.

10.9

IRISH PRESIDENCY DRAFT TREATY, DECEMBER 1996

http://europa.eu.int/en/agenda/igc-home/general/pres/index.html.

In its draft the Irish Presidency outlined the options for reform of qualified majority voting. The Amsterdam Treaty of 1997 postponed the hard decisions on this matter.

3. *One view* at the Conference is that the time has come for a very substantial extension of QMV [qualified majority voting] under Pillar 1. (Decision-making under Pillars 2 and 3 is dealt with in the relevant sections of this document.) This is seen as already desirable to improve decision-making in the existing Union; and even more necessary with each further enlargement if paralysis is to be avoided. A contrary view sees the further extension of QMV, at least to any significant degree, as an unacceptable inroad on national sovereignty and would wish to maintain the status quo or could accept, at most, minimal change. The view has also been expressed that agreement to the extension of QMV to new areas would depend on how far there may also be agreement to a re-weighting of votes (see below). Many Member States are at this stage reticent about showing their hands.

4. It appears to the Presidency that there are essentially three possible avenues of approach if progress is to be made on this issue:

   (a) approach the possible extension of QMV case by case taking each Treaty article in turn;

   (b) agree on more general criteria to be applied in a more systematic way;

   (c) accept a generalised move to QMV – subject to certain relatively limited exceptions.

5. In the view of the Presidency, it remains essential to make significant progress on QMV at the Conference both for the Union of today and in order to ensure that decision-making will not become paralysed in the larger Union of the 21st century. Merely starting with a case by case approach is unlikely to lead to satisfactory results. There has as yet been no indication of criteria which might

be agreed. The Presidency considers, however, that it may well be possible to find a basis for progress in the later stages of the Conference – but only if a clear political direction is eventually given from a high level at a stage when the likely balance of issues in the outcome of the Conference has become clear.

6. In the view of the Presidency, it might be possible to prepare for such a development, by an approach drawing on the following points:

   (a) seek general agreement to exclude some areas (such as constitutional or quasi-constitutional matters) *a priori* from QMV;

   (b) examine the extension of QMV to other areas under the Treaty establishing the European Community with the burden of proof being with those who do not consider an extension of QMV to be justified. As indicated in paragraph 5 above, this approach if it is to lead to successful results will eventually require political direction from a high level. In examining the specific Articles, particular attention should be given to matters bearing directly or Indirectly on the Internal Market;

   (c) work to define as precisely as possible within larger and more general areas of activity those particular aspects to which QMV might be extended;

   (d) explore the possibility of phasing in the extension of QMV over specified time periods as a way of facilitating progress.

_____10.10_____

SUMMARY OF THE EUROPEAN COMMISSION SUGGESTIONS ABOUT ITS FUTURE ROLE IN RELATION TO THE COMING ENLARGEMENT, MARCH 1997

Together in Europe, No. 105 (15 March 1997) http://europa.eu.int/en/comm/dg10/infcom/newspage/news-105.html

The prospect of enlargement called into question the existing arrangements for the appointment of Commissioners. Disagreement between member states led to postponement of decisions in the Amsterdam Treaty.

... the French government ... would like to see in the future a very restricted Commission, with only ten to twelve Commissioners, arguing that, in that case, the Commission's members would be less attached to their own country and thus be able to defend the interests also of smaller countries, even if the latter would not be able to send a Commissioner to Brussels any more. It remains clear that Commissioners do not 'represent' their own country, but are simply designated by them. 'Smaller' countries have fiercely opposed the idea of a Commission with fewer Commissioners than there are member states, and Santer's Commission has come up with an idea which should made it possible to appease them, and, at the same time, gain time. Thus, the present European Commission in its communication argues that, after this revision of the Maastricht Treaty, the number of Commissioners should be reduced to one per member state: the 'big' countries which have at present two Commissioners – France, Germany, Italy, Britain and Spain – all agree, except for Spain which, until now, has insisted on keeping two. The Santer Commission, on the contrary, thinks that the principle 'one country, one Commissioner', should undergo a review after a further enlargement of the Union, and in any case once there are more than 20 member states.

The Commission's communication stresses the need to preserve, in the revised Treaty, the independence and the collegial nature of the European Executive, as well as to strengthen its legitimacy. It, therefore, makes suggestions which go in both directions. First of all, it says that, in the future, the European Commission should remain accountable to the European Parliament. France would like it to be accountable also to the European Council, but only collectively. The issue of 'individual' accountability of Commissioners was raised by the European Parliament's inquiry committee on the 'mad cow' disease, and EP's members found, in their recommendations, that single Commissioners should be held responsible for their possible mistakes. The Commission disagrees arguing that this would disrupt the collegial nature of the European Executive.

The Santer Commission is also very sensitive to the question of the Executive's legitimacy and suggests provisions which would strengthen authority of the Commission's President over his colleagues. Chancellor Kohl was one of the first European leaders to acknowledge the need to do something about that, during the December 1995 European Council in Madrid. Thus, the Commission President, who has been until now a 'primus inter pares', would have in particular more say about the appointment of the different Commissioners.

_____10.11_____

THEO WAIGEL ON GERMANY AND MONETARY UNION, 10 APRIL 1997

http://www.bundesregierung.de/inland/bpa/bulletin/
bu97041802.html.

The debate on economic convergence and monetary union was especially acute in Germany, where monetary stability, presided over by the Bundesbank, was seen as the key to prosperity. In this statement, the German Finance Minister asserted German commitment to the convergence criteria.

A European free trade zone will not suffice for the challenges of the next decades. Monetary union is in our inherent interest. The export nation Germany profits from open markets without exchange rate risks, from a strong, stable Euro bloc in the world currency system. If the Euro does not arrive the Deutschmark will be under pressure to revalue. The export economy will be burdened, jobs will be lost and the public coffers will be burdened . . .

With the creation of the Euro a currency area of global significance will arise, which will offer a real alternative to the US dollar. Thereby Europe's dependence on the exchange rate of the dollar and dollar interest rates will be reduced. Europe will be able to orient itself towards its own circumstances and have an important voice in the concert of world currencies. But for this the markets and the citizens of our own country must be convinced of the stability of the Euro . . .

Much is at stake. For the almost DM five billion [in this context, five million million] in private hands in Germany each percentage point of inflation means a capital loss of around DM fifty milliard [fifty thousand million]. For that reason we have in the Maastricht treaty clear rules about monetary policy. They are modelled on the German Bundesbank and in some respects go even further. This includes the convergence criteria which guard against 'unwarranted entry' . . .

The European Council, at the suggestion of the Finance Ministers, will take the decision at the beginning of May 1998. Until then speculation about the group of participants is futile. One thing however is clear: no-one has an automatic right to participate. Convergence determines the timetable for every individual country . . .

I have not changed my own view. I will oppose every divergence from the criteria: 'three is three'.

_____10.12_____

SPEECH BY JACQUES SANTER, AMSTERDAM, 21 APRIL 1997

http://europa.eu.int/rapid//cgi.ksh (22 April 1997)

This speech caused consternation amongst the Euro-sceptics

As to the functioning of the institutions, nobody is beyond criticism, nor should be. But if these institutions had not existed, forcing Member States to focus on promoting their common interest, if the Union's founding fathers had not devised this original and effective legislative, supervisory, jurisdictional and democratic framework, *there would be no European Union today*. The formidable advantages of the internal market would not exist. We would probably have achieved no more than a modest free trade zone. And even that would be doubtful.

Those who criticise, do they know what they are talking about? Do they have an equally stimulating alternative? If so, what is it? Do these doom-merchants want us to step backwards towards a Europe only composed of simple trading arrangements? Even the countries which in the fifties wanted to go no further than a European free trade association, have now virtually all opted for the benefits of European Union membership. And for good reason.

No one can seriously suggest that we turn back the clock and deprive ourselves of the strength and advantages of belonging to the world's first economic power, especially as we witness the globalization of our economies and the emergence of ever more numerous and strongly performing actors on increasingly open world markets.

If regression is unthinkable, what other options are left? We can stick to the status quo or move on. But is there such a thing as the status quo? Every day we must adapt ourselves to changing circumstances, correct deficiencies, fill gaps – in short, manage our daily business. Moreover, our Treaty, our legislation, the political decisions taken by Heads of State or Government, by our Ministers, contain commitments which still must be delivered ...

In other words, ladies and gentlemen, there is no such thing as the status quo. As a consequence of our own decisions, the European Union is always at the stage of 'work in progress'. We have only one option: to move on.

THE NEW EUROPEAN ARCHITECTURE AFTER 1989

INTRODUCTION

The reunification of Germany, the collapse of the multilateral organizations of the eastern bloc, the Warsaw Pact and Comecon, seemed to some to herald a return of Europe to its pre-1945 state of multipolar rivalry. Such sentiments were embodied in the title of a provocative article in the summer of 1990: 'Back to the future: instability in Europe after the Cold War'.[1] The reassertion of sovereignty by the post-communist states of central and east Europe and even more so the resurgence of nationalism, especially in its virulent form in Yugoslavia, seemed to confirm this pessimistic prognosis.[2] Yet there were fundamental differences, above all in the persistence of the western organizations. The problem, of course, was that they were purely western. Fearful of the reassertion of Russian hegemony, the central and east European states rebuffed attempts to find substitutes for the disintegrating economic and military systems of the cold war era. That they would resist Russian attempts to replace the Warsaw Pact with a system of bilateral alliances, or Comecon with an Organization for International Economic Cooperation, was perhaps predictable.[3] The fact that they were Russian initiatives was sufficient to arouse suspicion. Western initiatives were scarcely any more successful. When the EC Commissioner for External Affairs took up the idea of a Central European Payments Union, in the hope that this might mimic the highly successful western-based European Payments Union of the 1950s, even this was seen as an artificial attempt to prolong Comecon.

The disintegration of the old order and the refusal to find a more acceptable substitute for it raised the prospect of the newly liberated states languishing in an economic and security vacuum. Again the images which this conjured up were laden with analogies and historical connotations, none of them pleasant. Reference to these states as the 'land in between' – that is, between Germany and Russia – recalled the inter-war experience which ended in conquest and occupation. The notion of the substitution of a wall of prosperity in place of the iron curtain suggested that they would be condemned to a permanent state of underdevelopment, locked out of the charmed circle of western prosperity (Document 11.4). Prosperity and security were the most immediate issues at stake. But there was more to it than that. It was also a matter of self-identity. This was evident in the avowed puzzlement of Czech Prime Minister Václav Klaus about talk of enlarging Europe (Document 11.5). His point was that his country's European identity was not dependent upon membership of any international organization, no matter how desirable membership might be for other reasons.[4] Klaus's confident assertion of Czech European identity was one response. Elsewhere there was a fear that the perpetuation of the division of Europe, the perpetuation of Yalta, was in fact bound up with the denial of the European vocation of these states.

Amidst the initial fluidity and uncertainty of the disintegration of the cold war barriers, the Czech President Václav Havel discerned an apparently straightforward solution. Both military alliances, the Warsaw Pact and NATO, should, he argued, be dissolved and replaced by a pan-European security system. The obvious building block for this overarching organization was the CSCE. There was, in fact, little prospect for Havel's vision. His presupposition, the demise of NATO, ignored the role that it had played in integrating the Federal Republic of Germany into the western system, and would play in integrating a reunified Germany.[5] Yet the settlement of the German question was bound up with some strengthening of the CSCE, albeit nothing close to what Havel had desired. The CSCE was really a rolling conference programme, kept going by lack of any alternative forum which bridged the cold war divide and brought together all states with an interest in the fate of Europe. It was no more than the sum of its parts.[6] The Charter of Paris, signed on the same day as the Conventional Forces in Europe (CFE) treaty, celebrated the end of the cold war but provided little institutional embodiment of a new order. Beyond the Council (which was to meet at least once a year), a Committee of Senior Officials and a Secretariat, there were only two *ad hoc* attempts to respond to the rapidly changing situation: a Conflict Prevention Centre, largely restricted to monitoring and consultation, and an Office for Free Elections. The specific provisions of the Charter of Paris were not substantial, but it had played a significant symbolic role in facilitating German reunification and drawing a formal line to mark the end of the cold war.

A similar symbolic declaration had come from NATO in its July 1990 London Declaration (Document 11.1). According to this, NATO proposed a joint declaration with the Warsaw Pact states, 'in which we solemnly state that we are no longer adversaries and reaffirm our intention to refrain from the threat or use of force against the territorial integrity or political independence of any state'.[7] Despite the

central role played by NATO in German reunficiation, there was extensive speculation about the Alliance's future, or lack thereof. NATO, according to one report,
was 'struggling against obsolescence'.[8] This was not the first crisis of identity which
NATO had undergone. Indeed, its history was one of recurrent crises, speculation
about its loss of purpose and the creation of committees and reviews to re-endow it
with a sense of direction. Nevertheless, the existence of adversaries on the other side
of the iron curtain had provided a constant reference point, with the argument
centring on how best to deal with the eastern bloc. The absence of that reference
point added greater urgency to the debate, although the options and many of the
concerns were familiar ones. In the United States, financial considerations and
commitment to what many regarded as ungrateful Europeans were used to question
continued involvement. On the other hand, as one official explained to Congress in
February 1990, NATO enabled the United States to 'play an active role in shaping
the emerging political and security architecture of Europe'.[9] In Europe the debate
about a European security and defence identity predictably divided the Europeans,
with the more Atlanticist British and Dutch worrying about the potential damage to
NATO from too ambitious an emphasis on a European profile. The Maastricht
negotiations and the associated review of the WEU's role provided the context for
these arguments. The debate also caused concern in the United States, which
responded with an ill-considered and counterproductive warning to the Europeans
in February 1991.[10] France, the most vigorous promoter of a European security
profile, was also angered by the decision of NATO's Defence Planning Committee
to create a Rapid Reaction Force. All of this was sufficient to postpone agreement on
the Alliance's new strategic concept until November. At the November Rome
summit, the 'new Strategic Concept' acknowledged that 'In contrast with the
predominant threat of the past, the risks to Allied security that remain are multi-
faceted in nature and multi-directional, which makes them hard to predict and
assess.'[11] The summit did attempt to introduce a new element of order in this
increasingly unpredictable environment by offering to establish a North Atlantic
Cooperation Council (NACC), incorporating the Soviet Union and the central and
east European states. President George Bush, reassured that the Europeans wanted
the Americans to stay, was notably enthusiastic about the summit and the Alliance's
prospects.

The significance of the Rome summit was, however, subject to diverse interpretations. The Russian President, Boris Yeltsin, responded by writing to the newly
created NACC suggesting that Russia might become a member of NATO and
expressing support for a security system extending from Vancouver to Vladivostok.[12] Yeltsin's radical suggestion was one option in a volatile debate going on inside
his country, whose struggle to find a new orientation became increasingly desperate
as its military power declined. Elsewhere other conclusions were drawn. The
Secretary General of the WEU opined that 'the Alliance's new strategy . . . created an
opportunity for Europeans to regain the ground which had been lost when the
European Defence Community failed in 1954'.[13] These radical and excessively
ambitious speculations were united by a sense that the framework agreed at Rome
was insufficient. Both also reflected the desire for some bold step which, albeit in

different ways, would cut through the complexity of the post-cold war world. The reality, the complexity and hesitation, were better reflected by NATO's reference to 'a framework of interlocking institutions which complement each other since the challenges we face cannot be comprehensively addressed by one institution alone' (see Document 12.3).

While NATO members argued over the way forward, the central European states – Poland, Hungary and the Czech and Slovak Republic – had coordinated their stance at the Visegrad Summit of 15 February 1991. The Solemn Declaration invoked the memory of a medieval meeting in Visegrad, and the three states set out a broad agenda of cooperation, extending from consultation on security issues to economic cooperation and the protection of minorities.[14] There were, however, quite severe limits to what these countries could do, or wished to do, on their own. The Visegrad Triangle, as it was known, could not dispel what Václav Havel described as a 'political, economic and security vacuum'.[15] Even less so could an older form of cooperation which went back to the Alpine-Adriatic Association of 1978, providing for cooperation between the provinces of Austria, Italy, Hungary and Yugoslavia. After several changes of name associated with the disintegration of Yugoslavia and the addition of new members, it became know as the Central European Initiative. Again the agenda was broad, but the lack of financial resources, despite the change from an interprovince arrangement to an intergovernmental agreement in 1989, meant that most of its projects remained on the drawing board.

Minority rights, one of the issues mentioned at the Visegrad Summit, had long plagued the region. The violence in Yugoslavia was a painful reminder of the potential consequences of failure to provide some provision for minorities. Europe's record, however, was one of neglect punctuated by what became known as ethnic cleansing: that is, forcible expulsion and the suppression of minorities. The protection of minorities was helped on to the agenda by the link between it and democracy. Here, the Council of Europe played a key role. Admission to the Council of Europe was widely regarded as a litmus test of a state's democratic credentials, and this gave the Council considerable leverage in its attempt to have repressive legislation removed. More importantly, the Council finally agreed, at its October 1993 Vienna Summit, to codify protection of minorities. The mechanism for doing this, a Framework Convention for the Protection of National Minorities, did have its limitations. Unlike the Human Rights Convention, its provisions were not subject to enforcement by the Court of Human Rights. It merely specified principles which signatory states undertook to respect. Yet even this was a major change. The issue of minority rights raised questions about citizenship and identity which many states, both west and east, found uncomfortable. Those concerns were dramatically formulated in Václav Havel's warning not to 'let in the demon of national collectivism with a seemingly innocent emphasis on the rights of minorities and on their right to self-determination', which, he continued 'inevitably leads to questioning of the integrity of the individual states and the inviolability of their present borders'.[16] Despite these hesitations the Council concluded its Framework Convention, which was duly opened for signature at the beginning of 1995. For all its limitations the Framework Convention contributed to what one author has called the 'increased obtrusiveness of monitoring'.[17]

One of the major forces behind this 'increased obtrusiveness', upon whose work the Council of Europe built, was the CSCE. At its Helsinki Conference in July 1992, agreement had been reached, if only with the insertion of several qualifications and reservations, on the creation of a High Commissioner on National Minorities (HCNM). The Commissioner had no authority to impose measures, but he did have substantial independence to initiate enquiries and issue warnings where he 'concludes that there is a *prima facie* risk of potential conflict'.[18] Prior to the Helsinki Conference, in June 1991, the CSCE had agreed that it could discuss emergencies without the consent of the state in which the emergency was deemed to have occurred. In the same vein, the Moscow Conference of December declared 'that the commitments undertaken in the field of the human dimension of the CSCE are matters of direct and legitimate concern to all participating states and do not belong to the internal affairs of the State concerned'.[19] These were important steps towards the 'increased obtrusiveness of monitoring' even if they did nothing to remedy the CSCE's lack of any enforcement mechanism. The other major function of the CSCE, arms negotiation and confidence-building measures, also received a boost at the 1992 Helsinki Conference, through the creation of a Forum for Security Cooperation. The remit of the Office of Free Elections had already been expanded in January 1992, when it was also renamed the Office for Democratic Institutions and Human Rights (ODIHR). Much of its work, and indeed that of the HCNM and the Council of Europe, could be categorized under the heading of the promotion of civil society: that is, of a set of values and common standards of behaviour in place of the crude consideration of interest and the balance of power.[20] For the CSCE's defenders, such an emphasis has more long-term prospects of ensuring stability than the more traditional methods of defence alliances.

Other attempts to regulate the European agenda through an ever more complex network of treaties and agreements were soon forthcoming. The initiative this time was French. In April 1993, Edouard Balladur launched the idea of a Stability Pact and, at the June 1993 Copenhagen Council, won the support of the EC states for the idea. The proposed pact was really a framework for a series of more specific pacts, many of them bilateral, intended to promote stability by resolving grievances, especially over minorities and borders. As the Final Document of the May 1994 Paris Opening Conference made clear, the proposed Pact for Security and Stability in Europe was itself an embodiment of the complexity of Europe's new architecture. The EU had not only played an active role in bringing about the Conference but, according to Article 2.4, was willing to act as a moderator at the request of parties seeking to reach an agreement. In addition, the document called on the CSCE to monitor the agreements. The pressure of a more complex European environment was also forcing France to reconsider some long-established policies, namely its attitude towards NATO. In September 1992, Defence Minister Pierre Joxe publicly suggested that France should reconsider its empty chair policy towards key NATO committees. He also indicated that the price for this would be reform of NATO.[21]

NATO itself was finding it difficult to live within the 'framework of interlocking institutions' which it had acknowledged as a necessity in December 1991. The Alliance had agreed to provide the military means to enforce UN resolutions in the former Yugoslavia, thereby seeming to accept a hierarchical relationship between the various international organizations. However, in May 1993 the NATO Secretary General was warning that 'these actions in support of the UN do not mean that NATO now sees its role mainly as that of a "sub-contractor" for international peacekeeping duties'. The experience of involvement in Yugoslavia was evident when he added, 'it cannot commit itself to supporting every peacekeeping operation; especially where the conditions for success are absent, where it believes that the mandate and rules of engagement are inadequate and where it cannot exercise unity of command'.[22]

NATO's agenda was also being complicated by pressure to admit east European states into the Alliance (Document 11.6). This raised the difficult question of NATO's relations with Russia. To refuse to admit new members meant leaving them in the uncomfortable security vacuum. But to admit them meant pushing NATO's eastern border towards Russia. In the summer of 1993 the problem seemed to have been resolved, when Yeltsin assured the Polish President, Lech Walesa, that Polish membership of the Alliance did 'not run counter to the interests of any state, including Russia'.[23] It was not long before the optimism vanished. Yeltsin's conciliatory offer was disavowed by his own ministers and generals. The return to the orthodox position of Russian opposition to NATO expansion divided the western states and caused alarm in central and east Europe. Václav Havel invoked the memory of the Munich Agreement of 1938 and, drawing a pointed analogy, claimed that NATO concessions to Russia 'would mean selling out the nations that have invested so much in the struggle for their own freedom, and selling out the West's own freedom as well'.[24] A little later the electoral support received by the nationalist Russian politician Vladimir Zhirinovsky induced more references to the past. The Estonian President, Lennart Meri, had some direct cause for concern – Zhirinovsky had openly called for the reassertion of Russian authority over the Baltic states – when he compared the nationalist's electoral advance with that of Hitler.[25] Even in the absence of any direct threat, the history of war and occupation was sufficient to generate a general sense of insecurity. It was this which NATO membership was meant to alleviate.[26] The western response was divided. Germany's Defence Minister Volker Rühe continued to press for NATO enlargement but ran into opposition from the United States. American policy at the end of 1993 was heavily influenced by President Clinton's adviser, Strobe Talbott, who argued for a 'Russia first' policy. This meant giving priority to Russian concerns, lest precipitate action induced a nationalist backlash. Talbott's influence was evident in Clinton's statement in January 1994 that 'We cannot afford ... to draw a new line between east and west that would create a self-fulfilling prophecy of confrontation.'[27]

At the January 1994 NATO Council, the western states sought to reconcile the demands for a European Security and Defence Identity, without compromising the integrity of the Alliance, and the security concerns of the central and east Europeans, without alienating Russia. The strategy for dealing with the former was the development of combined joint task forces. These were to draw upon elements of the NATO command structure which could be detached and put at the service of the WEU, if NATO as a whole decided not to commit itself. The underlying idea, and its ambiguity, were summed up in the slogan of 'separable but not separate' military forces.[28] Nevertheless, Paris was pleased with the outcome and inaugurated a review of its defence policy. There was greater emphasis on the need for cooperation, but formal reintegration into the NATO command structure was not on Defence Minister François Leotard's agenda. As he put it, 'We cannot put the 1966 decision in question. It is now part of our military/cultural heritage.'[29] To the central and east Europeans, NATO offered the principle that the Alliance remained open to new membership, but then provided a substitute in the form of the Partnerships for Peace (PfP). These were to be programmes negotiated with individual countries, and focused on democratic control of the military, budgetary transparency and joint planning and exercises with NATO in preparation for peacekeeping missions. The response from the prospective partners was varied. There were expressions of guarded welcome. On the other hand, Lech Walesa openly accused the west of desertion.[30] Ironically, the package did not please Russia either, which resented being placed on the same level as lesser powers.

Despite such reservations, the various countries began to sign their PfP agreements, while pressing ever more vigorously for membership. As with the EU, another unresolved issue was that, if there was to be an enlargement, the question of whom to include would have to be answered. Here the basic choice was between opening negotiations with all applicants or selecting the more promising, or less problematic, candidates. Although the problem did not have to be faced yet, the sensitivities involved were already evident in the disappointment of the Visegrad states that their greater progress towards democracy and a market-based economy was not recognized by the indiscriminate PfP offer. The fact that it was all-embracing remained one of the major attractions of the CSCE. There were several initiatives in 1994 aimed at strengthening the CSCE. A joint German–Dutch text was submitted in May and called on member states to 'commit themselves "to make every effort to achieve pacific settlement of local disputes" through the CSCE before referring them to the United Nations. "CSCE first" should thus become the aim.'[31] It also called for strengthening the role of the Chairman-in-Office and the formulation of a code of conduct. The following month, the Russian Foreign Minister Andrey Kozyrev proposed that the CSCE should be transformed into an international organization with an executive committee of ten members. The strengthened CSCE was also to have a 'coordinating role' and 'overriding responsibility' for stability. This suggestion was watered down in July, when the Russians explained that Kozyrev's letter had been misinterpreted and that the CSCE should be regarded as the 'leading partner' of the UN.[32] Both initiatives were made in preparation for the Budapest Conference, which opened in October and concluded with a summit meeting on 5–6 December 1994.

Shortly before the CSCE summit, the NATO Council met in Brussels. The debate on enlargement in preparation for the December Council had continued to be divisive. Clinton had been confronted with strong domestic criticism of his Russia-first policy. As this failed to produce the desired results, American policy swung behind advocates of enlargement. Indeed, just before an Alliance meeting at the end of September 1994, the Defense Secretary William Perry was scarcely less enthusiastic than Volker Rühe. At the meeting itself, however, Rühe's call for opening negotiations with the Visegrad states was rebuffed by Perry. Vigorous Russian opposition had once again forced the Americans to retreat. Nevertheless, the NATO Council did take a hesitant step forward. Although there was no timetable and no specification of who would be invited to the negotiating table, the Council decided 'to initiate a process of examination inside the Alliance to determine how NATO will enlarge'.[33]

The CSCE Budapest summit sanctioned the transformation of the CSCE into the Organisation for Security and Co-operation in Europe (OSCE). The significance of this was somewhat undermined by the announcement that it did not entail any changes in the rights and obligations of member states. On the other hand, it provided a better platform for subsequent reforms and, equally important, was a symbolic confirmation of the fact that the OSCE was seen as a permanent feature of the new European architecture (Document 11.7). The more radical reforms proposed by, among others, Russia, The Netherlands and Germany, were not approved, although they failed only by the narrowest margin. Among the new documents adopted was a Code of Conduct on Politico-Military Aspects of Security. Three days after the Code was approved, Yeltsin ordered military action against the autonomous republic of Chechnya. The war in Chechnya involved violation of numerous articles of the Code by both sides, but there was a noted reluctance of other states to invoke OSCE mechanisms. That did not demonstrate the irrelevance of the Code. It did demonstrate once again that in most fields the OSCE inevitably faltered in the absence of the political will of the member states.[34]

The war in Chechnya soured relations on all fronts. The EU declined to sign an interim trade agreement in protest at human rights violations in Chechnya. Volker Rühe advised the Russians that their Defence Minister, General Grachev, would not be welcome at a security conference in Germany after the General had denounced Russia's own human rights ombudsman for criticism of the army's behaviour. In March, Russian military figures were even questioning the CFE treaty and linking its fate with the issue of NATO enlargement.[35] The apparent intractability of the problems divided the western allies and divided the political actors within the states. In a replay of the arguments between advocates of a Russia-first policy and advocates of rapid enlargement in the United States, the German Foreign Minister and Defence Minister openly supported different lines. The Foreign Ministry, with an eye to Russia's presidential elections scheduled for 1996, argued that 'We cannot push Yeltsin into a corner, which would play into the hands of the nationalists. There is too much to lose.'[36] The Defence Ministry, referring to the indecision shown by the west over Yugoslavia and Chechnya, insisted on a more robust stance.

The atmosphere improved towards the middle of 1995 with agreement between NATO and Russia on a document promising enhanced cooperation between the two. This was still not the wide-ranging treaty sought by the Russians but it was a step in the right direction. EU signature of the postponed trade agreement also helped to diffuse tension. Yet none of this solved the underlying dispute. Each hesitant step or public call for enlargement risked provoking a strong Russian response and setting off a new round of the now well rehearsed arguments in western capitals. The long-awaited *Study on NATO Enlargement*, completed in September 1995, was one such hesitant step. There were no surprises in the document, and no timetable or indication of who would be considered for membership. There was evidence of the inherent problems of expanding an alliance based on unanimity. As the *Study* noted, 'Concerns have already been expressed ... that a new member might "close the door" behind it to new admissions in the future'.[37] That problem was solvable by seeking express commitments not to take such action. It was, however, indicative of a general problem.

As with the EU, it was clear that enlargement would have to be accompanied by institutional reform, even if the extent of reform was less drastic than in the case of the EU. Pressure here came from France, which was continuing its rapprochement with NATO's institutions. At the December 1995 Council, France declared its willingness to participate in 'appropriate NATO military bodies', but also wanted a redistribution of decision-making to maximize its influence, while declining to participate in what it considered to be inappropriate bodies (Document 11.8). There were other analogies with EU enlargement. The admission of new members was to be conditional upon willingness to undertake not only the formal commitments involved in membership, but also domestic reforms, to ensure civilian control over the military, and potentially expensive moves to standardize equipment and ensure interoperability with NATO forces. Enlargement also raised questions about the geographic focus of the Alliance, and fears that enlargement towards the north and east would detract attention from the Mediterranean. Some of these issues were taken up at the December 1995 Council. Setting out the agenda for 1996, it promised 'intensified' dialogue, 'enhancement' of the PfP process and consideration of 'what internal adaptations and other measures are necessary to ensure that enlargement preserves the effectiveness of the Alliance'.[38] There was also a reassertion of the Alliance's interest in the Mediterranean.

Russia, the stumbling block to enlargement, continued to lash out. According to General Grachev, the Russian response to enlargement would be to 'seek partners among the countries of east and central Europe, and among the member states of the Commonwealth of Independent States in order to form a future military-political alliance'.[39] In reality there were few, if any, prospective partners in east and central Europe, and such speculation served more to encourage the majority to clamour ever more loudly for admission to NATO. In Germany, though, Kohl was sensitive to Yeltsin's position and, seeking to keep enlargement out of the forthcoming Russian electoral campaign, stressed that he would not imperil Russo-German relations. At the same time, Germany's dynamic Defence Minister was pushing hard for the development of a European defence identity, arguing that this would strengthen Atlantic relations. Ideally, he wanted a full merger of the EU and the WEU, but was well aware of the reluctance of Britain even to contemplate this.[40] The WEU, very much the junior partner of western defence cooperation, had already expanded its membership and its remit. In doing so it incorporated the diversity of Europe into its own structures. That was evident in the existence of three tiers of membership in addition to the presence of Observers. Alongside full membership, the WEU, as of its May 1994 Kirchberg Declaration, recognized Associate Partners, the central and east Europeans, and Associate Members. In the light of such divergence, the WEU's Assembly cast doubt upon the desirability of absorbing the WEU within the EU, describing plans to do this as 'dangerous'.

The WEU's future status was improved by the decision at the Berlin NATO Council in June 1996 to proceed with the CJTF concept. The eventual agreement was warmly welcomed by France, though there had been considerable wrangling over the precise wording of the commitment. The formation and deployment of a CJFT would in fact still require authorization by the NATO Council, and hence still require American consent. The determination of the United States not to lose control over the process even led to the curious assertion by its spokesman that 'We are also a European country and a European power and we are determined to remain here.'[41] Issues of command, status and identity continued to trouble France's relationship with NATO as the Alliance moved towards enlargement. As part of its internal review, NATO slowly moved towards a streamlining of its command structure. In the surrounding debate France pushed for the nomination of a European as head of the NATO Naples-based southern command, a position traditionally held by an American. American reluctance to relinquish control was equally obdurate. Again the resonance of the past was notable, for it was issues of control and status in the Mediterranean which had induced de Gaulle's first moves away from the integrated command structure at the end of the 1950s.

At Berlin in June 1996, Russia, which had been invited along with the other ex-Warsaw Pact states, began to show more signs of flexibility about enlargement. Russia continued to oppose enlargement in principle, but the rhetorical tone was softened and there was more talk of the conditions under which enlargement would take place. The change in atmosphere was far from unequivocal, and there were still periodic reassertions of a more vigorous opposition. Later in 1996, with both the Russian and the American presidential elections out of the way, Clinton began to press for an end to the hesitation about enlargement. It was increasingly clear that the United States favoured opening negotiations with the Czech Republic, Hungary and Poland, with Slovenia being a possible fourth candidate. That still left several others, including the exposed Baltic states (Document 11.10). In an attempt to offer these some compensation, the United States even encouraged the EU to include them in its first phase of an eastern enlargement (Document 11.11).[42]

The December 1996 round of summits saw NATO take the long awaited step with the decision to issue invitations to negotiations at the scheduled Madrid Summit in July 1997, with a view to incorporating the new members in time for the Alliance's fiftieth anniversary in 1999. Discussions with Russia were increasingly focusing on some kind of charter formalizing Russia–NATO relations. After years of delay, negotiations moved at considerable speed. Confronted with greater NATO resolve, Russia salvaged what it could. It failed to obtain a binding commitment never to incorporate the Baltic states, never to restrict the deployment of NATO forces in new member states and never to exercise any kind of veto over NATO actions. On the other hand, there were reassurances that NATO had 'no intention, no plan and no need to station nuclear weapons on the territory of any new members'.[43] There was also agreement on the need to modify the CFE treaty to take account of changes since its signature in 1990. This sufficed to enable the two parties to sign the Founding Act on Mutual Security Relations between NATO and the Russian Federation on 27 May 1997. The Act provided for a Permanent Joint Council through which 'NATO and Russia will promptly consult . . . in case one of the Council members perceives a threat to its territorial integrity, political independence or security.'[44]

Amidst the preparations for issuing the invitations to negotiations there was disagreement within the Alliance over the extent of enlargement. The United States insisted on restricting the offer to the Czech Republic, Hungary and Poland. France, Germany and Italy – the last out of concern to balance northern enlargement with southern enlargement – argued for extending the offer to Slovenia and Romania, but to no avail.[45] Prior to the formal offer, the Council met in Sintra and established the new Euro-Atlantic Partnership Council (EAPC) to succeed the NACC. The document offered an 'expanded political dimension of consultation and co-operation' to those who wished to take it up. It also noted that it would continue the NACC practice of 'self-differentiation, in that Partners will be able to decide for themselves the level and areas of co-operation with NATO'.[46] The Madrid Summit in July 1997 welcomed the EAPC and finally issued the invitations to negotiations.

There was some irony in the fact that it was NATO, the product and embodiment of the cold war whose fate was cast in doubt by the supposed disappearance of its *raison d'être*, and not the EU, which led the eastern enlargement of the western-based institutions. The EU Commission's recommendations on enlargement, *Agenda 2000*, did not appear until after the Madrid Summit, and identified Poland, Hungary, the Czech Republic, Slovenia and Estonia as candidates for the first wave of negotiations. The EU, however, was not scheduled to take a decision on those recommendations until December 1997. Both organizations, especially the EU, had grown in complexity as they met the challenges of the post-cold war world. Moreover, they continued to exist alongside other bodies – the OSCE, WEU and Council of Europe – which typically received less headline attention but nevertheless were seen as fulfilling essential functions. The relationship between these organizations was complex, as was revealed by the OSCE Secretary General's comment that 'the envisaged security model is non-hierarchical and the OSCE complements the mutually reinforcing efforts of other European and transatlantic organisations, particularly NATO, which operate in the same geographic area and/or realm of activities'.[47] The suggestion of smooth, mutual reinforcement glossed over the reality of awkward, often *ad hoc*, adjustments made under the pressure of events.[48]

Yet the momentous changes following on from the collapse of the cold war order had been managed with relatively little bloodshed and uncertainty. Much, of course, depends upon the reference point which such terms as 'relatively' conjure up. Compared, however, with the breakdown of the old Europe of the pre-1914 balance of power, the management of the breakdown of the cold war order was impressive indeed. That achievement was due in no small measure to the existence of the institutions which inhibited a return to the strategies of the pre-1914 world.

NOTES

1. John Mearsheimer, 'Back to the future: instability in Europe after the cold war', *International Society*, Vol. 15 (1990), pp. 5–56.
2. For early examples of such pessimism see Marcin Krol, 'A Europe of nations or a universalistic Europe?' and Laszlo Lengyel, 'Europe through Hungarian eyes', both in *International Affairs*, Vol. 66 (1990), pp. 285–90 and 291–7.
3. For a concise survey of these issues see Christian Meier, 'Cooperation initiatives in eastern central Europe', *Aussenpolitik*, Vol. 45 (1994), pp. 254–62.
4. Invocation of cultural tradition and identity is still common. See the lecture given by the Polish President to the French Insitute of International Politics, Paris, 4 December 1996.
5. The same point was made in the context of criticism of an American Senator's assertion that NATO had been purely a response to an expansionist Soviet Union. Jan Petersen, 'Towards a security strategy for Europe', Draft General Report, WEU, October 1995, para. 46.
6. Thus, Walter A. Kemp, *The OSCE in a New Context* (London, 1996), p. 11.
7. London Declaration.
8. *The Guardian* (20 September 1990).
9. Quoted in Frank Costigliola, 'An "arm around the shoulder": the United States and German reunification, 1989–90', *Contemporary European History*, Vol. 4 (1995), p. 102.
10. This was the 'Bartholomew' paper. See Alexander Moens, 'Behind complementarity and transparency: the politics of the European security and defence identity', *Journal of European Integration*, Vol. 16 (1992), pp. 16–17.
11. *The Alliance's Strategic Concept* (Brussels, NATO, November 1991), p. 4.
12. *Financial Times* (21 December 1991).
13. 'WEU's post-Maastricht agenda', *NATO Review*, No. 2 (1992), p. 17.
14. Hungarian Minstry of Foreign Affairs, Press Release 4/1991 (15 February 1991).
15. Quoted in Rudolf Tökes, 'From Visegrad to Krakow', *Problems of Communism*, no. 6 (November–December 1991), p. 108.
16. *Financial Times* (11 October 1993).
17. Kemp, *The OSCE in a New Context*, p. 13.
18. CSCE, *Helsinki Documents 1992* (Helsinki, 1992), p. 20.
19. *Document of the Moscow Meeting of the Conference of the Human Dimension of the CSCE* (Moscow, 1991), p. 29.
20. Ernst-Otto Czempiel, 'Die Neuordnung Europas', *Aus Politik und Zeitgeschichte*, nos. 1–2 (1997), pp. 34–45.
21. *Financial Times* (30 September 1992).
22. NATO Press release, 10 May 1993. The importance of unity of command was stressed at the Athens NATO Council of June 1993. NATO Press release M-NACC 1 (93)40.
23. *Financial Times* (27 August 1993).
24. *Guardian* (19 October 1993).

25. *Guardian* (16 December 1993).
26. The point was still evident in the calmer atmosphere of 1996, when the Polish Prime Minister wrote that 'We are not making a bid for membership of NATO or the European Union out of fear of some immediate, unexpected threat. Our actions are guided by our historical experience', *NATO Review*, no. 3 (1996), p. 4.
27. *Financial Times* (12 January 1994). On Talbott's influence see Peter Rudolf, 'The USA and NATO enlargement', *Aussenpolitik*, Vol. 47 (1996), pp. 340–1.
28. Manfred Wörner, 'Shaping the Alliance for the future', *NATO Review*, no. 1 (1994), p. 4.
29. *Financial Times* (24 January 1994).
30. Alfred Reisch, 'Central Europe's disappointments and hopes', *RFE/RL Research Report*, no. 3 (1994), p. 25.
31. Press Release, Embassy of the FRG 48/94, 24 May 1994.
32. Michael Mihalka, 'Restructuring European security', *Transition*, Vol. 1, no. 11 (1995), p. 6.
33. *NATO Review*, no. 1 (1995), p. 26. This was sufficient to produce a strongly worded reaction from Yeltsin, *Financial Times* (6 December 1994).
34. For a useful survey of the Code see Michael R. Lucas, 'The OSCE Code of Conduct and its relevance in contemporary Europe', *Aussenpolitik*, Vol. 47 (1996), pp. 223–35.
35. *Guardian* (7 March 1995), *Financial Times* (6 February 1995 and 18 March 1995).
36. *Financial Times* (5 May 1995).
37. *Study on Enlargment* (September 1995), para. 30.
38. *NATO Review*, no. 1 (1996), p. 23.
39. *Financial Times* (11 February 1996).
40. Report of the Political Committee, *Organising Security in Europe* (26 January 1996).
41. *Guardian* (4 June 1996).
42. *Guardian* (25 November 1996).
43. *Financial Times* (11 December 1996).
44. 'Founding Act on Mutual Security Relations between NATO and the Russian Federation', *NATO Review*, no. 4 (1997), p. 8.
45. *Guardian* (6 May 1997), *Financial Times* (30 May 1997, 16 June 1997).
46. 'Basic Document of the Euro-Atlantic Partnership Council', 30 May 1997, *NATO Review*, no. 4 (1997), p. 11.
47. *OSCE Newsletter*, Vol. 4, no. 4 (April 1997), p. 3.
48. Thus, while the OSCE Chairman welcomed the creation of a multinational protection force for Albania as an example of the idea of 'OSCE first' (ibid., p. 2), Russia added to the authorizing decision the proviso that 'any operation envisaging the use of an element of compulsion or force must be sanctioned by the United Nations Security Council', OSCE, *PC Journal*, no. 108 (26 March 1997).

FURTHER READING

S. Duke, *The New European Security Disorder* (Basingstoke, 1994).
A. Hyde-Pryce, *European Security Beyond the cold war* (London, 1991).
W. A. Kemp, *The OSCE in a New Context* (London, 1996).
H. D. Kurz (ed.), *United Germany and the New Europe* (Aldershot, 1993).
V. Mastny (ed.), *The Helsinki Process and the Reintegration of Europe 1986–1991* (New York, 1992).
H. Miall (ed.), *Redefining Europe* (London, 1994).
H. Miall (ed.), *Minority Rights in Europe* (London, 1994).

A. A. Michta, *East Central Europe after the Warsaw Pact* (New York, 1992).

G. Pridham *et al.* (eds), *Building Democracy? The International Dimension of Democratisation in Eastern Europe* (London, 1997).

G. W. Rees, *International Politics in Europe. The New Agenda* (London, 1993).

L. Roucek, *After the Bloc* (London, 1992).

O. Waever, 'Three competing Europes: German, French, Russian', *International Affairs*, Vol. 66 (1990), pp. 477–93.

A. J. Williams (ed.), *Reorganizing Eastern Europe* (Aldershot, 1994).

11.1

LONDON DECLARATION ON A TRANSFORMED NORTH ATLANTIC ALLIANCE, 5–6 JULY 1990

NATO. London Declaration on a Transformed North Atlantic Alliance (July 1990). (5–6 July 1990)

This statement was issued by the North Atlantic Council in London. It symbolized the end of the cold war.

---

4. We recognise that, in the new Europe, the security of every state is inseparably linked to the security of its neighbours. NATO must become an institution where Europeans, Canadians and Americans work together not only for the common defence, but to build new partnerships with all the nations of Europe. The Atlantic Community must reach out to the countries of the East which were our adversaries in the cold war, and extend to them the hand of friendship.

5. We will remain a defensive alliance and will continue to defend all the territory of all of our members. We have no aggressive intentions and we commit ourselves to the peaceful resolution of all disputes. We will never in any circumstance be the first to use force.

6. The member states of the North Atlantic Alliance propose to the member states of the Warsaw Treaty Organization a joint declaration in which we solemnly state that we are no longer adversaries and reaffirm our intention to refrain from the threat or use of force against the territorial integrity or political independence of any state, or from acting in any other manner inconsistent with the purposes and principles of the United Nations Charter and with the CSCE Final Act. We invite all other CSCE member states to join us in this commitment to non-aggression.

_____11.2_____

CHARTER OF PARIS FOR A NEW EUROPE, NOVEMBER 1990

Bull. EC, 11-1990, pp. 126–9, 131–2

The Paris Charter of the CSCE, together with the Treaty on Conventional Forces in Europe and the Treaty on the Final Regulation in Relation to Germany, set the seal upon the end of the cold war division of Europe in time for the unification of Germany on 3 October 1990.

The era of confrontation and division of Europe has ended. We declare that henceforth our relations will be founded on respect and cooperation. Europe is liberating itself from the legacy of the past. The courage of men and women, the strength of the will of the peoples and the power of the ideas of the Helsinki Final Act have opened a new era of democracy, peace and unity in Europe ...

The 10 principles of the Final Act will guide us towards this ambitious future, just as they have lighted our way towards better relations for the past 15 years ...

Freedom and political pluralism are necessary elements in our common objective of developing market economies towards sustainable economic growth, prosperity, social justice, expanding employment and efficient use of economic resources ...

The participation of both North American and European States is a fundamental characteristic of the CSCE; it underlies past achievements and is essential to the future of the CSCE process. An abiding adherence to shared values and our common heritage are the ties which bind us together ...

Although the threat of conflict in Europe has diminished, other dangers threaten the stability of our societies. We are determined to cooperate in defending democratic institutions against activities which violate the independence, sovereign equality or territorial integrity of the participating States ... our common efforts to consolidate respect for human rights, democracy and the rule of law, to strengthen peace and to promote unity in Europe, require a new quality of political dialogue and cooperation and thus development of the structures of the CSCE.

The intensification of our consultations at all levels is of prime importance in shaping our future relations. To this end, we decide on the following:

(a) We, the Heads of State or Government, shall meet next time in Helsinki on the occasion of the CSCE follow-up meeting 1992. Thereafter, we will meet on the occasion of subsequent follow-up meetings.

(b) Our Ministers of Foreign Affairs will meet, as a Council, regularly and at least once a year. These meetings will provide the central forum for political consultations within the CSCE process. The Council will consider issues relevant to the Conference on Security and Cooperation in Europe and take appropriate decisions ...

(d)   A Committee of Senior Officials will prepare the meetings of the Council and carry out its decisions. The Committee will review current issues and may take decisions, including in the form of recommendations to the Council ...

(h)   In order to provide administrative support for these consultations we establish a Secretariat in Prague ...

(j)   We will create a Conflict Prevention Centre in Vienna to assist the Council in reducing the risk of conflict.

(k)   We establish an Office for Free Elections in Warsaw to facilitate contacts and the exchange of information on elections within participating States.

(l)   Recognizing the important role parliamentarians can play in the CSCE process, we call for greater parliamentary involvement in the CSCE, in particular through the creation of a CSCE parliamentary assemble, involving members of parliaments from all participating States ...

11.3

FINAL COMMUNIQUÉ OF THE NORTH ATLANTIC COUNCIL, 19 DECEMBER 1991

Ministry of Foreign Affairs, Republic of Hungary, Current Policy, no. 4 (1991)

This announcement reflects the complexity of the new European architecture.

A security architecture for Europe

8.   The peace and security of Europe will increasingly depend on a framework of interlocking institutions which complement each other since the challenges we face cannot be comprehensively addressed by one institution alone. We are determined to ensure that our Alliance will play its full part in this framework.

CSCE

9.   We are actively pursuing the initiatives taken by our Heads of State and Government in Rome to strengthen the CSCE process ... We further believe that the CSCE should fulfill its increasingly important role in furthering cooperation and security in Europe by fostering democratic change, securing freedom, and developing and applying effective instruments for conflict prevention, the peaceful settlement of disputes and crisis management ...

European security identity and defence role

11. In the spirit of our Alliance's Rome Declaration, we welcome the decisions taken at Maastricht by the European Council on the common foreign and security policy of the European Union which shall include all questions related to the security of the European Union, including the eventual framing of a common defence policy, which might in time lead to a common defence, and by the member states of the Western European Union on the role of WEU and its relations with the European Union and with the Atlantic Alliance. We note with satisfaction the European Council's agreement that the common foreign and security policy of the European Union shall be compatible with the common security and defence policy established within the framework of the North Atlantic Treaty. Enhancing European responsibility on defence matters while strengthening the solidarity and cohesion of the transatlantic partnership will greatly contribute to our common security.

_____11.4_____

A HUNGARIAN VIEW OF THE NEW EUROPEAN ARCHITECTURE, 1991

NATO Press Communiqué M-NAC-2(91)110

This statement by the Hungarian Minister of Foreign Affairs reflects the fears of a new division of Europe.

... let me refer to a speech recently delivered by the Prime Minister of Hungary at the Paris Summit in which he drew the attention of major European leaders to the fact that we should not allow Europe to be jeopardized by the existence of what he called the Wall of prosperity dividing the Western half of Europe from the former Communist countries. Neither recent changes which helped to bring down the Iron Curtain nor the important steps taken towards a United Europe should be undermined. From this it follows naturally that we are also aware of the dangers which another Wall of Prosperity or Wall of Welfare represents and which does exist to a large degree between the so-called North and the so-called South. Certainly neither Europe nor Hungary would like to live in a world where people would simply shut themselves in ivory towers and make their life as pleasant as possible. We are very much aware that the world is interdependent, that there is only one world and that no one can live in prosperity if other countries are on the brink of famine.

We, as the newest member of the Council of Europe, will certainly support all efforts, inside and outside the Council, to draw the attention of both Europeans and non-Europeans to the very grave problems of these countries. Certainly the importance of co-operation not only between East and West, but also between North and South must be emphasized. This is something the Republic of Hungary and

European society as a whole should show sufficient interest in. This is particularly the case for former Communist countries because they are now aware of the discrepancy which exists between the developed and less-developed countries. We in fact hope that these former Communist countries will adopt an intermediate position between the developed and less developed world.

I would also like to mention that we in Hungary as well as our neighbours in Central and Eastern Europe have also been schooled in the value of co-operation and experienced the lack of it. In the last three decades there was within our political bloc, a lot of talk of mutual co-operation which rarely materialised either in economic or political matters. So on the one hand we learned that mere phrases brought no results if they were uttered only by leaders and were not based on the constitutional and practical reality of the countries concerned. On the other hand, however, the interdependence of the countries, whether on economic, political, cultural or environmental issues, has been brought home to the societies in Central and Eastern Europe very clearly in these last few decades. The Central and Eastern European countries suffered for a long time because of their lack of real national sovereignty. They were in fact under a kind of dependency which without a doubt paralysed the energies of those nations. It was natural for us that after subordination, all those nations wanted to establish full sovereignty. However, full sovereignty cannot be the ultimate aim. I think full sovereignty has to be achieved first only so that one may then surrender voluntarily certain elements of national sovereignty in the field of international co-operation.

_____11.5_____

VÁCLAV KLAUS ON THE FUTURE SHAPE OF EUROPE, 11 FEBRUARY 1994

Czech Republic, Press Release, no. 02/94 (11 February 1994)

In this press release, the Czech Prime Minister pointed to the gap between Europe as a cultural and historical entity and the 'Europe' represented by the European Union.

I have to confess that I am puzzled by the title (or subtitle) of our session. I refer to the term 'an enlarged Europe'. It seems to me, however, that Europe cannot be enlarged. Europe is as it is, and as it always was, and the authors of the title had in mind, probably, the enlargement not of Europe but of some European institutions only. This difference is important. Some of us tend to underestimate it and it is an error.

The future position of Europe in the world, the success or failure of Europe, or better to say, the success or failure of citizens of this beautiful continent we Czechs regard so highly, does not depend so much as it is usually assumed on the existence, scope and activities of multilateral European institutions because it depends on the quality and structure of political, social and economic systems we have or will have in our countries. This is exactly the message I wish to bring here from a country which was a member of one powerful multilateral institution and which has been in the most radical way eliminating the irrational and oppressive communist regime and which has already created basic institutions of a free society. The source of our tragedy was communism, not COMECON.

Our success (and I now have in mind success of all Europeans) depends on the degree of freedom, on the degree of free market and free trade, on our ability to get rid of unnecessary government interventionism introduced in the past in the name of socialism in one part of Europe or of welfare state in its second part, on our ability to get rid of various forms of bureaucratic manipulations with all of us, on our determination to suppress the powerful, social welfare endangering, lobbying, rent seeking groups, on our capability to put economic 'fundamentals' in order, which especially means to bring into accord our own performance with the rewards we are getting for it. Those are, in my opinion, the preconditions for either success or failure of all of us.

Technically speaking the positive role of multilateral European institutions (especially of the EC) in our economic and social development depends on the validity of three hypotheses:

1. European institutions are more in favour of free markets, free trade, less interventionism, less bureaucracy, less rent-seeking, etc. than governments of individual European countries (both in intentions and in their implementation).
2. European institutionalized integration succeeds in creating economies of scale (which will outweigh the non-negligible diseconomies of scale connected with huge organizations).
3. The idea of integrated (unified) Europe will be the true idea of European citizens and not of European politicians.

We mostly believe in the power of these hypotheses but we must formulate them explicitly and test them carefully.

Czech Republic (and similarly all other Central European countries, especially countries which a year ago formed the so called CEFTA) starts with the assumption the country is and has always been part of Europe and, therefore, does not want to be deprived of advantages stemming from membership in European institutions. I strongly believe that my country has already crossed the Rubicon dividing the two, totally different political, social and economic systems, that the country should be taken seriously and that the country is prepared for further steps in the direction of reasonable European integration. When I say reasonable integration I do not mean absolute unification.

The countries known as the Czech Republic intend to be 'equal partners', they don't want just to get, they are ready to give as well. We know that it is our task to solve our own problems and we do not expect Europe will solve them instead of us. We hope the European countries will not stop the search for the optimal nature and form of their integration, and I am convinced that the countries known as the Czech Republic will be able to participate in this endless searching process and will be able to contribute to its outcome. Our communist past gives us a very special degree of sensitivity to several issues which have been in west Europe – because they were lucky not to experience them – underestimated. We feel it our duty to repeat them again and again here and hope we will have a chance to do it.

11.6

LET US RECALL 'NEO-GAULLISM': A VIEW OF RUSSIA'S PREDICAMENT, JULY 1995

Sergei Kaganov, 'Let us recall "Neo-Gaullism"', *Current Digest of the Soviet Press*, Vol. 47, no. 27 (1995), pp. 22–3.

The end of the cold war and collapse of the CMEA and Warsaw Pact created new uncertainties for Russia, as seen here by Sergei Kaganov, Deputy Director of the Russian Academy of Science Institute of Europe.

A great deal has already been said to the effect that, outwardly, the Halifax meeting of the Group of Seven went rather well for Russia. One can agree with much of this. Indeed, another step was taken toward our country's becoming a regular participant in the political 'half' of the meeting. As Russia's economic revival proceeds, it will also become possible to raise the question of participation in the more significant part of these 'summits' – the economic part. None of this, however, dispels skepticism regarding the usefulness of Moscow's participation not only in meetings of the G-7, but also in the entire system of organizations dominated by the West.

In part this skepticism is a reaction to the 'whatever-you-say' diplomacy that was openly pursued by the Russian Foreign Minister during the first years of Russian statehood and continues to be pursued to this day under a cover of militant-nationalistic philippics. This 'diplomacy' has done tremendous damage to Western-oriented Russian political thinking and Russian policy, weakening support for them in society and among the elite.

But there are even more significant doubts.

Won't our desire to join organizations dominated by the West at a time when we are weak – and hence as a junior partner – only consolidate our position of weakness?

Won't our presence as a kind of associate, as opposed to full, member of the G-7 or NATO amount to shared responsibility for various decisions but very limited opportunities to influence the way those decisions are made?

Won't our joining some of these organizations – for example, the new COCOM [Coordinating Committee on Multilateral Export Controls] – tie our hands in both diplomacy and trade?

The people who are asking these reasonable questions propose two lines as an alternative to the policy of engagement: partial self-isolation, or neo-Gaullism.

The reasoning behind the first line is rather simple: We leave, gather strength, and return on more advantageous terms. The logic is outwardly attractive, but it is counterproductive, unfortunately. If we leave, the vacuums – both political and economic – will be filled in, and it will be difficult, if not impossible, to return.

Here are some examples. For several years we did a brilliant job of ignoring the countries of Central and Eastern Europe. The result is plain to see – in our policy of opposing NATO expansion, we have almost no levers or allies in those countries.

We were extremely passive in Ukraine, and Western countries now have very serious positions there, despite the fact that their actual ability to influence that country is only a fraction of our potential ability to do so.

We have left some traditional arms markets. It is very difficult to reclaim a place there.

And now for the second line, which can be called neo-Gaullism. Its proponents, by contrast, call for vigorously defending our interests and positions, sometimes pointedly, but within the framework of a strategic alliance with the West. This line, in my view, is a more attractive strategy.

Theoretically, It would enable us to maximize our influence in a position of weakness. Partners interested in keeping such a 'neo-Gaullist' country in an alliance would be forced to make concessions incommensurate with its real strength. This line would also be advantageous from a domestic policy viewpoint.

In principle, Russia should use elements of this policy; at the same time, it should not overdo it, bearing in mind that we are not France of the time of de Gaulle. The French President could afford to play that game because he knew that France was a key member of the alliance opposing the USSR and France's allies couldn't manage without it.

We, however, are not a member of such of an alliance. Russia is more useful to the West as a partner, but nothing more. It would be difficult for the West to solve many problems without us, but such problems could at least be blocked or skirted. For a while, at any rate.

What is the solution? Can Russia have a clear cut, unambiguous strategy? Under current conditions, apparently not, We need to combine a policy of deepening our relations with the West with a policy of independence, to gain time to build up our economic and political strength, and to prevent situations that could perpetuate our weakness.

We need a diplomacy that is active in all areas but not costly, one that entails maximum use of the potential of the neo-Gaullist line.

Needless to say, pursuing such a complex policy will be difficult. And so efforts to strengthen our personnel and, most importantly, to carry out organizational reform of the Foreign Ministry are all the more important.

_____11.7_____

THE ROLE OF THE OSCE, 12 FEBRUARY 1996

Dr Wilhelm Höynck, Speech at the Ninth Meeting of the
International Security Forum, Tokyo, 12 February 1996, in *From
CSCE to OSCE* (Vienna, Secretariat for the OSCE, n.d.), p. 193.

The OSCE Secretary-General, Wilhelm Höynck, sought to delimit the role of the
OSCE on several occasions. In this speech at the ninth meeting of the International
Security Forum, Tokyo, he emphasized its complementarity with other bodies.

Looking at this multitude of regional Structures, one may ask whether there is not
a high degree of redundancy. Where do all of these organizations find their proper
place? Actually, co-operation and co-ordination work rather smoothly.

Let me cite as an example the case of the OSCE. There is no danger that the OSCE
will one day become a UN-type body for Europe. Like NATO, the OSCE can
provide co-operative and collective security, but not, as opposed to NATO, collective defense. Its relationship with NATO and other western security structures is
clearly complementary and not an alternative. EU and NATO memberships will
most likely never be all-inclusive in the OSCE area. Therefore, a balanced security
structure must include a strong, all-inclusive, co-operative security organization
where all States of the OSCE area find their place. It is an essential function of the
OSCE to allow all participating States to work in full respect of OSCE principles
and commitments for their legitimate interests and, at the same time, to make their
contribution to overall stability. We will not be able to manage today's extremely
complex situation successfully if important aspects of comprehensive security are
dealt with in an isolated, exclusive way. As an overarching principle, 'inclusion' is a
key element of a co-operative security system.

It is increasingly evident that no one organization, global or regional, can go it
alone. I think that within the OSCE area only a 'pluralistic' structure will lead to
long-term stability, for reasons of substantive and formal competence, for reasons
of historically based differences in membership and – in the final analysis – for
reasons of power-sharing. Hence, the great number of institutions and organizations is a strength, not a weakness of Europe's post-confrontation situation.

However, a central issue in the developing new security order in Europe is the
relationship between this multitude of international organizations. While some
basic elements are already in place, co-operation between the OSCE and other
regional organizations is still complex, both politically and in practice.

The Helsinki Summit of the OSCE in 1992 stressed complementarity and
excluded any form of hierarchy. The OSCE approach *vis-à-vis* other regional
organizations is co-operative and not competitive. Peacekeeping operations are a
case in point. The Helsinki Document expresses explicitly the OSCE's interest in co-
operative support from NATO and other organizations in OSCE-led peacekeeping.

The OSCE could go as far as giving a 'mandate' to another regional organization for a peacekeeping operation within the OSCE area, although this has not yet been done. On the other hand, the central role of the OSCE in the European security architecture has been recognized in political statements by NATO and other regional organizations. The Budapest Summit in 1994 directed the OSCE to pursue more systematic and practical co-operation between itself and other regional and transatlantic organizations and institutions that share its values and objectives.

What does all this mean in practice? Representatives of the United Nations and other international organizations attend major OSCE meetings. They contribute to seminars held within the OSCE framework. The OSCE is invited to attend meetings of other organizations. It enjoys observer status at the UN General Assembly. Officials of the organizations at all levels have direct and often daily contacts on a broad range of issues. In the field of the Human Dimension, multilateral meetings involving the United Nations, UNHCR, the ICRC and the Council of Europe are a regular practice.

But in spite of these many contacts and ties, the present situation falls short of fully using the potential of mutually reinforcing co-operation. It is sometimes difficult to agree concretely on the specific distribution of tasks and a division of labour based on comparative advantages.

Some of the underlying problems can be qualified as bureaucratic. International organizations, like all bureaucracies, are tempted with 'empire building'. They may look for new tasks in order to become more relevant or more powerful. For the same reasons, they may be concerned with 'empire-maintaining' and therefore reluctant to share responsibilities with other organizations.

More difficult to overcome are obstacles of a political nature. Some elements of the developing European architecture are controversial. There are differing views on the role of NATO and the scale and pace of its possible expansion. The perception of the nature and political perspectives of the CIS [Commonwealth of Independent States] is another controversial issue. Like the future role of NATO, it is directly related to a still unresolved problem of the transition period: the position of the Russian Federation within the European and transatlantic security structures.

_____11.8_____

FRANCE AND NATO, JULY 1996

Charles Millon, Minister of Defence of France, 'France and the renewal of the Atlantic Alliance', *NATO Review*, no. 3 (May 1966), pp. 13, 15–16.

Charles Millon, Minister of Defence in France, here set out France's relationship with NATO.

At the meeting of the North Atlantic Council on 5 December 1995, France announced that she would resume her role in appropriate NATO military bodies which do not encroach on her sovereignty. Henceforth, she will also participate in the meetings of the Council of Defence ministers and is fully involved in the Military Committee, while intensifying her working relations with the military structure ...

Our participation in the Military Committee – full participation, as it now is – is all the more important in that this is an essential, central body in the Alliance's decision-making structure ...

We should emphasize, however, that this strengthening of the role of the Military Committee in no way changes France's relationship with the integrated military structure of NATO. This will continue to be regulated by bilateral agreements, updated as necessary to keep pace with the changing international context. The present situation of the Atlantic organization, and the position of our forces relative to it remains unchanged.

With regard to the new organization of the Alliance that should be set up, we have no preconceived idea and no hard-and-fast procedural plan. We do, however, have one conviction: taking due account of the European dimension must be one of the Atlantic Alliance's priorities for 1996 and beyond.

The political scheme for European integration necessarily means that security and defence matters will increasingly be dealt with at European Union level. This ambition is certainly no threat to Alliance. On the contrary, it must be interpreted as a means of consolidating the Alliance and placing transatlantic solidarity on a sounder footing. There can be no European defence policy that does not take account of the Atlantic dimension; there can be no lasting Alliance without the affirmation of a strong European pillar. The purpose is to arrive at a form of collaboration between Europe and North America within NATO.

The 'European pillar', an image portrayed by President Kennedy, is not a predetermined organizational plan. It is a political concept whose relevance is acutely apparent today. It relates to the founding of a lasting Alliance based on a more visible and operationally more effective European contribution, both politically and militarily.

Let there be no ambiguity from the outset: the affirmation of a European defence identity must not find expression in a binary Alliance, with the European Union states on one side and the North American nations on the other. Not only would such duplication of resources and procedures be costly and inefficient but, more to the point, it would be tantamount to rejecting the very concept of a transatlantic alliance. The solution, then, lies in the establishment of a more flexible organization. In future, the Europeans must be able to prepare and undertake the commitment of a European force, supported where necessary by the resources and structures existing within NATO, in accordance with the decisions reached at the January 1994 Summit. In other words, the 'Europeanization' of the Alliance has to be effective not only when an operation is actually mounted but also in time of peace. It must be able to take effect not only within the framework of the actual military operation but also in the planning and preparatory stages, and in the politico-military decision process.

11.9

A DUTCH VIEW OF NATO ENLARGEMENT, 1996

Frits Bolkestein, 'NATO: deepening and broadening?',
NATO Review, no. 4 (July 1996), pp. 21–2.

This statement by Frits Bolkestein, leader of the Liberal Party in The Netherlands, illustrates the strong Atlanticist sentiment in The Netherlands, as well as the inherent problems of NATO's enlargement.

In December, the North Atlantic Council is expected to take further decisions on how NATO enlargement should take place. However, the process of bringing new members into the Alliance must be handled with care. If events move too quickly, the significance of membership will be watered down and, in any case, there is no cause for haste.

The geopolitical position of Poland, for instance, is undisputed for the first time in centuries. Nor are other candidate states for membership under any direct or indirect threat. Above all, there is a need for consensus on enlargement among the member states themselves. We must not give any guarantees which we will not or cannot fulfil. Recent history has shown where this would lead us. No one would benefit from 'fair weather' membership, and a scaled-down form of membership which is intended to allow prospective members to join more quickly would undermine the Alliance and, what is more, this distinction would be lost on Russia. The difference between full membership and limited membership is quickly swept aside by political rhetoric. Thus, those who join must become full members, with all the rights and obligations of the NATO Treaty.

As I see it, three important conditions need to be fulfilled before a country can join the Alliance. Firstly, all member states must be prepared to accept the new members. NATO is still based on consensus.

Secondly, the enlargement process should enhance stability and security in Europe. Relations with Russia, which is still the largest military power on the European continent, are vitally important here. The recent visit to Moscow by Secretary General Javier Solana made it clear once again that relations with Russia could be seriously upset if the enlargement process is not handled carefully.

The third condition is that the new member states will have to satisfy a number of admission criteria . . .

At last year's *Wehrkunde Tagung* – the annual high-level conference on security policy held in Munich – the US Secretary of State and the German Foreign Minister clearly called for the enlargement of NATO to include Central European countries. The flames of enthusiasm for enlargement were fanned by a lobby which has strong links with Central European countries, particularly Poland. Indeed, these arguments are not based on security policy alone, but more on emotional factors.

The strong preference in Germany for countries to join as soon as possible is based on considerations of security policy. Germany wants to extend the zone of stability as far east as possible. The German Minister of Defence, Volker Rühe, has indicated on several occasions that a stable Central Europe is in Germany's vital interest. This is of course also in the interest of the West, if we want to prevent Germany from 'going it alone' in the event of any instability occurring on its eastern border . . .

Before making moves to enlarge the Alliance, the member states will therefore have to answer the fundamental question of whether they are willing to accept the associated risk. Their declaration of intent must not be restricted to the conference rooms of Brussels.

_____11.10_____

A LITHUANIAN VIEW OF NATO ENLARGEMENT, 1996

Ceslovas V. Stankevicius, 'NATO enlargement and the indivisibility of security in Europe: a view from Lithuania', *NATO Review*, no. 5 (September 1996), pp. 22, 24–5.

This was an unsuccessful plea by a Lithuanian diplomat, Ceslovas Stankevicius, for the inclusion of all central and east European countries in the enlargement negotiations.

Despite 50 years of suppression, the Lithuanian, Latvian and Estonian nations have managed to preserve their affinity to west European civilisation and they are basing their development on the model of Western democracy. The integration of Lithuania and the other two Baltic States into the community of Western nations means a return to their natural places in the international community. In contrast, the Eurasian commonwealth represented by the CIS is foreign to most Lithuanians, as it is to Latvians and Estonians.

A hundred years of experience prompts Lithuania to exercise caution and the Lithuanian Constitution explicitly forbids the country from joining any post-Soviet Eastern military, political or economic alliances, commonwealths or areas. Lithuania has rejected the model of the so-called bridge between East and West or the role of any type of buffer state. Moreover, any form of mixed integration into both Eurasia and Europe would be unacceptable to Lithuania. Thus, Lithuania will only be a part of the Eurasian sphere as a result of direct or indirect force.

Throughout its history, Lithuania has been dominated three times by Russia: in 1795–1914, 1940–1941 and 1944–1990, when Russia and the West shared this part of Europe among themselves. If Russia's interests were satisfied once again and Lithuania were excluded from the NATO enlargement process, this would deal a serious blow to the Lithuanian nation.

Sometimes, in discussions on NATO enlargement, one hears voices in the West warning that the Baltic States are 'indefensible'. However, the concept of indefensible European states is in complete discord with modern principles of European democracy. This would imply that the realm of European democracy can be divided into 'defensible' and 'indefensible' democracies ...

On this score, I would refer to President Bill Clinton's letter of 27 November 1994 to Estonia's President Lennart Meri, in which President Clinton wrote that the goal of the United States was to expand across all of Europe the area of democracy, stability and welfare that had been achieved in west Europe after the Second World War. The US President emphasized that he believed in a 'New Europe' united by common values, where there is no room for 'spheres of influence' ...

... the issue of how to avoid a dangerous division of the unifying region of Central and Eastern Europe at a time when individual countries of the region begin their accession process becomes particularly imperative. To this end, it is important to ensure that those countries whose defence capabilities are relatively weaker do not become even more insecure due to the accession of stronger countries ...

Thus, to avoid making the border between Lithuania and Poland an external NATO border, it is necessary to pursue a policy of non-differentiation and equal opportunity. To this end, it is important that all the countries of the region enter simultaneously the first stage of the process leading to membership.

_____11.11_____

REBALANCING TRANSATLANTIC RELATIONS, 1997

Klaus Francke, 'Rebalancing transatlantic relations', *NATO Review*, no. 5 (September–October 1997), pp. 18–19.

This assessment by Klaus Francke, Head of the German delegation to the North Atlantic Assembly, deals with the impact of the new European architecture upon transatlanctic relations.

An equal partnership will require the US to relinquish some of its responsibilities. However this would also ease some of its burdens ... From a European perspective, the US still has some ground to make up in terms of the experience of multilateral integration which the European states have acquired over recent decades within the European Union.

The Europeans, in their turn, must create the conditions which enable them to take on more responsibility. They can only expect to be acknowledged by the US as an equal partner if they speak with one voice. Although I believe that the Europeans are likely to demonstrate their unity more and more frequently ... the reliability of this unity, from the US's perspective, has yet to be tested ...

... an accelerated process of accession to the EU, which the US has called for in respect to the Baltic states, cannot be an alternative [to membership of NATO]. The European Union is currently less able than NATO to fulfil the security aspirations of applicant countries. However, I am convinced that in the long term, EU membership and hence participation in the European area of economic prosperity, will offer as much stability, and therefore security, as the guarantees contained in Article 5 of the North Atlantic Treaty.

INDEX